Cost and Managerial Accounting in Government and Nonprofit Organizations

To remain financially viable, all organizations, including government and nonprofit organizations, need to maximize efficiency, improve performance, and deal with complex problems. Managing costs and operations are two of the most essential elements for the successful operation of an organization. This timely book provides an introduction to cost and managerial accounting in government and nonprofit organizations, with an emphasis on cost basics, cost accounting methods, and cost management and control.

The book is divided into three parts: Part I deals with cost basics, with an emphasis on basic cost concepts, cost behavior, and cost analysis. Part II discusses methods commonly used in cost accounting. Included in this category are job costing, contract costing, process costing, cost allocation, and activity-based costing. And Part III looks at cost management and control. Three topics are discussed here: standard costing, quality control, and budgeting for planning and control. The book concludes with a brief discussion of emerging trends in cost and managerial accounting. With an emphasis on relatability and practical applications, examples have been drawn from real government and nonprofit organizations. Graduate students in public administration and management, as well as practitioners in government and nonprofit organizations, will find this book an essential foundation for understanding public accounting's unique challenges.

Aman Khan is Professor of Political Science and Public Administration at Texas Tech University, USA, where he teaches public budgeting, financial management, and cost and managerial accounting in government and nonprofit organizations. He is the author and co-author of several dozen publications in professional journals and edited volumes, including seven books. His most recent publications include *US Infrastructure: Challenges and Directions for the 21st Century* (with Klaus Becker, Routledge, 2019) and *Fundamentals of Public Budgeting and Finance* (2024). Trained as an economist and planner, Dr. Khan previously served as Director of the Graduate Program in Public Administration at Texas Tech University and also taught graduate finance at a business school. Dr. Khan is the founder and current Director of the Institute of Governmental Finance, which provides professional training to elected officials and middle- and upper-level managers in government.

Cost and Managerial Accounting in Government and Nonprofit Organizations

Aman Khan

Routledge
Taylor & Francis Group
NEW YORK AND LONDON

First published 2026
by Routledge
605 Third Avenue, New York, NY 10158

and by Routledge
4 Park Square, Milton Park, Abingdon, Oxon OX14 4RN

Routledge is an imprint of the Taylor & Francis Group, an informa business

ISBN: 978-1-032-78054-2 (hbk)
ISBN: 978-1-032-78053-5 (pbk)
ISBN: 978-1-003-48609-1 (ebk)

DOI:10.4324/9781003486091

Typeset in Sabon
by Newgen Publishing UK

To my wonderful wife

Terri Khan

with love and affection

Contents

Figures

Tables

Preface

This book is about cost and managerial accounting in government and nonprofit organizations, with an emphasis on cost basics, cost accounting methods, and cost management and control. Managing costs and operations are two of the most important elements essential for successful operation of an organization – public, private, and nonprofit. While cost has always been the focal point of business organizations, it has not received the same level of attention in government until recently. There is a simple reason for this: The private sector is driven by profit-maximizing incentive and cost is an integral part of it. Without knowing how to manage costs, it will be impossible for any firm or business to survive, let alone make a profit. In fact, there is an inverse relationship between cost and profit: For a firm to maximize profit, it must keep its costs to a minimum. This plain and unassumingly simple principle that lies at the heart of all business operations explains why firms and businesses must remain efficient at all times.

However, there has been a shift in focus in recent years from profit maximization, especially in the short run, to revenue maximization in the long run. This apparent shift in business practice has been necessary to ensure that firms build up a clientele that remains loyal to it for a long time. Since consumer satisfaction is essential for the long-term viability of a firm, most firms are willing to sacrifice their short-term profit maximization objective for a long-run revenue maximization goal. In contrast, the government does not operate to maximize profit either in the short run or in the long run. Therefore, it does not necessarily have the same incentive to undertake measures that will increase efficiency in the same way the private sector does. Additionally, government provides a wide array of goods and services, the net gain of which to society cannot be measured in precise monetary terms yet they are essential to maintain social order, improve public health, revitalize the economy, and raise the level of living for its citizens. In other words, they are necessary to improve the welfare of society vis-a-vis the public, assuming one is able to measure 'welfare' in some meaningful ways. In reality, it is almost impossible to measure welfare that would be consistent and sufficiently reflective of the social, economic, and political differences that exist in society. This makes it even more difficult for the decision makers to determine how efficiently the resources of society should be allocated to achieve the desired level of welfare.

From a theoretical point of view, the question of efficiency in resource allocation should not pose any major problems, so long as the resources of a government are sufficient to meet the needs of its citizens. From a practical point of view, however, it is only when a government does not have sufficient resources to address the needs of the public or when public expectations exceed the ability of the government to meet its needs, which is often the case, that it becomes a major concern of the public and the government. This also applies to organizations such as nonprofits that have become increasingly important in public service provision. Even without resource limitations or public expectation, it is still necessary, from the point of view of good management, for a government as well as nonprofit organizations to function efficiently and effectively. Inefficiency in operation can not only contribute to poor performance, but also cause serious economic and financial problems, leading eventually to financial bankruptcy and default. What this means is that, to remain financially viable, all organizations, including the government and nonprofits, must be willing to undertake measures and adopt methods and approaches that will increase their efficiency, improve performance, and enable them to deal with complex problems with relative ease. Cost and managerial accounting play an important role in all this.

The book is divided into three parts: Part I deals with cost basics, with an emphasis on basic cost concepts, cost behavior, price and rate structure of cost, and cost analysis. Part II discusses methods commonly used in cost accounting. Included in this category are job costing, contract costing, process costing, cost allocation, and activity-based costing. Part III looks at cost management and control. Three topics are discussed here: standard costing, quality control, and budgeting for planning and control. The book concludes with a brief discussion of emerging trends in cost and managerial accounting. While many of the topics discussed in the book appear to be analytical in content, every effort has been made to keep them simple. Furthermore, examples have been drawn primarily from government and some from nonprofit organizations so that readers can relate to them without much difficulty.

In putting together the chapters, this book has drawn heavily from several disciplines; in particular, from economics, accounting, statistics, and operations management. Each of these disciplines play an important role in cost studies: how they are defined, measured, analyzed and evaluated.

For instance, there is a direct relationship between cost and economics, in particular microeconomics which studies the economic behavior of individuals, firms and businesses (individual consumers and individual firms). Cost plays a critical role in the determination of that behavior. To give an example, when economists study the behavior of individual consumers and firms, they measure costs in terms of resource scarcity. What this means is that when resources are used for one purpose, they cannot be used for anything else at the same time. Therefore, the cost of resource use is the cost of alternatives forgone. In other words, it is the sacrifice individuals, as well as firms and businesses make by forgoing the opportunities they could have availed of.

On the other hand, accounting, which has long claimed an exclusive interest in costs, measures costs in absolute terms. From an accounting point of view, costs are regarded as historical outlays rather than as opportunities forgone. This has an intuitive appeal since no one quite knows all the opportunities that are available to a decision maker at any given time. This does not mean that that economists' notion of cost is irrelevant. What this means is that both perspectives are necessary to study the cost behavior of an organization, similar to the cost behavior of individual consumers and firms. For instance, historical costs are important where legal, operational, and financial requirements of an organization are concerned, whereas opportunity costs are important where predictions have to be made on future costs, based on alternative courses of action. In fact, to be able to make good and reliable cost forecasts, one must have good historical data. Therefore, the two views on costs are complementary, not conflicting.

As an applied branch of mathematics, statistics is concerned with two things: providing summary information and drawing inferences about the characteristics of a population based on a sample drawn from the same population. The former is called descriptive statistics, and the latter inferential statistics. Both descriptive and inferential statistics are useful in cost studies, especially in measuring the cost behavior of an organization such as measuring the characteristics of cost and related variables, analyzing their relationship, setting up confidence intervals, testing the significance of the estimated cost parameters, and so forth. Knowledge of statistics is also important in dealing with cost variables whose behavior is difficult to predict with certainty.

Like statistics, operations management can provide valuable information on cost and related variables that are important in decision making in government as well as nonprofit organizations, but operations management is much broader in scope than statistics. It deals with the management of organizational practices and processes to improve efficiency and productivity. This is achieved through planning, organizing, and overseeing activities that convert resources into products and services. Examples of areas that are directly impacted by operations management are quality control, productivity, and inventory management, among others. However, the real advantage of using operations management in cost studies lies in its ability to experiment with solutions by sensitizing them to alternative scenarios without altering the basic structure of the relationship.

Finally, a good management system must be in place to appreciate the critical need for integrating diverse knowledge into a coherent whole. Without this integration, these goals will not produce the kinds of results one would expect from their use. It is essential that the management understands this critical need and is supportive of those who are directly responsible for utilizing them to solve everyday problems. Proper communication between those who set up organizational policies and those who carry them out is critical to the success of an organization. Particularly in government, where acceptance of new ideas and innovations is more gradual, such openness can provide a real welcome change.

Lubbock, Texas, USA Aman Khan

Acknowledgements

This book would not have been possible without the help and unfailing support of several individuals at Routledge of Taylor & Francis Group. First and foremost, Ms. Laura Varley, the publisher of Routledge, a wonderful and gracious individual in the literal sense of the term, who had the patience to bear with me and never failing to extend her support at every turn when I needed it. Ms. Lauren Powell, the ever so delightful editorial assistant, for her patience, help, and unending support in every sense of the word. My deep gratitude and sincere thanks to Ms. Powell. Mr. Francis Norman, the copy editor, did a good job of copyediting. A special thanks to Mr. Norman. Thanks are also due to three outstanding production managers, Ms. Noorjahan Begum, Ms. Shruthi Maniyodath, and Ms. Shamli Priya, as well as the entire production team for making sure that everything was done in order and in a professional manner during the production process. I owe each one of them my heartfelt thanks and appreciation.

Finally, my heartfelt thanks to my family, especially my wife and our children - Junaid, Jasmine, and Tyler - for their love and affection, which has been a constant source of inspiration in my personal and professional life. I am ever so grateful to have them in my life.

1 Introduction and Background Discussion

1.1 Introduction

There is not a single organization anywhere – public, private, quasi-public,[1] and nonprofit, that is not concerned about costs and how to account for them. As organizations become complex, requiring diverse and intelligent information to function efficiently and effectively, the need for cost studies, in particular accounting for costs, or simply cost accounting, becomes more important. The primary objective of cost accounting is to provide cost and related information that is essential for an organization to determine how best to run its internal operations. This includes, among others, how to explain cost behavior, how to analyze, assign, allocate and control costs, and what measures to take to improve cost performance. In government, where efficiency and accountability have always been a concern, cost accounting fills an important gap by producing information that is critical to the economic and financial success of the government.

Cost accounting is often discussed in conjunction with two other areas of accounting – managerial and financial, although they are not the same. This chapter presents a brief background discussion of cost accounting, as it relates to government, as well as nonprofit organizations. This is followed by an overview of the differences between cost, managerial, and financial accounting, the rules of cost commitment, cost accounting standards, and cost reporting. The chapter concludes with a brief discussion of ethics in cost and managerial accounting.

1.2 Contextual Framework

Cost accounting is the process of accounting for costs an organization incurs in carrying out its routine and non-routine operations. The process is detailed, with distinct, interrelated, and well-defined activities. These activities include gathering, recording, analyzing, summarizing, evaluating, and interpreting cost and related information, and communicating

DOI: 10.4324/9781003486091-1

the results to those who would directly benefit from them (Lanen et al., 2020). In government, this would mostly include the chief administrator, elected officials, various agency heads, internal auditors, plus any other individual who is directly involved in the operations of the government. Although individuals and entities outside of government may benefit from the information the process generates, it is primarily used for internal consumption.

1.3 Relationship with Other Disciplines

There is a direct relationship between cost and managerial accounting and disciplines that benefit from the information they generate. For instance, cost information is particularly useful for budgeting and economic decision making which is concerned with how best to allocate the limited resources of a government to meet its competing needs (Marburger, 2013). Information, especially cost data, is frequently used in the production and delivery process, pricing strategies, as it draws heavily from economic principles such as marginal analysis, benefit-cost analysis, cost-effectiveness analysis, and other similar methods to evaluate the cost implications of government decisions.

Similarly, cost information plays an important role in the financial management and reporting activities of a government and nonprofit organization. For instance, the result of financial management activities is an annual report consisting of a number of financial statements that summarize the financial condition of a government (Mead, 2018). This also applies to nonprofit organizations and the financial reports they prepare at the end of the year. The information cost accounting gathers on costs of materials, labor, and work-in-process in the production and delivery of a good or service are often incorporated in preparing some of these statements (Smith, 2014).

The information cost accounting produces is also useful in operations management which deals with how best to manage and control the internal operations of a government for increased efficiency and effectiveness. This is where tools used in fields such as operations research for efficiency and performance measurement become useful in cost studies (Kriens et al., 1983; Vatter, 1967). Cost accounting works closely with operations research, by identifying areas within production and delivery processes where costs can be optimized through improved efficiency and resource allocation.

Besides budgeting and economic decision making, financial management and reporting, and operations management and control, cost accounting is also important in planning, especially strategic planning and management (Shank and Govindarajan, 2008). Strategic planning deals with the best ways to direct (plan) and manage the financial and nonfinancial resources

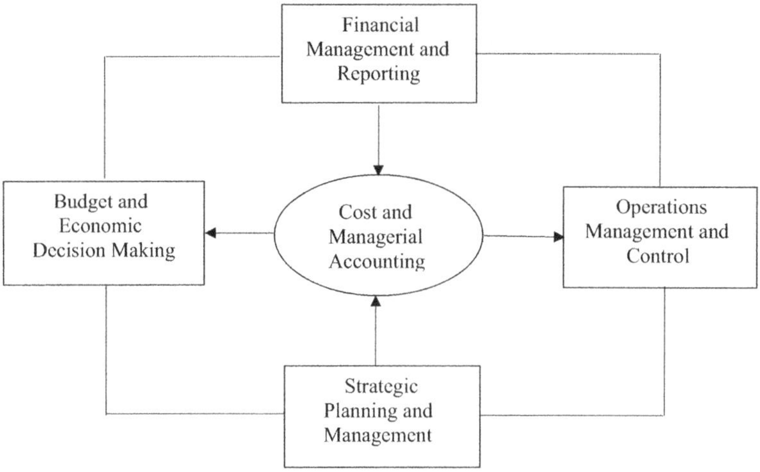

Figure 1.1 Relationship between cost accounting and other areas of operation

of an organization to achieve its mission, goals, and objectives. The information cost accounting produces, such as direct costs, indirect costs, operating costs, and so forth, are extremely useful in developing a strategic plan; in particular, strategies. This is understandable since the strategies a strategic plan uses frequently rely on cost information to determine the best course of action to achieve the mission, goals and objectives of an organization. Figure 1.1 shows this relationship between cost accounting and other areas of government operations.

1.4 A Brief Historical Development

Cost accounting has a relatively short history compared to other fields of study in government, although it has been extensively used in the private sector, especially in Western Europe, going back to at least the 14th century (Garner, 1954; Brown, 1905). In the US, it was not formally introduced until the late 19th century (Metcalf, 1895), although interest has been growing in recent years, especially with outsourcing and contracting out of services becoming common place at all three levels of government.

This is particularly reflected at the federal level, where cost accounting has received considerably more attention than at the state and local level, in part because the federal government has strict guidelines for contracting services, where it is mostly used (Manos, 2020; AGA-CPAG, 2009). For instance, the Chief Financial Officers Act of 1990 requires the government to integrate and modernize its financial systems and to provide for the development and reporting of cost information (Holm, 2018; Smith, 2014; Oracle, 2010). Additionally, government legislation such as the Government Performance and Results Act of 1993 also requires the government to develop strategic plans and performance goals, based on unit costs and other types of cost information, to be able to measure and compare costs with outputs and outcomes (Oracle, 2010).

The Federal Financial Accounting Standards in particular highlight the importance of cost accounting in managing government programs. For instance, according to one of the standards (Standard 4), cost information is necessary in several areas of government operations, especially in budgeting and control, as well as performance measurement, in determining and setting fees and prices, evaluating programs, and making economic decisions (Oracle, 2010). The standards specifically recognize the importance of tracing the use of government resources to an agency's performance goal, where managerial cost accounting is considered the recommended method of achieving this goal.

Interestingly, cost accounting has been widely used at the local level for a long time, going as far back as the early twentieth century, especially for measuring efficiency in service provision, but it was never implemented in a systematic and structured fashion (Rivenbark, 2005), which partly explains why it has not received the same level of attention as it did at the federal level. The passage of Statement 34 by the Governmental Accounting Standards Board (GASB) in 1999 generated renewed interest in cost accounting. The statement expanded the existing financial reporting model by including government-wide financial statements to provide a broad overview of the financial condition of a government that was lacking in the earlier reporting model. The new statements include cost information, such as the total cost of government services, to enable the jurisdictions to make comparisons against other service providers (Rivenbark, 2005). With recent developments in outsourcing and public-private partnership, the interest in cost accounting is likely to grow even further.

Similarly, cost and managerial accounting in nonprofit organizations has a long history that goes back to the beginning of the 20th century with the passage of the Tariff Act in 1913 that granted tax-exempt status for certain charitable organizations. This was followed by the War Revenue Act of 1917 providing tax benefits to donors contributing to non-profits. In 1941, the Internal Revenue Service (IRS) introduced Form 990, which became mandatory for most nonprofit organizations to file annually, providing increased transparency regarding their financial activities and operations. It was reinforced further in 1954 when the IRS Code established the 501(c) classification system, defining different types of nonprofit organizations and their eligibility for tax-exempt status (Sanches et al., 2020). There have been additional changes and requirements since then and in all likelihood, it will continue in the coming years, depending on the demand and changes in government-nonprofit partnership.

At the procedural level, the American Institute of Certified Public Accountants (AICPA) played an important role in developing accounting standards, specifically for nonprofit organizations (Deloitte, 2024). This included, among others, the Standards of Accounting and Financial Reporting for Voluntary Health and Welfare Organizations, which provided a framework for reporting financial information. With growing public scrutiny, both nonprofit organizations and the government have increasingly emphasized the importance of sound financial management practices, including cost analysis, budgeting, and performance metrics to demonstrate the effectiveness of their programs (AICPA, 2019).

1.5 Cost, Financial, and Managerial Accounting

As noted earlier, cost accounting is often discussed in conjunction with two other fields of accounting – financial and managerial. Although the three are discussed in the same way, they are not quite the same, especially financial accounting. What distinguishes them is the basis of use (who uses the information generated by the accounting process and the purpose it serves). For instance, financial accounting produces information that is primarily used for external consumption to meet the needs of outside individuals and organizations such as bond rating institutions, investors in government securities, upper-level governments which provide financial assistance to lower-level governments to fill their revenue gaps, concerned citizens, and other external evaluators. Much of the information financial accounting produces is presented in the form of financial statements that contain detailed accounts of the financial position of a government (Libby et al., 2019; Patton et al., 2019). To ensure that these statements are presented fairly, consistently, and accurately, they are prepared according to a set of prescribed guidelines, known as Generally Accepted Accounting Principles (GAAP).

GAAP consists of a set of rules, conventions, and procedures that define the accepted accounting principles in operational terms (FASAB, 2024). In government, the responsibility for establishing these rules falls on the Governmental Accounting Standards Board (GASB), an autonomous organization headed by a chairman, a full-time director, and several part-time members (Ingram, 1991). The board reports directly to the central accounting organization called the Financial Accounting Foundation (FAF). The foundation, in turn, selects its members and raises funds to support its activities and those of its private sector counterpart - the Financial Accounting Standards Board (FASB).

In contrast, managerial accounting produces information that is mostly used by the chief administrator, the agencies, internal auditors, elected officials, and others who are directly involved in the day-to-day operations of a government (Martin, 2016). Since the information produced by managerial accounting is largely used for internal consumption, it is not governed by GAAP and, as such, is considered more flexible than financial accounting. It is also more eclectic, drawing heavily from other disciplines such as economics, decision science, statistics, finance, and management. In this respect, there is a similarity between cost and managerial accounting in that both rely heavily on other disciplines for substantive growth, both provide information that is used for internal consumption, and in both cases their practices are not governed by GAAP.

Perhaps the most interesting aspect of cost and managerial accounting, which separates them from financial accounting, is that they both are tools oriented and analytical in content. Because of these apparent similarities, the two fields are often treated as one, with one major difference: Cost accounting is more concerned with routine operations of an organization, whereas managerial accounting is more finance oriented.

1.6 Rules of Cost Commitment

When costs are incurred by an organization, it is due to one of two things: due to a commitment made by the organization or owing to a third-party effect. Most costs are due to the commitments an organization makes and, as such, they cannot be avoided in most instances. This is particularly true for government where costs result from policy decisions, often with long-term consequences. Therefore, it is important that these decisions are made with a sound understanding of the costs that underlie them.

The following provides some basic rules of cost commitment:

There should be a direct relationship between cost and the purpose it serves. This is the first rule of cost commitment. There must be a clearly defined objective for an activity for which costs will be ascertained. Setting clear-cut objectives can not only help an organization identify the costs it will incur for specific activities, but also facilitate its resource allocation, improve organizational performance, and increase accountability in the long run.

Costs should be charged only when they are incurred. Although most organizations are careful about it, occasional glitches can occur in an accounting system where a cost unit could be charged before a cost has been actually incurred. This can happen especially where programs or activities are recurring. Regular monitoring of accounting and related activities can easily correct this problem.

Costs should be properly segregated to avoid the problems of multiple counting. Serious problems can arise if costs are not properly traced to their sources of origin, especially in government, where revenues and expenditures are required by law to be segregated by funds. Therefore, any mix-up in costs can affect fund balance, which, in turn, can affect future financial management decisions of an organization. With good record-keeping practices, this can easily be avoided.

Past costs should be avoided in cost calculations. It is an axiom in cost studies that only those costs that are relevant to a specific activity should be included in cost calculations. Past costs, while they may be significant, are not considered relevant except when they are used for forecasting purposes since they have already been incurred. However, if a cost has been incurred, it can be included in cost calculation, provided it still has some realizable values left that can be retained or replaced.

All cost transactions should be recorded on a double-entry accounting system, where possible. The double-entry accounting system has become standard practice for most organizations, including government. However, for cost accounting, a lot of organizations still use a single-entry accounting system. In a single-entry system, cost ledgers are prepared differently from financial ledgers (as in fund accounting), yet the two use the same basic data. This creates a discrepancy in cost analysis, but it can be corrected with a double entry-accounting system.

Unusual cost data should be treated separately from normal data. This is more of a statistical than an accounting problem, but it can easily influence the outcome for the latter. From time to time, organizations may encounter costs that are clearly outside the realm of normal data. In statistics, they are called outliers. Their presence in normal data can distort cost calculations and provide misleading information to the decision makers. They should not be totally thrown out of cost calculations but, like most outliers, they should be treated separately.

Data used in cost studies should be verified periodically for validity and reliability. Like any financial data, cost data should be verified on a regular basis to see if it is correct and follows proper cost accounting procedures. This is part of the auditing process. Cost auditing ensures that the data used in accounting is correct and that cost units, cost centers, and cost accounts have been appropriately charged.

Cost statements should be presented fairly and accurately. Finally, all financial organizations, including government and nonprofit organizations, are required to provide fair and full disclosure of all their transactions and changes in financial position, which, as noted earlier, can also be extended to include cost statements. Failure to accurately measure costs and present them in a consistent manner can have serious impacts on organizational performance both in the current and in future years. Inaccuracy can enter cost statements when, for instance, contingencies are added to cost calculations. If contingencies are necessary, they should be maintained in a separate account and not merged with accounts for regular and normal activities.

1.7 Cost Accounting Standards

All organizations use standards to ensure quality, consistency, and safety of the goods and services they produce and deliver. Likewise, cost accounting has standards, which, in addition to the rules of cost commitments, are necessary for an organization when dealing with cost data. The standards set guidelines that organizations must follow to account for costs. The idea behind standards is to produce cost information that is clear, accurate, and reliable. They are designed to improve the accuracy of cost data by ensuring that they are based on consistent definitions and principles. More importantly, they provide a benchmark against which actual costs can be compared and measured for accuracy, determine inefficiency, control expenses, and help organizations make informed decisions.

Cost Accounting Standards (CAS) in government, especially at the federal level, are set by the Cost Accounting Standards Board (CASB), an independent legislatively established entity,[2] and part of the Office of the Federal Procurement Policy (OFPP). Developed primarily for government contractors, the standards consist of a series of 19 standards, with associated rules, conditions, and regulations issued by the government.[3] These standards were put in place to ensure that government contractors maintain uniformity and consistency in how costs associated with government contracts are computed, allocated, and reported. The CAS requires contractors to maintain accurate and complete records of their costs, allocate costs appropriately, and disclose any changes in accounting practices. Compliance with CAS is required for all contractors and subcontractors engaged in business with any federal government agency and covers all types of contracts. State and local governments also have cost standards, consistent with those of the federal government.

Nonprofit organizations, like the government, are also required to strictly follow the accounting standards, especially when receiving government funding. This is necessary to ensure consistency and transparency in financial reporting; more importantly, to ensure that they follow the Generally Accepted Accounting Principles (GAAP).

1.8 Cost Reporting and Audit

Historically, the information generated by cost and managerial accounting has been used for internal consumption but in recent years there has been a growing interest in external reporting of cost information, especially where contracts are concerned. Whereas in the past the reports were mostly ad hoc, governments now require the use of formal standards, such as the Generally Accepted Accounting Principles (GAAP), especially for federal contracts. State and local governments receiving federal funding are also required to use GAAP for reporting purposes.[4] There may be exceptions, however, depending on the type of funding.

Once a cost report has been prepared, it is necessary for an organization to conduct a cost audit. The purpose of such an audit is to help the organization verify that the cost records and accounts used in a study are consistent with the established standards and that they have followed prescribed cost accounting procedures. In situations where standards are not clearly specified for cost audits, reporting entities, including governments, can follow the guidelines used for financial audits. To illustrate the point, financial audits are based on two essential conditions: fairness and compliance. The former requires that the audited entities have presented their basic financial statements fairly, in conformity with GAAP, while the latter requires that they are in compliance with the stated laws, regulations, and contractual obligations. In addition to financial audits, organizations often conduct performance audits to assess the efficiency and economy of the audited entities' operations and to determine the extent to which they have achieved their stated goals and objectives. The objective is to ensure accuracy of cost records (fairness), statutory requirements (compliance), and efficiency and economy (performance) based on standard or prescribed accounting procedures.

Put simply, the benefits of a cost audit, even an informal audit, are enormous. If properly conducted, a cost audit can easily help improve an organization's internal control, increase efficiency of its operation, and create cost consciousness among its employees. Additionally, a formal cost audit can help ensure maximum utilization of available resources and, more importantly, provide the decision makers with information for effective financial decision making.

1.9 Ethics in Cost and Managerial Accounting

It is almost impossible to discuss any subject or discipline without having any reference to ethics. This is more so for public and nonprofit organizations where ethical norms and behavior remain the central focus of how employees in these organizations should conduct themselves. Ethical conduct generally includes behavior that one would consider "right" or "proper", but it is not quite as simple to define what is right or proper. Nevertheless, there are some commonalities (core values) that bind individuals within an organization, which frequently provide the basis for designing ethical norms and standards.

In a now famous article on ethics in management accounting, James Brackner, (1992) recognized ten such core values for organizational ethics, which also applies to accounting practice: honesty, integrity, promise keeping, fidelity, fairness, caring for others, respect for others, responsible citizenship, pursuit of excellence, and accountability. Collectively, all these values appear to make sense, but it is difficult to say whether they would be most prudent from an individual perspective. For instance, while responsible citizenship may require caring and respect for others, it can be in direct conflict with the pursuit of excellence. Theoretically, in pursuing excellence one does not necessarily have to care for or have respect for others so long as one carefully observes the remaining values. But in practice, lack of responsible citizenship can affect collective performance which may not be in one's own best interest or the interest of the organization as a whole.

Although suggested for private organizations, Brackner's core values can be applied to any organization. To ensure that public organizations carry out their responsibilities ethically and professionally, the American Society for Public Administration (ASPA) also developed several core values for organizational ethics that would apply to all professional activities, including cost accounting (Svara, 2013). They are (1) advance the public interest, (2) uphold the constitution and the law, (3) promote democratic participation, (4) strengthen social equity, (5) fully inform and advise, (6) demonstrate commitment to duty, principle, and personal integrity, (7) promote ethical organizations, and (8) strive for professional excellence. Two of these codes (5 and 6) have a direct bearing on accounting practices as they focus on efficiency and standards of behavior. Code 5, for instance, emphasizes accurate, honest, comprehensive, and timely information and Code 6 on the highest standards of conduct to inspire public confidence and trust in public service. Collectively all these values are important in public organizations as they focus on striving for and always maintaining the highest ethical and professional standards.

Similarly, nonprofit organizations are required to maintain high ethical standards. The standards by and large include honesty (accountability in financial reporting), integrity (ethical behavior in all aspects of management), objectivity (decisions based on data), transparency (fair presentation of financial information), and confidentiality (safeguard sensitive information) to maintain public trust and ensure responsible use of resources. However, unlike government and business organizations, unethical conducts for nonprofit organizations can lead to severe penalties, loss of trust, and even tax-exempt status.

1.10 Chapter Summary

Cost lies at the heart of all financial activities of an organization. Without some knowledge of costs, in particular cost accounting, it will be difficult for an organization to carry out its routine and non-routine operations. The information that cost accounting generates is extremely useful for an organization, in particular, government, that ranges from budgeting and economic decision making, to financial statements and reporting, to operations management and control, to strategic planning and management, among others. This chapter has provided a brief background discussion of cost accounting, as it relates to government and nonprofit organizations, followed by a discussion of the differences between cost, financial and managerial accounting. The chapter concluded with a brief discussion of cost reporting and audit, rules of cost commitment, and ethics in cost accounting.

1.11 Review Questions

1.1 What is accounting? How does cost accounting differ from financial and managerial accounting?
1.2 Why is cost and managerial accounting important in government? Discuss briefly the history of cost accounting in government and nonprofit organizations.
1.3 What is GAAP? What role does GAAP play in cost and managerial accounting?
1.4 What is audit? What are the benefits of audit and reporting in government? Why is it difficult to develop a uniform set of codes for cost audits and reporting in government?
1.5 What are some of the rules of cost commitments in government? Why is it necessary to follow these rules?
1.6 What role does ethics play in government? How does ASPA address the ethical issues in government that also apply to cost and managerial accounting?

Notes

1 These are organizations that are neither completely public nor completely private. In reality, they are mostly private organizations that may have been a part of government at one time but are no longer a part of it and have government mandates to provide specific services. A good example would be the Federal National Mortgage Association (FNMA).
2 The Cost Accounting Standards Board (CASB) mandates consistency and uniformity in cost accounting activities for government grants and contracts.

Established by Congress in 1970, under Public Law 91–379, it was dissolved in 1980 but was permanently re-established in 1988. The CASB is a function of the Office of Federal Procurement Policy (OFPP). It serves three specific objectives: (1) create, update, and enforce cost accounting standards, (2) ensure consistency in how costs are measured, assigned, and allocated, and (3) require contractors and subcontractors to comply with CAS, and, more importantly, as a condition of contracting, to disclose in writing their cost accounting practices (Rayburn, 1996).

3 There are currently 19 standards, 10 of which were introduced in 1982. The standards have changed over the years under successive administrations.

4 GAAP has a number of principles, 10 or so, that serve as the main principles. Here are examples of some of the principles: Matching Principle – matching expenses related to the revenue in the same period, assuming a cause-and-effect relationship. Accrual Principal – recording transactions when they occur, not when received in cash or paid out in cash. Recognition Principal – recognizing revenue when the service is provided, not when planned or scheduled. Consistency Principle – applying accounting methods consistently for similar items across time. Full Disclosure Principle – disclosing all material information in financial statements. In addition, there are other principles, such as materiality (ignoring minor expenses that will not significantly affect financial statements), going concern (the entity will continue to operate in the foreseeable future), historical cost (assets should be recorded at their original cost when acquired), and so forth.

References

AGA-CPAG. (2009). *Managerial cost Accounting in federal government: Providing useful information for decision making*. Washington, DC: AGA-CPAG Research Series, Report No. 22.

AICPA. (2019). *Audit and Accounting Guide: Healthcare Entities*. Durham, NC: American Institute of Certified Public Accountants.

Brackner, J.W. (1992). Consensus values should be taught. *Management Accounting*, August, Page 19.

Brown, R. (1905). *History of accounting and accountants*. London: Ballantyne, Hanson & Company.

Deloitte. (2024). AICPA Audit and Accounting Guide: Not-For-Profit Entities. https://dart.deloitte.com/USDART/home/auditing/aicpa/audit-accounting-guides-audit-risk-alerts/aicpa-audit-accounting-guide-not-for

FASAB. (2024). *FASAB Handbook of Federal Accounting Standards and Other Pronouncements, as Amended*. Washington, DC: Federal Accounting Standards Advisory Board.

Garner, S.P. (1954). *Evolution of cost account to 1925*. Tuscaloosa, AL: The University of Alabama Press.

Holm, L. (2018). *Cost accounting and financial management for construction project managers*. New York: Routledge.

Ingram, R.W. et al. (1991). *Accounting and financial reporting for governmental and nonprofit organizations: Basic concepts*. New York: McGraw-Hill.

Lanen, W., Anderson S., and Maher, M. (2020). *Fundamentals of cost accounting*. New York: McGraw Hill Education.

Libby, R., Libby, P., and Hodge, F. (2019). *Financial accounting*. New York: McGraw-Hill.

Kriens, J., van Lieshout, J.T., and Verheyen, R.P. (1983). Management accounting and operations research. *European Journal of Operations Research*, 13(4): 339–352.

Manos, K.L. (ed.). (2020). *Government contract costs and pricing handbook*. Washington, DC: Thomson West.

Marburger, D. (2013). *Economic decision-making using cost data*. New York: Business Expert Press.

Martin, J.R. (1916). *Management Accounting: Concepts, Techniques, and Controversial Issues*. Management and Accounting Web: http://maaw.info/MAAWTextbookMain.htm (undated).

Mead, D. (2018). *An analyst's guide to government financial statements*. Norwalk, CT: Government Accounting Standards Board.

Metcalf, H. (1885). *Cost of manufactures*. New York: John Wiley.

Oracle. (2010). *Federal government managerial cost accounting*. Oracle White Paper. Washington, DC: Oracle.

Patton, T., Patton, S., and Ives, M. (2019). *Accounting for governmental & non-profit organizations*. Cambridge, England: Cambridge Business Publishers.

Rayburn, F.R. (1996). Cost Accounting Standards Board (1970–1980–; 1988–), in M. Chatfield and R. Vangermeersch (eds) *History of accounting: An international encyclopedia*. New York: Garland Publishing, 170–180.

Rivenbark, W.C. (2005). A historical overview of cost accounting in local governments. *State and Local Government Review*, 37(3): 217–227.

Sanches, L.C, Brown, S.A., and Izzo, J.A. (2020). A century of not-for-profit accounting: A historical perspective. *The CPA Journal*. www.cpajournal.com/2020/12/09/a-century-of-not-for-profit-accounting/

Shank, J.K. and Govindarajan, V. (2008). *Strategic cost management: The new tool for competitive advantage*. New York: Free Press.

Smith, L.R. (2014). *Financial accounting and reporting*. New York: Wolters Kluwer Tax & Accounting.

Svara, J.H. (2013). *Public administrator's code of ethics*. Phoenix, AZ: Lincoln Center for Applied Ethics, Arizona State University.

Vatter, W.J. (1967). Operations research and management accounting. *Nebraska Journal of Economics and Business*, 6(2), Autumn: 65–79.

Part I

Cost Basics

- Cost Terms and Concepts
- Price and Rate Structure of Cost
- Cost Behavior and Estimation
- Break-Even Analysis
- Differential analysis

DOI: 10.4324/9781003486091-2

2 Cost Terms and Concepts

2.1 Introduction

Cost is central to effective decision making in an organization. It is the cement that holds together the different elements of an organization into a viable operating structure. For governments, as well as for non-profit organizations, it serves as the principal guiding force that underlies most decisions they make, especially those related to the provision of goods and services. More specifically, without some knowledge of costs it will be difficult for these organizations to know what kinds of goods and services to provide, the level of their provision, the length of time for which they will be provided, and the costs the provisions will incur. Even for those goods and services that are considered meritorious, such as education and healthcare, cost remains the single most overriding concern. This chapter introduces several key concepts that are useful in cost studies and defines and distinguishes between different types of costs. It also illustrates the contrast between cost, expense, and expenditure, and how to reconcile the differences. A term that often appears alongside cost is depreciation. This chapter highlights the relationship between cost and depreciation, followed by a detailed discussion of some of the commonly used depreciation methods in cost studies.

2.2 What Is Cost?

Cost ordinarily means the value of economic resources used in the production and delivery of goods and services. The use of the word "value" has a special meaning in cost studies; it indicates the actual dollar amount spent on materials, labor, and other factors of production. Since a government does not produce goods for direct public consumption, with some exceptions such as water, electricity, and a few others, the costs a government incurs in providing goods and services include the costs of acquisition, maintenance, and delivery.

DOI: 10.4324/9781003486091-3

Costs are generally expressed in cost units. A cost unit is a unit of a good or service in relation to which costs are ascertained. It is the basic unit of measurement used in all cost calculations. Examples of cost units in government will be the number of accidents prevented, gallons of water supplied, tons of garbage collected, and so on. For nonprofit organizations, this will typically include the number of individuals served, percentage of goals reached, rate of donor retention, average donation amount, cost per donor acquisition, program impact metrics, such as literacy rates or improved health outcomes, and fundraising efficiency ratios, and so forth. Additionally, costs can also be expressed in terms other than cost units such as costs incurred by an agency, a department, a function, a program, and a product. These individual units of a government, or a nonprofit organization, and their functions, programs, and services to which costs are frequently charged are called cost objects. Theoretically a cost object can be anything so long as it is possible to attribute costs to a responsible body unit.

When costs are charged to a cost object, it entails only those costs that belong to it and not to any other entity. On occasion, however, one may find two or more cost objects sharing a service responsibility and, therefore, the costs associated with it. These types of costs are generally known as joint costs. An example of joint costs in government will be a public safety program that is jointly provided by a police department and a county sheriff's office, where both organizations share the responsibility as well as the cost. Cost sharing for joint provision is an old concept, but has become increasingly common in recent years, especially for communities that are financially strapped.

2.3 Cost Classification

Classification generally means organizing activities with the same attributes into distinct groups or categories. In cost studies, classification means maintaining effective record keeping and establishing proper linkage to cost objects. Interestingly, there is no one specific cost that can uniformly apply to all government and non-governmental activities; different types and variations of costs exist, depending on the purpose they serve. This section presents several different types of costs that are used in varying degrees in government and nonprofit organizations, depending on the purpose they serve, the time frame of use, types of goods and services, their relevance to planning, degree of controllability, and so forth. By and large, they include (1) direct versus indirect, (2) fixed versus variable, (3) mixed versus step, (4) current versus historical, (5) sunk versus future, (6) incremental versus total, (7) implicit versus explicit, (8) product versus period,

(9) standard versus actual, (10) relevant versus irrelevant, (11) controllable versus uncontrollable, and (12) one time versus life cycle.

2.3.1 Direct versus Indirect Cost

A cost is considered direct if it can be unequivocally traced to a cost object. Since direct costs can be unequivocally traced or attributed to a cost object, they do not involve any cost sharing between cost objects. This makes it possible to calculate them with relative ease compared to other types of costs. Examples of direct costs will include personnel costs such as wages, salaries, fringe benefits, and other non-personnel costs such as materials and supplies. In contrast, an indirect cost, also known as an overhead, cannot be unequivocally attributed to a specific cost object because these often involve multiple cost objects, although the cost may be necessary for the completion of an activity. Examples of indirect costs will be rent (if a facility is used for more than one purpose), supervision (if responsibility is shared between different activities and operating units), supplies (if purchased in bulk for multiple activities and units), insurance, and utilities.

2.3.2 Fixed versus Variable Cost

A cost is considered fixed if it does not change in relation to the quantity produced or consumed. This condition for fixed costs is true only in the short run (throughout the relevant range) because in the long run all costs are variable, meaning that they do not remain fixed over a long period of time. Examples of fixed costs will include salary, rent, interest payments on debt, and depreciation on structure and equipment (if depreciated at a fixed rate). A variable cost, on the other hand, changes in direct proportion to changes in the quantity produced or consumed. It is fixed per unit of output but varies in total as quantity or output level changes (Figure 2.1). Suppose that a government purchases 20 units of an item that costs \$15 a unit, the total variable cost of the item will be \$300 (\$15 × 20). Wages, utilities, materials and supplies are typical examples of variable costs.

2.3.3 Mixed versus Step Cost

There are circumstances where the cost is neither entirely fixed nor completely variable. These types of costs are called mixed costs. Mixed costs, also known as semi-variable costs, are a common occurrence in government. For instance, a public utility's billing rate may contain a flat (fixed) charge per month that is independent of consumption, plus a rate per unit in excess of the fixed monthly rate that may change with the changes in the

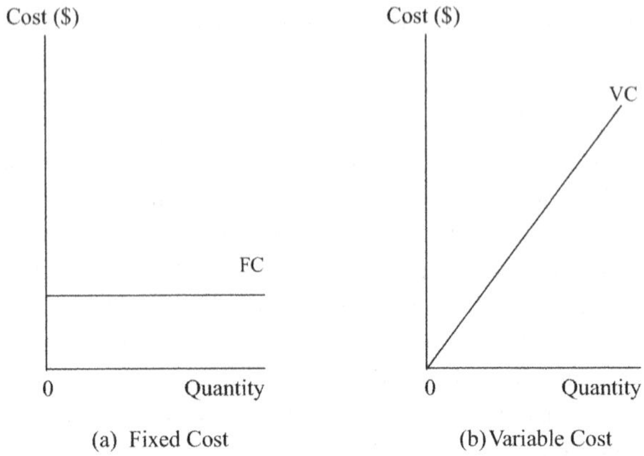

Figure 2.1 Fixed and variable cost

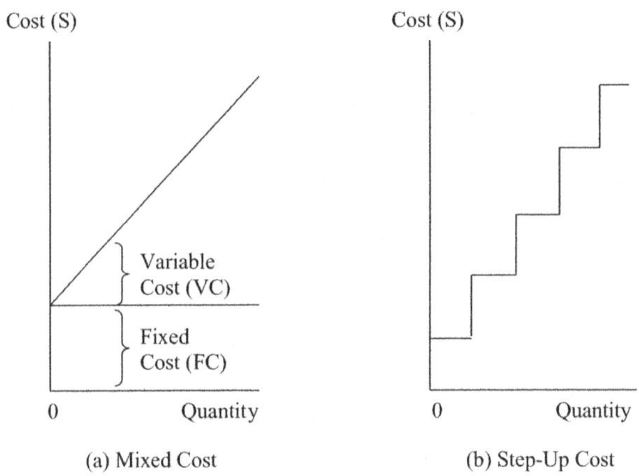

Figure 2.2 Mixed and step-up cost

level of production or delivery.[1] A step cost, on the other hand, is a cost that does not change continuously as the quantity increases, but rather increases at discrete points, as in a staircase (Figure 2.2). For instance, the construction cost of a building remains steady until the next level is added when it increases to a higher level as new costs are incurred, then becomes steady again until the next level is added, and so forth.

2.3.4 Current versus Historical Cost

Current cost represents the value of a good produced or service consumed at the present time. The term 'current' means that costs incurred in the past have no bearing on production or consumption at present. An example of current costs will be a desktop computer that a government purchased, say, for \$1,800 a year ago, which, if purchased today, would cost \$1,500. The current cost of the item will be \$1,500, even though the government purchased it for \$1,800. Historical cost, on the other hand, represents the cost incurred at the time of purchase. Thus, the \$1,800 the government paid a year ago for the computer will be the historical cost, regardless of how much it costs today. In accounting, it is the historical cost that is mostly used. There are two simple reasons for that: Firstly, it is important for reporting purposes, especially when preparing a financial statement or report and, secondly, it helps to prevent the over-estimation of costs, if, for instance, the current cost is due to temporary changes, or unstable conditions in the market.

2.3.5 Sunk versus Future Cost

A special case of historical cost, a sunk cost can be defined as the cost incurred in the past that has no resale or salvage value and, as such, it cannot be recovered. Thus, if the computer in our previous example has no resale value (assuming it has become obsolete) but it cost the government \$1,800 when first purchased, the sunk cost will be the entire amount of \$1,800. A future cost, as opposed to sunk or historical costs, will be incurred at certain points in time in the future. For instance, if the government decides to purchase a computer six months from now, the price it will pay for it at that time will be the future cost.

2.3.6 Incremental versus Total Cost

An incremental cost, also called a marginal cost, is the cost of producing an additional unit of a good or service. For instance, if it costs \$11 to produce 10 gallons of water and \$13 to produce 11 gallons, the incremental (marginal) cost or cost of producing the 11th gallon would be \$2 [\$13 - \$11 = \$2]. On the other hand, total cost is the sum of all costs involved in the production and delivery of a good or service. For instance, if it costs a government \$500 in fixed costs and \$1,500 in variable costs to provide a good or service, the total cost of the provision will be \$2,000 [\$500 + \$1,500 = \$2,000].

2.3.7 Implicit versus Explicit Cost

Implicit cost, also known as imputed or implied cost, is the cost of what one must give up in order to produce or consume a good or service. The term is often used synonymously with opportunity cost. It is not really the cost one incurs in the true sense of the term but is essential for making economic decisions. Since these are not actual costs, they do not show up in accounting records. For instance, if a government uses internally generated funds for which it receives no interest, but had the funds been invested they would have earned an interest income of, say, $1,500; the loss of interest income will be the implicit (opportunity) cost, which is the cost of opportunity forgone. Opportunity cost, therefore, is the cost one incurs by not selecting the alternative; in fact, all costs, in some sense, are opportunity costs. Explicit cost, on the other hand, is the cost one incurs in carrying out an activity and is recognized as such. Thus, if a government pays $500 in rent for a piece of equipment it uses to carry out an activity it will be an explicit cost. Other examples of explicit costs will be salaries and wages, payments for materials and supplies, interest payments on debt, and so forth.

2.3.8 Product versus Period Cost

Product costs are costs of labor, materials, and overhead that can be attributed to the production or delivery of a good or service. In other words, they will not be incurred if there are no goods and services produced or delivered at the end of the process. Examples of product costs are costs of direct labor, direct materials, and overhead (indirect labor and indirect materials that are not directly related to production or delivery). Period costs, on the other hand, include all costs other than product costs. Although useful, they are not necessary for the production or delivery of a good or service. Marketing costs, the costs of legal research and development are good examples of period costs.

2.3.9 Standard versus Actual Cost

Standard costs are predetermined costs based on standards that most practitioners or stakeholders would agree with, also called industry standards.[2] They are usually established on a unit cost basis and often serve as benchmarks for comparing actual costs. Actual costs, on the other hand, are costs an organization incurs when carrying out an activity and are frequently compared against standard costs to determine the extent of variation in costs between the two. For instance, let us say that a government purchases 20 units of an item at a cost of $150 a unit, while the standard cost of the item is \$125, if purchased at a discount for bulk purchase. Therefore, the actual cost of the items to the government would be \$3,000 (\$150 × 20), and the standard (discount) cost would be \$2,500 (\$125 × 20).

2.3.10 Relevant versus Irrelevant Cost

A cost is considered relevant if its value changes in the course of an action. Relevant costs are decision specific such as acquiring an asset, producing a good, or delivering a service; as such, it has a direct bearing on the cost of operation. An irrelevant cost, on the other hand, does not change with a change in the course of action (producing a good or delivering a service). Sunk costs are good examples of irrelevant costs. This does not mean that they should not be recognized, but only that they do not have any quantitative effect on a decision. There is often a tendency to confuse fixed costs with irrelevant costs since both remain unaffected by changes in the quantity produced or delivered, but the two are not the same. In a fixed cost, the cost is relevant but remains the same regardless of the quantity produced or delivered, whereas for an irrelevant cost it has no bearing on the decision.

2.3.11 Controllable versus Uncontrollable Cost

A cost is considered controllable if there exists a significant degree of control on its incurrence. In general, for a cost to be controllable, an organization must have sufficient discretion over it. Wages, salaries, fringe benefits, and various non-personnel costs are good examples of controllable costs. However, controllable does not mean 100 percent controllable, only that the organization has sufficient influence over it. Uncontrollable costs, on the other hand, are costs over which an organization does not have any discretion. Interest payment on debt, contract obligations, and entitlements are among the best-known examples of uncontrollable costs. They are called uncontrollable because when an organization, in particular a government makes a commitment to purchase an item or provide a service guaranteed by legislative actions, the government is obligated to pay for the item or provide the service. In other words, it cannot avoid the cost of purchase or the provision of the service without violating any legal or contractual obligations.

2.3.12 One-Time versus Life-Time Cost

A cost can be one time, or it can extend over the entire useful life of an asset, a service, or a program. One-time costs are those costs that do not involve any additional commitment of resources once a good has been produced or service delivered. In other words, there are no subsequent obligations, including repair and maintenance, except for the initial cost of procurement. Seasonal contracts, with no direct or indirect benefits, are good examples of one-time costs. In contrast, a life-cycle cost includes all costs that are associated with the ownership of an asset, including acquisition, operation, and maintenance over its useful life. Costs associated with buildings, equipment, and service vehicles are typical examples of life-cycle costs.

It should be worth noting that, although they appear distinct, costs are not necessarily mutually exclusive, in that costs can have more than one characteristic. For instance, a cost can be direct as well as fixed, or it can be current as well as uncontrollable. A good example of cost that is direct and fixed would be rent for a facility (assuming it is used for a single purpose). And an example of cost that is current and uncontrollable would be the tax we pay on gasoline or tax we pay on property we own. It is important to note that when dealing with cost items with multiple characteristics, one pays attention to the inherent differences that exist in their characteristics and treats them in a manner that will avoid duplication in cost calculations.

2.4 Cost, Expense, and Expenditure

It is often necessary to make a distinction between three terms that frequently appear in cost calculations: cost, expense, and expenditure. As noted earlier, a cost is the value of economic resources used in the production or delivery of a good or service. An expense, on the other hand, is a cost an organization incurs or a cost it has incurred from the productive use of an asset (resource). An asset is defined as anything of value acquired or owned. Since most public goods and services are provided for direct and immediate consumption by the public, they do not have any acquired value and, consequently, are not regarded as assets. When assets are expended in the course of producing a good or delivering a service such as the use of a patrol vehicle for traffic safety, or an X-ray machine for diagnosing a health problem, or a fire truck for preventing fires, they benefit the community that a government serves; as such, they serve a productive purpose that is necessary for the welfare of the public. Consequently, they are considered an expense. If such provisions do not result in any benefit, direct or indirect, they are considered a waste or loss. Finally, an expenditure is the payment for a good or service that an organization received or provided. As such, it represents an outflow of cash and other resources for payment. From an accounting point of view, expenditures are unadjusted costs that do not reflect any change or adjustments in the consumption of an asset, or in the course of providing a good or a service.

2.4.1 Reconciling the Difference

There is a fundamental reason why it is necessary to understand this distinction between cost, expense, and expenditure: When a government acquires an asset or purchases a cost item, it does not always consume it in the same period, or it may consume it at different rates over time. This creates a lag in consumption but also affects the way in which costs and expenditures are calculated (Cory and Rosenberg, 1984). From an accounting point of view, the lag indicates the amount of adjustment that is necessary for cost calculations. If there is no time lag, that is, if goods purchased in one period are consumed in the same period, then expenditures and costs will be the same, but when they are not consumed in the same period, an adjustment is necessary to maintain consistency in cost calculations.

Let us look at a simple example to illustrate this. Suppose that the Public Works department of a government spent $1.25 million last year on street cleaning, including $84,000 on a new vehicle, $26,000 on materials and supplies, and the rest went to wages, salaries, insurance, and miscellaneous other costs. Since most vehicles have a life expectancy of several years, let us assume that the vehicle purchased has a life expectancy of seven years in that it can be used next year, the year after, and so forth, and will lose some of its use value each year from wear and tear. By the same token, we can assume that not all the materials and supplies will be fully consumed in the current year such that a portion of the materials and supplies will be available for consumption next year or the year after. Assume that $10,000 worth of materials and supplies were used, and the rest remain unused. Therefore, to determine the cost of street cleaning for the government we will need to make some adjustments to the total expenditure by taking into account these changes.

The adjustments typically involve a two-step process: First, we subtract the costs of the items, such as the cost of the vehicle as well as the materials and supplies, from total expenditure for the year when they were purchased. The rationale for this is simple: since these items were not fully consumed in the year in which they were purchased, a portion of them will be available for consumption in the future. Therefore, subtraction would allow for the adjustments to be made for the portion of resources that remain unused during the accounting period. Second, add the portion of materials and supplies as well as the vehicle used for the year. For the vehicle, since it will experience wear and tear, it is important to depreciate it to account for the wear and tear. The cost of street cleaning for the year, therefore, would be the residue. In other words, it is the balance after all

Table 2.1 Cost and expenditure calculation

Street Cleaning: FY 2XXX *($)*		
Total Expenditure		$1,250,000
(-) Vehicle[1]	72,000	
(-) Materials and supplies[2]	16,000	($88,000)
Total Cost		$1,162,000

[1] Unused portion of the vehicle: $84,000 - $12,000* = $72,000
[2] Unused portion of materials and supplies: $26,000 - $10,000 = $16,000
* Depreciation for the first year: $12,000

the adjustments have been made to the total expenditure. This is shown in Table 2.1.

As the table shows, the total cost of street cleaning after all the adjustments have been made came out to be $1,162 million, which is $88,000 less than the total expenditure for the year. The $88,000 is the unused portion of the resources ($72,000 for vehicle + $16,000 for materials and supplies) that will be available for future use. To see if our calculation is correct, we can add $88,000 to $1,162 million, which will produce the total amount of expenditure for the year of $1.25 million [$1,162,000 + $88,000 = $1,250,000].

Thus, we can formally define the cost of operation (street cleaning in our example) as the total expenditure for a given year minus the value of the equipment, materials and supplies that remain unused. However, one must be careful when using approaches such as the one used here because it can complicate the adjustment process if too many cost items are involved with different life spans and levels of use.[3]

2.5 Cost and Depreciation

In our discussion of the street cleaning example, recall that we adjusted the cost of the service by depreciating the value of the vehicle for the year during which it was used. Without this adjustment, we would have had a different cost figure than the one we obtained. Depreciation, therefore, plays an important role in all cost calculations, especially where physical assets are involved with several years of useful life. As noted earlier, depreciation occurs because of wear and tear as well as for technological obsolescence. When an asset depreciates, it loses some, or all of its use value, because it is wearing out and, as such, fails to perform to its fullest capacity. On the other hand, an asset may be slow in wearing out but may still lose its usefulness and in the process its value because of obsolescence such as changes in technology. Thus, the loss of value either because of wear and tear or because of technological obsolescence must be considered when calculating the depreciation of an asset.

There are different ways to depreciate an asset. This section discusses four frequently used depreciation methods in cost studies: straight-line, declining balance, sum-of-the-years-digits, and units of production (Corporate Finance Institute, 2021; Kalfayan, 2012). Of these, declining balance and the sum-of-the-years-digits belong to a category of depreciation, known as accelerated depreciation (Wade and Herman, 2021; Johnson, 1982).

2.5.1 Straight-Line Depreciation

The depreciation method we used in the street-cleaning example is the classic straight-line depreciation. An important characteristic of straight-line depreciation is that it is uniformly distributed over an asset's useful life, which means that depreciation will be the same for each year of the useful life of the asset, regardless of the nature of wear and tear. Determining the depreciation for straight line depreciation is quite simple. All we need to do is divide the initial value of an asset by the number of years of its useful life; that is, V_0/T, where V_0 is the initial value of an asset, and T is the number of years in the useful life of the asset. However, in practice, it is obtained by multiplying the beginning book value of an asset by the depreciation rate. The book value, on the other hand, is the difference between the value of an asset and its accumulated depreciation, while the depreciation rate is obtained by taking the reciprocal of the number of years in the useful life of an asset. In other words, one divided by the numbers of years in the useful life of an asset, 1/T, where T is the total useful life of an asset, which in our case would be 0.1429 or 14.29 percent; that is, $(1/7) \times 100 = 0.1429 \times 100 = 14.29$ percent.

We can formally express depreciation using the straight-line method as

$$d_t = BBV_{Beg} \times DR \tag{2.1}$$

where d_t is the depreciation at time t, BBV_{Beg} is the beginning book value, and DR is the depreciation rate.

To illustrate how the method is used, let us return to the street-cleaning example. We know that the vehicle has a useful life of seven years. Let us assume that the vehicle has no salvage value; the depreciation for the vehicle for the first year thus will be \$12,000 [\$84,000 × 0.1429 = \$12,000 (after rounding off), where \$84,000 is the initial value or purchase price of the vehicle, also known as the beginning book value, and 0.1429 is the depreciation rate. The net or ending book value (at the end of the

Table 2.2 Straight-line depreciation (without the salvage value)

Year	*Annual Depreciation*[1] *($)*	*Accumulated Depreciation*[2] *($)*	*Ending (Net) Book Value ($)*
0	---	---	84,000
1	84,000 × 0.1429 = 12,000	12,000	72,000
2	84,000 × 0.1429 = 12,000	24,000	60,000
3	84,000 × 0.1429 = 12,000	36,000	48,000
4	84,000 × 0.1429 = 12,000	48,000	36,000
5	84,000 × 0.1429 = 12,000	60,000	24,000
6	84,000 × 0.1429 = 12,000	72,000	12,000
7	84,000 × 0.1429 = 12,000	84,000	0

[1] Beginning book value × Depreciation rate; [2]Rounded to the nearest thousand

year) will be $72,000, obtained by subtracting the depreciation from the beginning book value; that is, $84,000 - $12,000 = $72,000. Since the vehicle depreciates at the same rate for each of the seven years of its useful life, the depreciation will be the same for each of the seven years; that is, $d_1 = d_2 = \ldots = d_7$. For T years, it will be $d_1 = d_2 = \ldots = d_T$ and the sum of the depreciations will the equal to its initial value or purchase price; that is, Σd_i (i =1, 2, ..., 7) = $\$12,000_1 + \$12,000_2 + \$12,000_3 + \$12,000_4 + \$12,000_5 + \$12,000_6 + \$12,000_7 = \$84,000$. It should be worth noting that the ending book value at the end of the useful life of the asset (which is the seventh year for our vehicle) will be zero because we are depreciating the asset by the same percentage or DR against the full value or purchase price. The results of the depreciation calculation are shown in Table 2.2.

We made an assumption early in the example that there is no salvage value at the end of the useful life of the vehicle. Let us assume that there is a salvage value. In that case, we will need to adjust the book value by subtracting the salvage value from the initial value. Assume that the vehicle has a salvage value of $14,000, the adjusted book value will therefore be $70,000 [$84,000 - $14,000 = $70,000], which is our initial or beginning book value. The depreciation for the first year will be $10,000, obtained the same way, as before; that is, $70,000 x 0.1429 = $10,000 (after rounding off). This is the amount by which we would have depreciated the vehicle to obtain the cost of street cleaning instead of the $12,000 we used, had we taken the salvage value into consideration. This is shown in Table 2.3.

The greatest advantage of using the straight-line method is that it is simple and easy to use. Also, forecasting the future operation of an asset is much easier when it depreciates at a constant rate. On the other hand, it may not accurately reflect how an asset depreciates, as some assets may depreciate faster than others. Additionally, since it depreciates at the same

Table 2.3 Straight-line depreciation (with the salvage value)

Year	*Annual Depreciation*[1] *($)*	*Accumulated Depreciation*[2] *($)*	*Ending (Net) Book Value ($)*
0	---	---	70,000
1	70,000 × 0.1429 = 10,000	10,000	60,000
2	70,000 × 0.1429 = 10,000	20,000	50,000
3	70,000 × 0.1429 = 10,000	30,000	40,000
4	70,000 × 0.1429 = 10,000	40,000	30,000
5	70,000 × 0.1429 = 10,000	50,000	20,000
6	70,000 × 0.1429 = 10,000	60,000	10,000
7	70,000 × 0.1429 = 10,000	70,000	0

[1] Beginning book value × Depreciation rate; [2]Rounded to the nearest thousand

rate, it is difficult to know when an asset needs to be replaced. Finally, it may not be useful for assets that go through periodic improvements such as land, buildings, and physical plants.

2.5.2 Accelerated Depreciation

While straight-line depreciation is simple and easy to use, it is not realistic because most physical assets do not depreciate at the same rate over time. Accelerated depreciation is a good case in point. In an accelerated depreciation, depreciation is usually high during the early years of an asset's useful life and then declines gradually, as time progresses. Accelerated depreciation is frequently used by firms and businesses because there is an underlying tax advantage. In general, assets are highly productive when they are new; as such, they are more heavily used during the early years which allow businesses to write off the assets before the end of their useful lives or before they become obsolete. Consequently, it is mostly used by firms and businesses rather than by the government.

This section looks at several methods that are frequently used in accelerated depreciation. They are declining balance, double-declining balance, sum-of-the-years-digits, and units of production depreciation.

2.5.2.1 Declining Balance Depreciation

In a declining depreciation balance, the depreciation is usually high during the early years of an asset's useful life. The rationale for this is that it reflects the use-pattern of assets that" are highly productive during the early years of their useful lives and their productivity declines gradually with time. In general, the depreciation in a declining balance tends to decrease with the book value of an asset. As noted earlier, the book value of an asset is the difference between the initial value of an asset and the accumulated depreciation over time. To give an example, suppose that we have an asset whose acquired value at the beginning of the year was \$1,800 and the accumulated depreciation at the end of the year was \$300. The ending book value of the asset at the end of the year will be \$1,500.

We can formally illustrate this with the help of a simple expression: Let DR be a fixed percentage of the initial value (purchase price or cost of acquisition) of an asset, the depreciation for the first year will then be the beginning book value times DR (the fixed percentage of the initial value of the asset). That is,

$$d_1 = BBV_{Beg1} \times DR \tag{2.2}$$

where d_1 is the depreciation in year 1, BBV_{Beg1} is the beginning book value in year 1, and DR is the depreciation rate.

The depreciation for the second year is calculated very much the same way; that is, multiply the beginning book value of the asset in year 2, which is the ending book value for Year 1, by the depreciation rate, so that

$$d_2 = BBV_{Beg2} \times DR \tag{2.3}$$

where d_2 is the depreciation in year 2, BBV_{Beg2} is the beginning book value of the asset in Year 2, and DR is the depreciation rate, as before.

The depreciation for the third year is calculated similarly, as

$$d_3 = BBV_{Beg3} \times DR \tag{2.4}$$

and so forth. The process usually stops when the salvage value is reached. Note that we deliberately used the term fixed percentage of book value for the depreciation rate because the rate can vary depending on where the fixed percentage is set, or how fast one wants to depreciate an asset. Tables 2.4 and 2.5 show the declining balance depreciation with and without the salvage value, with a discount rate of 14.29 percent, which is the rate we used for the straight-line method.

As the tables show, the depreciation is high during the early years of the asset, as one would expect, then declining gradually with time. Since it declines gradually, it usually takes a longer time for the ending book value to be zero than the straight-line depreciation. For depreciation with salvage value, especially since there is a salvage value at the end of the useful life of the asset, one could stop the process once the salvage value is reached.

Table 2.4 Declining balance depreciation (without the salvage value)

Year	*Annual Depreciation ($)*[1]	*Accumulated Depreciation ($)*	*Ending (Book) Value ($)*
0	---	---	84,000
1	84,000 × 0.1429 = 12,004	12,004	71,996
2	71,996 × 0.1429 = 10,288	22,292	61,708
3	61,708 × 0.1429 = 8,818	31,110	52,890
4	52,890 × 0.1429 = 7,558	38,668	45,332
5	45,332 × 0.1429 = 6,478	45,146	38,854
6	38,854 × 0.1429 = 5,552	50,698	33,302
7	33,302 × 0.1429 = 4,759	55,457	28,543

[1] Rounded to the nearest integer

Table 2.5 Declining balance depreciation (with the salvage value)

Year	*Annual Depreciation ($)*[1]	*Accumulated Depreciation ($)*	*Ending (Book) Value ($)*
0	---	---	70,000
1	70,000 × 0.1429 = 10,003	10,003	59,997
2	59,997 × 0.1429 = 8,574	20,292	51,423
3	51,423 × 0.1429 = 7,348	28,865	44,075
4	44,075 × 0.1429 = 6,298	35,234	37,777
5	37,777 × 0.1429 = 5,398	40,692	32,379
6	32,379 × 0.1429 = 4,627	45,370	27,752
7	27,752 × 0.1429 = 3,966	49,380	23,786

[1] Rounded to the nearest integer

2.5.2.2 Double Declining Balance Depreciation

A special case of declining balance depreciation is the double declining balance depreciation, where the DR is obtained by doubling the depreciation rate used for straight line depreciation; hence, the term double declining balance depreciation. What this means is that depreciation will be much higher during the early years of an asset's useful life, as one would expect since we are doubling the depreciation rate, then declining gradually in the later years.

We can now apply the method to the vehicle in our street-cleaning example to obtain the annual depreciation over its useful life. The depreciation rate we will be using is double the rate of the straight-line depreciation, which will be 28.57 percent $[((1/7) \times 2) \times 100 = (0.1429 \times 2) \times 100 = 0.2857 \times 100 = 28.57\%]$. Once we have

Table 2.6 Double declining balance depreciation (without the salvage value)

Year	*Annual Depreciation*[1] *($)*	*Accumulated Depreciation*[2] *($)*	*Ending (Net) Book Value ($)*
0	--	--	84,000
1	84,000 × 0.2857 = 23,999	23,999	60,001
2	60,001 × 0.2857 = 17,142	41,141	42,859
3	42,859 × 0.2857 = 12,245	53,386	30,614
4	30,614 × 0.2857 = 8,746	62,132	21,868
5	21,868 × 0.2857 = 6,248	68,380	15,620
6	15,620 × 0.2857 = 4,463	72,843	11,157
7	11,157 × 0.2857 = 3,188	76,031	7,969

[1] Beginning book value × Depreciation rate; [2]Rounded to the nearest thousand

determined the depreciation rate, the calculation of the depreciation and the ending book value is straightforward. Table 2.6 shows the schedule of annual depreciation and the ending book value for each of the seven years. As the table shows, depreciation is high in the early years of the vehicle, like the declining balance depreciation, and begins to decrease as time progresses. However, the level of depreciation is much higher since we are depreciating at twice the rate of the declining balance depreciation. Also, like the declining balance depreciation, the ending book value at the end of the seventh year is not zero because, as before, we are depreciating the asset by the balance of the beginning value for each successive year, even though it is decreasing at a much higher rate in the early years than the declining balance depreciation.

Table 2.7 shows the double declining balance depreciation with salvage value. It should be worth noting that salvage value is not generally used for declining balance depreciation calculation. Part of the reason for this is that depreciation does not technically reduce the ending book value to zero, although it eventually will but will take much longer than the useful life of the asset. Since the ending book value does not reach zero at the end of the useful life of an asset, as in straight-line depreciation, it does not make much sense to continue the depreciation calculation once it has reached the salvage value. This is because, as noted earlier, the asset has no more use value for the organization after that, which will be approximately year 5 (Table 2.6).

It should be worth noting that while the double declining balance is useful in situations when an asset is consumed at a much higher rate during the early years of its useful life than simple declining balance depreciation, it is obviously not suitable when the asset is consumed at a constant rate, as in straight-line depreciation. An alternative would

Table 2.7 Double declining balance depreciation (with the salvage value)

Year	*Annual Depreciation*[1] *($)*	*Accumulated Depreciation*[2] *($)*	*Ending (Net) Book Value* *($)*
0	--	--	70,000
1	70,000 × 0.2857 =19,999	19,999	50,001
2	50,001 × 0.2857 = 14,285	34,284	35,716
3	35,716 × 0.2857 = 10,204	44,488	25,512
4	25,512 × 0.2857 = 7,289	51,777	18,223
5	18,223 × 0.2857 = 5,206	56,983	13,017
6	13,017 × 0.2857 = 3,719	60,702	9,298
7	9,298 × 0.2857 = 2,656	63,358	6,642

[1] Beginning book value × Depreciation rate; [2]Rounded to the nearest thousand

be to use a moderate rate, such as 1.5, which will better reflect the rate of consumption than a double declining balance, depending on the nature of the asset. From the point of view of business organizations, depreciating an asset at a faster pace, although attractive from a tax perspective, can distort investment decisions if the depreciation fails to accurately reflect profitability. Consequently, most firms and businesses prefer to use a variation of accelerated depreciation, called the Modified Accelerated Cost Recovery System (MACRS), that allows annual deductions for depreciation to recover the costs of a tangible asset over its specified life.[4]

2.5.3 *Sum-of-the-Years-Digits Depreciation*

Unlike the declining balance or double declining balance depreciation, the Sum-of-the-Years-Digits (SYD) depreciation is a much slower version of accelerated depreciation. The difference between SYD and the declining balance depreciation is that it depreciates against the full (initial) value of an asset rather than against its declining values. The result produces a rate of depreciation that is much slower than the double declining balance depreciation, but still higher than the straight-line depreciation. The way it is calculated is that each year the beginning book value of an asset is multiplied by a fraction, called fractional depreciation, d_f, to obtain that year's depreciation. That is,

$$d_{SYD} = BBV_{Beg} \times d_f \qquad (2.5)$$

where d_{SYD} is the sum-of-the-years-digits depreciation, BBV_{Beg} is the beginning book value, and d_f, is the fractional depreciation. Fractional depreciation, in turn, is obtained by dividing the years remaining in the useful life of an asset by the sum-of-the-years-digits, as shown below:

$$d_f = t_R/SYD \tag{2.6}$$

where d_f is the fractional depreciation, t_R is the year(s) remaining in the useful life of an asset, and SYD is the sum-of-the-years digits.

In general, the denominator of the fractional depreciation remains constant, since it is the sum of the number of years (total), while the numerator changes from year to year representing the number of years remaining in the useful life of an asset. The calculation of SYD is straightforward in that it is obtained by simply adding the number of years in the useful life of an asset; that is, $SYD = 1+2+3+\ldots+T$. The t_R, on the other hand, is obtained by subtracting the year(s) remaining from the useful life of an asset; that is, $t_{R1} = T-0 = T$, $t_{R2} = T-1$, $t_{R3} = T-2$, ..., and so forth.

We can use the same street cleaning example to illustrate the method. Since the vehicle in our example has a useful life of seven years, the denominator of the fraction, which is the sum-of-the-years-digits, will be 28 ($1+2+3+4+5+6+7 = 28$). From this, we can express the fractional depreciation for each year, as follows: Year 1: $t_{R1}/SYD = (7-0)/28 = 7/28 = 0.250$; Year 2: $t_{R2}/SYD = (7-1)/28 = 6/28 = 0.214$; Year 3: $t_{R3}/SYD = (7-2)/28 = 5/28 = 0.179$; Year 4: $t_{R4}/SYD = (7-3)/28 = 4/28 = 0.143$; Year 5: $t_{R5}/SYD = (7-4)/28 = 3/28 = 0.107$; Year 6: $t_{R6}/SYD = (7-5)/28 = 2/28 = 0.071$; and Year 7: $t_{R7}/SYD = (7-6)/28 = 1/28 = 0.036$. Note that since each depreciation represents a fraction of the time remaining in the useful life of an asset, the sum of the fractions must be equal to 1; that is, $0.250+0.214+0.179+0.143+0.107+0.071+0.036 = 1.000$. Obviously, the higher the fraction, which happens to be in the early years of the life of the asset, the depreciation will be greater in the early years, then declining gradually in the later years.

Next, we multiply the beginning book value of the vehicle by its corresponding fractional depreciation to obtain the depreciation for that year and repeat the process, as shown in Table 2.8 (without the salvage value). As the table shows, the ending book value at the end of the seventh year is zero. This is because, like the straight-line depreciation, we are depreciating the asset against its full value or purchase price and not against the beginning book value, as in declining or double declining balance depreciation.

Table 2.9 shows the sum-of-the-years digits depreciation with the salvage value. As before, the ending book value becomes zero at the end of the seventh year of the vehicle. To see if our calculation is correct, we can add the depreciation for every single year of the asset and if the sum of these depreciations equals the initial cost of the asset, the result should be considered correct. The results presented in the table clearly show

Table 2.8 Sum-of-the-years-digits depreciation (without the salvage value)

Year	*Annual Depreciation*[1] *($)*	*Accumulated Depreciation*[2] *($)*	*Ending (Net) Book Value ($)*
0	---	---	84,000
1	84,000 × 0.250 =21,000	21,000	63,000
2	84,000 × 0.214 = 17,976	38,976	45,024
3	84,000 × 0.179 = 15,036	54,012	29,988
4	84,000 × 0.143 = 12,012	66,024	17,976
5	84,000 × 0.107 = 8,988	75,012	8,988
6	84,000 × 0.071 = 5,964	80,976	3,024
7	84,000 × 0.036 = 3,024	84,000	0

[1] Beginning book value × Depreciation rate; [2]Rounded to the nearest thousand

Table 2.9 Sum-of-the-years-digits depreciation (with the salvage value)

Year	*Annual Depreciation*[1] *($)*	*Accumulated Depreciation*[2] *($)*	*Ending (Net) Book Value ($)*
0	70,000 × 0 ---	---	70,000
1	70,000 × 0.250 = 17,500	17,500	52,500
2	70,000 × 0.214 = 14,980	32,480	37,520
3	70,000 × 0.179 = 12,530	45,010	24,990
4	70,000 × 0.143 = 10,010	55,020	14,980
5	70,000 × 0.107 = 7,490	62,510	7,490
6	70,000 × 0.071 = 4,970	67,480	2,520
7	70,000 × 0.036 = 2,520	70,000	0

[1] Beginning book value × Depreciation rate; [2]Rounded to the nearest thousand

that the sum of the depreciations for all seven years adds up to $70,000, which is the initial book value of the vehicle, adjusted for the salvage value; that, $17,500 +14,980 + $12,530 + $10,010 + $7,490 + $4,970 + $2,520 = $70,000.

Although it has some of the same attributes of the declining balance depreciation and is relatively easy to use, it can be conceptually problematic because of the use of sum of the digits to calculate the depreciation rate. One can construe this as somewhat arbitrary because the rate may not reflect the actual usage or decline of the asset value. There are other complications besides this, which have resulted in its loss of appeal over the years, but it is still used in government, along with other forms of depreciation, as well as by a wide range of financial organizations such as banking and regulated industries.

2.6 Units of Production Depreciation

The final method, which is occasionally used in depreciation calculation in the private sector but often used in government, especially for utilities, is the units of production depreciation. Unlike the methods we have discussed so far, the units of production depreciation use output as the basis for depreciation. The advantage of using output is that it avoids the problem of depreciation calculation using a predetermined rate or the number of years. Output is generally defined by the quantity or amount of goods or services an asset produces within a specified time. For instance, if the asset is a power generator, it will be how many kilowatt hours of electricity it can produce, say, in a month; if it is a patrol vehicle, it will be how many miles the vehicle could be driven a year; if it is an X-ray machine, how many X-rays it can take a year, and so forth.

Since the method is based on output, the depreciation calculation is different from the previous methods. It is usually done in two steps: First, find the depreciation cost per unit of production, which is obtained by dividing the book value of an asset by the output the asset will produce, and then multiply it by the (estimated) output to obtain the annual depreciation, as shown below:

$$d_{UP} = O \times DC_{PUP} \tag{2.8}$$

$$DC_{PUP} = BV/O = (V_0 - SV)/O \tag{2.7}$$

where d_{UP} is the unit of production depreciation, O is the output, DC_{PUP} is the depreciation cost per unit of production, BV is the book value, V_0 is the initial value of an asset, and SV is the salvage value,

Let us look at a simple example to illustrate the method. Suppose that a government purchased a patrol vehicle last year at a cost of $40,000, with all the state-of-the-art equipment, and has a salvage value of $10,000. It has a useful life of five years, although it could be less, depending on the community it serves. Assume that the vehicle would be driven on average 50,000 miles a year, for a total of 250,000 miles over a five-year period. The depreciation cost per unit of production will, therefore, be

$$DC_{PUP} = (V_0 - SV)/O = (\$40{,}000 - \$10{,}000)/250{,}000 = \$0.12$$

which is 12 cents per mile.

Next, we multiply the vehicle miles for a given year by the cost per unit of production to obtain the depreciation for that year, which will be $6,000 [$O \times DC_{PUP} = 50{,}000 \times \$0.12 = \$6{,}000$] for the first year and repeat the process for the remaining years. If we assume the miles driven to remain constant for each of the seven years, as we have in the current example, the depreciation will remain the same for all seven years, in which case it will give the appearance of a straight-line depreciation. This is where the method has an inherent weakness in that in order to obtain the correct depreciation one must be able to accurately estimate the output; that is, the estimated units of production (miles to be driven in our example) over the useful life of the asset. If not, one could use an average, as we did here.

2.7 Other Methods of Depreciation

In addition to the declining balance, sum-of-the-years digits, and the units of production methods of depreciation, there are other methods that one can also use to depreciate an asset. A good example will be sinking fund depreciation. A sinking fund is a fund in which money is deposited at regular intervals to pay for the principal and interests on a debt (debt service). According to this method, the depreciation for any year is the increase for that year, which is the deposit for the year plus any interest accrued for that year. The method produces a yearly depreciation schedule, which increases systematically with time, and hence can be viewed as the opposite of accelerated depreciation. Another method used, although not as frequently as the methods described above, is the annuity method, which allocates the cost of an asset as a series of cash payments over the useful life of the asset, as in annuity. Given the range of methods available for depreciation calculation, which method an organization will use depends on the nature of the assets and the accounting purpose for which they will be used.

2.8 Chapter Summary

Cost lies at the heart of financial activities of an organization. Without some knowledge of costs and how to account for them, it will be difficult for an organization to carry out its normal activities. Understanding the basic cost concepts is an important first step toward that. This chapter has presented an overview of several key cost concepts that are frequently used in government and nonprofit organizations. In presenting these concepts, the chapter made a distinction between terms that appear alongside cost such as expense, expenditure, and depreciation, which are not the same. The terms are often used interchangeably that can create confusion in cost calculations. This chapter has provided a brief explanation of what contributes to their differences and how to reconcile them. Another term that also appears alongside cost is depreciation. Depreciation allows an organization to spread the costs of a physical asset over its life span rather than trying to recover the initial cost or purchase price immediately. This, in turn, helps the organization determine how much of the asset's value has been used up. In other words, it helps an organization to accurately value physical assets, track expenses, and report financial information. Finally, the chapter provided a detailed discussion of some of the methods frequently used in depreciation calculations.

2.9 Review Questions

2.1 Define cost. How is cost measured? What is a cost object? Can cost be charged to more than one cost object? If so, give an example.

2.2 Define cost. How would you distinguish between (a) direct and indirect costs, (b) fixed and variable costs, (c) sunk and future costs, (d) implicit and explicit costs, (e) mixed and step costs, (f) current and historical costs, and (g) controllable and uncontrollable costs? Give an example of each.

2.3 How does a cost differ from expense and expenditure? How would you reconcile their differences? Explain with an example.

2.4 What is depreciation? Why is depreciation necessary in government? What depreciation method is commonly used in government? Why?

2.5 A state highway patrol department spent $1,500,000 last year on patrols, which included, among others, the purchase of a new vehicle in the amount $65,000 with a salvage value of $7,500. It also spent $28,000 on materials and supplies, but used only 65% for the year, the rest spent on wages and salaries. The vehicle has a life span of six years. What was the actual cost of providing the service to the department, assuming a straight-line depreciation, with and without the salvage value?

2.6 What is the difference between a straight-line and an accelerated depreciation? Under what circumstances would a government use straight-line, as opposed to an accelerated depreciation?

2.7 The Public Works Department of a local government has just purchased a heavy-duty vehicle for $75,000 with an estimated useful life of seven years and a salvage value of $15,000. The department decided to use the straight-line method of depreciation.

   a. Calculate the depreciable amount.

   b. Calculate the annual depreciation with and without the salvage value for all seven years.

2.8 What is the difference between a declining balance and a double-declining balance depreciation? At what point in time is a depreciation calculation no longer necessary? Why?

2.9 A local public library has recently purchased a multi-purpose copying machine at a cost of $4,500. It has a standard life span of five years and a salvage value of $1,250. What would be the annual depreciation expense for the machine under (a) straight-line depreciation, (b) declining balance depreciation, and (c) the sum-of-the years-digits depreciation, with and without the salvage value?

2.10 A local United Way has recently purchased a minivan at a cost of \$45,000 to provide free transportation services to elderly people who could not otherwise move around. The organization plans to trade it in for \$10,000 after it has done 80,000 miles. The following information is available on the vehicle for miles traveled over a five-year period: 15,000 miles in year 1, 17,000 miles in year 2, 20,000 miles in year 3, 15,000 miles in year 4, and 13,000 miles in year 5. Calculate the depreciation expense for each of the five years using the units of production method.

2.11 For the problem in 2.7, suppose the Department wants to use the double declining balance method for depreciation.

a. Determine the double-declining rate.
b. Calculate the annual depreciation without the salvage value for all seven years

2.12 For the problem in 2.7, let us further suppose that the vehicle would be driven on average 25,000 miles a year, for a total of 175,000 miles over a seven-year period. Assume now that the government wants to use the Units of Production method for depreciation.

a. Calculate the depreciation cost per unit of production.
b. Calculate the annual depreciation for the vehicle.

Notes

1 Operationally, a simple regression equation for a cost function (discussed later) is a example of mixed cost in that it contains elements of both fixed and variable cost: $Y = a + bX$, where Y is the total cost of a good or service, a is the fixed cost, b is the variable rate (cost) per unit of the good or service, and X is the number of units of the good or service.

2 Based on a set of conditions or requirements that are considered acceptable across organizations such as consistency, reliability, quality, and the like.

3 When discussing the life span of an asset it may be necessary to make a distinction between types of life such as economic life, ownership life, physical life, and useful life. Economic life is the time (usually expressed in years) over which an asset is expected to operate with minimum cost to its owner. The ownership life will vary depending on how long an asset is held by the owner. If the ownership changes hands three times, then the time the asset is held by an owner will be the ownership life of the asset for the owner. Physical life is the time when an asset is acquired to the time when it is no longer able to produce goods or services. If an asset is managed properly with due care, the chances are that the

physical life of an asset will coincide with the time of its acquisition to the time it is abandoned or replaced. Finally, useful life is the time when an asset is kept in productive use with normal repair and maintenance. In the current context, useful life is used.

4 According to this method, assets are divided into classes by type of asset or by the type of business in which the asset is used. The idea is to create greater incentives for firms and businesses to refurbish their capital to remain competitive. Following the passage of the 1986 Tax Reform Act, the government began to allow greater accelerated depreciation for tangible assets (properties) over their specified lives, ranging from three to fifty years, called Modified Accelerate Cost Recovery System (MACRS). The lives of the properties are broadly specified by the Internal Revenue Code of the government.

References

Corporate Finance Institute. (2021). *Depreciation methods: The four main types.* https://corporatefinanceinstitute.com/resources/knowledge/accounting/types-depreciation-methods/ [Accessed March 15, 2021].

Johnson, J.M. (1982). *Handbook of depreciation methods, formulas, and tables.* New York: Prentice-Hall.

Kalfayan, F.G. (2012). *Mastering depreciation.* New York: American Institute of Professional Bookkeepers (AIPB).

Wade, J. and Herman, M. (2023). Accelerated depreciation. *Investing Answers.* https://investinganswers.com/dictionary/a/accelerated-depreciation [Accessed February 23, 2023].

3 Price and Rate Structure of Cost

3.1 Introduction

A term that frequently appears alongside cost is price. Price is simply a measure of value. It is the premium we pay for the goods and services we consume. However, determining price for public goods is far more complex than it is for private goods (Lee, 1982). In the private sector, price is generally determined by calculations that reflect the profit-maximizing interest of a firm or business. These calculations typically include factors such as the target return on an investment, the market share the firm must maintain, the price it must charge to match competition, the need to maintain a stable price to avoid fluctuations in demand, and so forth (Lanzillotti et al. 1958). But the same calculations do not readily apply to public goods because of congestion costs, the free-rider problem, and the difficulty of producing them in discrete units, which makes it difficult to determine the price the public must pay for their consumption (Samuelson, 1954; Davis and Whinston, 1967). However, there are goods a government provides that have some of the same characteristics as private goods in that they can be produced in discrete units, thus making it possible to provide them in a business-like manner. These are referred to as proprietary goods.

This chapter focuses on the price and rate structure of cost. It begins with an introduction to pricing strategies for delivering goods and services, followed by a detailed discussion of some of the commonly used pricing methods in government, along with a brief discussion of the rate structure of cost. The chapter concludes with a brief discussion of cost and inflation.

3.2 Pricing Strategies

Pricing decisions are not arbitrary. They are based on the goals and objectives of an organization. For private organizations, the goal is to maximize profit or return on investments, subject to the constraint that it does not fall below a level at which they will incur loss and not survive

DOI: 10.4324/9781003486091-4

in a competitive market. Accordingly, they design strategies based on pricing methods that will (1) allow them to maximize profit, (2) earn a normal profit, or (3) break even. While government and nonprofit organizations do not operate to maximize profit, it is expected at a minimum that they do not incur a loss to be able to provide the goods and services. Therefore, the best strategy for these organizations would be to select a pricing method or a combination of methods that will keep the operation financially viable.

There is also a dynamic aspect of pricing in that the same method may not be applicable to all services within the same organization, depending on the types of goods and services that it provides. For instance, if an organization provides five different services that are qualitatively different, then it is quite likely that the same method would not apply to all five. In the same vein, the same method may not be applicable for the same service over time. The condition of the market, the internal structure of the organization, and the nature of demand for services may change over time requiring new strategies and pricing methods.

3.3 Pricing Methods

As noted above, there is no one specific method for determining the price of a good or service. There are different methods an organization can use depending on the nature of the goods, but all pricing methods have an accounting basis, where costs serve as the basis for determining the price. The price is not the same as the cost. It can be higher than the cost, lower than the cost, or equal to the cost. If the price is higher than the cost of production or delivery of a good or service, the organization makes a profit. If it is less than the cost, it incurs a loss. If it is equal to cost, it breaks even. In general, no organization would like to provide goods and services at a price that is less than their cost of production or delivery, which also applies to government as well as to nonprofit organizations.

A number of pricing methods have been developed over the years that have come to rely on this basic approach. Although most of these methods are designed for private goods they can also be applied to public goods, especially those that are provided in a business-like manner such as water, sewerage, electricity, parking meters, traffic citations, patient care, and so forth. Important among these methods are (1) marginal cost pricing, (2) average cost pricing, (3) total cost pricing, (4) cost-plus pricing, (5) levelized pricing, and (6) transfer pricing. All these methods, except for marginal cost pricing, are non-incremental in that they do not base their analysis on incremental change.

3.3.1 Marginal Cost Pricing

One of the most widely used concepts in price behavior is marginal cost pricing. Marginal cost pricing is based on a simple microeconomic rule that resources are best allocated when the price of goods and services is set equal to their marginal cost, MC (the cost of producing an additional unit of a good or delivering a service); that is, P = MC. For instance, if it costs a firm $100 to produce 10 units of a good and $109 to produce 11 units of the same good, then the marginal cost (the cost of the 11th or last unit) will be $9 ($109-$100). The $9 will then serve as the price at which the good should be sold in the market. If this were a public good, then the marginal cost would measure the cost of resources to society (the public) for producing an additional unit of the good and the price would measure the value of the additional unit to the public (Tyndall, 1951).

The economic rationale for setting the price equal to the marginal cost is that at that level the profit will be maximum, but for the profit to be maximum the rule further suggests that the marginal cost must be equal to the marginal revenue, MR (the revenue earned from an additional unit of a good sold or service delivered); that is, MC = MR. The explanation for this is quite simple: so long as MC<MR, the firm should continue to produce because there is a net gain from additional production until the marginal cost becomes equal to marginal revenue; that is, MC = MR. If, on the other hand, MC>MR, it should continue to lower production because there is a net loss from additional production until the marginal cost becomes equal to the marginal revenue; that is, MC = MR. Thus, at the point where MC = MR, the profit will be maximum. Therefore, if MC = MR and P = MC, then by extension, P = MR. In other words, MC = MR = P. What this means is that the price a firm receives from selling an additional unit of a good is the same as the revenue it earns from selling one more unit of the good. In other words, P = MR. Since MC = MR, and MR = P, then P = MC; hence the term MC pricing. It should be worth noting that the relationship described above holds good for a perfectly competitive market, which may not hold for a noncompetitive market.

As noted earlier, an important requirement for marginal cost pricing to work is that the goods produced must be divisible, so they can be measured in discrete units and a price can be assigned to individual units. To give an example, suppose that an outpatient clinic does 25 chest X-rays a day. The procedures do not require much time. It costs their clinic $250 an X-ray, which is the price it charges the patients. Assume that the price the clinic charges is the marginal cost of the 25th X-ray (the last X-ray of the day);

that is, P = MC. Assume further that the cost of an additional X-ray, the 26th X-ray, would produce a revenue loss for the clinic. Therefore, at 25 X-rays, P = MC = MR, and the profit that the clinic will earn from the X-rays will be maximum. Since we know the price of an X-ray and the number of X-rays for a day, we can easily calculate the revenue the X-rays will produce for the clinic, which will be $6,250; that is, ($250 × 25 = $6,250). In other words, it is the maximum revenue the clinic will earn from the X-rays, *ceteris paribus*.

However, the clinic could do additional X-rays, so long as the marginal cost of an X-ray is less than the marginal revenue, MC<MR, but it will not be profitable if the marginal cost of an additional X-ray exceeds the marginal revenue, MC>MR, while the price remains the same at $250; that is, P = $250|MC>MR. Therefore, from the clinic's point of view, the maximum number of X-rays it should do is 25 at the current price of $250 each.

Although as a concept marginal cost pricing makes good sense when applied to firms and businesses, it does not necessarily work well in government; in particular, where public goods are concerned. Most public goods, as noted earlier, except for those provided in a business-like manner, are not divisible, which makes it difficult to assign a price to individual units. At the same time, it may not be possible for a government not to provide additional services because of higher marginal cost, if there is a demand for it. For instance, the clinic may not be able to refuse additional X-rays if the cost of additional X-rays goes up, while the price it charges the patients remains the same, thereby producing a revenue loss, even if the patients cannot afford the additional price. The alternative is to subsidize the price, which is a common practice in government for many of the services it provides, such as water, sewerage, electricity, the postal service, and so forth.

3.3.2 Average Cost Pricing

Unlike the private sector, a government is not necessarily in the business of making profit in that so long as the government is able to break even, it will have achieved its basic economic and financial goal (although that may not necessarily be the case for proprietary goods that are provided in a business-like manner). The pricing method that is most suitable where break-even is concerned is the average cost pricing, which is determined by setting the price of an item of goods or service at a level where it is equal to the average cost; that is, P = AC.

To give an example, suppose that it costs a state-run four-year college with 10,000 students $45 million annually to operate, 50 percent of which comes from the state, 40 percent from tuition fees, and the remaining

10 percent from a variety of other sources such as charitable contributions. Students take on average 30 credit hours during an academic year, including summer. Therefore, the price per credit hour for a student will be \$150, which is the average cost for a credit hour, obtained in the following way:

$$
\begin{aligned}
AC &= TC/Q \\
&= \text{Total Cost/N of Credit Hours} \\
&= \$45{,}000{,}000/(10{,}000 \times 30) \\
&= \$45{,}000{,}000/300{,}000 \\
&= \$150
\end{aligned}
$$

Thus, at a price of \$150 per credit hour, the total revenue ($TR = P \times Q$) for the college will be \$45 million [$TR = P \times Q = (\$150)(30 \times 10{,}000) = \$150 \times 300{,}000 = \$45{,}000{,}000$], which is the same as the total cost, TC = TR. In other words, it will break even. However, given that 40 percent of the cost is covered by tuition fees and charges, the actual price the student will pay for each credit hour of college education will be \$60 [$\$150 \times 0.40 = \$60$], excluding books, supplies, transportation, accommodation, meals, and so on. This means that 40 percent of \$45 million, or \$18 million [$\$45{,}000{,}000 \times 0.40 = \$18$ million] will come from tuition fees and the rest from other sources, although theoretically the college could charge the students the entire \$150 for each credit hour, which would be the theoretical break-even price.

Since the average cost pricing is primarily used in situations where the goal is to break even, it will not produce maximum profit like marginal-cost pricing. Also, since the price is set equal to average cost, it means that some would pay more and some less depending on the level of consumption, but on average the price of the item of goods will be the same for all consumers. Going back to the tuition fee example, since the college needs 300,000 credit hours to generate the break-even revenue ($\$150 \times 300{,}000 = \$45{,}000{,}000$), those taking more hours are essentially subsidizing those taking less hours for the college to be able to charge \$150 per credit hour. This is known as cross subsidization. Cross subsidization is a common practice in government such as water, sewerage, electricity, the postal service, and so forth, where revenue generated from a particular service area, or a group of consumers, is used to compensate for the loss in other areas or by other consumers.

It should be worth noting that an area where average cost pricing is frequently used by the government is in regulating the behavior of natural monopolies.[1] Since monopolies, in general, tend to produce less than the optimal quantity thereby pushing the prices up, government can use the average cost pricing as a tool to regulate the price the monopolies would otherwise charge. Put simply, the average cost pricing (P = AC) can force a monopoly firm to reduce price to a point where the firm's average cost would equal marginal revenue, since marginal revenue works differently for a monopoly firm. For a monopoly firm, the price is usually higher than the marginal revenue. Thus, setting the price equal to marginal revenue will work as a disincentive for the firm to maximize profit. Alternatively, the government could provide the goods itself, so long as it breaks even.

3.3.3 Total Cost Pricing

Total cost pricing is the price the consumers must pay, or an organization must charge the consumers to recover the full cost of a good or service. It is called total cost pricing because the focus is on the recovery of the full cost of a good or service. rather than a fraction of it. A typical example of total-cost pricing in government would be the cost of infrastructure such as roads, bridges, highways, and other physical assets that are produced as a lump sum. The fact that these goods cannot be produced in discrete units and once produced cannot exclude individuals from their consumption, thereby creates a free-rider problem that makes it difficult for government to determine the exact price it must charge the consumers vis-à-vis the public for their use. Consequently, governments often use tax as an instrument to generate the necessary revenue to provide them, although there are exceptions such as toll roads and other high-end public goods. Therefore, taxes can be construed as a form of price the public must pay for the consumption of public goods.

To illustrate, suppose that a state highway department wants to construct a 50-mile long, four-lane highway, at a cost of $5 million a mile. The total cost of the highway is $250 million ($5 million per mile × 50). The state will cover 50 percent of the cost, which will be $125 million; the federal government will cover another 20 percent, which will be $50 million, and the remaining $75 million or 30 percent ($75/$250 = 0.3) the government will recover through toll. So, basically the state will cover 80 percent of the cost [$125 million + $75 million)/$250 million) × 100 = ($200 million/$250 million) × 100 = 0.80 × 100 = 80%)]. Assume that on average 50,000 vehicles will use the highway every day, and the government sets the toll at 30 cents a mile, which will include the cost of repair and maintenance. At that rate, it will take the government roughly 13.70 years to recover the 30 percent of the cost; that is, $TC / (TVM_{Year} \times P)$ = $75,000,000/(50,000 × 365)($0.30) = $75,000,000/(18,250,000)($0.30) = $75,000,000/ $5,475,000 = 13.70 years, where TC is the total cost, TVM is the total vehicle miles per year, and P is the price (toll) per mile.

On the other hand, if the government wants to recover 80 percent of the cost through toll, which is \$200 million (\$250,000,000 × 0.8 = \$200,000,000), it will take much longer, roughly 36.53 years; that is, $TC/(TVM_{Year} \times P)$ = \$200,000,000/(50,000 × 365)(\$0.30) = \$200,000,000/(18,250,000)(\$0.30) = \$200,000,000/\$5,475,000 = 36.53 years. However, the government can adjust the recovery period by increasing or decreasing the toll rate.

Assume now that it is not a toll road and the government plans to recover the full cost of \$200 million from gasoline tax, earmarked for highway construction and maintenance. Therefore, the revenue the government will generate from the gasoline tax to cover the government's share of the cost will be the price the public must pay for the consumption of the road. Since the entire amount of \$200 million will be coming out of gasoline tax, we can think of the gasoline tax as a form of price the public must pay for the consumption (use) of the good (road). And like the toll rate, the government can determine the tax rate the public will pay for each gallon of gas to cover the cost of construction and the number of years to recover the cost, once they know the estimated gallons of gas the vehicles will use for the length of the highway for the year.

3.3.4 Cost-Plus Pricing

Cost-plus pricing is basically an extension of total cost pricing and is obtained by adding a predetermined margin to the total cost of a good or service, called markup. The rationale for cost-plus pricing is that government, like most private firms and businesses, often needs a cushion to provide safeguards against uncertainty, especially where fixed costs are concerned since these costs cannot be automatically adjusted for quantity produced. Cost-plus pricing provides that cushion, known commonly as the safety margin, to ensure that these costs can be eventually recovered. The margin is essentially a predetermined "markup" on an organization's estimated per unit cost of production at the time of setting the price.

To determine the cost-plus price, one must first determine the per unit variable cost, then determine the total variable cost, and add it to the fixed cost, to obtain the total cost of production. Next, multiply the total cost by the markup percentage to determine the total cost with the markup. Finally, divide the total cost with the markup by the (estimated) quantity to determine the cost-plus price, as shown below:

$$\begin{aligned} P_{\text{Cost-Plus}} &= [(FC + VC(Q))(1 + k)]/Q \\ &= [(TC)(1 + k)]/Q \end{aligned} \tag{3.1}$$

where $P_{Cost\text{-}Plus}$ is the cost-plus price, FC is the fixed cost, VC is the variable cost, TC is the total cost, Q is the quantity, and k is the markup percentage.

To give an example, suppose that a government wants to determine the price of garbage collection next year, t+1. The variable cost of garbage collection is $5.25 a ton and the fixed cost is $750,000 a year. Assume that the government has estimated the volume of collection for next year to be 1.25 million tons. Let us assume further that the government plans to use a 5 percent markup as the safety margin to estimate the cost of collection. The total cost of garbage collection for next year will then be

$$\begin{aligned}
P_{Cost\text{-}Plus,\, t+1} &= [(FC + VC(Q))(1 + k)]/Q \\
&= [(\$750{,}000 + (\$5.25)(1{,}250{,}000))(1 + 0.05)]/Q \\
&= [(\$750{,}000 + \$6{,}562{,}500)(1.05)]/Q \\
&= [\$7{,}312{,}500](1.05)] \\
&= \$7{,}678{,}125
\end{aligned}$$

which includes the markup. Therefore, the cost-plus price for each ton of garbage will be $6.14 [$7,678,125/1,250,000 = $6.14], which is the price the consumers vis-à-vis the public must pay for each ton of garbage collection.

As a pricing method, cost-plus pricing is the surest way to recover the cost of a good or service, but it raises an interesting question as to how one determines the markup price. Ideally, it should be determined in such a way as not to have any negative effect on demand. This is possible in situations where demand is price inelastic, meaning that an increase in price will not have any effect on consumption, which is possible only if there are no substitutes for the goods and the consumers have no alternative but to consume goods. However, if there are substitutes with a lower price, it is quite likely that the consumers will change their preference for goods with a lower price, known as the substitution effect. Alternatively, they may lower their consumption. In either case, a higher markup or safety margin will have a dampening effect on consumption which, in turn, will have a negative effect on net return for the government. Interestingly, there are not too many substitutes for most goods that a government provides which allows it greater control in determining the markup price. One way to avoid the problem is to use the inflation rate or the level of service usage as a basis or simply tailor it to the financial needs of the government without overburdening the public.

3.3.5 Levelized Pricing

Levelized pricing is used mostly for public utilities such as electricity. It is unique in the sense that unlike most other pricing methods the price the public utilities charge is often regulated by a regulatory commission. Consequently, utility companies as well as others who are responsible for these services are careful about what they include in setting their prices. Since investments in utilities can cost large sums of money, utility companies are allowed a return on their investments. In most instances, they are allowed to treat the interest cost as part of investment as well as other costs, such as depreciation as expense, and include them in the price the consumers will pay for these services. Therefore, the price the consumers pay reflects the cost they must absorb to compensate the producers for interest and other costs.

To give an example, consider a case where a government expects to earn \$1.525 million in net revenue from electricity provision next year, based on an estimated production of 35 million kilowatt hours of electricity. The levelized price per kilowatt of electricity will be a little over 4 cents, obtained by dividing the estimated revenue by the estimated output; that is, \$1.525 million/35 million kWh = \$0.04, which includes interest (assuming the utility company had to borrow funds, say, to upgrade the facility) and other costs. This is the amount of cost the consumers must absorb for each unit of electricity they will consume.

It is worth noting that the calculation of levelized pricing is somewhat more involved than most other pricing methods because it takes into consideration a variety of factors that are directly associated with the asset used in the production of a good over its entire life span. This would include initial investment, operations and maintenance, cost of fuel, cost of capital such as debt, and so on. Since the calculations run over the lifetime of an asset, it is useful to take into consideration the time value of money.

3.3.6 *Transfer Pricing*

A pricing method that applies to both public and private goods is transfer pricing. Transfer pricing is usually applied to a situation where there is a transfer of service between different units within the same organization. It can be defined as the price an organization (or any of its units) charges other units for rendering a service. Since the service provided is internal to the organization and no cash transfer takes place, it is also known as internal service pricing. To give an example, suppose that the Highway Department of a government buys \$10,000 worth of legal services from the Public Attorney's office, which it records as internal service transfer. The government did not spend any cash on the transaction but, from an accounting point of view, it needs to move the amount from the Highway Fund to the Legal Services Fund where the transaction (payment) will be recorded. This will allow the government to keep track of the cost it incurred in providing the service, similar to other service transactions, for instance, it had during the fiscal year, except that it was provided internally.

There are several ways in which one can determine the transfer price. The simplest way to determine it, assuming the item of goods or the service the government provides is divisible, would be to add a margin of profit or net return to the cost of production or delivery. That is, transfer price = cost of production + (cost of production × profit margin). Thus, if the cost of production for a unit of the goods is \$20, and the profit margin or net return is 10 percent, then the transfer price for the unit of the good would be \$22; that is, \$20 + (\$20 × 0.10 = \$20 + \$2 = \$22). It is the price the service provider must charge for the service. On the other hand, if it is not divisible, then one can use one's professional judgment, since there are no actual monetary transactions involved in these transfers and administer it from the top.

However, the problem with any judgmental or qualitative price determination is that it could lead to inefficiency in service provision since the price would not necessarily reflect the real worth of the service. It could also lead to accounting problems for the organization if the price is artificially inflated or deflated, which would distort the actual cost of the service. An ideal alternative would be to use the market price; that is, the price the service would have charged if it were sold in a competitive market (assuming there is an actual demand for the service outside of the organization). Another alternative would be for the units to negotiate among themselves and settle at a price that is realistic and will be satisfactory for all parties concerned. This is known as a negotiated price. The rationale for using negotiation as a tool to establish a price is that it can stimulate competition and encourage non-competitive units to be more competitive.

3.3.7 *Other Pricing Methods*

In addition to the methods discussed above, there are other pricing methods a government can use, depending on the nature of the goods and the circumstances to which the methods are applied. Examples of some of these prices will be strategic price (short-run price which may or may not be used in the long run), penalty price (the price an individual or a firm pays for delinquent behavior such as pollution or delinquent taxes), target price (the price set equal to a predetermined target such as the return on an investment), value-based price (the price determined by the value an item of goods or which a service will produce for the public), and subsidized (the price support a firm or business receives from government to compensate for the difference between a prevailing price in the market and what they would have earned under normal conditions).

As noted previously, there is no one specific method that can uniformly apply to all goods and services that a government provides since they vary in number and characteristics. This explains why it is not uncommon to find a government using not one, but multiple different pricing methods.

3.4 Pricing Methods in Nonprofit Organizations

Like the government, nonprofit organizations use different pricing methods for the range of services they provide. Nonprofit organizations are mission-driven, which is reflected in their pricing strategies. The primary objective of nonprofit pricing is to ensure sustainability and maximize their impact, while maintaining the mission-driven focus. There is a wide range of pricing methods the organizations use, depending on the services they provide. This section discusses five such methods: cost-based pricing, differential pricing, cost-recovery pricing, sliding-scale pricing, and pay-what-you-can-afford.

Cost-based pricing. It is essentially a cost-plus pricing method, discussed earlier. It involves calculating the total cost of a service and then adding a mark-up to cover the overhead and a margin of safety. The mark-up is usually a fixed percentage of the total cost. For instance, if a service costs $1,500, then a fixed percentage, say 10 percent, is added to the total cost to determine the price.

Differential pricing. According to this method, individuals pay a different price based on their ability to pay. For instance, a nonprofit organization providing legal services may charge different fees for different individuals based on their ability. It is somewhat discriminatory in nature since different individuals pay at different rates; as such, organizations need to ensure that the practice does not violate ethical norms in service provision. Because of its differential nature, another term used for this method is discriminatory pricing.

Cost-recovery pricing. As with the government, the method is primarily used to recover the cost of service. This includes both direct and indirect costs. A good example is the training programs that organizations run. Since the objective is to recover the cost, it is important for the organizations to do a careful analysis of the costs, such as the salary of the instructor, cost of instruction materials, and overhead costs.

Sliding scale pricing. This method offers individuals a range of prices from which to determine the price that would best meet their needs and ability to pay. Health care clinics are good examples, where individuals with low income pay at a lower rate than individuals who can pay a higher rate. The method is more involved in that it requires the organizations providing the service to have a system in place that can verify individual income to ensure their affordability and fair pricing.

Pay-what-you-can-afford. According to this method, individuals decide what they can afford to pay. The method is somewhat restrictive in the sense that it is available where price is not the primary determining factor for the service, although it is important. Good examples where the method applies are museums and art galleries.

Given the range of pricing methods nonprofit organizations can choose from, and the need to maintain a sound financial health, this can create a real challenge for them. As such, like the government, the nonprofit organizations design strategies that would produce the best possible return for the services they provide, subject to financial and other constraints. They are typically based on the need to (1) assess the current pricing strategy based on the information on gains, losses, barriers to growth, and unmet goals, (2) determine the optimal pricing model from the range of pricing options they have, and (3) execute the new strategy (Alkhas, 2021). Success of the strategies depends on how well the organization designs the strategies and executes them (Robinson and Foreman, 2011).

3.5 Rate Structure of Cost

Besides price, the government uses other means to collect revenue such as a user fee or charge. Although the term price is used across the board for goods and services that a government provides, it is important to make a distinction between price and user charge. Price is the money one pays for the consumption of a good or service. User charge is a form of price one pays for those goods and services where it is possible to establish a one-to-one correspondence between the amount of goods one consumes and the price one pays for their consumption. These are mostly goods that are provided in the business-like manner we defined earlier as propriety goods such as water, sewer, electricity, parking meters, and so forth. Since these goods are divisible in that they can be produced in discrete units, it is possible to establish a rate structure for their provision.

Rate structure is a pricing mechanism a government uses to charge the public for the goods and services they consume. Just like price, there is no single or uniform rate that applies to all goods and services that a government provides. Different types of rates are used by the government depending on the nature of goods and the level of provision (consumption). The rates can be used independently, by themselves, or in combination. Four types of rates are commonly used by a government: flat rate, uniform rate, block rate, and seasonal rate.

3.5.1 Flat Rate

In a flat rate the consumers are charged at the same rate, regardless of the quantity of goods and services they consume. All consumers within a given class, such as residential, commercial, and industrial, are charged the same rate as others in the same class at a predetermined rate. Flat rates are easier to use in that they do not require meter readings such as those required for electricity, gas, or water. The classic example of a flat rate is the rate the US Postal Service uses for different size boxes such as $7.50 for a small box, $12.50 for a medium box, and so forth.

3.5.2 Uniform Rate

Under a uniform rate, the rate remains constant, the same as the flat rate, but the amount charged has a time dimension that depends on the amount of service consumed over time and is commonly used for utilities such as water. Thus, the total amount the consumers will pay for the consumption of water is proportional to the quantity consumed plus a fixed charge. To give an example, suppose that a household uses on average 5,000 gallons of water a month at a rate of $4.50 per 1,000 gallons, it will pay $22.50 [$4.50 × 5 = $22.50] plus a fixed charge, called the base price. Fixed charges are mandatory and used primarily to recover the fixed cost of operation such as maintaining the service connections, billing, and customer service.

However, the charges often vary by consumer types such as residential consumers using a certain sized water meter, such as 0.75 inch, 1 inch, and 1.5 inch, as opposed to commercial or industrial consumers who use a different size, usually larger. Going back to the water consumption example, let us suppose that the household uses a 0.75 inch water meter and the fixed charge for a 0.75 meter is $15. Therefore, the price the consumer will pay for water consumption for a given month is $37.50 [$4.50 × 5) + $15 = $22.50 + $15 = $37.50], plus the fixed cost of operation. If we add to this the fixed cost of operation, say, $5, the price the consumer will pay is $42.50 ($37.50 + $5). In general, fixed charges are used to recover the fixed cost, while the variable costs are recovered through consumption (the quantity consumed).

3.5.3 Block Rate

Used mostly for utilities, a block rate is a schedule of rates or charges used for different levels of consumption. For instance, if the first 5,000 gallons of water in our example are charged at one rate, then any consumption over that level will be charged at a different rate. Returning to the water consumption example again, let us say that the government divides water consumption into three blocks – Block 1 for the first 5,000 gallons, Block 2 for the next 10,000 gallons, and Block 3 for the next 8,000 gallons. The rate the government charges is $4.50 for Block 1, $6.50 for Block 2, and $7.50 for Block 3. Assume now that our consumer (household) uses 7,000 gallons for the month instead of 5,000 gallons; therefore, the price the consumer will pay for consuming 7,000 gallons of water is $55.50 [(($4.50 × 5) + ($6.50 × 2)) + $15 + $5 = ($22.50 + $13.00) + $15 = $35.50 + $15.00 + $5 = $55.50], where 5 and 2 represent per thousand gallons, and $15 and $5 represent the fixed charge for the meter used and fixed cost of operation, respectively.

Block rates are not constant; they can be declining or inclining. In a declining block rate, the rate decreases as consumption increases. Reversing the rate for our water consumption example, $7.50 for the first 5,000 gallons, $6.50 for the next 10,000 gallons, and $4.50 for the next 8,000 gallons is a good example of declining block rate. Under this rate, consumers often receive a volume discount. High-end users, especially those consumers who use large quantities or volumes, tend to prefer this rate because it produces the greatest savings for them. In an inclining block rate, on the other hand, the rate increases with consumption. The rate structure we used for water consumption, $4.50 for the first 5,000 gallons, $6.50 for the next 10,000 gallons, and $7.50 for the next 8,000 gallons is a good example of an inclining block rate. Inclining block rates are often used to incentivize the consumers to lower their consumption such as to reduce average and peak use, thereby making it an effective tool for conservation plans.

3.5.4 *Seasonal Rate*

Finally, under seasonal rates, the rate changes depending on the time of the year. A good example is water use during the summer months for lawn maintenance when the demand is high. The inclining rate mentioned above is a good example, where the government charges $4.50 for the first 5,000 gallons in the winter, $6.50 for the next 10,000 gallons in the spring, and $7.50 for the next 8,000 gallons in the summer. Governments often restrict the day and time of use to optimize water consumption, especially during the summer months.

3.6 Cost and Inflation

Inflation is an increase in the general price level. Inflation affects both the consumer and the producer in the same way by lowering the value of money they spend on goods and services. From a cost point of view, inflation is a factor in how costs are measured, evaluated, and compared. Variations in costs over time reflect the changes in inflation, assuming everything else remains the same. Therefore, to get an accurate measure of costs unaffected by inflation, called the real cost, one must take out the effects of inflation from costs.

The simplest way to remove the effect of inflation from costs is to deflate it by a price index. An index is a statistical measure used to track changes in a representative group of observations or data points. The price index compares the average price of a group of commodities (goods and services) in one period with the average price for the same group in another period. In general, the prices are determined first for the base year and the prices of all subsequent years are then measured in relation to the base-year price. The price index that is most used in cost adjustment is the Consumer Price Index (CPI), which is based on the price of a group of basic items required by an average family. In reality, we do not have to calculate the price index because the US Bureau of Labor Statistics (BLS) produces the CPIs on a regular basis.[2]

3.6.1 Determining the Real Cost

Let us look at the street-cleaning example again to illustrate the effect of inflation on the cost of providing the service. As shown in Table 3.1, it cost the government, say, \$945,000 six years ago, t-6, to provide the service, \$961,000 in year t-5, \$982,000 in year t-4, and so forth. Let us assume that we have the CPI for each of the six years. We can use this information to determine first the inflation rate, and then use the rate to determine the real (adjusted) costs of street cleaning, as shown below:

$$\text{Inflation rate} = (\text{CPI}_{t\text{-}i} - \text{CPI}_{\text{Base Year}}) / \text{CPIt}_{\text{Base Year}}) \tag{3.2}$$

$$\text{RC} = (\text{NC}) / (1 + \text{Inflation rate}) \tag{3.3}$$

Table 3.1 Cost of street cleaning (with CPI)

Year	*Nominal Cost (\$)*	*CPI*	*Inflation Rate[1] (%)*	*Real Cost[2] (\$)*
t-6	945,000	110	0.0	945,000
t-5	961,000	115	0.0454 (4.54)	919,265
t-4	982,000	122	0.1091 (10.91)	885,403
t-3	1,117,000	130	0.1818 (18.18)	945,168
t-2	1,135,000	140	0.2727 (27.27)	891,805
t-1	1,162,000	152	0.3818 (38.18)	840,932

[1] Base Year, t-6;[2]Rounded to the nearest thousand

where CPI_{t-i} at time t-i is the year in which we are interested, $CPI_{BaseYear}$ is the base year, NC is the nominal (unadjusted) cost, and RC is the real (adjusted) cost.

It is important to note that the selection of the base year is critical in determining the real cost. The rule of thumb for selecting the base year is to select the year that serves the cost objective. To illustrate, we will use t-6 as the base year. We can apply the expressions in Equation 3.2 to the street cleaning problem, with t-6 as the base year, to determine the inflation rate for each of the six years. For instance, for the year t-5, it will be 0.0454 (4.54%); that is, $[(CPI_{t-i} - CPI_{Base\ Year})/CPIt_{Base\ Year})] \times 100 = [(115-110)/110] \times 100 = 0.0454 \times 100 = 4.54\%$, indicating that there has been a 4.54 percent increase in inflation in t-5 from the previous year, t-6.

We can now use this information to determine the real cost of street cleaning for t-5 using the expression in Equation 3.3; that is, (NC)/(1 + inflation rate) = \$961,000/(1 + 0.0454) = (961,000/1.0454 = \$919,265. What this means is that had there been no inflation, the nominal cost and the real cost of street cleaning for the year t-5 would have been the same. We do the same for the year t-4. The real cost of street cleaning for t-4 would be \$885,403 and continue the process. Table 3.1 shows the inflation rates and their corresponding real costs for all six years.

Interestingly, we could have used a more direct measure, without determining the inflation rate first, to obtain the real cost: Real Cost = (Nominal Cost)(CPI_0) / CPI_t), which would have produced the same result. For instance, applying the expression above to the street cleaning problem for t-5, with t-6 serving as the base year, the real cost of street cleaning will be \$919,160. That is, Real Cost = ((Nominal Cost)(CPI_0 / CPI_t) = (\$961,000)(110/115) = (\$961,000)(0.9562) = (919,196) for t-5, which is close to what we obtained using the expression in Equation 3.2. We can repeat the process to determine the real costs for the remaining years. It should be worth noting that the real cost can be higher or lower than the nominal cost, depending on what we use as the base year.

In determining the real costs of street cleaning, we assumed that we knew the CPIs but, what if we did not know the CPIs? In that case we can use the same procedure we used above, first, to obtain the inflation rate and then use the rate to determine the real costs. To illustrate, let us look at the water supply example. Suppose that the rate the government charged for residential property six years ago, t-6, was \$3.50 per one thousand gallons of water, which we will use as the base year; it was \$3.70 five years ago, t-5. The inflation rate for the year t-5, in light of the year t-6, which is the base year, will then be 0.0571 (5.71%). That is, $[\$3.70 - \$3.50)/\$3.50] \times 100 = (\$0.20/\$3.50) \times 100 = 0.0571 \times 100 = 5.71\%$, indicating that there has been an increase in inflation by 5.71 percent in t-5 from the previous year,

Table 3.2 Cost of water supply (without CPI)

Year	*Nominal Cost ($)*	*Water Rate ($)*	*Inflation Rate (%)*	*Real Cost ($)*
t-6	2,000,000	3.50	0.0	2,000,000
t-5	2.250,000	3.70	0.0571 (5.71)	2,128,465
t-4	2,700,000	4.10	0.1714 (17.14)	2,304,934
t-3	3,250,000	4.30	0.2286 (22.86)	2,645,287
t-2	3,500,000	4.60	0.3143 (31.43)	2,663,014
t-1	4,000,000	5.00	0.4286 (42.86)	2,799,944

[1] Base Year, t-6; [2]Rounded to the nearest thousand

t-6, the base year. For the year t-4, in light of t-6, the base year, it will be 0.1714 (17.14%), and so forth.

As before, we use this information to determine the real cost of street cleaning for t-5; that is, (NC)/(1-+inflation rate) = \$2,250,000/(1+0.0571)=(\$2,250,000/1.0454=\$2,128,465. Again, what this means is that had there been no inflation, the nominal cost and the real cost of water supply for the year t-5 would have been the same. We can do the same for the year t-4, which will produce a real cost of \$2,304,934, and repeat the process for each of the six years. Table 3.2 shows the inflation rates and their corresponding real costs for all six years.

We can now use this information to determine, for instance, the average inflation rate for all six years, taken together, which for the water supply example would be 20 percent. That is, (5.71+17.14+22.86+31.43+4 2.86 = 120.00/6 = 20%. As noted earlier, it is not necessary to calculate the inflation rates, since the BLS publishes the inflation statistics on a regular basis.

Besides CPI, the government, in particular the federal government, has been using the GNP implicit price deflator instead of the traditional consumer price index for deflating costs. The GNP implicit price deflator is an index that takes into account not only the changes in prices, but also some changes in the quality of goods and services that individuals consume. In addition to the GNP implicit price deflator, the government also uses the GDP price deflator, which is calculated the same way as the GNP price deflator, except that it uses GDP.[3]

3.7 Municipal Cost Index

In recent years, local governments have been using a slightly different index to determine the effect of inflation on municipal services, called the Municipal Cost Index (MCI). Developed by American City and

County in 1978, the index draws on the monthly data collected by the US Departments of Commerce and Labor together with the data compiled independently to develop a composite index by factoring in the costs of labor, materials and contract services. To construct the index, MCI relies on three sets of indices: the Consumer Price Index (CPI) to reflect the fluctuations in the prices of goods and service the public consumes, especially the urban consumers (CPI–U), the Producer Price Index (PPI) to reflect the fluctuations in industrial commodity wholesale prices, and the Construction Cost Index (CCI) to reflect the changes in the costs of construction materials and skilled and unskilled labor (GFOA, 2010). The data for the first two indices are available from the BLS and the third index from the Department of Commerce.

To give an example, suppose that the base year for an MCI is t-3, and the cost index for t-1 is 117. This means that, based on this index, the cost of providing municipal services in the city has increased by 17 percent (117–100) since t-3. In fact, the American City and County Magazine publishes the MCI on a regular basis, using 1982 as the base year. There are numerous advantages to using MCI. For instance, local governments can use the MCI to estimate future spending needs and adjust budget allocations based on anticipated cost increases. Also, the data produced by MCI across different cities can help policymakers understand cost variations and identify areas for potential cost savings.

3.8 Chapter Summary

Price plays an important role in government. For many of the goods and services a government provides, especially those that are provided in a business-like manner, there is a price the public must pay for their consumption. Price is not the same as cost, although the two are interrelated. Price is the premium we pay for the consumption of a good or service, while the cost is what it costs to produce or deliver a good or service. However, there is not one specific price the government uses for the goods we consume, but multiple different prices, depending on the nature of the goods. This chapter has provided a general discussion on the different pricing methods used in government, along with a brief discussion of the rate structure of cost. Just like price, there are different types of rates that can be used for a good or service. The chapter has also provided a broad overview of different types of rates that are typically used in government. Finally, the chapter concluded with a brief discussion of cost and inflation; in particular, how to calculate the real costs of a service with and without the conventional Consumer Price Index (CPI).

Review Questions

3.1 Define price. Why is it difficult to determine the price of public goods? What pricing method would you use for (a) public utilities, (b) recreation facilities, and (3) a toll road? Why?
3.2 What is the difference between marginal cost, average cost, and total cost pricing? Why is it difficult to use marginal cost pricing in government. Give an example of each.
3.3 Suppose that it costs the Parking Department of a mid-sized government $200 for five parking tickets at $40 a ticket and $270 for six tickets, what would be the marginal cost for the sixth ticket? What would be marginal revenue? Assuming P = MC, what would be the price the department must charge for a ticket?
3.4 The cost of a heart procedure for a county-run hospital on average is $125,000, with a fixed cost of $50,000 and a variable cost of $75,000. The hospital completed 100 procedures last year. Assuming there are no changes in the number of procedures the hospital will perform next year, calculate the cost of surgery for next year, if (a) there is a 2% increase in variable and a 1.5% increase in fixed costs, and (b) it wants to maintain a 3.5% safety margin.
3.5 For the problem in 3.4, what would the cost be if the number of procedures (a) increases by 2%, and (b) decreases by 4%, with and without the safety margin. Assume no changes in cost conditions next year?
3.6 What is a cost-plus price? Suppose that a government currently charges $12.50 in entrance fee for a government-run amusement park (children under five are free), which includes a fixed cost of $2.50 and the rest is variable cost. The price is just enough to break even. The government wants to set the price for next year using a cost-plus price. How should the government determine the cost-plus? Should it be based on total cost, fixed cost, or the variable cost? What would be the difference?
3.7 What is the rate structure of cost? What are the differences between flat rate, uniform rate, and block rate? How is a seasonal rate different from a block rate?
3.8 The water department of a local government charges its residents the following rates for water consumption: (a) the first 5,000 gallons of water at $4.50 per 1,000 gallons, (b) the next 7,000 gallons at $6.00 per 1,000 gallons, and (c) more than 10,000 gallons at $7.50 per 1,000. Suppose that a family consumes 15,000 galls of water on average a month. What would be the monthly payment for the family of the consumption? Assume there is a fixed cost of $15 with each payment.

3.9 Suppose that the electric utility department of a large metropolitan government charges the residents the following rates for electricity consumption: (a) the first 20,000 kWh at $0.06 per kWh, (b) the next 50,000 kWh at $0.05 per kWh, and (c) more than 70,000 kWh at $0.04 per kWh. Suppose that a family home consumes 80,000 kWh on average a year. What would be the monthly payment for the family for their consumption?

3.10 Governments often use different pricing methods for different goods and services. Select a government that you are familiar with. Identify three of the services for which it charges a price.

a. Discuss the pricing method it uses for each service.
b. Do the methods generate revenues sufficient to cover the costs of the services?
c. If the answer to (b) is no, what pricing method would you recommend?

3.11 Returning to the example in 3.10, look at the rate structure the government uses for water, and indicate what rate it uses.

a. A block rate? If so, is it an inclining or declining rate?
b. What seasonal rate does the government use for different months?

3.12 Nonprofit organizations also use different pricing methods for the range of services they provide. Select a nonprofit organization that you are familiar with or interests you and discuss the pricing methods it uses. Would any of the methods it uses can be considered as discriminatory?

2.12 For Problem 3.9, suppose further that the department has experienced the following rate changes in the last 10 years, based on the monthly average rate per kilowatt hour (kWh) of electricity, with corresponding costs, as follows:

Year	*Rate Per kWh ($)*	*Departmental Cost ($ Million)*
1 (t-10)	0.075	10.5
2 (t-9)	0.078	10.5
3 (t-8)	0.080	11.4
4 (t-7)	0.083	11.6
5 (t-6)	0.085	12.0
6 (t-5)	0.087	12.6
7 (t-4)	0.090	12.9
8 (t-3)	0.092	13.3
9 (t-2)	0.095	13.5
10 (t-1)	0.098	13.7

Using the information above, calculate

A. a. the index for each of the ten years
   b. the adjusted cost of electricity for each of the ten years
   c. Interpret the results
   [Hint: Use t - 1 as the base year]
B. Calculate the inflation rates for all 10 years (a) taking two years at a time, and (b) using t - 1 as the base year. What would be the average inflation rate?

Notes

1 A natural monopoly is associated with activities with high start-up costs that make it difficult for small, competitive firms to enter the market. At the same time, unlike a pure monopoly, it allows for limited competition which makes it possible to keep the price low and increase efficiency of provision.

2 For a long time, BLS used a formula based on an index called the Laspeyres Index. The index is based on three sets of information: the average quantity of an item consumed in the base period, the price in the base period, and the price in the current period. It can be expressed as $L = \Sigma P_{jt}Q_{j0}/\Sigma P_{j0}Q_{j0}$, where L stands for Laspeyres Index, P_{jt} is the price of the jth item at time t, Q_{j0} is the quantity of the jth item at time 0 (which is the base year), and P_{j0} is the price of the jth item at time 0. However, the Bureau has discontinued using the Laspayres index; instead, it uses a hybrid. The hybrid index uses a geometric mean for the lower level and the Laspeyres for the upper level. The Bureau updates the index on a regular basis, which can be easily accessed from its web site.

3 It is obtained by dividing the nominal GNP by the real GNP and multiplying the product by 100. For instance, if nominal GNP is $175,000 and real GNP is $125,000, the deflator will be 140 [$175,000/$125,000) × 100 = 140]. If GDP is used instead of GNP, it will be GDP deflator.

References

Alkhas, E. (2021). Nonprofits need pricing strategies too. Logic 20/20. https://logic2020.com/insight/nonprofits-need-pricing-strategies too/#: :text=On%20 one%20hand%2C%20they%20want,leveraging%20pricing%20strateg ies%20is20essential, February 16.

Davis, O.A. and Whinston, A.B. (1967). On the distinction between public and private goods. *American Economic Review*, 57 (2): 360–373.

GFOA. (2010). Inflationary indices in budgeting, in *GFOA Best Practices*. Chicago, IL: Government Finance Officers Association. www.gfoa.org/materials/inflation ary-indices-in-budgeting [Accessed March 31, 2010].

Lanzillotti, R., Dirlam, J.B., and Kaplan, A.D.H. (1958). *Pricing in big business*. Washington, DC: Brookings Institution.

Lee, D.R. (1982). On the pricing of public goods. *Southern Economic Journal*, 49(1), July: 99–105.

Robinson, J.H. and Foreman, T. (2011). How to price strategically? *Nonprofit World*, 29(3): 24–25.

Samuelson, P.A. (1954). The pure theory of public expenditure. *The Review of Economics and Statistics*. May/June, 36 (4), November: 387–389.

Tyndall, D.G. (1951). The relative merits of average cost pricing, marginal cost pricing, and price discrimination. *The Quarterly Journal of Economics*, 65(3): 342–372.

4 Cost Behavior and Estimation

4.1 Introduction

A fundamental principle that underlies the cost behavior of an organization is that there exists a direct relationship between cost and quantity. Although variables other than quantity, such as the price of factors of production, the structure of an organization, and the latter's ability to efficiently utilize the input resources have a bearing on cost, they are usually held constant in most cost studies, especially in the short run. In the long run, all costs and related factors of production are variable because of changes in technology, price of labor, and so forth. Since organizations operate differently at different levels of production, it is difficult to determine a priori the time for the short run, but the rule of thumb is that it should be a year or less. However, the time frame for long run is not fixed and can easily vary depending on the relationship between inputs and the production or delivery process. This chapter discusses three basic elements of cost behavior that are important to understand the nature of costs and how they affect the functioning of an organization: time frame of costs, general properties of cost functions, and cost estimation. Of these, cost estimation is particularly important, as it provides the information necessary for determining the nature of current as well as future costs of an organization. The chapter provides a detailed discussion of cost estimation, followed by a brief discussion of cost forecasting.

4.2 Time Frame of Costs

Although it may be difficult to determine the exact time that separates a short-run from a long-run cost, the concept nevertheless has important implications for decision making in an organization. For instance, the short run is an operating concept. As an operating concept, it deals with the day-to-day operations of an organization. Thus, when an organization wants to deal with its routine activities, such as collecting garbage,

DOI: 10.4324/9781003486091-5

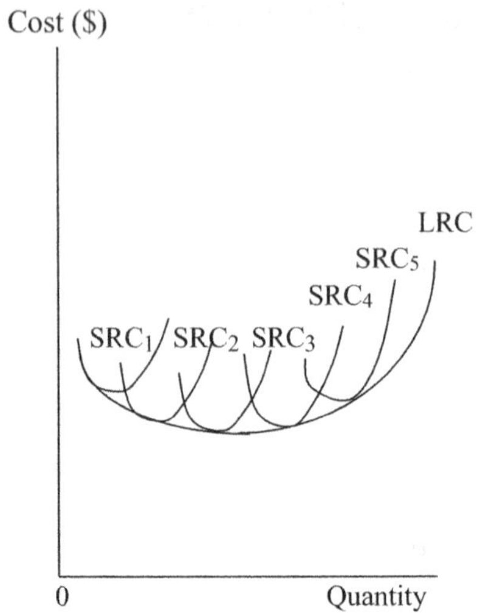

Figure 4.1 Short-run and long-run costs

providing water and sewer services, or fixing traffic lights, it relies on short-run cost functions.

On the other hand, the long run, which includes many short runs (Figure 4.1), is a planning concept and, as a planning concept, it deals with non-routine activities of an organization. These activities usually take a longer time to complete and often have impacts that extend over a long period of time. Thus, when an organization plans to make major changes in its operation such as improving traffic congestion on major highways or upgrading the delivery system for healthcare, it relies on its long-run cost functions.

Since in the long run all factors of production are variable, it is possible to adjust the factors more easily in the long run than in the short run. This is largely because once a production process has been set in motion it is not possible for an organization to easily change the usage of its input factors. Some inputs such as plants and equipment may have already been committed to the process, thus making it difficult for the organization to change these factors without affecting the efficiency of operation.

4.2.1 Short Run Costs

As noted previously, the short run is a period during which some of the input factors, such as machines, tools, and equipment remain fixed. Since they remain fixed, they produce a cost to the organization that is independent of the level of output. Two factors determine the cost behavior in the short run: the price of variable inputs, such as labor and capital, and the production function that underlies a production process. A production function shows the relationship between input and output based on the state of technology. If technology remains constant in the short run, it is likely that the production function will also remain constant in the short run.

To understand the cost structure of an organization and see how it affects decision making in the short run, it is necessary to reintroduce some of the cost terms we introduced earlier; in particular, Total Cost (TC), Fixed Cost (FC), Variable Cost (VC), Marginal Cost (MC), and Average Cost (AC). All these costs can be directly obtained from observations on total cost. For instance, since the total cost is expressed as the sum of fixed and variable costs using the standard expression $TC = FC + VC$, we can directly obtain the average cost by dividing the total cost by quantity, $AC = TC/Q$, and the marginal cost by taking the difference between two adjacent total costs, $MC = TC_2 - TC_1$. Similarly, since the variable cost depends on quantity, we can express it as a function of quantity; that is, $VC = f(Q)$, which means that as the quantity changes, so will the variable cost. Therefore, we can write total cost as $TC = FC + VC = FC + VC(Q)$.

The simplest way to understand how cost behaves is to look at the cost curves. Interestingly, both marginal and average cost curves are U shaped, with the marginal cost curve intersecting the average cost curve at its lowest point. The shapes of the curves indicate that they both tend to decrease with increased production or delivery up to a point and then increase. In the case of MC, it decreases at a lower rate than the average cost initially and then increases at a higher rate once it intersects the average cost curve at its lowest point (Figure 4.2).

Table 4.1 presents a cost schedule showing the relationship between fixed, variable, total, marginal, and average costs based on cost data for recycling water for the Water Department of a local government. Recycling water is a standard practice for local governments to improve the water quality for residential and commercial use. As the table shows, it costs the department \$20 in fixed costs and \$3.50 in variable costs to recycle the first thousand gallons of water.[1] While the fixed cost remains the same for any amount of water produced, the variable cost increases as the amount of water produced increases, but it does not increase at a constant rate. In fact, it increases at a slower rate with increased production (downward cost curve) because of economies of scale (lower average cost), then increasing at a higher rate as production increases. This is often due to resource limitations and other factors that can reduce efficiency, thereby raising the cost curve upward. However, since the fixed cost remains

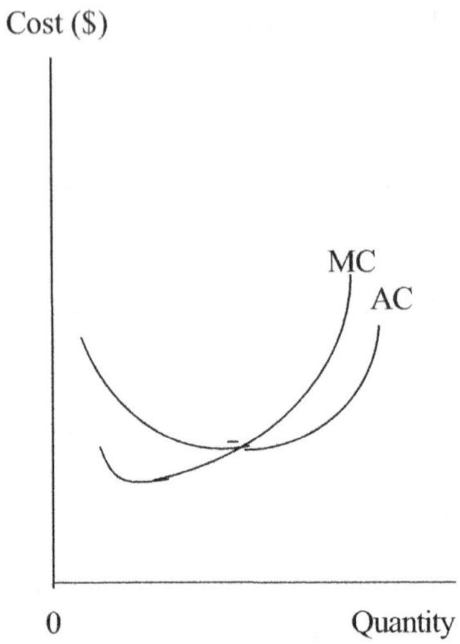

Figure 4.2 Marginal and average cost

Table 4.1 Cost schedule for recycling water for residential use

Quantity (Gallons)[1]	*Fixed Cost ($)*	*Variable Cost ($)*	*Total Cost ($)*	*Marginal Cost ($)*	*Average Cost (CPG)*[2] *($)*
1	20	3.50	23.50	--	23.50 (0.02350)
2	20	5.00	25.00	1.50	12.50 (0.01250)
3	20	6.00	26.00	1.00	8.67 (0.00867)
4	20	7.00	27.00	1.00	6.75 (0.00675)
5	20	8.75	28.75	1.75	5.75 (0.00675)
6	20	11.96	31.96	3.21	**5.33** (0.00533)
7	20	17.29	37.29	**5.33**	**5.33 (0.00533)**
8	20	26.69	46.69	9.40	5.84 (0.00684)
9	20	45.00	65.00	18.31	7.22 (0.00722)
10	20	73.20	93.20	28.20	9.32 (0.00982)

[1] In 1,000 gallons; [2]Cost per gallon (CPG), e.g., $23.50/1,000 = $0.02350

constant, the only factor that affects the total cost of recycling is the variable cost.

As can be seen from the table, both marginal and average costs continue to decrease, the marginal cost up to the 4th thousand gallons, increasing afterwards, and AC up to the 7th thousand gallons, increasing afterwards. Also, as can be seen from the table, at the 7th thousand gallons, where the cost is \$5.33, marginal cost equals average cost, MC = AC, after which MC increases at a higher rate than AC.

4.2.2 Long Run Costs

As we noted earlier, the short-run cost is an operating concept, which means that an organization has no control over the fixed costs it incurs for a given level of operation in the short run. Therefore, any effort to increase its efficiency must come from a reduction in its variable costs. In contrast, an organization dealing with long run costs does not have any such problem. Since all factors of production are variable in the long run, it is possible for the organization to select the most efficient (least cost) combination of factors at which its operation will be optimal.

An important implication of this behavior is that in the long run it is possible for organizations to have greater economies of scale. Economies of scale occur in an organization when the average cost of production decreases because of improvements in the production process, but economies of scale cannot be maintained continuously over time. Eventually, costs will rise. The eventual rise in costs is due to diseconomies of scale, which occur once the level of operation becomes too large making it difficult for the decision makers to efficiently coordinate all the activities of an organization.

4.3 Elasticity of Cost

Let us introduce a term that frequently appears in discussions on cost behavior called elasticity of cost. Elasticity, in general, measures the responsiveness of a variable (dependent) to a change in another variable (independent), and is usually expressed in percentage terms. In other words, how cost changes in response to changes the level of production (output). The responsiveness is measured by a coefficient, ϵ, called the elasticity coefficient, and is determined by two interrelated factors: its sign and magnitude. The sign reflects the direction of movement between two variables, and the magnitude indicates the degree of responsiveness of the dependent variable to a change in the independent variable.

Elasticity can be greater than, equal to, or less than 1. If it is less than 1, $|\epsilon| < 1$, it is inelastic, meaning that cost increases proportionately at a slower rate than the output (a 1 percent increase in output leads to less than 1 percent increase in cost). In behavioral terms, it means that there are economies of scale. If it is equal to 1, $|\epsilon| = 1$, it is unit elastic, meaning that cost and output increase proportionately, at the same rate (a 1 percent increase in output leads to a 1 percent increase in cost). In behavioral terms, it means that there are no economies or diseconomies of scale. If it is greater than 1, $|\epsilon|>1$ it is elastic, meaning that cost increases proportionately at a higher rate than the increase in output (a 1 percent increase in output leads to more than 1 percent increase in cost). Again, in behavioral terms, it means that there are diseconomies of scale.

The following presents a simple expression of cost elasticity to measure the responsiveness of cost to a change in output:

$$\epsilon_C = \frac{\Delta TC}{TC} / \frac{\Delta Q}{Q} \tag{4.1}$$

where Є is the elasticity of cost, ΔTC is the change in total cost, and ΔQ is the change in quantity, TC and Q are total cost and quantity, respectively.

We can simplify the expression in Equation 4.1 by rewriting it as

$$\epsilon_C = \frac{\Delta TC}{TC} / \frac{\Delta Q}{Q} = \frac{\Delta TC}{\Delta Q} \times \frac{Q}{TC} \tag{4.2}$$

where the first term (ΔTC/ΔQ) represents the marginal cost (MC) and the second term (Q/TC) represents the reciprocal of average cost, 1/AC, since AC = TC/Q. Thus, if we have information on both marginal and average costs, we can easily obtain the elasticity of cost. In general, if MC < AC, it is inelastic; if MC > AC, it is elastic; and if MC = AC, it is unit elastic.

To give an example, let us look at the water recycling problem again. For instance, at Q = 6, the elasticity of cost is 0.6; that is, ϵ_C = (ΔTC/ΔQ) × (Q/TC) = (MC) × (1/AC) = (3.21) x (1/5.33) = 3.21/5.33 = 0.6. In other words, for a one percent change in output, total cost will change by 0.6 percent, indicating that cost is inelastic. In common sense terms what this means is that it will cost the department less at a higher level of output. By the same token, cost is elastic at higher levels of output. For instance, at Q = 9, the elasticity is 2.54 [18.31/7.22 = 2.54], indicating a more than a proportionate change in output. In other words, it will cost the department more at a higher level of output, especially when it exceeds eight thousand gallons of water, than it will when the output level is low. Put simply, when the output reaches a level where the production cost increases at a faster rate it becomes necessary to adjust the production process to bring the costs down, which then becomes a long-run cost problem.

4.3.1 Point versus Arc Elasticity

The elasticity concept discussed above is known as point elasticity because it represents incremental movements from point to point along a cost curve, but there are situations where we may need to measure elasticity over a large segment of the curve. The elasticity that is commonly used for this is arc elasticity. The arc elasticity for a total cost function can be written as

$$\epsilon_C' = [\frac{TC_1 - TC_0}{(TC_1 + TC_0)/2}]/[\frac{Q_1 - Q_0}{(Q_1 + Q_0)/2}] \quad (4.3)$$

where ϵ'_c is the arc elasticity, and the subscripts 1 and 0 are the new and the initial costs and quantities, respectively. The purpose of dividing the denominator by 2 is that it measures the average distance, or the distance halfway between the designated end points of the arc.

To give an example, let us take two output quantities from the water recycling problem, $Q_0 = 5$ and $Q_1 = 8$, and two total costs corresponding to the outputs, $TC_0 = \$28.75$ and $TC_1 = \$46.69$, then substitute these values into Equation 4.3, as shown below:

$$\epsilon_C' = [\frac{TC_1 - TC_0}{(TC_1 + TC_0)/2}]/[\frac{Q_1 - Q_0}{(Q_1 + Q_0)/2}]$$

$$= \frac{(TC_1 - TC_0)(Q_1 + Q_0)}{(TC_1 + TC_0)(Q_1 - Q_0)}$$

$$= \frac{(46.69 - 28.75)(8 + 5)}{(46.69 + 28.75)(8 - 5)}$$

$$= \frac{(17.94)(13)}{(75.44)(3)}$$

$$= 1.03$$

which produces an elasticity of 1.03.

The result indicates that the total cost is elastic, although marginally, over the range of the cost curve designated by the end points of the arc, (TC_1, Q_1) and (TC_0 , Q_0). In other words, it represents the average elasticity for the range of output between Q_1 and Q_0 (between 8 and 5 thousand gallons of water). Interestingly, both point and arc elasticities serve as good examples of how costs respond to changes in output. Although our example has been limited to cost behavior in the short run, it can be used in any situation, including long-run costs, so long as there is a logical justification for it.

It is worth noting that when elasticity is used for long-run cost functions, the results may be less than precise because so many other factors may intervene in the relationship between a dependent and an independent variable. Also, since elasticity measures a one-to-one relationship, it cannot account for any intervention that may affect the responsiveness of the variable and the elasticity being measured.

4.4 Properties of Cost Functions

All cost functions have one characteristic in common in that they all contain two basic parameters: one representing the fixed cost and the other the variable cost. Fixed costs, as we know, are costs that do not change in the short run over a given range of output, whereas variable costs change in direct proportion to changes in output. The notion of range is important in cost functions because it sets the limits within which one's definition of cost remains valid. Since fixed costs are constant, they can be assumed away in a cost function in that if one would remove the parameter representing the fixed cost from a cost function, it would leave the function with the variable cost only, meaning that fixed cost does not have any effect on the function. It is tantamount to saying that the fixed cost is zero.

4.4.1 Linear Cost Function

We can explain the above relationship between cost and quantity with the help of a simple linear cost function, where we define Total Cost (TC) as a function of output quantity, Q, such that TC = f(Q). The linear equation corresponding to this function can be written as

$$TC = a + bQ \tag{4.4}$$

where a is the parameter representing fixed cost, and b is the term representing the variable cost per unit of output, Q.

In conventional algebraic terms, TC is the dependent variable and Q the independent variable. If, according to this relationship, the fixed cost does not have any effect on total cost, TC, the Equation 4.4 will become

$$TC = bQ \tag{4.5}$$

meaning that there is no fixed cost ($a = 0$). This also means that if we can draw a line corresponding to this equation on a two-dimensional plane, one representing Cost (C) on the vertical axis and the other representing Quantity (Q) on the horizontal axis, it will pass through the points of origin of the two axes (Figure 4.3).

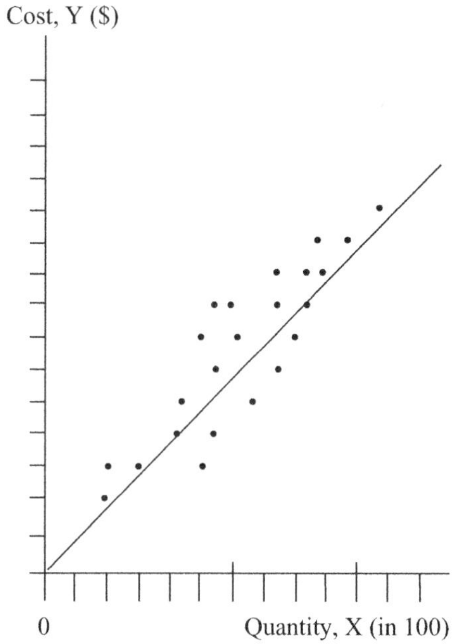

Figure 4.3 Cost and quantity relationship

4.4.2 Nonlinear Cost Functions

Although linear relationships are common in most cost studies, it is not uncommon to have a non-linear relationship such as quadratic, cubic, or a higher degree polynomial. While a linear cost function shows a straight-line relationship between cost and one or more independent variables, as in Equation 4.4, a nonlinear relationship shows changes in relation to the behavior of one or more independent variables such as the rate of change in output, change in direct labor, change in direct materials, and so on.

For instance, a typical quadratic function describing the relationship between cost and quantity can be expressed as

$$TC = a + bQ - cQ^2 \tag{4.6}$$

where TC is the total cost, Q is the quantity, and a, b and c are the parameters representing fixed and variable costs, respectively.

Similarly, a typical cubic function describing the cost behavior of an organization can be expressed as

$$TC = a + bQ - cQ^2 + dQ^3 \qquad (4.7)$$

where the terms of the expression are the same, as before. We can easily extend Equation 4.7 to show a higher degree polynomial cost function.

Nonlinear cost functions, by their very nature, are more complex than linear cost functions. As such, the cost terms one derives from these functions, in particular average and marginal costs, are also more complex. On the other hand, an advantage of using these functions is that once we know the average and marginal costs, we can use this information to estimate the elasticity of costs from these functions without having to go through the formalities of Equation 4.1 (since the terms b, c, and d, in essence, are elasticities). However, it should be worth noting that although most cost functions in the real world are nonlinear, the advantage of using a linear cost function is that it is easier to estimate costs with a linear function than with a nonlinear function. Nonlinear functions such as cubic functions often require theoretical generalizations which can make it difficult to fit the curves to empirical data.

4.5 Cost Estimation

Cost functions and their properties serve two important objectives in cost studies: One, they help us understand the patterns of cost behavior over time and, two, they provide us with the information necessary to estimate current as well as future costs of operation for an organization. Cost estimation is an important element of cost behavior. Without good estimates of cost, it will be difficult for an organization to effectively plan its current as well as its future activities. There is a wide range of methods with varying degrees of complexity that can be used for cost estimation (Mislick and Nussbaum, 2015). This section discusses three such methods that are often used in cost studies: the graphical method, the high-low method, and the least square method.

4.5.1 The Graphical Method

The graphical method is primarily used to show the relationship between two variables (a dependent variable and an independent variable) by fitting a visual line into a set of data on a two-dimensional plane. In general, the cost data is presented on the vertical axis and the quantity data on the horizontal axis, based on the conventional wisdom that cost depends on quantity. For instance, if we assume that there is a linear relationship

Table 4.2 Cost and quantity data for solid waste collection

Month	*Tons of Solid Waste Collected, X*	*Total Cost, Y ($)*
January	1,500	50,000
February	1,300	45,000
March	1,200	42,500
April	1,000	37,500
May	1,200	40,000
June	1,600	47,500
July	2,000	55,000
August	1,800	52,000
September	1,700	50,000
October	1,800	50,000
November	2,000	57,500
December	2,200	60,000

between Total Cost (TC), which we will call Y, and Quantity (Q), which we will call X, such that $Y = a + bX$, then using the graphical method we can estimate the parameters, a (which is the intercept) and b (which is the gradient or slope t) of this relationship by visually fitting a line to the plotted observations (referred to as the coordinates). The intercept represents the fixed cost (the value that the dependent variable Y will assume when the value of the independent variable X is zero), while the slope represents the variable cost (the amount by which the dependent variable Y will change for a unit change in the independent variable X).

We can use a simple example to illustrate this. Suppose that a small local government is trying to estimate the cost of solid waste collection for its residential units. Let us assume that the government has the data on solid waste collection (X) and the corresponding cost of collection (TC) over a twelve-month period. Our objective is to find the values of a and b, given the cost and quantity information we have on the two variables. Table 4.2 presents this data.

To estimate the values of a and b, we begin first by plotting the data on a graph with X (tons of solid waste collected) on the horizontal axis and Y (total cost of running the program) on the vertical axis, as shown in Figure 4.4. Next, we visually construct a line that would pass through the data points in such a way that some of the observations will lie above the line and some below, thus giving it the appearance of a good fit. Ideally, they should all lie on the line to show perfect fit, but that is seldom the case.

As the figure shows, the line intercepts the cost axis roughly at $15,000. This is the Fixed Cost (FC), a, of solid waste collection per month. The variable cost, b, is given by the slope of the line. We can obtain this

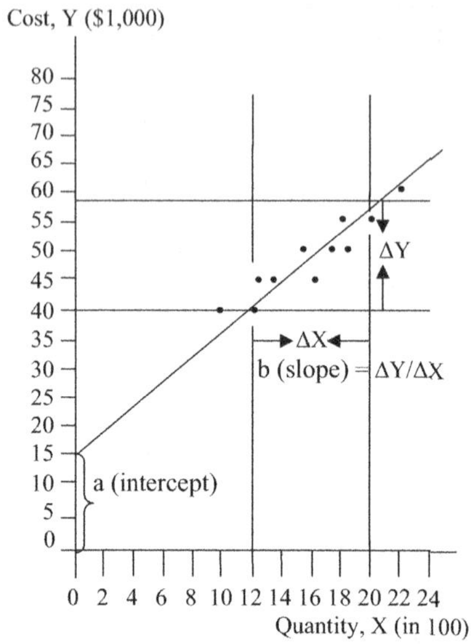

Figure 4.4 Cost and quantity relationship for the solid waste collection problem

slope by taking the ratio of two changes: Changes in total cost (ΔY) to changes in the amount of solid waste collection during a month (ΔX), as shown below:

$$b = \frac{\Delta Y}{\Delta X}$$

$$= \frac{\$57,500 - \$40,000}{2,000 - 1,200} = \frac{\$17,500}{800}$$

$$= \$21.875 \approx \$21.87$$

The result produces a value of $21.87 (after rounding). This is the variable cost, b, the cost of solid waste collection for an additional ton. In other words, it is the marginal cost of garbage collection. Although based on ‘ eye impression, we can formally present the estimated equation as

$$TC = \$15,000 + \$21.87Q$$

where $15,000 is the Fixed Cost (FC) and $21.87 is the Variable Cost (VC).

4.5.2 The High-Low Method

Unlike the graphical method, where one tries to visually fit a line to a set of sample observations, the high-low method uses two observations: one high and one low, to estimate the slope, b, and the intercept, a. The advantage of using this method is that it utilizes a minimum amount of information to estimate the parameters of the model. To illustrate how the method is used in practice, let us return to the solid waste collection example. As before, we assume that the relationship between Total Cost (TC) and the tons of solid waste collected (X) a month is linear; that is, $Y = a + bX$. In fact, the high-low method always assumes a linear relationship between the dependent and the independent variable.

Our objective is to find the values of a and b; in other words, the intercept and slope of this relationship. We use the following procedure to determine the values: Let Y represent the cost of solid waste collection and X the amount of garbage collected, Y_H and Y_L, represent the high and low cost of solid waste collection, and X_H and X_L the high and low amount of garbage collected during the year, respectively. Since we assumed a linear relationship between the two variables, we can set up the problem in terms of two linear equations

$$Y_H = a + bX_H \tag{4.8}$$

$$Y_L = a + bX_L \tag{4.9}$$

where a is the intercept, and b is the slope. The equations indicate that at both levels, Y_H and Y_L, the total cost consists of a fixed component, a, and a variable component equal to the rate, b, times the level of activity, so that $Y = FC + VC(X)$; in other words, $TC = FC + VC(Q)$.

We begin with the slope, the variable component of the total cost function since we need to have this information in order to determine the intercept. To obtain the slope, we subtract Equation 4.9 from Equation 4.8, and solve for b. That is,

$$\begin{aligned} Y_H - Y_L &= a + bX_H - a - bX_L \\ &= bX_H - bX_L \\ \therefore b &= \frac{Y_H - Y_L}{X_H - X_L} \\ &= \frac{\$60{,}000 - \$37{,}500}{2{,}200 - 1{,}000} \end{aligned}$$

$$= \frac{\$22,500}{1,200}$$

$$= \$18.75$$

The result produces a slope of \$18.75. This is how much it costs the government to collect a ton of solid waste, which is about three dollars less than what we obtained from the graphical method.

The calculation of the intercept term, a, is relatively straightforward once we know the slope, b. We can use any of the two equations (4.8–4.9) for this purpose. Equations 4.10–4.11, which are obtained from Equations 4.8–4.9, show how the intercept is obtained from the equations:

$$Y_H = a + bX_H$$

$$\therefore a = Y_H - bX_H \tag{4.10}$$

Alternatively,

$$Y_L = a + bX_L$$

$$\therefore a = Y_L - bX_L \tag{4.11}$$

Suppose now that we want to use Equation 4.10. Thus, substituting the respective values of the terms b, Y_H, and X_L into Equation 4.10, we can easily obtain the intercept (the estimate of a). That is,

$$\begin{aligned} a &= Y_H - bX_H \\ &= \$60,000 - (\$18.75)(2,200) \\ &= \$60,000 - \$41.250 \\ &= \$18,750 \end{aligned}$$

which produces a value of \$18,750. This is the fixed cost of solid waste collection, which turns out to be higher than the value we obtained with the graphical method (\$15,000).

Alternatively, we could have used Equation 4.11, which would produce the same result, since they are identical equations, except that we are using low, instead of high:

$$\begin{aligned} a &= Y_L - bX_L \\ &= \$37,500 - (\$18.75)(1,000) \\ &= \$37,000 - \$18,750 \\ &= \$18,750 \end{aligned}$$

We can now put all this information together and present the estimated equation as

$$Y = \$18,750 - \$18.75X$$

The result indicates that the fixed cost of solid waste collection, regardless of the amount collected, is \$18,750. The variable cost, on the other hand, is \$18.75, indicating that for each additional ton of solid waste collected the total cost of solid waste collection will increase by \$18.75 (the value equal to the variable cost of \$18.75). To see if our calculations are correct, we can plug in the observed values of the intercept (FC) and the slope (VC) into the estimated equation for any month, say April, which is \$37,500: that is, TC = FC + VC(Q) = \$18,750 + \$18.75(1,000) = \$18,750 + \$18,750 = \$37,500. The result appears to be correct, although it may deviate a little for the other months because of rounding errors.

What appears to be an obvious advantage for the high-low method can also be a disadvantage. Since the method does not utilize all the information in a data set, the estimated equation may not be an accurate representation of the exact relationship between the variables under study, especially if the difference between high and low can be considered, significant. In other words, it may not be the perfect line that can be fitted through the data points (coordinates). This is where the least square method becomes useful in that it makes full use of all the available information and, as such, provides a more accurate measure of the estimates than the high-low method.

4.5.3 The Least Square Method

Besides being able to fully utilize the available information in a data set, there are other advantages that make the least square method considerably better than either the graphical or the high-low method. For instance, it is computationally simple, although more involved than either method and it does not have excessive data requirements. Another advantage of the method is that its parameters have certain optimal properties that make it possible to apply various tests of significance. These tests are primarily used to determine the reliability of the estimated parameters as well as of the estimated equation. Furthermore, it is comprehensive in analytical details and frequently serves as the foundation for other more advanced methods used in cost studies.

This section focuses on a simple bivariate regression model involving two variables: a dependent variable, Y, representing the total cost, and an independent variable, X, representing the amount of garbage collection, as shown below:

$$Y = a + bX \tag{4.12}$$

where Y is the dependent variable and X is the independent variable, and a and b are the respective parameters (intercept and slope) of the model. As before, we assume a linear relationship between the two variables.

In general, the signs of the parameters in a regression model (the intercept and the slope) are always presented in positive terms, although in reality the values of the parameters can be positive, negative, or zero. In general, a positive slope indicates a positive relationship between X and Y, meaning that a change in X in a certain direction will lead to a change in Y in the same direction; that is, if X goes up, so will Y, and vice versa. A negative slope, on the other hand, indicates an inverse relationship between X and Y, meaning that a change in X in a certain direction will lead to a change in Y in the opposite direction; that is, if X goes up, Y will go down, and vice versa. The slope, however, cannot be zero because it will mean a total redundance of the independent variable, in which case it should not be included in the first place.

The intercept term, on the other hand, can be positive, negative, or zero. When it is positive, it means Y is positive, when X is zero. When it is zero, it means Y is zero, when X is zero. In other words, there is no intercept; that is, the line passes through the points of origin, where X and Y intersect at 0 (Figure 4.3). Finally, when the intercept is negative, it means that Y has a value that is less than zero, when X is zero, in which case it depends on the researcher whether to keep or ignore the negative portions of the equation.

4.5.3.1 The Error Term

When a linear equation is expressed as $Y = a + bX$, it implies that the relationship between X and Y is exact; that is, all the variation in Y is due entirely to the variation in X. If this were true, then all the data points on a two-dimensional plane would fall on a straight line. However, when observations come from the real world and are plotted on a graph, as we saw in our solid waste collection problem, one will most certainly observe that they will not fall on a straight line. In other words, there will be some deviations from the line, however small they may be.[2] To correct for these deviations (errors), the convention is to introduce an error term into the regression equation (4.12), so that the new equation will now appear as

$$Y = a + bX + e \tag{4.13}$$

where e is the error term. Therefore, the true relationship that connects the variables in this equation consists of two components: One represented by the line, $a + bX$, and the other by the error term, e.

4.5.3.2 The Least Squares Criterion

The linear equation we have just introduced, Y = a + bX + e, holds true for situations where one is dealing with population data, but we seldom deal with population data. Instead, we collect a sample of observations on X and Y, specify the distribution of the error term, and try to obtain a satisfactory estimate of the true value of the parameters of the relationship. As noted earlier, we do so by fitting a regression line through the observations of a sample, assuming that it would be a good approximation of the true line. Therefore, the true relationship between X and Y can be expressed as Y = a + bX + e, and the true regression line as Y = a + bX. On the other hand, the estimated relationship can be expressed as

$$Y = \hat{a} + \hat{b}X + \hat{e} \tag{4.13}$$

and the estimated regression line as

$$\hat{Y} = \hat{a} + \hat{b}X \tag{4.14}$$

where $\hat{Y}$is the estimate of Y, given a specific value of X, $\hat{a}$ is the estimate of the true intercept, a, and $\hat{b}$ is the estimate of the true slope, b, and $\hat{e}$ is the estimate of the true value of the error term, e. And the symbol ^ (hat) represents the estimated value of the parameters as well as of the regressed (dependent) variable in the equation

The weakness of this procedure is that we can obtain an infinite number of regression lines by assigning different values to the parameters a and b that will fit the data, but our objective in regression analysis is to choose a line that will best approximate the true line. Therefore, we need to use some guidelines or criteria by which we can determine this line. The criterion we generally use for this purpose is the least squares criterion, also known as the Ordinary Least Squares (OLS) method. According to this criterion, the line selected must be such that it will produce the smallest possible error for the observations from the line: it will be optimal. In other words, select the line for which the sum of the squares of the deviations of the observations from the line is the minimum.

4.5.4 Estimating the Parameters

The least squares criterion serves a very important purpose in regression analysis in that it allows us to estimate the parameters directly from it. The only requirement is that they must be estimated in such a way as to ensure that they are efficient (they have minimum variance). To illustrate, let us recall Equation 4.13 for the two variables, X and Y, $Y = \hat{a} + \hat{b}X + \hat{e}$ which, with slight reorganization, can be written as

$$\begin{aligned} \hat{e} &= Y - \hat{Y} \\ &= Y - (\hat{a} + \hat{b}X) \\ &= Y - \hat{a} - \hat{b}X \end{aligned} \tag{4.15}$$

Our objective is to find estimates of a and b in such a way as to ensure that the sum of the squared errors, $\sum(\hat{e}^2)$, where $\hat{e}$ is the estimated error (variance), will be minimum. That is,

$$\text{Minimize} \sum \hat{e}^2 = \sum (Y - \hat{a} - \hat{b}X)^2 \tag{4.16}$$

with respect to $\hat{a}$ and $\hat{b}$.

Equation 4.16 is what one would call a minimization function that can be easily solved using simple calculus, and with some algebraic manipulations (Appendix A), to produce the equations for the estimated intercept and slope, $\hat{a}$ and $\hat{b}$, that will satisfy the minimum variance requirement in Equation 4.16, as shown below:

$$\hat{a} = \frac{\sum Y}{n} - \frac{\hat{b}\sum X}{n} \tag{4.17}$$

$$\hat{b} = \frac{n\sum XY - \sum X \sum Y}{n\sum X^2 - (\sum X)^2} \tag{4.18}$$

Note that the expressions in Equations 4.17 and 4.18 do not require much information other than the values of X and Y, and the number of observations. This makes it easy to compute the estimated values of $\hat{a}$ and $\hat{b}$; as such, they are often called computational methods.

We can now apply the above expressions to the data in Table 4.2 to obtain the intercept and the slope for solid waste collection (Table 4.3), starting with the slope coefficient, as shown below:

$$\hat{b} = \frac{n\sum XY - \sum X \sum Y}{n\sum X^2 - (\sum X)^2}$$

Table 4.3 Calculation of summary statistics for intercept and slope

Month	*Tons of Solid Waste Collected, X*	*Total Cost, Y ($)*	X^2	*XY*
January	1,500	50,000	2,250,000	75,000,000
February	1,300	45,000	1,690,000	58,500,000
March	1,200	42,500	1,440,000	51,000,000
April	1,000	37,500	1,000,000	37,500,000
May	1,200	40,000	1,440,000	48,000,000
June	1,600	47,500	2,560,000	76,000,000
July	2,000	55,000	4,000,000	110,000,000
August	1,800	52,000	3,240,000	93,600,000
September	1,700	50,000	2,890,000	85,000,000
October	1,800	50,000	3,240,000	90,000,000
November	2,000	57,500	4,000,000	115,000,000
December	2,200	60,000	4,840,000	132,000,000
	ΣX = 19,300	ΣY = $587,000	ΣX^2 = 32,590,000	ΣXY = 971,600,000

nΣXY = (12)(971,600,000) = 11,659,200,000
ΣXΣY = (19,300)(587,000) = 11,329,100,000
$n\Sigma X^2$ = (12)(32,590,000) = 391,080,000
$(\Sigma X)^2$ = $(19,300)^2$ = 372,490,000

$$= \frac{(12)(971{,}600{,}000) - 11.329{,}100{,}000}{(12)(32{,}590{,}000) - 372{,}490{,}000}$$

$$= \frac{11{,}659{,}200{,}000 - 11.329{,}100{,}00}{391{,}080{,}000 - 372{,}490{,}000}$$

$$= \frac{330{,}100{,}000}{18{,}590{,}000}$$

$$= 17.757 \approx \$17.76$$

for $\hat{b}$. Similarly,

$$\hat{a} = \frac{\sum Y}{n} - \frac{\hat{b}\sum X}{n}$$

$$= \frac{587{,}000}{12} - \frac{(17.757)(19{,}300)}{12}$$

$$= 48{,}916.667 - 28{,}559.175$$

$$= 20{,}357.492 \approx \$20{,}357.49$$

for $\hat{a}$.

The estimated equation can be written as

$$\hat{Y} = 20{,}357.492 + 17.757X$$

4.5.4.1 *Alternative Formulation*

It should be worth noting that we could have also used the expressions in Equations 4.19 and 4.20 to estimate the intercept and slope; the results would have been the same. They are based on essentially the same set of information as the ones we used for the computational method, except that the equations are expressed in terms of the deviations from the means of the variables, X and Y. The following presents the equations for the intercept and the slope coefficients:

$$\hat{a} = \bar{Y} - \hat{b}\bar{X} \tag{4.19}$$

$$\hat{b} = \frac{\sum (X - \bar{X})(Y - \bar{Y})}{\sum (X - \bar{X})^2} \tag{4.20}$$

As before, we can apply the equations to the solid waste collection problem to obtain the estimated values of intercept and slope. Tables 4.4 and 4.5 present the summary measures that were used to estimate the parameters of the model and other relevant statistics. Thus, using the appropriate summary data from the table and substituting them into the respective terms in Equations 4.19 and 4.20, we can obtain the estimates of a and b, as shown below:

$$\hat{b} = \frac{\sum (X - \bar{X})(Y - \bar{Y})}{\sum (X - \bar{X})^2}$$

$$= \frac{27{,}508{,}333.32}{1{,}549{,}166.68}$$

$$= 17.757 \approx \$17.76$$

and

$$\hat{a} = \bar{Y} - \hat{b}\bar{X}$$

$$= 48{,}916.67 - (17.757)(1{,}608.33)$$

Table 4.4 Calculation of summary statistics for intercept and slope: the alternative formulation

Month	*X (Tons)*	*Y ($)*	*x*	*y*	*xy*	*x*^{2}	*Y*^{2}
January	1,500	50,000	-108.33	1,083.33	-117,357.14	11,735.39	1,173,603.89
February	1,300	45,000	-308.33	-3,916.67	1,207,626.86	95,067.39	15,340,303.89
March	1,200	42,500	-408.33	-6,416.67	2,620,118.86	166,733.39	41,173,653.89
April	1,000	37,500	-608.33	-11,416.67	6,945,102.86	370,065.39	130,340,353.89
May	1,200	40,000	-408.33	-8,916.67	3,640,943.86	166,733.39	79,507,003.89
June	1,600	47,500	-8.33	-1,416.67	11,800.86	69.39	2,006,953.89
July	2,000	55,000	391.67	6,083.33	2,382,657.86	153,405.39	37,006,903.89
August	1,800	52,000	191.67	3,083.33	590,981.86	36,737.39	9,506,923.89
September	1,700	50,000	91.67	1,083.33	99,308.86	8,403.39	1,173,603.89
October	1,800	50,000	191.67	1,083.33	207,641.86	36,737.39	1,173,603.89
November	2,000	57,500	391.67	8,583.33	3,361,832.86	153,405.39	73,673,553.89
December	2,200	60,000	591.67	11,083.33	6,557,673.86	350,073.39	122,840,203.89
	ΣX = 19,300	ΣY = $587,000	Σx ≈ 0	Σy ≈ 0	Σxy = 27,508,333.32	Σx^2 = 1,549,166.68	Σy^2 =514,916,666.68

$\bar{X} = 1{,}608.33$; $\bar{Y} = 48{,}916.67$; $x = (X - \bar{X})$; $y = (Y - \bar{Y})$; $xy = (X - \bar{X})(Y - \bar{Y})$; $x^2 = (X - \bar{X})^2$; $y^2 = (Y - \bar{Y})^2$

$$= 48{,}916.67 - 28{,}559.12$$
$$= 20{,}357.55\ (\$20{,}357.55)$$

As expected, the results appear to be the same as those obtained from the earlier expressions, except for the rounding errors. We can now put all this information together and present the estimated equation of the regression line as

$$\hat{Y} = 20{,}357.55 + 17.76X$$

What the result tells us is that, given the estimated values of the intercept and slope ($\hat{a}$ and$\hat{b}$), it will cost the government \$17.76 in variable costs to collect an additional ton of solid waste, and \$20,357.55 in fixed costs per month regardless of the amount of solid waste collected. Interestingly, the results compare relatively well with those we obtained earlier for the high-low method.

4.5.4.2 Tests of Significance of the Estimated Parameters

So far, our discussion has concentrated on estimating the values of the parameters of the regression equation, but we do not know how good these estimates are. Therefore, to establish the goodness (reliability) of these estimates we need to conduct a standard statistical test, called the *t*-test (used mostly for small samples involving 30 or fewer observations). The purpose of this test is to determine whether the estimates of a and b are significantly different from zero. In other words, whether the sample from which the data has been drawn and the parameters of the regression equation estimated could have come from a population whose true parameters are zero and, if so, what the chances are of observing this. What this means is that if the t-values could show, with a considerable degree of certainty, that they did not come from the population whose true parameters are zero, one should be able to consider the estimates as statistically significant (reliable), provided everything else remains the same.

In general, the *t* values are computed by taking the ratio of the estimated parameters to their corresponding standard errors (Appendix B). That is,

$$t_{\hat{a}} = \frac{\hat{a}}{S_{\hat{a}}} \tag{4.21}$$

$$t_{\hat{b}} = \frac{\hat{b}}{S_{\hat{b}}} \tag{4.22}$$

where $S\hat{a}$ and $S\hat{b}$ are the respective standard errors, and the values in parentheses indicate the *t* values.

The estimated equation, with the attendant t values can be written as

$$\hat{Y} = 20{,}357.55 + 17.76X$$

$$(9.4528)\ (13.5861)$$

From this compact form, we can test the significance of the estimated parameters, $\hat{a}$ and $\hat{b}$, by comparing the observed t values against their theoretical values, also called critical values (which can be found in a *t* table in any standard statistics textbook). The rule for comparison is simple: if the observed t is positive and greater than the critical value of t (for a two-tailed test) at a given level of *p*, called the *p* value (the probability or likelihood of obtaining the observed data or values under a null hypothesis in a hypothesis test), it is considered statistically significant at that level. The opposite is true when it is negative. Since our observed t is greater than the critical value of t at $p = 0.05$ (which is fairly standard); that is, $t(\hat{a}) = 9.4528 > t(a) = 2.228$, with $n-2 = 12-2 = 10$ degrees of freedom (number of independent observations or values to calculate a statistic), our estimated parameter $\hat{a}$ is statistically significant.

Similarly, since $t(\hat{b}) = 13.5861 > t(b) = 2.228$, then for the same level of *p* and the same degrees of freedom, the estimated parameter $\hat{b}$ is also statistically significant. What this means is that there is only a 5 percent chance that these results could have occurred by chance (due to error). Interestingly, the results would have been significant also at $p = 0.01$, given the size of observed *t* values.

4.5.4.3 *Confidence Intervals for the Estimated Parameters*

To say that our estimated coefficients $\hat{a}$ and $\hat{b}$ are statistically significant does not mean that they are correct estimates of the true population parameters, a and b. It simply means that our estimates have come from a sample drawn from a population whose parameters are different from zero. Therefore, to determine how close the estimated parameters are to the true population parameters, we need to construct a confidence interval for these parameters. What this means is that we need to establish, with a certain degree of confidence, two limiting values within which we can expect to find the true value of the population parameter, which we will call θ: one high value called the upper limit of the interval, and one low value called the lower limit of the interval.

The procedure for setting up a confidence interval is as follows:

$$C[\hat{\theta} - S_{\hat{\theta}} t_{\alpha/2} < \theta < \hat{\theta} + S_{\hat{\theta}} t_{\alpha/2}] = (1 - \alpha) \tag{4.23}$$

where C is the confidence statement, $(1 - \alpha)$ is the confidence level (degree of confidence), $\hat{\theta}$ is the estimated value of the parameter θ, $S_{\hat{\theta}}$ is the standard error of the estimate, and $t_{\alpha/2}$ is the critical t value for two-tails ($t_{\alpha/2}$), the probability of obtaining an observed statistic by error, for a given degree of freedom.

Using the expression in Equation 4.23, we can easily construct the confidence intervals for our estimated parameters $\hat{a}$ and $\hat{b}$, , say, at the 99 percent level of confidence. That is,

$$C[\hat{a} - S_{\hat{a}} t_{\alpha/2} < a < \hat{a} + S_{\hat{a}} t_{\alpha/2}] = (1 - \alpha)$$

$$C[20{,}357.55 - (2{,}153.56)(3.17) < a < 20{,}357.11 + (2{,}153.56)(3.17)] = 0.99$$

$$C[20{,}357.55 - 6{,}826.79 < a < 20{,}357.55 + 6{,}826.79] = 0.99$$

$$C[13{,}530.76 < a < 27{,}184.34] = 0.99$$

for $\hat{a}$.

Similarly,

$$C[\hat{b} - S_{\hat{b}} t_{\alpha/2} < b < \hat{b} + S\hat{b} t_{\alpha/2}] = (1 - \alpha)$$

$$C[17.76 - (1.307)(3.17) < b < 17.76 + (1.307)(3.17)] = 0.99$$

$$C[17.76 - 4.14 < b < 17.76 + 4.14] = 0.99$$

$$C[13.62 < b < 21.90] = 0.99$$

for $\hat{b}$.

The results indicate that at the 99 percent level of confidence, the true parameters of the estimated equations, a and b, will lie between \$13,530.76 and \$27,184.34 for a, and between \$13.62 and \$21.90 for b. In other words, we are 99 percent confident that the true parameters of the estimated equations will lie between these two intervals. This is how sure we are about the reliability of our estimates. In general, confidence intervals established at less than 90 percent are not considered significant (acceptable).

4.5.4.4 Goodness-of-Fit of the Regression Line

Once we have estimated the values of the parameters and set up the equation of the regression line, we need to determine how good the fit is to the sample observations; in other words, how closely the line fits the observed data points (coordinates). In general, the closer the line to the observed data points, the better the fit. However, to be able to precisely measure this fit we need to use a statistic called the coefficient of determination, or simply R^2. The coefficient of determination measures the amount of variation in the dependent variable that is explained by the variations in the independent variables (assuming there is more than one independent variable in the equation). In other words, it shows how well the observations fit the regression line.

Since the total variation in a regression is equal to the variation explained by the regression line and the error term, that is, total variance = explained (regression) variance + error variance, the R^2 can be computed by either of the following two expressions:

$$[1]\ R^2 = \frac{ExplainedVariance}{TotalVariance} \tag{4.24}$$

$$= \frac{\sum(\hat{Y} - \bar{Y})^2}{\sum(Y - \bar{Y})^2}$$

$$[2]\ R^2 = 1 - \frac{ErrorVariance}{TotalVariance} \tag{4.25}$$

$$= 1 - \frac{\sum(Y - \hat{Y})^2}{\sum(Y - \bar{Y})^2}$$

Table 4.5 shows how the explained and the error variances were obtained. Now, substituting the respective values from Tables 4.4 and 4.5 into the above expressions, we can easily obtain the R^2 for our solid waste collection problem, as shown below:

$$[1]\ R^2 = \frac{\sum(\hat{Y} - \bar{Y})^2}{\sum(Y - \bar{Y})^2}$$

$$= \frac{488,569,366.62}{515,024,450.04}$$

$$= 0.9486 \approx 0.95$$

Table 4.5 Calculation of summary statistics for solid waste collection

Month	*Y ($)*	$(\hat{Y})$	$(Y - \hat{Y})$	$(Y - \hat{Y})^2$	$(\hat{Y} - \bar{Y})$	$(\hat{Y} - \bar{Y})^2$
January	50,000	46,993.05	3,006.95	9,041,748.30	-1,923.62	3,700,313.90
February	45,000	43,441.65	1,558.35	2,428,454.72	-5,475.02	29,975,844.00
March	42,500	41,665.95	834.05	695,639.40	-7,250.72	52,672,940.52
April	37,500	38,114.55	-614.55	377,671.70	-10,802.12	116,685,796.50
May	40,000	41,665.95	-1,665.95	2,775,389.40	-7.250.72	52,572,940.52
June	47,500	48,768.75	-1,268.75	1,609,726.56	-147.92	21,880.33
July	55,000	55.871.55	-871.55	759,599.40	6,954.88	48,370,355.81
August	52,000	52,320.15	-320.15	102,496.02	3,403.48	11,583,676.11
September	50,000	50,544.45	-544.45	296,425.80	1,627.78	2,649,667.73
October	50,000	52,320.15	-2,320.15	5,383,096.02	3,403.48	11,583,676.11
November	57,500	55,871.55	1,628.45	2,651,849.40	6,954.88	48,370,355.81
December	60,000	59,422.95	577.05	332,986.70	10,506.28	110,381,919.28
	ΣY =$587,000		$\sum(Y - \hat{Y}) \approx 0$	$\sum(Y - \hat{Y})^2 = 26,455,083.42$	$\sum(\hat{Y} - \bar{Y}) \approx 0$	$\sum(\hat{Y} - \bar{Y})^2 = 488,569,366.62$

$\bar{Y} = 48,916.67$
$\hat{Y} = 20,357.55+17.757X = 20,357.55+17.757(1,500) = 20,357.55+26,635.50 = 46,993.05$

$\sum(Y - \hat{Y})^2 /(n\text{-}k) = 26,455,083.42/(12\text{-}2) = 26,455,083.42/10 = 2,645,508.34$

$$[2]\ R^2 = 1 - \frac{\sum (Y - \hat{Y})^2}{\sum (Y - \bar{Y})^2}$$

$$= 1 - \frac{26{,}455{,}083.42}{515{,}024{,}450.04}$$

$$= 1 - 0.0514$$

$$= 0.9486 \approx 0.95$$

The result indicates that approximately 95 percent of the variation in total cost (Y) is explained by the variation in the amount of solid waste collected (X), which is quite high considering that R^2 ranges between 0 and 1. The remaining 5 percent of the variation remains unaccounted for by the regression line and can be attributed to the error term, e. Overall, it appears that our equation was a good fit.

Although a high R^2 reflects the existence of a strong relationship between a dependent and a set of independent variables, it does not say anything about the significance of the coefficient itself. To ensure that our observed R^2 is significant, we use another test called the F test. The F-test tells us, from a statistical point of view, if the estimated regression line is a good fit; in other words, if the model sufficiently describes the variations in the data. The F statistic, the basis of this test, is computed by taking the ratio of the variance due to the regression line (the variance due to the independent variables) to the variance due to the error term, adjusted for appropriate degrees of freedom. That is,

$$F = \frac{\mathit{Explained\ Variance} / (k-1)}{\mathit{Error\ Variance} / (n-k)}$$

$$= \frac{\sum (\hat{Y} - \bar{Y})^2 / (k-1)}{\sum (Y - \hat{Y})^2 / (n-k)} \qquad (4.26)$$

where k is the number of parameters (the number of variables in a regression equation, including the dependent variable), and n is the sample size.

According to Equation 4.26, if the explained variance turns out to be the same as the error (unexplained) variance, the ratio will be equal to 1, meaning that the variability explained by the model is the same as vriability not explained by it (i.e., the independent variable is not a good predictor of the dependent variable). Put simply, the model is not a good fit. However,

Table 4.6 Analysis of variance (ANOVA) table

Sources of Variation (A)	*Sum of Squares (B)*	*Degrees of Freedom (C)*	*Mean Squares MS (D) = (B)/(C)*	*F-Value* (MS_{Reg}/MS_{Error})
Due to Regression	$\sum(\hat{Y}-\bar{Y})^2$ = 488,569,366.62	k - 1 = 2 - 1 = 1	488,569,366.62/1 = 488,569,366.62	488,569,366.62/ 2,645,508.34 = 184.679
Due to Error	$\sum(Y-\hat{Y})^2$ = 26,455,083.42	n - k = 12 - 2 = 10	26,455,083.42/10 = 2,645,508.34	
Due to Data (Total)	$\sum(Y-\bar{Y})^2$ = 515,024,450.04	n - 1 = 12 - 1 = 11	515,024,450.04/11 = 46,820,404.55	

as the explained variance increases in magnitude relative to the unexplained variance, the F statistic also increases in size. In general, the higher the explained variance in relation to the unexplained variance, the better the fit. Table 4.6, called the ANOVA or F table, shows how the F-statistic was computed. According to the table, the observed F came out to be 184.679.

To determine if the estimated equation $\hat{Y} = 20.357.55 + 17.757X$ is statistically significant, we need to compare the observed F, as we did with the observed t's, against the critical value of F. Since our observed F of 184.679, with 1 degree of freedom (k - 1= 2 - 1 = 1) for the numerator and 10 degrees of freedom (n - k = 12 - 2 = 10) for the denominator is greater than the critical value of F of 10.04 at the 0.01 level of *p* (which can be easily obtained from an F table found in any standard statistics textbook), we can say with 99 percent degree of certainty that our estimated equation is statistically significant; that is, there is only a 1 percent chance that it could have occurred by chance (due to error). To further determine if our observed F has been computed correctly, we can add the explained and the error variances together to see if they equal the total variance. If they do, we can say that it has been calculated correctly, which appears to be the case here except for rounding-off errors.

We can now write the estimated model for the solid waste collection problem in its complete form with the associated test statistics, as follows:

$$\hat{Y} = 20,357.55 + 17.76X$$

$$(9.4528)\ (13.5861)$$

$$R^2 = 0.9486\ F = 184.634$$

Overall, it appears that our model was good and reliable since all the tests results came out to be statistically significant.

4.5.5 Second Order Tests

All regression models are based on a set of assumptions.[3] To see that these assumptions are satisfied in a regression model, it is important to conduct additional tests. The tests are useful to ensure that the assumptions on which the regression models were built have not been violated. Conceptually, we can think of the first set of tests, which we will call the first order tests, as the necessary condition, and the second set of tests, which we will call the second order tests (not conducted here) as the sufficient condition for the soundness of a model. For the most part, especially when one is dealing with a simple regression model, such as the one in our example, the first order tests we conducted should suffice. However, for complex models with multiple independent variables and large time-series data, both first and second order tests would be appropriate. Although our model included time-series data, it was limited to only 12 months. Ideally, the number should be much larger to produce satisfactory results. The requirements for the second order tests are much more rigorous than the ones we have used here. (A detailed discussion of these tests can be found in any standard econometric textbook.)

4.5.6 Extension of the Simple Linear Model

So far, we have used only one independent variable (amount of solid waste collected each month) to estimate the fixed and the variable cost of the problem. In reality, we do not have one but multiple independent variables such as direct labor (the time spent collecting solid waste), indirect labor (additional support personnel), direct materials (fuel), indirect materials (safety equipment, maintenance tools), and so on that could have some effects on the dependent variable (cost of solid waste collection). Theoretically, we could have *n*-number of independent variables, instead of one, in which case we need to expand our simple linear model with one independent variable to incorporate multiple independent variables.

The general cost function with multiple independent variables for instance, can be written as

$$Y = a + b_1X_1 + b_2X_2 + \ldots + b_nX_n + e \tag{4.27}$$

Equation 4.27 is a typical expression for a regression model with n-independent variables in linear form. It should be pointed out that when we are dealing with a multiple regression model, it is not possible to use the same computational procedures we used for the simple regression model. It will involve far too many computations that will be difficult to solve by hand. The alternative will be to use matrix algebra, or statistical software, if the number of variables is considerably large, that can deal with the multidimensionality in a regression problem more efficiently.

4.6 Cost Forecasts

Once we have estimated the parameters of a cost function for an organization and tested for their statistical significance, we can easily extend the discussion by estimating (forecasting) the future costs of solid waste collection for the government. Two types of methods are commonly used in forecasting: time series and econometric. While both methods can produce good and reliable forecasts, time-series methods are relatively simple and have low data requirements, which make them much easier to use than econometric methods. For convenience, we will use time series forecasts for our purpose.

Time-series methods use past or historical observations to predict the future values of a forecast variable. They are particularly suitable for short-term rather than long-term forecasts, which means that time-series methods will produce reasonably accurate forecasts in the short-term but not necessarily in the long-term. There is a wide range of time-series methods, including some that are fairly advanced with greater analytical capabilities, but for our purpose we will use the simplest of the time series methods called simple moving average (SMA).[4] As the name implies, SMA relies on arithmetic average, but instead of using a single average it uses a series of averages, called Moving Averages (MAs), which are obtained by taking the average of the most recent observations in a series.

The procedure is quite simple: As new observations become available, a new average is calculated by dropping the oldest observation from the average and including the most recent one. The newest average is then used to forecast the value for the next time period. Thus, the number of observations used in the average always remains constant. However, the method requires that the number of observations included in the average is specified in advance, such as three months, six months, or any length of time. The number of months included in a series defines the type of moving average method being used for forecasting. Thus, a series containing three months of data is called a three-month moving average, six months of data is called a six-month moving average, and so forth.

The following presents the expression for the method:

$$\hat{Y}_{t+1} = \frac{Y_t + Y_{t-1} + \ldots\ldots\ldots\ldots + Y_{t-n+1}}{n} \tag{4.28}$$

where $\hat{Y}_{t+1}$ is the forecast Value of Y at time t+1, Y is the actual observation, $Y_{t\text{-}i}$ is the past observations (i = 1, 2, …, n), and *n* is the number of observations in the moving average.

Let us say that we will use a three-month moving average to obtain the amount of solid waste collection for the month of January, next year (t+1). We can use the expression in Equation 4.28 to forecast the collection for the month of January, as shown below:

$$\hat{Y}_{t+1(January)} = \frac{Y_{Dec} + Y_{Nov} + Y_{Oct}}{3}$$

$$= \frac{2{,}200 + 2{,}000 + 1{,}800}{3}$$

$$= 2{,}000$$

The result produces an average of 2,000 tons, which is the amount of solid waste the department will collect in January, next year. We can now plug this information into the estimated equation to obtain the cost of solid waste collection for January. That is,

$$\hat{Y}_{January} = 20{,}357.55 + 17.757\hat{X}$$

$$= 20{,}357.55 + 17.757(2{,}000)$$

$$= 20{,}357.55 + 35{,}514$$

$$= 55{,}871.55\ (\$55{,}871.55)$$

which is $55,871.55 but is much higher than what it cost the same month the previous year ($50,000). Part of the reason for this is the high collection amount in the three previous months used for the forecast. Had the collection in the previous months been lower, or close to the actual collection for the month of January, last year, the cost would have been lower. This is an important weakness in SMA, especially when data is too high or too low in a series. One way to avoid the problem would be to use weighted moving average. Another weakness of the time-series methods, such as SMA, is that they are not readily amenable to conventional statistical tests, but they can be used in conjunction with other methods and tests to gain insights into the series for underlying trends and patterns.

Alternatively, we could have used methods such as a simple trend line, $Y_t = a + bT$, where T is the time variable, that is relatively simple to use. However, it would typically require more observations (number of data points) than we used in the current example, so the results could be tested for statistical reliability, discussed earlier. In fact, there is a wide range of time-series methods, highly sophisticated, that can deal with forecasting problems far more complex than the one discussed in the current example.[5]

4.7 Chapter Summary

Cost behavior deals with the way in which costs behave in an organization in response to changes in variables that affect the costs. This chapter has provided a general discussion of cost behavior in government. Several aspects of cost behavior were discussed in the chapter, both in the short and long run as well as properties of cost functions. An important aspect of cost behavior is cost estimation. The basic idea behind cost estimation is to estimate the future costs based on the relationship between costs and the variables affecting the costs. This chapter has presented three of the most widely used methods of cost estimation: the graphical method, the high-low method, and the regression method. Of these, the regression method is detailed and analytically more sophisticated than either the graphical or the high-low method. This is due to the fact that it utilizes all the available information in a data set, the estimated parameters are more precise than those obtained by the other two methods and, more importantly, the estimated parameters can be tested for statistical significance. The greatest advantage of the regression method is that once the parameters have been estimated and tested for statistical significance, they can be easily used for forecasting. The chapter concludes with a brief discussion of cost forecasts.

4.8 Review Questions

4.1 What is the difference between a short-run and a long-run cost? Why, in the long run are all costs variable?

4.2 What is the difference between a linear and non-linear cost function, and what are their advantages and disadvantages? How can one linearize a non-linear cost function? Give an example of a linear and non-linear cost function.

4.3 What are the advantages and disadvantages of using a graphical, the high-low, and the least square method for estimating the cost behavior of an organization? Under what circumstances would one use the high-low method over the least square method?

4.4 What are the steps in constructing a regression model? What specific tests would one conduct to establish the significance of the regression coefficients and the estimated regression line?

4.5 What is the difference between first and second-order tests? Why is it necessary to do both sets of tests to establish the significance of an estimated regression model?

4.6 Define elasticity. What is the difference between a point and an arc elasticity? Give an example of each.

4.7 The State Fishing License Department conducted a study of the demand for fishing licenses. It was found that the average daily demand for licenses, Q, based on the licensing fee (P) is given by the equation

$$Q = 250 - 5P$$

a. How many permits can the department issue a day if the fee for the license is $30?
b. If the state wants to issue 150 permits a day, what fee should it charge for a license?
c. How many permits could the department issue if it decided not to charge a fee?

4.8 The Water Department of a large metropolitan government noticed that the demand, Q, for water consumption (in gallons) for a family per year is affected by changes in per capita family income (INC) in such a way that

$$Q = 2{,}500 + 0.5INC$$

Given the equation above,

a. Calculate the quantity demanded for water for a family for the year, as income changes from $1,000 of per capita family income to $15,000, and interpret the results
b. Calculate the income elasticity of demand, if per capita family income changes from $5,000 to $10,000 and from $15,000 to $20,000 and interpret the results.

4.9 The State Health and Human Services Department, one of the largest in most states, processes hundreds of applications for healthcare benefits each year. There is a cost associated with the processing, depending on the number of individuals or hours it takes to process the applications. Select a state agency of your choice, collect the number of applications it processed for the last 15 years, their corresponding costs, and do the following:

a. Determine the fixed and variable costs of processing.
b. Present the estimated equation and interpret the result.

c. Forecast the cost for the next three years and interpret the results. [Hint: Use the High-Low method]

4.10 For the problem in Question 4.10, do the same, using the least square method.

a. Determine the fixed and variable costs of processing.
b. Present the estimated equation and interpret the result.
c. Conduct the statistical tests for the estimated coefficients and the equation.
d. Forecast the cost for the next three years.
e. Interpret the results.

4.11 Suppose that a local Homeless Shelter wants to know the costs of running the facility, in particular the fixed and variable costs that include, among others, providing shelter and free meals throughout the year. It has the following information on the number of individuals served and the corresponding costs, by month:

Month	*Number of Individuals Served (Q)*	*Cost of Operation ($)*
January	350	140,000
February	400	150,000
March	300	120,000
April	250	120,000
May	200	100,000
June	150	70,000
July	150	80,000
August	150	80,000
September	200	90,000
October	200	100,000
November	250	110,000
December	300	120,000

a. Using the high-low method,

i. Estimate the fixed and variable costs of running the shelter, and interpret the results
ii. Determine the total cost of running the shelter for next year, assuming the shelter expects a 10% increase in the homeless population but no changes in fixed and variable costs
iii. Determine the total cost of running the shelter, assuming there will be no change in the homeless population, but the variable

cost will increase by 2.5% to keep up with the inflation rate next year

iv. Determine the total cost of running the shelter, assuming there will be no change in the homeless population, but the fixed cost will increase by 5%.

b. Repeat questions (i) through (iv) using the least square method and show the estimated model with associated t-values, R^2, and the F-Value. What do the results indicate as to the soundness of the estimated coefficients and the model?

4.12 Healthcare clinics provide a wide range of services. Select a government-run healthcare clinic of your choice, identify the types of services it provides. Select a service, collect data on the number of patients the clinic served the past 24 months, their corresponding costs, and do the following:

a. Determine the fixed and variable costs of processing.
b. Using the least square method, set up the regression equation, estimate the regression coefficients, and interpret the results.
c. Conduct the necessary statistical tests for the estimated coefficients, and the equation, and interpret the results.
d. Forecast the cost for the next three years and interpret the results.

4.13 Select a nonprofit organization of your choice and identify the types of services it provides. Select a service, collect data on the number of individuals who received the service each month of the past year, the corresponding costs for the service, and do the following:

a. Determine the fixed and variable costs of processing.
b. Present the estimated equation and interpret the result.
c. Forecast the cost for the next three years and interpret the results.

[Hint: Use the High-Low method]

Notes

1 The costs of recycling water for residential and commercial use are generally based on cost per 1,000 gallons; as such, we can easily factor out thousand and express the production costs in terms of 1, 2, 3, and so forth, with 1,000 implicit in cost calculation.

2 There are several explanations as to why these deviations occur; in particular, the following: 1. omission of variables, 2. random behavior of human beings; 3. imperfect specification of the mathematical form of the model; 4. errors in aggregation; and 5. errors in measurement. Of the five sources of deviations

(errors), the first four are called the errors of omission and the fifth is called the error of measurement.

3 Four assumptions are commonly associated with regression models; they are (1) normality (the error term is normally distributed with a zero mean $\mu = 0$ and constant variance, σ_e^2), (2) homoskedasticity (the variance of the error term is the same for all values of the explanatory variables), (3) serial independence (the error terms of one period are not related to the error terms of the preceding period), and (4) no multicollinearity (the explanatory variables are not perfectly correlated with each other). All four assumptions, except for no multicollinearity, are based on the distribution of the error term. Violation of these assumptions can often raise questions about the soundness of the model being used. There are specific tests one can conduct to determine if any of these assumptions have been violated in a regression model and the measures that can be undertaken to correct the problem when the assumptions are violated. (For a detailed discussion of these assumptions, their corresponding tests, and measures to correct the problem, see any standard econometric textbook.)

4 Moving average methods are particularly useful when one is dealing with seasonal data. While moving average methods can be useful for seasonal data, which is what we have in the current example, they are not ideal for directly capturing strong seasonality on their own. Therefore, to effectively analyze data with pronounced seasonal patterns, one will need to use more advanced methods such as seasonal decomposition or Holt-Winters, which specifically account for seasonality. However, moving averages can help smooth out short-term fluctuations and reveal underlying trends within seasonal data when used appropriately.

5 For an at length discussion of time-series methods for forecasting, including those that are more advanced, see Gilchrist (1976), Montgomery and Johnson (1976), Box and Jenkins (1976), Bails and Peppers (1982), Pindyck and Rubinfeld (1991), Makridakis et al. (1998), Green (2003), Enders (2014), and Rivera (2016), Hyndman and Athanasopoulos (2018).

References

Bails, D.G. and Peppers. L.C. (1982). *Business forecasting: Forecasting techniques and application.* Englewood Cliffs, NJ: Prentice-Hall.

Box, G.E.P. and Jenkins, G.M. (1976). *Time series analysis: Forecasting and control.* San Francisco, CA: Holden-Day.

Enders, W. (2014). *Applied econometric time series.* New York: John Wiley.

Gilchrist, W. (1976). *Statistical forecasting.* New York: John Wiley.

Green, W.H. (2003). *Econometrics.* New York: Prentice Hall.

Hyndman, R.J. and Athanasopoulos, G. (2018). *Forecasting Principles and Practice.* New York: Texts. Online, Open-Access Textbooks.

Makridakis, S.G., Wheelwright, S.C., and Hyndman, R.J. (1998). *Forecasting: Methods and applications.* New York: John Wiley.

Mislick, G.K. and Nussbaum, D.A. (2015). *Cost estimation: methods and tools.* New York: John Wiley.

Montgomery, D.C. and Johnson, L.A. (1976). *Forecasting time-series analysis.* New York: McGraw- Hill.
Pindyck, R.S. and Rubinfeld, D.L. (1991). *Econometric models and economic forecasts.* New York: McGraw-Hill.
Rivera, G. (2016). *Forecasting for economics and business.* New York: Routledge.

5 Break-Even Analysis

5.1 Introduction

An important financial consideration for firms and businesses in the private sector is to be able to determine the level of operation at which they will have the maximum profit on their investments or, at a minimum, earn just enough profit to break even. A government does not operate to maximize profit, but it is just as important for a government to know in advance the level of operation at which a project or activity will be economically and financially viable so that it does not incur a loss. However, to determine the level at which an operation will be viable one must be able to measure the costs and returns in precise monetary terms. Unfortunately, for most public goods and services that a government provides, except for those provided in a business-like manner, called proprietary goods, it is difficult to measure the costs and returns, especially returns, in precise monetary terms. Nevertheless, where it is possible to measure the costs and returns with a certain degree of precision, efforts should be made to do so to ensure the viability of a government activity. Break-even analysis plays an important role in this process.

Besides determining the level of operation at which it will break even, break-even analysis can be used for a wide range of economic and financial decisions, from expanding the level of activity, to lowering price, raising revenue, to dealing with multiple operations or activities, among others. Break-even analysis can be linear as well as non-linear. This chapter presents a detailed discussion of linear break-even analysis involving both single and multiple activities. It concludes with a brief discussion of non-linear break-even analysis.

5.2 Background Discussion

One of the oldest and most widely used techniques in cost analysis, break-even analysis was formally developed by Rautenstrausch in the late 1930s

DOI: 10.4324/9781003486091-6

in his classic work, Economics of Business Enterprise (Rautenstrausch, 1939)[1] Its purpose is to integrate the cost, revenue, and output of an activity to determine the effect it will have on alternative courses of action. The basic objective is to find a level of operation, for a given cost, at which there will be neither gain nor loss: it will break even (Shrotriya 2019; Lohmann, 1976). The fundamental rule that underlies this objective is that at the lowest level of an activity cost exceeds revenue producing a loss, but as the level of activity increases revenue will increase at a faster rate than cost leading to a point where the two would become equal, called the break-even point. If the level of activity continues to increase, revenue will eventually exceed cost, producing a net gain until a point comes when it begins to diminish again. This fundamental law of operation that serves as the basis for break-even analysis is universal, but for the law to be of any practical significance one must be able to illustrate how this relationship works in practice.

5.3 Linear Break-Even Analysis

We begin our discussion with a simple assumption that there is a linear relationship between cost, revenue, and output level of an activity. The linearity assumption sets up a mathematical relationship between cost, in particular fixed and variable costs, revenue, and output (quantity of goods and services produced or provided) that can be expressed in terms of a straight line, provided that the following conditions hold: (1) the variable cost is constant and hence is linearly dependent on output, (2) the fixed cost is independent of output, (3) there are no other financial costs, (4) output can be increased without significantly affecting the cost structure, and (5) all output units are charged or sold at the same price.

These conditions imply a constancy of rate scale that does not vary for different levels of output. What this means is that the price a government charges for a unit of a good or service it provides, or the cost it incurs in providing the unit of a good or service, does not change regardless of the quantity provided. Since the price does not change, the total revenue from an operation can be represented by a linear curve emanating from the point of origin (as in a two-dimensional plane). Similarly, since the cost per unit does not change, the total cost of operation can also be represented by a linear curve emanating from the point of origin. Figure 5.1 shows this relationship between total revenue, total cost, and break-even quantity.

As the figure shows, since both revenue and cost curves are straight lines, there is only one break-even point, which occurs at Q* It is the point at which Total Revenue (TR) equals Total Cost (TC). The shaded area above and below the total cost line represents net gain and loss, respectively.

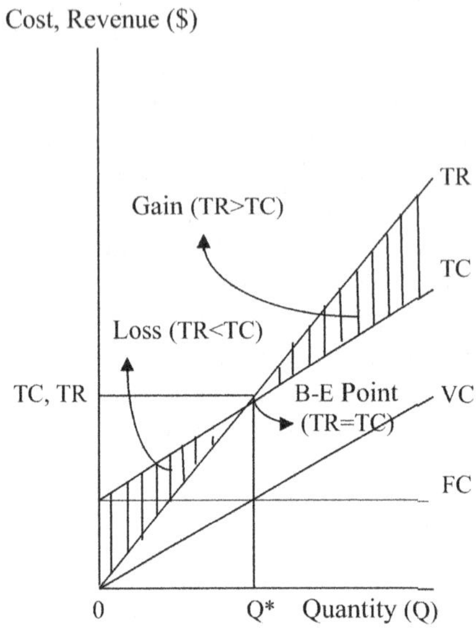

Figure 5.1 A linear break-even relationship

5.3.1 The Basic Structure

The mathematical relationships underlying the cost and revenue functions described above provide a basis for developing a set of simple algebraic expressions that can be used to deal with various break-even problems such as break-even quantity, break-even revenue, break-even price, and so forth. We begin with the simplest one, the break-even quantity, as shown below:

$$TR = pQ \tag{5.1}$$

$$TC = FC + VC(Q) \tag{5.2}$$

where TR is the total revenue, TC is the total cost, p is the price per unit of output, Q is the total quantity or output, FC is the fixed cost, and VC is the per unit variable cost associated with the output quantity, Q.

From these two simple equations, we can obtain the break-even quantity by setting TR = TC, since at the break-even point total revenue must be equal to total cost. We can formally express this relationship as

$$\begin{aligned} TR &= TC \\ TR - TC &= 0 \\ pQ - [FC + VC(Q)] &= 0 \\ pQ - [VC(Q) &= FC \\ Q(p - VC) &= FC \\ \therefore\ Q^* &= FC/(p\text{-}VC) \end{aligned} \tag{5.3}$$

where Q^* is the break-even quantity, and (p - VC), the difference between price and the variable cost, is the contribution margin (discussed in the next section).

With slight algebraic manipulation, Equation 5.3 yields the break-even price and break-even revenue, corresponding to Q^*. That is,

$$\begin{aligned} Q^* &= FC/(p - VC) \\ Q^*(p - VC) &= FC \\ pQ^* - VC(Q^*) &= FC \\ pQ^* &= FC + VC(Q^*) \\ \therefore\ p^* &= (FC/Q^*) + VC \quad (5.4) \\ \text{and } R^* &= p^*Q^* \quad (5.5) \end{aligned}$$

where Q^* is the break-even quantity, as before, p^* is the break-even price, and R^* is the break-even revenue. Since it is derived from Q^*, at the break-even price, p^*, total revenue must also be equal to total cost, TR = TC.

5.3.1.1 Contribution Margin

Contribution margin, a term that frequently appears in break-even analysis (Equation 5.3), has a special meaning in break-even analysis. It measures the contribution the difference, (p - VC), makes toward recovering the fixed cost of an operation as well as any net gain from it; hence, the term contribution margin. This is important because when an organization charges a fee or price for a service, it is important that it not only recovers the variable cost, but also the fixed cost to remain financially viable. Contribution margin helps us achieve that (Shim et al. 2011).

To give an example, suppose that a state Fishing License Department charges \$40 (price) for an inland fresh-water fishing permit, and it costs the department \$10 in Variable Cost (VC). Let us assume that we do not know the fixed cost. Thus, each permit issued recovers its variable cost, plus \$30. The \$30 is the contribution margin, (p - VC), obtained by subtracting the variable cost (VC) from price (p); that is, VC-p = \$40-\$10 = \$30. If, for instance, the fixed cost is \$30, then the contribution margin recovers the entire amount of fixed cost. On the other hand, if the fixed cost is \$25, then there would be a net gain of \$5 [p-(FC+VC) = \$40-(\$25+\$10) = \$5] per permit. In other words, the contribution margin will recover all \$25 of the fixed cost and produce a net revenue (net gain) of \$5 for each permit.

Let us further suppose that the department issues 5,000 fishing permits for the year, Q, with a fixed cost of \$70,000, and the variable cost of \$50,000 [VC(Q) = \$10×5,000 = \$50,000]. The contribution margin for the permits will be \$150,000 [Q(p-VC) = pQ-1VC(Q) = (\$40×5,000) -(\$10×5,000) = \$200,000-\$50,000 = \$150,000], of which \$70,000 will go toward recovering the fixed cost; thereby, producing a net revenue of \$80,000 [TR-TC = pQ-(FC+VC(Q) = (\$40×5,000)-[\$70,000+(\$10×5,000)] = \$200,000-(\$70,000+\$50,000) = \$200,000-\$120,000 = \$80,000] for the department.

Contribution margin is often expressed in percentage terms, called contribution margin ratio. We can use the above information to calculate the contribution margin ratio to show the revenue available to recover the fixed cost. It is obtained by taking the difference between price and the variable cost and dividing the difference by the revenue. Then multiply it by 100 to express it as a percentage, which for a single permit in our example would be 75% [(Q(p-VC)/Q(p))×100 = ((1)(\$40 - \$10)/(1)(\$40)) x 100 = ((\$40-\$10)/\$40) ×100 = (\$30/\$40)×100 = 0.75, or 75%], meaning that 75 percent of the revenue is available to recover the fixed cost for a single permit. For 5,000 permits, the ratio would be the same, 75%; that is, [(Q(p-VC)/Q(p)) ×100 = (5,0000) (\$40-\$10)/(\$5,000×40) ×100 = ((\$200,000-\$50,000)/\$200,000) ×100 = (\$150,000/\$200,000}×100 = 0.75 or 75%]. In general, the higher the percentage, the greater the amount of revenue available to recover the fixed cost.

5.3.2 Break-Even Analysis for a Single Activity

Break-even analysis can be used for single as well as multiple activities. The procedure is essentially the same for both, which makes it easy to apply it to any situation, so long as one has measurable information on cost, quantity, and revenue. This section looks at three important applications of break-even analysis involving a single activity: (1) break-even quantity, price and revenue, (2) changes in capacity level, and (3) changes in revenue, quantity, and price.

5.3.2.1 Break-Even Quantity, Price, and Revenue

Let us look at a simple example, citations for traffic infractions by the Public Safety department of a large local government, to illustrate how to use break-even analysis to determine break-even quantity, price, and revenue. Besides maintaining public safety, citations for traffic infractions constitute an important source of revenue for most local governments. Suppose that the number of citations the department gives for minor traffic infractions, such as not stopping at the stop sign, is 100,000 a year. Suppose also that the fixed cost of the activity is \$2 million, with a variable cost of \$25 per citation. The department charges \$50 for each citation. Assume that the department is working at 100 percent of its capacity (labor and capital, namely, vehicles and equipment used).

Since the first and foremost objective of any organization (public, private, or nonprofit), is to break even before determining additional revenue, profit, or net gain from an operation, our objective is three-fold: One, find the break-even quantity for the department, two, determine the break-even price, and three, and determine the net revenue from operation at the current as well as the break-even level of citations for the year.

Let us start with the break-even quantity for the department first. Since we already know the price one will pay for an infraction, we can determine the break-even quantity by directly applying Equation 5.3 to the problem, so that

$$\begin{aligned} Q^* &= FC/(p-VC) \\ &= \$2{,}000{,}000/(\$50-\$25) \\ &= \$2{,}000{,}000/\$25 \\ &= 80{,}000 \end{aligned}$$

which is 80,000. It is the break-even quantity, Q^*, which is the number of citations the department must produce to break even at the current price of \$50 per citation, and \$25 is the contribution margin, $(p-VC)$.

We can use the information on break-even quantity to determine the break-even price, p^*, using the expression in Equation 5.4, so that

$$\begin{aligned} p^* &= (FC/Q^*)+VC \\ &= (\$2{,}000{,}000/80{,}000)+\$25 \\ &= \$25+\$25 \\ &= \$50 \end{aligned}$$

which is \$50, since the break-even quantity, Q^*, was produced at the current price of \$50.

Now, multiplying p^* by Q^* produces a break-revenue, R^*, for the department of \$4,000,0000 [$p^*Q^* = \$50 \times 80{,}000 = \$4{,}000{,}000$]. We know that at the break-even point, revenue must be the same as the cost, producing a net revenue of 0. To see if this is correct, we substitute the value of Q* into Equations 5.1 and 5.2 for TR and TC, and set them equal to each other, so that

$$\begin{aligned} TR &= TC \\ p^*Q^* &= FC + VC(Q^*) \\ (\$50)(80{,}000) &= \$2{,}000{,}000 + (\$25)(80{,}000) \\ (\$50)(80{,}000) &= \$2{,}000{,}000 + \$2{,}000{,}000 \\ \$4{,}000{,}000 &= \$4{,}000{,}000 \\ \therefore\ TR &= TC = \$4{,}000{,}000 \end{aligned}$$

which comes out to be the same at $4,000,000.

What this means is that at the break-even level of citations, Q*, and the break-even price, p*, there is no gain or loss for the department, since the total revenue is the same as the total cost; that is, TR = TC = $4,000,000. In other words, the net revenue from the operation is 0.

$$\begin{aligned} \pi^* &= TR - TC \\ &= \$4{,}000{,}000 - \$4{,}000{,}000 \\ &= 0 \end{aligned} \tag{5.6}$$

where π^* is the net revenue at the break-even price and quantity.

On the other hand, the net revenue at the current level of output, Q, is positive, not zero, since the department is producing 20,000 more citations than the break-even quantity of 80,000 [100,000 - 80,000 = 20,000], as shown below:

$$\begin{aligned} \pi &= TR - TC \\ &= pQ - [FC + VC(Q)] \\ &= [(\$50)(100{,}000)] - [\$2{,}000{,}000 + (\$25)(100{,}000)] \\ &= (\$50)(100{,}000) - (\$2{,}000{,}000 + (\$2{,}500{,}000) \\ &= \$5{,}000{,}000 - \$4{,}500{,}000 \\ &= \$500{,}000 \end{aligned}$$

which is $500,000.

Interestingly, we could have obtained the same result by taking the difference between the two net revenues, $\pi - \pi^*$. That is,

$$\begin{aligned} \pi - \pi^* &= \$500{,}000 - 0 \\ &= \$500{,}000 \end{aligned}$$

Table 5.1 Contribution margin and net revenue for traffic citations

	Cost/Price Per Unit	*Total*	*CM Ratio*[1]
Revenue (100,000 citations)	$50	$5,000,000	50 (%)
(-) Variable cost	$25	$2,500,000	
= Contribution margin	$25	$2,500,000	
(-) Fixed cost	---	$2,000,000	
= Net revenue	---	$500,000	

[1](50-$25)/(50) = 0.5 (50%); ($5,000,000-$2,500,000)/$5,000,000 = 0.5 (50%)

5.3.2.2 Contribution Margin

As noted earlier, the contribution margin plays an important role in break-even analysis. In fact, it is a more effective way to determine the net revenue from an operation. Returning to the example on traffic citation, contribution margin per citation, using the expression (p-VC), is $25; that is, $50-$25 = $25. Therefore, for the total number of citations the department gives, which is 100,000, the net revenue would be $500,000. In other words, CM - FC = (p-VC)Q - FC = (pQ-VC(Q)) - FC = (TR-VC) - FC = (($50)(100,000) – (100,000)($25)) - $2,000,000 = ($5,000,000 - $2,500,000) - $2,000,000 = $2,500,00 - $2,000,000 = $500,000. Table 5.1 shows the contribution margin and net revenue for traffic citations. It also shows the contribution margin ratio.

Interestingly, we could have also used the contribution margin to obtain the break-even quantity and break-even revenue for the department, as follows:

$$\begin{aligned} Q^* &= \text{Fixed Cost/Contribution Margin} \\ &= \$2{,}000{,}000/(\$50-\$25) \\ &= \$2{,}000{,}000/\$25 \\ &= 80{,}000 \end{aligned} \tag{5.7}$$

$$\begin{aligned} \text{and } R^* &= p^*Q^* \\ &= (\$50)(80{,}000) \\ &= \$4{,}000{,}000 \end{aligned}$$

which is what we obtained without the use of contribution margin.

Similarly, we could have used contribution margin ratio to obtain the break-even revenue, as follows:

$$R^* = \text{Fixed Cost/Contribution Margin Ratio} \tag{5.8}$$
$$= \$2{,}000{,}000/0.5$$
$$= \$4{,}000{,}000$$

which is what we obtained earlier without the contribution margin ratio.

There is an added advantage of using contribution margin in that it can produce a single break-even point for multiple activities. This is particularly useful if, for instance, the goal is to determine a single break-even point for an entire organization, such as break-even price, break-even quantity, rather than individual units for the organization. We will look at an example later in the chapter for an organization with multiple activities.

5.3.2.3 Changes in Capacity Level

All organizations have a capacity level at which they operate that has a direct impact on output (number of citations given, in our example), costs of operation (fixed as well as variable cost), revenue, and net gain or loss. Capacity level indicates the fullest level at which an organization is using its labor, machines, tools and other resources to produce an output quantity. We made an implicit assumption in our current example that the department is working at 100 percent of its capacity. In reality, very few organizations work at their fullest capacity level. For instance, if we assume that the department is working at 90 percent of its capacity, instead of 100 percent, the net revenue from operations will be \$250,000, instead of \$500,000. That is,

$$\pi = k(PQ) - [FC + k(VC)(Q)]$$
$$= [(0.90)(\$50)(100{,}000)] - [\$2{,}000{,}000 + (0.90)(\$25)(100{,}000)]$$
$$= \$4{,}500{,}000 - [\$2{,}000{,}000 + \$2{,}250{,}000]$$
$$= \$4{,}500{,}000 - \$4{,}250{,}000$$
$$= \$250{,}000$$

where k is the capacity level, and π is the net revenue.

If, on the other hand, we assume that its capacity level has increased to 105 percent from the current level of 100 percent, the net revenue for the department will also increase from \$500,000 to \$625,000, provided that no changes have taken place in its operating costs or the price it charges for an infraction. That is,

$$\pi = k(PQ) - [FC + k(VC)(Q)]$$
$$= [(1.05)(\$50)(100{,}000)] - [\$2{,}000{,}000 + (1.05)(\$25)(100{,}000)]$$

$$= \$5{,}250{,}000 - [\$2{,}000{,}000 + \$2{,}625{,}000]$$
$$= \$5{,}250{,}000 - \$4{,}625{,}000$$
$$= \$625{,}000$$

However, at the break-even level of output, where the net revenue is zero, the capacity level for the department, given the current level of output, is 80% [Q*/Q = 80,000/100,000 = 0.80]. In other words, to break even the department only needs to work at 80 percent of its capacity, as shown below:

$$\pi = k(PQ) - [FC + k(VC)(Q)]$$
$$= [(0.80)(\$50)(100{,}000)] - [\$2{,}000{,}000 + (0.80)(\$25)(100{,}000)]$$
$$= \$4{,}000{,}000 - [\$2{,}000{,}000 + \$2{,}000{,}000]$$
$$= \$4{,}000{,}000 - \$4{,}000{,}000$$
$$= 0$$

The result also indicates that any drop in capacity from the current level of 80 percent will produce a loss (net negative return) for the department. Thus, if the department operates, say, at the 70 percent level of its capacity (assuming everything else remains the same), it will produce a net loss of $250,000. That is,

$$\pi = k(PQ) - [FC + k(VC)(Q)]$$
$$= [(0.70)(\$50)(100{,}000)] - [\$2{,}000{,}000 + (0.70)(\$25)(100{,}000)]$$
$$= \$3{,}500{,}000 - [\$2{,}000{,}000 + \$1{,}750{,}000]$$
$$= \$3{,}500{,}000 - \$3{,}750{,}000$$
$$= -\$250{,}000$$

It would obviously be higher if the capacity level dropped even further, which is unlikely, since no organization, public, private, or nonprofit, would like to operate at a loss.

5.3.2.4 Determining the Break-Even Capacity

While organizations can operate at different levels of capacity, the question that is often asked is: does an organization have to operate at the fullest capacity level to break even? The answer obviously is "no," if the goal is to break even. In the current example, it was 80 percent, which we obtained by simply dividing the break-even quantity by the current level of citations, Q*/Q; that is, 80,000/100,000 = 0.80. But what if we do not know the break-even quantity, in which case we could have obtained this capacity level directly from the current level of citations by slightly rearranging the expression for break-even quantity in Equation 5.3. That is,

$$k = \frac{FC}{pQ - VC(Q)} \tag{5.9}$$

where k is the capacity level and the rest of the terms are the same, as before.

Thus, applying the expression in Equation 5.9 to the citation problem with corresponding information on costs, price, and the current number of citations, we can obtain the break-even capacity level for the department, as shown below:

$$\begin{aligned} k &= \frac{FC}{pQ - VC(Q)} \\ &= \frac{\$2,000,000}{(\$50)(100,000) - (\$25)(100,000)} \\ &= \frac{\$2,000,000}{\$5,000,000 - \$250,000} \\ &= \frac{\$2,000,000}{\$2,500,000} \\ &= 0.80 \end{aligned}$$

which is what we obtained earlier, indicating that the department needs to operate at the 80 percent level of capacity to break even.

A couple of things are worth noting about capacity level. For instance, when an organization works at the capacity level, it means that labor, machines and equipment are working at the fullest capacity. Similarly, when it is operating above or below the capacity level, it means that they are working above or below the fullest level. However, it is possible that only one of the factors of production (labor or machines and equipment, but not both) is working at the capacity level. For instance, when labor is working above the capacity level, while machines and equipment are working at the capacity level, the organization is overusing labor. On the other hand, when labor is working below the capacity level, it is quite likely that machines and equipment are also working below the capacity level, in which case it is underusing labor as well as machines and equipment. There is a term in operations planning, called capacity management, that organizations often use to determine the optimal use of labor, machines and equipment to produce the desirable level of output, return, etc.

5.3.2.5 Changes in Revenue, Quantity, and Price

Financial necessities often require that a government must find ways to achieve a desired level of net revenue to provide a good or service. To achieve this, it must first increase its revenue. Theoretically, a government can increase its revenue in one of three ways: (1) by raising taxes, (2) by increasing the price of goods and services it provides, and (3) by increasing the quantity of goods and services. But most governments are reluctant to increase revenue by increasing price or taxes. The alternative is to increase the quantity where the potential exists for an increase. For instance, a government can install more parking meters, issue more permits, give more citations, produce more electricity, collect refuse more frequently, add more hospital beds, and so on, to increase the output quantity, so long as it is possible to establish that such efforts will be economically viable in that they will increase the revenue vis-à-vis the net revenue of the government.

Next, use the information to generate the target net revenue, π'. The simplest way to achieve this is to treat the target level as an increment of fixed cost, rather than a variable cost, since it does not change during the course of an activity, while a variable cost changes with quantity, VC(Q), which is what we are trying to determine. We can use the expression in Equation 5.10 to obtain the output quantity, as shown below:

$$Q' = (FC + \pi')/(p - VC) \tag{5.10}$$

where Q' is the quantity, which it must produce to generate the target revenue, and the rest of the terms are the same, as before

To illustrate, let us return to the traffic citation example. Suppose that the department now sets as its goal of net revenue at \$1 million (π'), instead of the \$500,000 it obtained earlier from 100,000 citations. Assuming no changes in price or costs and all other conditions remaining the same, the projected break-even quantity, Q', will be 120,000, as shown below:

$$\begin{aligned} Q' &= (FC + \pi')/(p - VC) \\ &= (\$2{,}000{,}000 + \$1{,}000{,}000)/(\$50 - \$25) \\ &= \$3{,}000{,}000/\$25 \\ &= 120{,}000 \end{aligned}$$

This is the total number of citations the department must give to generate the target revenue of $1 million. That is,

$$\begin{aligned}\pi' &= TR - TC\\ &= PQ - [FC + VC(Q)]\\ &= (\$50)(120{,}000) - [\$2{,}000{,}000 + (\$25)(120{,}000)]\\ &= \$6{,}000{,}000 - [\$2{,}000{,}000 + \$3{,}000{,}000)]\\ &= \$6{,}000{,}000 - \$5{,}000{,}000\\ &= \$1{,}000{,}000\end{aligned}$$

5.3.2.6 Using Price instead of Quantity

A question that becomes relevant here is what if the department does not have the physical capacity to raise its output from 100,000 citations a year to 120,000 but, at the same time, it needs to increase its net revenue to $1 million. This would obviously mean that the department must increase the price it presently charges for each citation to bring the revenue to the desired level, while keeping the level of output (the number of citations) constant at 100,000. To achieve this, we can easily reorganize the expression in Equation 5.10, so that

$$\begin{aligned}Q &= (FC + \pi')/(p' - VC)\\ \text{or } (p' - VC)Q &= (FC + \pi')\\ \therefore\ p'Q - VC(Q) &= (FC + \pi')\\ p'Q &= (FC + \pi') + VC(Q)\\ p' &= [(FC + \pi')/Q] + VC \qquad (5.11)\end{aligned}$$

where p′ is the new price, and the rest of the terms are the same as before.

Now applying the expression in Equation 5.11 to the citation problem, will produce the new price, p′, for the department, as shown below:

$$\begin{aligned}p' &= [(FC + \pi')/Q] + VC\\ &= [(\$2{,}000{,}000 + \$1{,}000{,}000)/100{,}000] + \$25\\ &= (\$3{,}000{,}000/100{,}000) + \$25\\ &= \$30 + \$25\\ &= \$55\end{aligned}$$

which is $55. This is the price the department must charge for each citation to produce the target net revenue of $1 million. To see if the result is correct (if it produces the target net revenue), we can substitute the value of p′ into the expression for net revenue. That is,

$$
\begin{aligned}
\pi' &= TR - TC \\
&= p'Q - [FC + (VC)(Q)] \\
&= [(\$55)(100{,}000)] - [\$2{,}000{,}000 + (\$25)(100{,}000)] \\
&= \$5{,}500{,}000 - \$4{,}500{,}000 \\
&= \$1{,}000{,}000
\end{aligned}
$$

The result produces a net revenue of $1 million, as expected.

5.3.2.7 Safety Margin

As noted earlier, organizations often have targets such as target revenue and target costs that they would prefer, but that is seldom the case. Inflation, unforeseen costs, poor estimates, and so forth, can produce deviations from the targets. One way to address the problem is to include a margin of safety to break-even revenue, income, and cost, called the Safety Margin (SM). The rule of thumb for revenue is to lower the target revenue by a margin to avoid the problem of overestimation and increase it by a margin for cost to avoid the problem of underestimation.

The following expressions show how to include the safety margin for revenue and cost calculations:

$$SM_{Revenue} = \text{Target Revenue} + (\text{Target Revenue} \times \text{Safety Margin}) \quad (5.12)$$

$$SM_{Cost} = \text{Target cost} + (\text{Target Cost} \times \text{Safety Margin}) \quad (5.13)$$

To give an example, let us look at the revenue of $5 million the public safety department collects or expects to collect from 100,000 citations, at $50 a citation ($50 × 100,000), which it may or may not collect. To be on the safe side, the department adds a safety margin of five percent. Thus, applying the expression in Equation (5.12) to the expected revenue, with a safety margin of five percent, would increase the revenue by $275,000 to $5.275 million, as shown below:

$$
\begin{aligned}
SM_{Revenue} &= \text{Target Revenue} + (\text{Target Revenue} \times \text{Safety Margin}) \\
&= \$5{,}000{,}000 - (\$5{,}000{,}000 \times 0.05) \\
&= \$5{,}000{,}000 - \$275{,}000 \\
&= \$5{,}275{,}000
\end{aligned}
$$

Similarly, we can look at the cost of \$4.5 million the department incurs or expects to incur, which it may or may not incur. As before, to be on the safe side, the department adds a safety margin of five percent to the expected cost. Therefore, applying the expression in Equation (5.13) would increase the expected cost by \$725,000 to \$4.725 million, as shown below:

$$\begin{aligned} SM_{Cost} &= \text{Target Cost} + (\text{Target Cost} \times \text{Margin of Safety}) \\ &= \$4{,}500{,}000 + (\$4{,}500{,}000 \times 0.05) \\ &= \$4{,}500{,}000 + \$225{,}000 \\ &= \$4{,}725{,}000 \end{aligned}$$

The result, as one would expect, will lower the net revenue for the department from \$1 million, without the safety margin, to \$500,000 [\$5,225,000 - \$4,725,000], with the safety margin.

5.3.2.8 Operating Leverage

A term that also appears alongside break-even analysis is operating leverage. In ordinary parlance, it means the degree to which an organization can increase its operating income by increasing its revenue. More specifically, operating leverage measures the degree to which an organization can increase its operating income (adjusted for costs) by increasing the price or quantity of goods and services it provides; in other words, by increasing its revenue. There is a direct relationship between operating leverage and the cost of an operation, in particular the fixed cost. For instance, if the cost structure of an organization has more fixed costs than variable costs, it indicates a higher degree of operating leverage, and if it has more variable costs than fixed costs, it indicates the opposite. Operationally, it is expressed as a ratio indicating the degree by which the operating income will increase (decrease) with an increase (decrease) in quantity, given the fixed cost relative to the variable cost. We can formally express this ratio as

$$\begin{aligned} OL &= (Q \times CM)/((Q \times CM) - FC) \\ &= Q(p - VC)/Q(p - VC) - FC \qquad (5.14) \end{aligned}$$

where OL is the operating leverage, $(p - VC)$ is the contribution margin (CM), and $Q(p - VC) - FC$ is the net revenue; that is, $[(pQ - VC(Q)) - FC = TR - VC(Q) - FC = TR - (VC + FC) = TR - TC = \pi]$.

Let us look at the fishing license example we introduced earlier to determine the operating leverage for the department:

OL = Q(p - VC) / (Q(p - VC) - FC)
= ((5,000)($40 - $10)) / ((5,000)($40 - $10)) - $70,000
= ($150,000 - $50,000) / (($200,000 - $50,000) - $70,000
= $150,000 / ($150,000 - $70,000)
= $150,000 / $80,000
= 1.875

which produces an operating leverage of 1.875, indicating that a 1% increase in fishing license will increase operating income (revenue) for the department by 1.87%.

In general, the higher the operating leverage, the greater the ability of an organization to increase its operating income (revenue). High operating leverage is usually associated with high fixed cost but low variable cost, and low operating leverage is associated with low fixed cost but high variable cost. However, low operating leverage does not necessarily imply inefficient operation; it depends on the nature of the activity. Labor intensive activities by and large have high variable costs and capital-intensive activities have high fixed costs. In the example above, if the fixed cost for the department was higher than $70,000, it would increase the operating leverage further.

To illustrate, let us look at the traffic citation example which has a high fixed cost, that of $2 million. Thus, applying Equation 5.14 to the example would produce an operating leverage of 5.833 for the department, as shown below:

OL = Q(p - VC) / (Q(p - VC) - FC)
= ((100,000)($50 - $25)) / ((100,000)($50 - $25)) - $2,000,000
= $2,500,000 / (2,500,000 - $2,000,000)
- $70,000 / 500,000
= 5.833

The result indicates that a 1% increase in citations will increase operating income (revenue) for the department by 5.83%. It should be worth noting that the increase in operating income from increasing citations is not linear. Eventually, diminishing returns will set in.

5.3.3 Break-Even Analysis with a Flexible Cost Structure

All organizations, including government and nonprofits, need to have a flexible cost structure to allow them the flexibility to make operating decisions, as situations demand. Since fixed costs cannot be changed or adjusted, especially in the short run, flexibility can come only from variable costs. One way to achieve this is to substitute variable costs for fixed costs. A good example of where variable costs can be substituted for fixed costs is outsourcing. Outsourcing has a long history in government, where a government allows a private firm or business to provide a good or service because it would be more cost-effective (saving the government money) to outsource than to provide it. However, before deciding to outsource, it is important for a government to determine if outsourcing will be cost-effective (saving the government money).

Let us look at a simple example to illustrate this: Snow removal, which is a common winter measure in many parts of the country. Suppose that a local government in one of these states operates a small department that is responsible for removing snow and ice from snow-covered streets during the winter months. Since snow removal is not a year-long activity, the government can outsource it to a private organization or provide the service directly. If the government wants to provide the service directly then it will need to include both fixed and variable costs (costs of labor, materials and supplies, vehicles to remove snow and ice, and other personnel costs such as health benefits, safety insurance, vacation pay, and so forth). On the other hand, if it wants to outsource, it will include only the variable cost, based on, say, the miles of snow removed, or to be removed.

Let us say that we have the following information on the cost structure of service provision for the government, as well as for the private organization (if outsourced):

1. If provided by the government:
$$\text{Total Cost} = FC + VC(Q) = \$750{,}000 + \$50Q$$
2. If outsourced:
$$\text{Total cost} = VC(Q) = \$80Q$$

where \$50 and \$80 represent the cost per mile of snow removal, and Q is the quantity (the miles of snow removal).

Our goal is to find the break-even quantity (break-even miles of snow removal) and use the information to determine whether the government should provide the service directly or outsource it. To determine the break-even quantity, we set the cost functions for the two provisions equal, as before, and solve for Q. That is,

$$\text{TC (if provided)} = \text{TC (if outsourced)}$$
$$\$750{,}000 + \$50Q = \$80Q$$

$$\$750{,}000 = \$80Q - \$50Q$$
$$\$750{,}000 = \$30Q$$
$$Q^* = 25{,}000$$

where Q* is the break-even quantity; that is, break-even miles of snow removal for the year.

We can now use this information to determine the total cost of snow removal for the two options. Let us suppose that the actual miles of snow removal for the year are 30,000. The total cost of snow removal by the two options will therefore be

$$\begin{aligned} TC &= FC + VC(Q) \\ &= \$750{,}000 + \$50(30{,}000) \\ &= \$750{,}000 + \$1{,}500{,}000 \\ &= \$2{,}250{,}000 \end{aligned}$$

if provided by the government, and

$$\begin{aligned} TC &= \$80Q \\ &= \$80(30{,}000) \\ &= \$2{,}400{,}000 \end{aligned}$$

if outsourced.

Since it would cost the government less to provide the service, $\$2{,}250{,}000 < \$2{,}400{,}000$, the government should provide the service. On the other hand, if the miles of snow removed for the year, say, is 20,000, it would be more cost-effective for the government to outsource rather than to provide it because it would cost the government $150,000 more to provide than to outsource, $1,750,000 as opposed 1,600,000; that is, $[(FC + VC(Q)) > VC(Q)] = (\$750{,}000 + (\$50 \times 20{,}000)) > (\$80 \times 20{,}000) = (\$750{,}000 + \$1{,}000{,}000) > \$1{,}600{,}000 = \$1{,}750{,}000 > \$1{,}600{,}000$. Finally, if we assume the miles of snow to be removed are the same as the break-even quantity, the decision would be indeterminate. There is a caveat to the example. Since it is difficult to predict the behavior of variables such as weather, it would be useful to use examples where it is relatively easy to predict such as water consumption, solid waste collection, electric utility consumption, use of toll roads, and so forth, and use professional judgment or past experience to deal with variables that are difficult to predict.

5.3.3.1 Break-Even Analysis Under Uncertainty

Up to this point, we have assumed that organizations know for certain the amount of goods or services they will provide, such as the number of fishing permits to be issued, traffic citations to be given, miles of snow to be removed, and the corresponding revenue or income they will earn, but that may not always be the case. Organizations may not know the exact number of permits they will issue, citations they will give, or amount of snow they will remove (Downen, 2020). Instead, they may have an estimate or likelihood of the number, in which case they will need to find the expected value and use the information to determine the likely operating revenue or income.

To give an example, let us look at the number of fishing licenses the department issued this year and the number it is likely to issue next year. Assume that there has been an increase in demand for permits in the state. We know that the department issued 5,000 permits this year, and it has a sense of the number it will issue next year, and the revenue or income it is likely to earn. The information is necessary for the department to plan, as most organizations do, especially when preparing their annual operating budget. Let us say that the department expects to issue a minimum of 5,250 permits, or as high as 5,500. Since it does not know for certain the number it will issue, it assigns a probability (P) that there is a 30 percent probability (P_1) it will issue 5,500 permits (Q_1), and a 70 percent probability (P_2) that it will issue 5,250 permits (Q_2). For convenience, let us assume that the permits to be issued are events, since probabilities are often associated with events, such as the probability that an event will or occur (the number of permits will be issued).

We can now use this information to determine the expected value, as shown below:

$$EV = (P_1 \times Q_1) + (P_2 \times Q_2) \tag{5.15}$$

where P_1 and P_2 are the probabilities corresponding to Q_1 and Q_2 (the number of permits that are likely to be issued), respectively. Since there are only two likely permits, there are only two probabilities: P_1 and P_2. If we had, say, n probabilities corresponding to n permits, then it will be $(P_1 \times Q_1) + (P_2 \times Q_2) + \ldots + (P_n \times Q_n) = \sum_{i=1}^{n} P_i Q_i$. It should be worth noting that the sum of the probabilities must always be equal to 1, or 100 percent.

The expected number of permits, therefore, will be

$$\begin{aligned} EV &= (P_1 \times Q_1) + (P_2 \times Q_2) \\ &= (0.3 \times 5{,}500) + (0.7 \times 5{,}250) \\ &= 1{,}650 + 3{,}675 \\ &= 5{,}325 \end{aligned}$$

which is the number of permits the department is likely to issue next year. We can now use this information to determine the expected operating income for the department, assuming there is no change in fixed and variable costs (Table 5.2).

According to the table, the expected operating income for the department next year, corresponding to the expected number of permits of 5,325, will be \$89,750. The income will be much higher at \$126,500, for 5,500 permits, than at \$106,000 for 5,250 permits. The reason the expected operating income is the lowest for the expected total number of permits is because the expected variable cost is much higher (\$53,250)

Table 5.2 Expected operating income for the state fishing license department

Data		*Q1*	*Q2*
Event-Permits to be issued, Q		5,500	5,250
Probability (P)		0.30	0.70
Expected value or number of permits, Q		1,650	3,675
Expected value or number of permits, Q	5,325	---	---
Fixed cost, FC	\$70,000	\$70,000	\$70,000
Expected variable cost, (VC × Q)	\$53,250[1]	\$16,500	\$36,750
Break-Even Analysis			
Price (Fee) per permit, p	\$40	\$40	\$40
Variable cost per permit, VC	\$10	\$10	\$10
Contribution margin, CM	\$30	\$30	\$30
Expected Value Analysis			
Expected revenue, (p × Q)	\$213,000[2]	\$213,000	\$213,000
Expected variable cost, (VC × Q)	\$53,250	\$16,500	\$36,750
Expected contribution margin, CM	\$159,750	\$196,500	\$176,250
Fixed cost, FC	\$70,000	\$70,000	\$70,000
Expected operating income	\$89,750	\$126,500	\$106,000

[1] $VC \times Q = \$10 \times 5{,}325 = \$53{,}250$; [2] $p \times Q = \$40 \times 5{,}325 = \$213{,}000$

than the expected variable costs for the other two numbers. Therefore, when adjusted for the costs, fixed as well as variable, the expected operating income turned out to be much lower, as one would expect. As for the department, which alternative income it should consider would depend on the decision makers. If the decision makers are risk neutral, they would look at all three operating incomes. Since risk neutral decision makers value gain or loss equally, the chances are they will select the highest operating income, that of $126,500, corresponding to 5,500 permits.

5.3.2 Break-Even Analysis for Multiple Activities

Our discussion of break-even analysis up to this point involved single activities, but as noted earlier, break-even analysis can be applied to multiple operations or activities within the same organization, as well as multiple organizations providing similar goods and services Cleverley, 1979). Let us look at a simple example to illustrate this: Our goal is to determine the break-even quantity and break-even revenue. We will use the contribution margin to determine the break-even points.

Suppose that the Outpatient Clinic of a local county hospital provides three different types of services: X, Y, and Z. Service X serves 1,000 patients a year, Service Y serves 3,000 patients, and Service Z serves 5,000 patients. The price (fee) the clinic charges for the three services per visit is $100 for X, $75 for Y, and $50 for Z. The variable costs for the services, respectively, are $60, $40, and $25, with a fixed cost of $180,000 (for all three services, combined). We will start with the Contribution Margin (CM) and then use the margin to determine the break-even quantity, and break-revenue for each service. Table 5.3 shows the results.

According to the table, the Contribution Margin (CM) for the three services, with corresponding break-even quantity (Q^*) and revenue (R^*), are as follows:

Service X: $CM_X = \$40\ (40\%);\ Q_X{}^* = FC/CM = \$180{,}000/\$40 = 4{,}500;\ R_X{}^* = \$100 \times 4{,}500 = \$450{,}000$

Service Y: $CM_Y = \$35\ (47\%);\ Q_Y{}^* = FC/CM = \$180{,}000/\$35 \approx 5{,}143;\ R_Y{}^* = \$75 \times 5{,}143 = \$385{,}725$

Service Z: $CM_Z = \$25\ (50\%);\ Q_Z{}^* = FC/CM = \$180{,}000/\$25 = 7{,}200;\ R_Z{}^* = \$50 \times 7{,}200 = \$360{,}000$

Table 5.3 Break-even analysis for multiple activities

Service X	*Units (Q)*	*Price-VC ($)*	*Total Revenue ($)*
Revenue	1,000	100	100,000 (TR)
Variable Cost	1,000	60	60,000 (TVC)
CM	1,000	40 (P-VC)	40,000 (TCM)
CM (%)	$40/$100 = 0.40 (40%)		
Service Y	*Units*	*Price ($)*	*Total Revenue ($)*
Revenue	3,000	75	225,000 (TR)
Variable Cost	3,000	40	120,000 (TVC)
CM	3,000	35 (P-VC)	105,000 (TCM)
CM (%)	$35/$75 = 0.47 (47%)		
Service Z	*Units*	*Price ($)*	*Total revenue ($)*
Revenue	5,000	50	250,000 (TR)
Variable Cost	5,000	25	125,000 (TVC)
CM	5,000	25 (P-VC)	125,000 (TCM)
CM (%)	$25/$50 = 0.50 (50%)		
Service: X+Y+Z	*Units*	*Price ($)*	*Total Revenue ($)*
Revenue	9,000[1]	63.89[2]	575,000[3] (TR)
Variable Cost	9,000	33.89[5]	305,000[4] (TVC)
CM	9,000	30.00	270,000 (TCM)
CM (%)	$30/$63.89 = 0.47 (47%)		

[1] $Q_{X+Y+Z} = 1{,}000_X + 3{,}000_Y + 5{,}000_Z = 9{,}000$ (Total number of patients)
[2] $P_{X+Y+Z} = TR/Q = \$575{,}000/9{,}000 = \$63.89$ (Average price)
[3] $TR_{X+Y+Z} = \$100{,}000 + \$225{,}000 + \$250{,}000 = \$575{,}000$ (Total revenue)
[4] $TVC_{X+Y+Z} = \$60{,}000 + \$120{,}000 + \$125{,}000 = \$305.000$ (Total variable cost)
[5] $AVC = TVC/Q = \$305{,}000/9{,}000 = \$33.89$ (Average variable cost)

To see if our calculations are correct for each service, the break-even cost, C*, must be equal break-even revenue, R*:

$$\text{Service X: } C^* = FC + VC(Q^*) = \$180{,}000 + (\$60)(4{,}500) = \$180{,}000 + \$270{,}000 = \$450{,}000$$

$$\text{Service Y: } C^* = FC + VC(Q^*) = \$180{,}000 + (\$40)(5{,}143) = \$180{,}000 + \$205{,}720 \approx \$385{,}720$$

Service Y: $C^* = FC + VC(Q^*) = \$180{,}000 + (\$25)(7{,}200) = \$180{,}000 + \$180{,}000 = \$360{,}000$

which is what we obtained. Note that the discrepancy for Service Y by \$5 is due to rounding off the break-even patients.

Given the information above, we can easily obtain the Contribution Margin (CM), the break-even quantity, Q*, and the break-even revenue, R*, for the entire clinic, taking all three services, together, as shown below:

Service X + Y + Z:

$CM = \$30;\ Q^* = FC/CM = \$180{,}000/\$30 = 6{,}000;\ R^* = \$63.89 \times 6{,}000 = \$383{,}340$

5.3.2.1 Sensitivity Analysis

Oftentimes, especially from a policy perspective, it may be necessary for an organization to look at various alternatives under different conditions to determine what would be the best course of action if the current conditions were to change. This is commonly known as sensitivity analysis. Let us look at three simple scenarios for our clinic: what will be the break-even quantity and revenue, if (1) the fixed cost of operation were to increase by 10 percent, (2) the variable cost were to increase by 5 percent across the board with no change in fixed cost, and (3) the price were to increase by 10 percent across the board, with a Safety Margin (SM) of 5 percent, and no change in fixed cost?

The results of the scenarios are shown below:

- Scenario 1:

  Change in $FC = \$180{,}000 + (\$180{,}000 \times 0.10) = \$180{,}000 + \$18{,}000 = \$198{,}000$

  $Q^*_{X+Y+Z} = \$198{,}000/\$30 = 6{,}600;\ \mathbf{R}^*_{X+Y+Z} = \$63.89 \times 6{,}600 = \$421{,}674$

- Scenario 2:

  Change in $VC_X = \$60 + (\$60 \times 0.05) = \$60 + \$3.00 = \$63.00;\ CM_X = \$100 - \$63 = \$37.00$

  Change in $VC_Y = \$40 + (\$40 \times 0.05) = \$40 + \$2.00 = \$42.00;\ CM_Y = \$75 - \$42 = \$33.00$

  Change in $VC_Z = \$25 + (\$25 \times 0.05) = \$25 + \$2.50 = \$27.50;\ CM_Z = \$50 - \$27.50 = \$22.50$

$Q_X{}^* = \$180{,}000/\$37.00 \approx 4{,}865$; $R_X{}^* = \$100 \times 4{,}865 = \$486{,}500$
$Q_Y{}^* = \$180{,}000/\$33.00 \approx 5{,}455$; $R_Y{}^* = \$75 \times 5{,}455 = \$409{,}125$
$Q_Z{}^* = \$180{,}000/\$27.50 = 6{,}545$; $R_Z{}^* = \$50 \times 6{,}545 = \$327{,}250$

- Scenario 3:

Change in $\text{Price}_X = \$100 + (\$100 \times 0.10) = \$100 + \$10.00 = \$110.00$;
$CM_X = \$110 - \$60 = \$50.00$
Change in $\text{Price}_Y = \$75 + (\$75 \times 0.10) = \$75 + \$7.50 = \$82.50$;
$CM_Y = \$82.50 - \$40 = \$42.50$
Change in $\text{Price}_Z = \$50 + (\$50 \times 0.10) = \$50 + \$5.00 = \$55.00$;
$CM_Z = \$55 - \$25 = \$30.00$

$Q_X{}^* = \$180{,}000/\$50.00 = 3{,}600$; $R_X{}^* = \$110 \times 3{,}600 = \$396{,}000$
$Q_Y{}^* = \$180{,}000/\$42.50 \approx 4{,}235$: $R_Y{}^* = \$82.50 \times 4{,}235 = \$349{,}388$
$Q_Z{}^* = \$180{,}000/\$30.00 = 6{,}000$; $R_Z{}^* = \$55 \times 6{,}000 = \$330{,}000$

SM_X: $Q_X{}^* = 3{,}600 + (3{,}600 \times 0.05) = 3{,}600 + 180 = 3{,}780$
SM_Y: $Q_Y{}^* = 4{,}235 + (4{,}235 \times 0.05) = 4{,}235 + 212 = 4{,}447$
SM_Z: $Q_Z{}^* = 6{,}000 + (6{,}000 \times 0.05) = 6{,}000 + 300 = 6{,}300$

SM_X: $R_X{}^* = \$396{,}000 + (\$396{,}000 \times 0.05)$
$= \$396{,}000 + \$19{,}800 = \$415{,}800$
SM_Y: $R_Y{}^* = \$349{,}388 + (\$349{,}388 \times 0.05)$
$= \$349{,}388 + \$17{,}469 = \$366{,}857$
SM_Z: $R_Z{}^* = \$330{,}000 + (\$330{,}000 \times 0.05)$
$= \$330{,}000 + \$16{,}500 = \$346{,}500$

The results presented above show how break-even analysis can be used under different conditions or scenarios. For instance, we could have easily extended the analysis to include additional scenarios, additional services the clinic provides, besides the three, and develop a comprehensive picture of the financial viability of the organization under varying conditions. This is where the appeal of the method lies in that it is simple in approach yet produces valuable information about the financial viability of an organization under different conditions.

5.4 Nonlinear Break-Even Analysis

Although it is relatively easy to deal with a linear break-even analysis, the real relationship between cost, revenue, and output may not be linear; it may be nonlinear. The notion that per unit price or cost will always be a constant, regardless of the quantity of output consumed is not a realistic assumption since, in reality, costs related to labor, maintenance, and utility change disproportionately, rather than in fixed, constant amounts. Figure 5.2 shows a typical non-linear breakeven relationship between cost, revenue, and output. Non-linear break-even relationship, as shown in the figure, is much more complicated because the rate scale is not constant, as in a linear model, but changes for different levels of output. What this means is that the price an organization charges for a unit of a good or service, or the cost it incurs in providing the unit of the good or service will change with the quantity provided. One way to address the problem would be to transform the variables by taking their logs, natural or to the base 10, and then converting them back to their original terms.

However, most non-linear models used in practice are much simpler. A good example is a quadratic model that produces two break-even points; for instance, two breakeven quantities. To give an example, recall

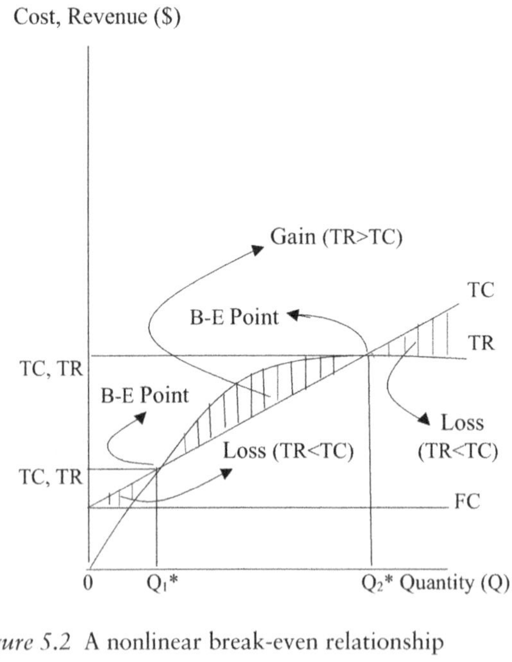

Figure 5.2 A nonlinear break-even relationship

the citation problem again. Assume now that we have total revenue and a total cost function for citations given by a single officer, rather than the entire department. We can express the two functions in terms of two simple equations, one linear and one nonlinear (quadratic), as given below:

$$TR = 50Q \tag{5.16}$$

$$TC = 0.08Q^2 - 10Q + 750 \tag{5.17}$$

where the price of an infraction is \$50, as before, with a fixed cost of \$750 and a variable cost that varies with different levels of output of the quadratic cost function. Our objective is to obtain a break-even quantity for the officer, given the information we have on the price and the cost of operation for the department.

To obtain the break-even quantity (citations) for the officer, we set up a net revenue function for the terms in Equations 5.16 and 5.17, so that

$$\begin{aligned}\pi &= TR - TC\\ &= 50Q - (0.08Q^2 - 1OQ + 750)\\ &= 50Q - 0.08Q^2 + 10Q - 750)\\ &= -0.08Q^2 + 60Q - 750\end{aligned}$$

The result resembles a typical quadratic function of the form

$$aQ^2 + bQ + c = O \tag{5.18}$$

where a and b are the parameters (constants) associated with Q. What this means is that Equation 5.18 has two solutions, called roots, one high and one low that are determined by a standard expression used for solving quadratic equations, given by the expression

$$Q = \frac{-b \pm \sqrt{b^2 - 4ac}}{2a} \tag{5.19}$$

Now, applying the expression in Equation 5.19 to the net revenue function, would produce two break-even quantities, one low and one high, as shown below:

$$\begin{aligned}Q &= [-b \pm [\sqrt{}(b^2 - 4ac)]\ /2a\\ &= [-60 \pm \sqrt{}(60)^2 - (4)(-0.08)(-750)]\ /[(2)(-0.08)]\\ &= [-60 \pm \sqrt{}(3{,}600 - 240]\ /(-0.16)\end{aligned}$$

$$= [-60 \pm \sqrt{3,360}] \,/(-0.16)$$
$$= [-60 \pm 57.9655] \,/(-0.16)$$
$$\therefore\ Q_1^* = 12.7156 \approx 13.0$$
$$Q_2^* = 737.2844 \approx 737.0$$

That is, 13 and 737 citations, respectively, since you cannot have fractional citations. Although both solutions produce positive break-even quantities, it is obvious that the department will not go with the lower quantity of 13 citations because it makes no sense to issue only 13 citations for the year for a single officer; it will also not generate enough revenue for the department. Therefore, the second solution, Q2 = 737, will be the preferred break-even quantity.

To see if the break-even points obtained for the problem are correct, we can substitute these quantities into the expression for π = TR - TC; if the result produces a net revenue of zero, it should be considered correct. We can start with Q^{2*} = 737.2844. That is,

$$\pi = TR \times TC$$
$$= 50Q^* - [0.08Q^2 - 10Q + 750]$$
$$= (50)(737.2844) - [(0.08)(737.2844)^2 - (10)(737.2844) + 750]$$
$$= \$36.864.22 - [\$43,487.0629 - \$7,372.844 + \$750]$$
$$= \$36,864.22 - \$36,864.22$$
$$= 0$$

which comes out to be 0, as expected. We could do the same for Q_1^* = 12.7156, but it would not be necessary since we do not think the department will go with 13 citations.

5.5 Chapter Summary

All organizations need to analyze their cost behavior on a regular basis to ensure that there are no cost overruns and that they are making cost decisions that are financially viable. While there are different ways to analyze the cost behavior of an organization, this chapter has presented a measure that is frequently used in cost analysis, known as break-even analysis. The primary objective of break-even analysis is to bring together the cost, revenue, and output of an activity to determine the level at which there will be no loss or gain: it will break even. This is an important first step in cost decisions to see if an operation will be financially viable before deciding whether to undertake the operation or expand it. Break-even analysis can be linear and non-linear, but the linear model is most frequently used because it is simple to use and easy to analyze. Also, like most cost analysis, it can be used for both single and multiple activities. The chapter focused mostly on linear break-even analysis for single as well as multiple activities and concluded with a brief discussion of non-linear breakeven analysis.

5.6 Review Questions

5.1 What is break-even analysis? What is the difference between a linear and non-linear break-even analysis? Discuss the assumptions that underlie break-even analysis and explain what happens if the assumptions are relaxed?

5.2 What is contribution margin? How does it differ from an operating leverage? Discuss, with an example, how contribution margin is used to determine a break-even quantity?

5.3 A city operates a downtown parking garage throughout the year, including holidays. The fixed cost of operating the garage is $750,000 with a variable cost of $2.50 per vehicle. The garage charges $8.50 each time a vehicle is parked.

a. Given this information,

  i. Calculate the number of vehicles that must be parked each year for the city to break even.
  ii. Calculate the break-even cost of operating the garage for the city for the year.
  iii. Calculate the break-even revenue from the operation of the garage for the year.

b. Assume that revenue from the operation of the garage will increase by 5% next year. What would be the net gain for the city next year?

c. Assume further that revenue as well as fixed and variable costs of operation will also increase by 5, 3, and 4 percents, respectively, next year. What would be the net gain for the city next year?

5.4 The Parking Meter Department of a local government gives on average 700,000 tickets a year, with a variable cost of $15 per ticket and a fixed cost of $700,000. The department charges $85 per ticket.

a. Given the information above,

  i. Determine the break-even quantity for the department.
  ii. Determine the break-even revenue and break-even cost.
  iii. Determine the net revenue at the current level of tickets.
  iv. Determine the net revenue at the break-even level.

b. Suppose that the department wants to increase its revenue by 10 percent next year. For the department to achieve its goal, determine

(1) the number of tickets it must issue, assuming there is no change in price, (2) the price it must charge per ticket without changing the current quantity.

5.5 What is operating leverage? Suppose that a government is looking into its revenue situation for the Water Department. Let us say that the department has an operating leverage of 3.75, based on recent water production and price. What does the operating leverage 3.7 mean? Also, if the government wants to raise revenue of the department by 3.5 percent, how much will the operating leverage have to increase?

5.6 What is outsourcing? Can a government use break-even analysis to determine if it should outsource a service that it currently provides to a private firm or a nonprofit organization? How? Give an example.

5.7 While break-even analysis is primarily used in situations where the conditions are certain, it can also be used under conditions of uncertainty. Given an example of break-even analysis under conditions of uncertainty.

5.8. What is a non-linear break-even analysis? Why is non-linear model more difficult to use than a linear model? Can you linearize a non-linear break-even model into a linear break-even model? How? Give an example.

5.9 Suppose that a local government is planning to undertake four new programs: a. A new bus route, b. An after-school math and science program, c. Building a new community center, and d. Expand the recycling program. Using hypothetical data for each program, do the following:

a. Determine the break-even number of riders needed to cover the costs of the expansion, such as new buses, drivers, fuel, plus any other.
b. Assess the break-even number of students needed to cover the costs of the program, in particular the cost of staff, supplies, equipment, and facility rental.
c. Determine the break-even participants needed to cover the costs of construction, staffing, and operation.
d. Determine the break-even number of households needed to offset the costs of setting up collection points and processing facilities.

5.10 A senior health rehabilitation program, operated by a nonprofit organization, received $1.2 million in grant from the federal government. The organization charges each person $500 a month for board and care. The program has a fixed cost of $800,000 and a variable cost of $600. Determine the break-even number of seniors the organization can serve and stay within the budget.

Note

1 According to available information, the concept of break-even analysis is credited to economists Karl Bücher and Johann Friedrich Schär, who developed the framework for calculating the "break-even point" where total costs equal total revenue, resulting in neither profit nor loss. However, the term itself is most commonly attributed to Walter Rautenstrauch who used "break-even point" in his book *The Successful Control of Profits* in 1930. A paperback version of the book, with a Forward by W.C. Dickerman, was published in October 2011 by Literary Licensing.

References

Cleverley, W.O.(1979). Cost/volume/profit analysis in the hospitality industry. *Health Care Management Review*. 4 (3): 29–36.

Downen, T. (2020). Accounting for uncertainty in cost-volume-profit analysis. *Management Accounting Quarterly*. 22 (1): 25–30.

Lohmann, R.A. (1976). Break even analysis: Tool for budget planning. *Social Work*. 21(4): 300–307.

Rautenstrausch, W. (1939). *Economics of business enterprise*. New York: John Wiley.

Shim, J.K., Siegel, J.G., and Shim, A.I. (2011). *Budgeting Basics and Beyond*. New York: Wiley.

Shrotriya, V. (2019). Break even analysis – The concept and its utility. *International Journal of Research and Analytical Reviews*. 6(1): 66–75.

6 Differential Analysis

6.1 Introduction

While break-even analysis serves as an important first step in the financial decision-making of an organization, it should be combined with other decision tools in order to gain a better understanding of the decision process. For a decision maker to be able to make the best possible decision, it is important to have more than one alternative to compare. From a financial and accounting perspective, comparison allows the decision makers to evaluate different alternatives against a criterion or criteria to determine the alternative that would produce the best possible choice for the organization such as the greatest amount of return, the greatest amount of savings, best value, and so forth. There is a wide range of methods that can be used in cost analysis that would fall into this category, referred to as differential analysis. The term differential analysis seems appropriate because the decision to select the best alternative is based on a comparison of the differences between two or more alternatives. This chapter discusses four methods that are frequently used in differential analysis: differential cost analysis, buy or lease, benefit-cost analysis, and life-cycle costing. Of these, benefit-cost analysis has a long and established history that precedes most methods of cost analysis.

6.2 Differential Cost Analysis

Like break-even analysis, differential cost analysis deals with cost, revenue, and output of an activity. Its purpose is to use cost and other related information to determine the course of action that will produce the best possible return from that decision for an organization. For instance, when a government wants to initiate a new program or eliminate an existing one, or when it wants to reduce a service charge or buy a piece of equipment, it must compare these decisions against the existing conditions to determine if the net return is higher in each instance to justify that course of action.

DOI: 10.4324/9781003486091-7

Without this comparison, it will be difficult for a government to determine the relative worth of its decisions. In general, a decision is considered worthwhile if it produces a return that is higher than the return under the existing conditions. This section discusses a situation where differential cost analysis makes the most sense in order to determine the effects of a change in cost on net return.

Earlier in the chapter on break-even analysis, we defined net return as the difference between total revenue and total cost, but in differential cost analysis it is defined as the difference between two differentials: differential return (revenue) and differential cost. Differential revenue is the difference between current revenue and the revenue one will earn under an alternative. Similarly, differential cost can be defined as the difference between current cost and the cost under an alternative. Thus, in calculating net revenue, the emphasis is placed on the differentials rather than on the simple difference between cost and revenue.

The calculation of net returns from these differentials is simple, provided one has all the information one needs on differential costs and returns. Equation 6.1 presents a simple expression for calculating the net return, as shown below:

$$\pi_D = (\Delta R \times T) - [C_0 + (\Delta C \times T)] \tag{6.1}$$

where π_D is the net return from differentials, ΔR is the change in revenue, C_0 is the one-time cost, such as construction cost, ΔC is the change in cost, excluding onetime cost, and T is time.

We can use a simple example to illustrate this. Suppose that a large metropolitan government owns and operates a parking garage with a capacity for parking 150 cars at any given time. The government charges $10 a day for parking, which runs from 7:00 in the morning to 7:00 in the evening; the garage remains closed after that time. The number of cars parked on average is 200 a day, including weekends. Suppose that demand for parking space has been increasing steadily in recent months. To deal with the problem, the government has three options: (1) outsource the garage, (2) privatize it (sell it to a private provider, say, for $3 million), or (3) upgrade it. Let us assume that before considering outsourcing or privatizing, the government wants to look at upgrading the garage because it provides a consistent source of revenue for the government. However, the government may consider the other two options if upgrading turns out to be more costly than the revenue the government will earn from the upgrade.

Suppose now that upgrading will involve increasing the capacity by another 150 parking spaces, which will raise the number of cars that can be parked on average to 400 a day. It will cost the city $1 million to upgrade the garage, which it will borrow as an intermediate-term loan from a local bank at a six percent interest rate payable in three years. Suppose further that the government plans to increase the parking fee by $2.50 to recover some of the costs of construction, thereby raising the current price from $10 to $12.50 a day. Table 6.1 presents a three-year differential on costs and returns from the upgrade.

According to the table, the city revenue from the upgrade will increase by $1,095,000 a year, resulting in part from price increase and in part from the revenue generated from additional parking spaces, as shown below:

Table 6.1 Differential-cost analysis (without discounting)

	Existing Condition ($)	*Alternative Proposal ($)*	*Difference ($)*
I. Operating Revenue from			
1. Parking Space	730,000[1]	1,460,000[2]	730,000
2. Price Increase	0	365,000[3]	365,000
Total Revenue/Year	730,000	1,825,000	1,095,000[4]
II. Operating Cost due to			
1. Construction	0	1,000,000	1,000,000
2. Interest Payment	0	60,000[5]	60,000
3. Repair & Maintenance	5,000	10,000[6]	5,000
4. Payroll Increase	20,000	30,000[7]	10,000
5.3 Miscellaneous	2,500	5,000	2,500
Total Cost/Year	27,500	105,000[8]	77,500[9]
III. Three-year differential			
Total Differential Revenue[10] ($1,095,000 x 3 = $3,285,000)			$3,285,000
Total Differential Cost[11] [$1,000,000 + ($77,500 x 3)] = $1,232,500			1,232,500
Net Return from Differential			$2,052,500

[1] ($10 × 200)(365) = $730,000
[2] ($10 × 400)(365) = $1,460,000
[3] ($2.50 × 400)(365) = $365,000
[4] $1,825,000 - $730,000 = $1,095,000 (Annual return from upgrade)
[5] Assuming an annual interest payment at 6%
[6] Assuming double the current cost (no adjustment made for inflation)
[7] Assuming $10,000 increase in payroll
[8] Excludes the construction cost
[9] Differential cost from upgrade (excluding one-time construction cost of $1 million)
[10] Based on an annual differential from upgrade of $1,095,000 (See Equation 6.2)
[11] One-time construction cost + Differential cost from upgrade

$$
\begin{aligned}
R_u &= R_{AP} - R_{EC} \qquad (6.2)\\
&= [(400)(365)(\$12.50)] - [(200)(365)(\$10)]\\
&= \$1,825,000 - \$730,000\\
&= \$1,095,000
\end{aligned}
$$

where R_u is the revenue from upgrade, R_{AP} is the revenue from alternative proposal, and R_{EC} is the revenue from the existing circumstances.

The differential cost from operating the garage will also increase by \$77,500 a year for three years, due to an increase in payroll, costs of additional repair and maintenance, and interest payments on debt. The table also shows a three-year differential revenue and cost of \$3,285,000 and \$1,232,500, respectively, with a net return from the differentials of \$2,052,500 (total differential revenue minus total differential cost). Does this mean that the government would be better off not selling the garage? The answer is "yes," because it will take the government less than a year (0.879 years) after the initial three years, or a total of 3.879 years (3 + 0.879) to recover the \$3 million it would have earned had it decided to sell the garage, while retaining its ownership. That is, (\$3,000,000 - \$2,052,500) / (1,095,000 - 77,500) = 947,500 / \$1,077,500 = 0.879 years. Note that \$2,052,500 is the net return from differentials, \$1,095,000 is the differential revenue, and \$77,500 is the differential cost for a year. Incidentally, the differential cost of \$77,500 would be lower after the first three years because there is no interest payment after three years.

It should be worth noting that when we are estimating the costs and returns over time, whether differential or otherwise, it is important to discount them to determine what the future values will be in today's term because money loses its value over time. For instance, a gallon of milk that cost \$3.75 two years ago may cost \$4.50 today because of the loss of value of money over a two-year period. The same is true for many of the goods and services we consume on a regular basis. The term that is commonly used for this purpose is the time value of money.

6.2.1 Time Value of Money

The time value of money simply means the value a given sum of money will have over time. In general, the value of money decreases as time progresses, indicating that money loses its value over time. Several factors contribute to this apparent loss of value of money over time such as inflation (it will cost us more to buy the same bundle of goods and services tomorrow than what it costs us today), our unwillingness to defer current consumption for future consumption (we are better off consuming the resources today than postponing them for tomorrow because they will cost more), uncertainty (we do not know what awaits us in the future), and so forth.

Because of the fact that money loses its value over time, it is necessary to make some adjustments in the costs and returns to get an accurate picture of its real worth. The simplest way to accomplish this is to discount the costs and returns by an appropriate discount rate (the rate by which we discount a stream of costs and returns). The result would produce a discounted stream of costs and returns, called the Present Value (PV) of costs and returns. By present value, we mean the value a future stream of costs and returns will produce in today's terms: Why in today's terms? Because when we make a decision to acquire or invest in an asset it involves a resource commitment at the time when the decision is made to invest or acquire it, although the actual returns from the decision will take place over a period of time.

To give an example, suppose that we want to invest an amount, say, X, today, t = 0, at 5 percent rate of interest (rate of return, r) that will produce exactly $100 a year from now, t + 1, the Present Value (PV) of $100 a year from now in today's terms will be $95.24. That is,

$$PV = \frac{X_1}{(1+r)^1} \tag{6.3}$$

$$= \$100/(1+0.05)^1$$

$$= \$100/1.05$$

$$= \$95.24$$

Note that $100 is the Future Value (FV) of $95.24 a year from now, t + 1. In other words, if we invest $95.24 today at a 5 percent rate of interest (return), it will produce $100 next year (the value a current investment will produce at some future point in time, called the future value).[1]

Similarly, if we invest an amount, X, today that will produce exactly $100 two years from now, t + 2, the PV of $100 in today's term will be $90.70. That is,

$$PV = \frac{X_2}{(1+r)^2} \tag{6.4}$$

$$= \$100/(1+0.05)^2$$

$$= \$100/1.1025$$

$$= \$90.70$$

which is how much \$100 two years from now would be worth today. In future value terms, if we invest \$90.70 today at 5 percent rate of interest (return), it will produce \$100 two years from now, t+2, and so forth. The interest rate (the rate of return) we used to discount the amount X is called the discount rate, described earlier.

Since costs and returns (benefits) extend over multiple years, we can extend the expression in Equation 6.3 to discount a stream of benefits, B_t, and costs, C_t, and take the difference between the two, which would produce the Net Present Value (NPV), as in net return or net benefit, except that it is expressed in discount terms, as shown below:

$$NPV = \sum_{t=0}^{T} \frac{B_t}{(1+r)} - \sum_{t=0}^{T} \frac{C_t}{(1+r)} \tag{6.5}$$

where B and C are benefit and cost streams, respectively, r is the discount rate, and t is time (for t = 1, 2, ..., T). The first part of the equation represents the discounted sum of benefits (returns) and the second part represents the discounted sum of costs.

Alternatively, we could have written Equation 6.5 as

$$NPV = \sum_{t=0}^{T} B_t \frac{1}{(1+r)^t} - \sum_{t=0}^{T} C_t \frac{1}{(1+r)^t} \tag{6.6}$$

which is the same as the expression in Equation 6.5, except that it is obtained by multiplying a stream of costs and benefits by a term 1/(1+r), called the Discount Factor (DF), and then taking their difference to obtain the net present value. As such, it is often called the computational formula. Thus, according to Equation 6.6, to obtain the discounted stream of costs and benefits, we simply multiply the streams of costs and benefits by the corresponding Discount Factor (DF). That is,

$$NPV = [(B_1 \times DF_1) + (B_2 \times DF_2) + \ldots + (B_T \times DF_T)] - [(C_1 \times DF_1) + (C_2 + DF_2) + \ldots + (C_T \times DF_T)] \tag{6.7}$$

6.2.1.1 Applying Time Value of Money to the Parking Garage Example

We can now apply the time value of money to our parking garage example. Table 6.2 shows the discounted differential costs and returns for the parking garage. According to the table, the discounted sum of returns (benefits) from the upgrade would be higher than the discounted sum of costs, producing a positive net present value of \$1,719,777.50

Table 6.2 Differential-cost analysis (with discounting)

Differential cost and return under alternative condition					
Year	*Differential cost ($)*	*Discount Factor (DF)*[1]	*Discounted Cost ($)*	*Differential Return ($)*	*Discounted Return ($)*[1]
0	1,000,000.00	1.0000	1,000,000.00	--	--
1	77,500.00	0.9434	73,113.50	1,095,000	1,033,023.00
2	77,500.00	0.8900	68,975.00	1,095,000	974,550.00
3	77,500.00	0.8396	65,069.00	1,095,000	919,362.00
Total	$1,232,500.00		$1,207,157.50	$3,285,000	$2,926,935.00

[1] Based on 6% discount rate; Example: $1/(1+i)^1 = 1/(1+0.06)^1 = 1/(1.06)^1 = 1/1.06 = 0.9434$

[$2,926,935.00 - $1,207,157.50 = $1,719,777.50] for the first three years. In general, a positive NPV means the project is producing more returns than costs over time, indicating that the project is worth undertaking.

In terms of recovering the $3 million if the government decided to sell it, it would take a little longer to recover because of the discounted costs and returns. It would take an additional 1.334 years, instead 0.879 years, after the first three years. That is, [$3,000,000 - ($2,926,935.00 - $1,207,157.50)]/($1,033,023.00 - $73,113.50) = ($3,000,000 - $1,719,777.50) / ($1,033,023.00 - $73,113.50) = $1,280,222.50/$959,909.50 = 1.334 years, with a total of 4.334 years (3 + 1.334), instead of 3.879 years without discounting.

6.3 Buy or Lease

Buying or leasing is a special case of differential cost analysis in which costs are compared not between an existing condition and an alternative, but between two alternatives: buy or lease. Like any business organization, when a government decides to acquire an asset, it has the option to buy or lease. Which option it should use depends on several factors such as the cost of the asset, the length of time for which it will be used, the salvage value it will have at the end of its useful life, and so on. Although as a financial option leasing has been around for a long time, more governments are using it today than ever before because of its viability as an alternative to buying.

Leasing can be defined as a process, whereby the owner of an asset, called lessor, enters into an agreement (lease) with the user of the asset, called lessee, to allow the latter to use the asset for a specified time at an agreed upon cost. Theoretically, the lease cost must be less than the purchase price to justify the option to lease, but there are situations where buying is a better alternative to leasing even if it costs a government more initially, provided that in the long run it will save the government more money.

There are several explanations as to why leasing is considered a better alternative to buying:

1. It provides a viable alternative for acquiring assets for governments that have limited resources. Without the opportunity to lease, many of these governments will not be able to obtain the facilities and equipment they need.
2. It can conserve or free up existing resources of a government that can be used to meet other financial needs.
3. It offers a fast and flexible alternative to raising taxes or borrowing funds to pay for the facilities and equipment a government needs.
4. It provides 100 percent financing in most cases. In addition to that, costs such as delivery fees and installation charges are frequently included in lease payments, thereby reducing the cost burden for the government.
5. It avoids the risk of obsolescence. In an age of rapid technological changes, ownership does not have a distinct advantage every time a new and improved product is introduced in the market.
6. It does not affect a government's ability to borrow and does not reduce its credit rating.

6.3.1 Steps in Determining Buy or Lease

Although the advantages are obvious, a government considering leasing as an option must do some financial analyses to see if it has a definite cost advantage over buying. In reality, the actual analysis does not have to be all that complicated and can be accomplished in three simple steps: (1) determine the cost of buying, as well as leasing; (2) calculate the difference between the two options; and (3) select the one that produces a lower cost to the government. We can formally express this relationship between buying and leasing in terms of a simple algebraic expression, as shown below:

$$C_W = \left[\left(P_0 + \sum_{t=0}^{T} OC_t\right) - SV_T\right] - \sum_{t=0}^{T}\left(LC_t + OC_t\right) \tag{6.8}$$

where CW is the net cost of ownership, P_0 is the purchase price at time 0, LC_t is the cost of leasing at time t, Ct is the operating cost at time t for the duration of the time the asset will be in use, SV_T is the salvage value at time T (t = 0, 1, 2, ..., T). Operating costs typically include the costs of utility, personnel such as custodial services, which are different from maintenance costs such as insurance, major repair, regular maintenance to keep the asset in good working condition, and so forth. Note that while maintenance costs are usually included in lease cost, the operating costs are not. As such, they are included in cost calculations whether the asset is owned or leased.

Equation 6.8 has two parts: The first part represents the cost of ownership, and the second part represents the cost of leasing. While the equation seems simple enough to be useful for everyday purposes, it has one major weakness in that it does not take the time value of money into consideration, which is important if the item in question has a useful life that extends over several years. Since leasing involves resource commitments that extend several years into the future, it is necessary to discount the cost of ownership as well as the cost of leasing to determine the net present value of ownership. Equation 6.9 shows the net present value of ownership, below:

$$NPV_W = [(P_0 + \sum_{t=0}^{T} \frac{OC_t}{(1+i)^t}) - \frac{SV_T}{(1+i)^T}] - [\sum_{t=0}^{T} \frac{(LC_t + OC_t)}{(1+i)^t}] \tag{6.9}$$

where NPV_W is the net present value of ownership (defined as the difference between the present value of purchase, namely, ownership, and the present value of lease), i is the rate of discount, and the rest of the terms are the same, as before.

Note that the expression $OCt/(1+i)^t$ in Equation 6.9 can also be written as $(OCt)[1/(1+i)t]$, so that

$$NPV_W = [(P_0 + \sum_{t=0}^{T} (OC_t)(\frac{1}{(1+i)^t}) - (SV_T)(\frac{1}{(1+i)^T})] - [\sum_{t=0}^{T} (LC_t + OC_t)(\frac{1}{(1+i)^t})] \tag{6.10}$$

where $1/(1+i)$ is called the Discount Factor (DF). A discount factor is the value by which the costs and returns of an asset are multiplied to obtain a discounted stream of costs and returns. In general, if the net present value of ownership is positive, leasing should be preferred since it will cost more to own than to lease. On the other hand, if it is negative, purchasing should be preferred since it will cost more to lease than to own.

We can use a simple example to illustrate this. Suppose that the Public Works department of a government needs a heavy-duty truck to carry out its normal repair and maintenance work. If the department has to buy the truck, it will cost it $65,000. If it has to lease, the rental cost will be $18,000 a year, payable at the end of each period for three years (assuming the department will lease the truck for three years). If purchased, there is a salvage value of $23,500 at the end of the asset's useful life. There is also an operating cost of $5,000, regardless of whether the vehicle is purchased or leased. Assume a discount rate of 9 percent. Table 6.3 shows the present value of ownership for the problem.

As can be seen from the table, the net present value of ownership will be $2,788.97, obtained by taking the difference between the sum of the present value of purchase and the sum of the present value of lease. That is,

$$
\begin{aligned}
NPV_W &= \Sigma PV \text{ of Purchase} - \Sigma PV \text{ of Lease} \\
&= [(\$65{,}000 + \$4{,}587.40 + \$4{,}208.40 + \$3{,}860.92) - \$16{,}647.00] \\
&\quad - [\$21{,}100.91 + \$19{,}358.64 + \$17{,}760.21] \\
&= \$61{,}008.73 + \$58{,}219.76 \\
&= \$2{,}788.97
\end{aligned}
$$

where NPV_W is the net present value of ownership. Now to determine whether the department should buy or lease the vehicle, we can apply the decision rule we established earlier; that is, if the net present value of ownership is positive, it should lease; if not, it should purchase. Since the

Table 6.3 Present value of ownership vs. lease

Year	*Purchase Price ($)*	*Operating Cost ($)*	*Salvage Value ($)*	*Discount Factor (DF)*[1]	*PV of Purchase ($)*
0	65,000	--	--	--	65,000.00
1	--	5,000	--	0.917431	4,587.40
2	--	5,000	--	0.841680	4,208.40
3	--	5,000	--	0.772183	3,860.92
4	--	--	23,500	0.708425	16,647.99

Year	*Lease Price ($)*	*Operating Cost ($)*	*Total Cost ($)*	*Discount Factor*	*PV of Lease ($)*
0	--	--	--	--	--
1	18,000	5,000	23,000	0.917431	21,100.91
2	18,000	5,000	23,000	0.841680	19,358.64
3	18,000	5,000	23,000	0.772183	17,760.21
4	--	--	--	--	--

[1] Example: $1/(1+i)^1 = 1/(1+0.09)^1 = 1/(1.09)^1 = 0.917431$

net present value of ownership is positive, it should lease. In other words, since the cost of ownership is higher than the cost of lease, the department should go with the option to lease.

We have taken a rather simplistic approach here to determine the cost of ownership. Although somewhat easy to understand, there is a weakness in this approach in that it tends to ignore intangible factors such as convenience, location, and the personal relationship between a lessee and a lessor that can affect the final cost. Another problem with this approach is that it is too broad and fails to include a host of other requirements that may also have an important determining influence on the final cost. For instance, a government may be required to pledge a collateral against an existing asset before acquiring the asset, or there may be restrictions on the use of the asset once acquired, or there may be a special clause requiring the government to buy safety insurance to protect the asset against potential loss, theft, or damage. In each of these instances, there is a monetary implication that must be incorporated in the final calculation before making the decision whether to buy or lease.

6.4 Benefit-Cost Analysis

One of the earliest decision tools used in cost analysis with a long history that goes back at least to the 17th century is Benefit-Cost Analysis (BCA) and despite its long history, it is still amongst the most popular decision tools in government (Thompson, 1982). Benefit-cost analysis is particularly suitable where resources are scarce and the demand for goods and services exceeds the available resources. Constrained by resource limitations, the rational choice facing a decision maker is to undertake those activities that will produce the greatest amount of return for the resources utilized. This fundamental rule of efficiency that guides the allocation decision of a household or firm also guides a government to allocate its resources among competing needs and interests. Without this measure of efficiency, there will be very little basis for determining how best a government can utilize its resources or what it can do to improve its allocation decisions in the future.

6.4.1 Steps in Benefit-Cost Analysis

As with any decision involving (project) investments, the benefit-cost analysis follows several distinct steps. These steps typically are (1) define the goals and objectives of the analysis, (2) identify the project or projects to be analyzed, (3) determine the costs and benefits associated with each project, (4) find the present value of costs and benefits for each project, (5) evaluate the projects using one or more decision rules or criteria, and (6) select the project(s).

All benefit-cost analysis begins with a clear statement of goals and objectives. Unlike the private sector, where the goals are generally stated in terms of maximizing profit for a firm or business, defining goals and objectives for government is much more complex. The complexity arises from the imprecise and often conflicting nature of the goals a government tries to achieve as well as the projects whose costs and benefits are not always easy to measure. Once the goals and objectives have been defined, the next step in the process is to identify and select the project or projects for evaluation. Theoretically, there is no limit to the number of projects a government can consider, but, in practice, it depends on the goals and objectives of the government as well as the resources the projects will consume and the benefits they will produce.

Once the goals and objectives have been defined, projects have been identified for evaluation, and some determinations have been made as to their costs and benefits, the next step in the process is to evaluate the projects. The convention is to use one or more criteria, we will call them decision criteria, for convenience, to analyze and compare projects. Comparison makes it possible for the decision makers to assess the merit of each project individually or against each other before selecting the one that will meet the goals and objectives of the organization. The process is completed with the selection of the project, or projects.

6.4.2 Decision Criteria in BCA

Three sets of criteria are generally used in benefit-cost analysis to determine if a project or activity is worth undertaking: Benefit-Cost ratio (B:C), Net Present Value (NPV), and Internal Rate of Return (IRR). A benefit-cost ratio is simply a ratio of sum of benefits to the sum of costs, and when the time value of money is incorporated it becomes a ratio of the sum of Present Value of Benefits (PV_B) to the sum of Present Value of Costs (PV_C). The ratio indicates the return the funds invested in a project, or projects, will produce for an organization. In general, the higher the ratio the greater the return and the more attractive the investment is.

Net Present Value (NPV), as discussed earlier, is the difference between a discounted stream of benefits and costs (the difference between the sum of present value of benefits and the sum of present value of costs). A positive NPV indicates that the benefits are greater than the costs, thereby making a project worth undertaking, while a negative NPV indicates the opposite. Like benefit-cost ratio, the higher the net-present value, the greater the attractiveness of an investment (project or projects under consideration).

Finally, the internal rate of return is the rate at which the sum of a discounted stream of benefits equals the sum of a discounted stream of costs. In other words, it is the rate at which the net present value will be zero, NPV = 0. In general, the higher the rate of return, the greater is the attractiveness of a project, as the rate is frequently associated with the growth rate of a project.

The following provides a summary of the three decision criteria, and the corresponding decision rules:

(1) Decision Criterion: B:C

$B{:}C = \Sigma B/\Sigma C$ (undiscounted)

$B{:}C = \Sigma PV_B/\Sigma PV_C$ (discounted)

Decision Rule:

1. For a single project: Select the project if $B{:}C>1$
2. For multiple projects: Select the project with the highest positive B:C (assuming the projects are mutually exclusive); if not, select those with $B{:}C>1$

(2) Decision Criterion: NB, NPV

$NB = \Sigma B - \Sigma C$ (undiscounted)

$NPV = \Sigma PV_B - \Sigma PV_C$ (discounted)

Decision Rule:

1. For a single project: Select the project if its $NPV>0$
2. For multiple projects: Select the project with the highest NPV (assuming the projects are mutually exclusive); if not, select those with positive NPV

(3) Decision Criterion: IRR

IRR: $\Sigma PV_B = \Sigma PV_C$

or IRR: $NPV = \Sigma PV_B - \Sigma PV_C = 0$

Decision Rule:

- For both single and multiple projects, the rule of thumb is to use IRR if it is higher than the required rate of return (known commonly as cost of capital)

Several things are worth noting about the decision criteria used in benefit-cost analysis. For instance, when B:C is used the rule of thumb is to select a project or projects so long as the ratio is greater than one, $B{:}C>1$, meaning that a dollar invested would produce more than a dollar worth of return. Thus, a B:C = 1.67 means that each dollar invested will produce a return of \$1.67, indicating a profit or net return of \$0.67. In the case of government, the ratio can be set at greater than or equal to one; that is, $B{:}C \geq 1$, which makes sense because, unlike private firms and businesses, a government does not operate to make profit. However, for goods and services that are provided in a business-like manner, most governments would prefer a net positive return.

Like B:C, the net present value tells us whether an investment will create value for an organization, but its greatest advantage lies in the fact that it explicitly takes into consideration the time value of money. As such, it produces a more realistic picture of whether a project is worth undertaking. Finally, the internal rate of return is considered good for a single project but not for multiple projects, because when multiple projects are involved, it is difficult to determine which IRR will produce the correct result since we can have more than one rate for a project, depending on the nature of cash flow (costs and benefits). In general, an IRR would produce correct results when there is an initial positive cash flow, followed by a series of negative flows. On the other hand, it tends to produce mixed results with inconsistent IRRs when the cash flows are mixed such as with some positives and some negatives, and in no precise order.

To illustrate how the rules are used, in particular the net present value since it is the most frequently used method in government, let us look at an example of where a government is considering two mutually exclusive projects, A and B, each with a life span of five years. Let us say that the initial cost of both projects is \$1 million. Both projects have one-time costs but produce benefits that occur in different amounts over time. We will use NPV, assuming a discount rate of 6 percent. Since our example involves a one-time cost and does not include any Salvage Value (SV) at the end of the useful lives of either of the two projects, we can write the NPV as

$$NPV = \sum_{t=0}^{T=5} \frac{B_t}{(1+i)^t} - C_0 \tag{6.11}$$

where C_0 is the one-time cost and the rest of the terms are the same, as before.

It is worth noting that a one-time cost means that there are no subsequent costs a project would incur, except for normal repair and maintenance which, in principle, should be treated as operating and maintenance costs for the government. However, if these costs occur over the entire length of a project's useful life, rather than one time, then they should be discounted the same way as one would discount a stream of costs and benefits.[2] Table 6.4 shows the benefits and costs for both projects, along with their corresponding net present value and benefit-cost ratio. According to the table, Project B produces a higher B:C (1.681B > 1.6263A) as well as a higher NPV (\$681,143B > \$626,308A); therefore, it should be selected.

Table 6.4 Benefit-cost analysis with time value of money

Project A				
Year	*Cost ($)*	*Benefit ($)*	*Discount Factor*	*PV of Benefit ($)*
0	1,000,000	-	-	-
1	-	700,000	0.9434	660,380
2	-	450,000	0.8900	400,500
3	-	325,000	0.8396	272,870
4	-	275,000	0.7921	217,828
5	-	100,000	0.7473	74,730
Total:	1,000,000	1,850,000	-	1,626,308

Project B				
Year	*Cost ($)*	*Benefit ($)*	*Discount Factor*	*PV of Benefit ($)*
0	1,000,000	-	-	-
1	-	125,000	0.9434	117,925
2	-	200,000	0.8900	178,000
3	-	475,000	0.8396	398,810
4	-	750,000	0.7921	594,075
5	-	525,000	0.7473	392,333
Total:	1,000,000	2,075,000	-	1,681,143

NPV_A = \$1,626.308 - \$1,000,000 = \$626,308
NPV_B = \$1,681,143 - \$1,000,000 = \$681,143

$B{:}C_A$ = \$1,850,000/\$1,000,000 = 1.8500 (w/o Time Value of Money)
$B{:}C_A$ = \$1,626,308/\$1,000,000 = 1.6263 (w/Time Value of Money)
$B{:}C_B$ = \$1,207,000/\$1,000,000 = 1.2075 (w/o Time Value of Money)
$B{:}C_B$ = \$1,681,143/\$1,000,000 = 1.6811 (w/Time Value of Money)

Assume now that Project A costs \$900,000, while B costs \$1 million and the benefit streams remain the same for both, as before. The resulting NVP and B:C for Project A will be: NPV_A = \$1,626,308 - \$900,000 = \$726,308; $B{:}C_A$ = \$1,850,000/\$900,000 = 2.0556 (without the time value of money); and $B{:}C_A$ = \$1,6266,308/\$900,000 = 1.8070 (with time value of money). This creates an interesting problem for the decision makers since Project A has a lower NPV than B, as before, but produces a higher B:C, with and without the time value of money. The final decision will depend on what the decision makers plan to achieve for the projects. If the objective is to have maximum (highest) net present value, then they should select Project B since it has a higher net present value. If, on the other hand, the objective is to get the most return for each dollar of investment, Project A should be selected since it has a higher benefit-cost ratio of the two.

Note that no attempt was made here to calculate the internal rate of return for the two projects. However, one way to obtain the rate would be to use trial and error until a rate is found at which NPV = 0. It can also be obtained using spreadsheets such as Microsoft Excel or from any standard financial calculator.

6.4.3 *Accounting Rate of Return*

An important concern with benefit-cost analysis is the selection of the discount rate because the rate one uses can have a significant effect on whether a project or investment will be worth undertaking. Cost and managerial accountants often use a method of discounting that is much simpler than the conventional methods economists and others use,[3] called Accounting Rate of Return (ARR). Its simplicity comes from the fact it does not use discounted streams of costs and returns; instead, it takes into consideration depreciation to provide some recognition of the role time plays in an asset's useful life. Operationally, it measures the return on an investment not in terms of cash flows, but in terms of income or return an investment will produce for an organization.

The following provides the expression for ARR:

$$\text{ARR} = \text{Net Income}/I_0 \tag{6.12}$$

where I_0 is the initial investment, and net income is the difference between average income (average cash flow, namely, sum of inflows minus outflows, divided by the number of years the investment or project will remain in place), adjusted for depreciation.

To give an example, suppose that a government is planning to invest in a project, say, a piece of heavy-duty road maintenance equipment for a toll road which will require an initial outlay of \$100,000 with no salvage value. The equipment has a useful life of five years and will produce the following cash flows: $\$20{,}000_1$, $\$30{,}000_2$, $\$40{,}000_3$, $\$30{,}000_4$, and $\$30{,}000_5$, respectively, with a total cash flow of \$150,000. The average cash flow or income from the use of the equipment will be \$30,000 [\$20,000 + \$30,000 + \$40,000 + \$30,000 + \$30,000)/5 = \$150,000/5 = \$30,000]. The depreciation for the equipment, based on straight line depreciation, will be \$20,000 [\$100,000/5 or \$100,000 × 0.20 = \$20,000]. The difference between the two will produce a net income for the government from the investment, after depreciation, of \$10,000 [\$30,000 - \$20,000]. We can now use this information to obtain the ARR by dividing the average (net) income by the investment, as follows:

$$\begin{aligned} ARR &= \text{Net Income}/I_0 \\ &= (\$10{,}000)/\$100{,}000 \\ &= 0.10 \end{aligned}$$

which will be 10 percent.

In the example above, we assumed that there is no salvage value but if there is a salvage value at the end of the useful life of the project, or for the time the government wants to use the equipment, we can easily incorporate it in the expression in Equation 6.7, as shown below:

$$ARR = \text{Net Income}/(I_0 + SV) \tag{6.13}$$

where SV is the salvage value, and the rest of the terms are the same as before. Note that we added the salvage value, instead of subtracting it, because the salvage value in ARR represents the residual value of the asset at the end of its useful life, which is considered part of total return.

Let us now suppose that the equipment has a salvage value of $15,000, the ARR for the investment will, therefore, be 8.7 percent. That is,

$$\begin{aligned} ARR &= \text{Net Income}/(I_0 + SV) \\ &= \$10{,}000/(\$100{,}000 + \$15{,}000) \\ &= 0.087 \end{aligned}$$

which is 8.7 percent.

6.4.4 Some Common Concerns with BCA

Despite its long history and use, there are several problems inherent in benefit-cost analysis, besides selecting an appropriate discount rate. The first and foremost is the requirement that the costs and benefits are expressed in precise dollar terms to make an easy comparison of the alternatives. The problem with this is that it is not always possible to find the dollar value of costs and benefits. However, the problem can be considerably overcome with surrogate or proxy variables and, where possible, with imputed or shadow prices for costs and benefits (Khan and Farias, 1996). Besides surrogates or proxy variables, when the when the dollar values of costs and benefits are not available, one can also use cost-effectiveness analysis, which does not require one to express the costs and benefits, especially the benefits in precise dollar terms; they can be expressed in their original units (Cellini and Kee, 2010).

Another frequent problem in benefit-cost analysis is that the projects being compared may not have identical life spans, unlike the example we discussed above, which can make comparison difficult. One way to overcome the problem would be to take a number of short-lived projects that are similar and compare them against several larger projects such that they would produce an approximate common time (Aronson and Schwartz, 1981)[4].

While it is generally assumed that the costs and benefits associated with a project are known with certainty, it is quite possible that there will be risks and uncertainties associated with them, in which case they must be expressed in terms of probabilities and their present value computations must also reflect this (Staehr, 2006). Perhaps the real challenge in benefit-cost analysis, as noted earlier, is determining the discount rate because what rate one would use can have a significant effect on the selection of a project (Mikesell, 1977). This is where IRR has an advantage in that the rate is determined "objectively" rather than by the decision makers which may explain why it is preferred by private firms and businesses (although in recent years there has been a shift toward net present value). In general, low discount rates tend to make a project more attractive than high discount rates, because at lower rates the consumers vis-à-vis the public will be more willing to give up their current consumption in favor of consumption in the future. The opposite is true when the rates are higher.

6.5 Life-Cycle Costing

Earlier in our discussion of differential cost analysis as well as benefit-cost analysis, we compared two alternatives, although we could have compared multiple alternatives, to determine the best course of action. Life Cycle Costing (LCC), and to an extent the differential cost analysis, is an extension of benefit-cost analysis in that it takes into consideration the total cost of an asset, from the initial cost of acquisition to all subsequent costs the asset will incur during its entire life span until it is replaced, sold, or no longer in use (US Department of Transportation, 2002). In other words, it takes into consideration all possible costs, including those that are hidden and not readily apparent at the time of acquisition. Formally, it can be defined as the total cost of an asset, including the costs of acquisition, operation, and maintenance (Lee, 1996). As a concept, life-cycle costing is nothing new; it was introduced by the US Logistics Management Institute in 1965, as part of defense-related expenditure analysis (US LMI, 1965). This was followed by a number of publications by the Defense

Department on the subject in the 1970s and 1980s. Today, it is widely used by all levels of government as well as by various firms and businesses.

6.5.1 Stages of Life Cycle

All physical assets, in particular machines, tools, equipment, vehicles, and buildings, go through several stages during their life span that begin with their acquisition, construction, or installation and end when they are no longer in use called the physical life of an asset. The stages typically begin with planning and development, followed by acquisition and break-in, growth, maturity, and decline (Figure 6.1). They are most productive during their maturity when they are operating at their fullest capacity. There is a direct relationship between the physical life of assets and how they are maintained: assets that are not maintained properly will deteriorate faster than those that are maintained properly and, as such, will cost an organization more over the longer term.

Assets also have an economic life that is directly related to the cost of ownership and the cost of operation. The cost of ownership typically includes the cost of owning an asset as well as its operating cost, plus any cost of disposal when it is no longer worthwhile to keep. In general, the cost of ownership tends to decrease as the operating cost begins to increase with time. Economic life represents the time when the two become equal.

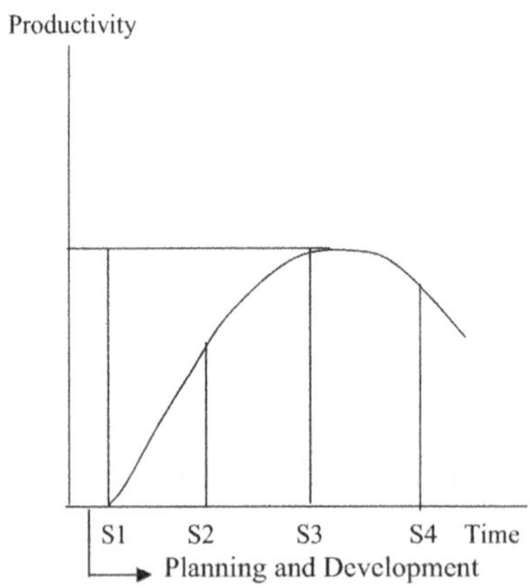

S1 = Acquisition S2 = Growth S3 = Maturity S4 = Decline

Figure 6.1 Physical life of an asset

Put differently, when the operating cost of an asset exceeds the cost of ownership, it costs an organization more to operate the asset than to own it. The opposite is true when the cost of ownership exceeds the operating cost. Ideally, an asset should be replaced before it reaches the end of its economic life (Douglas, 1978).

From a cost perspective, the life cycle has a direct cost effect on an organization. During the early years of an asset's life, the net return from operation is usually positive (assuming the operation has costs as well as benefits that can be measured in dollar or related terms) which continues to grow until maturity, at which point it becomes maximum and then begins to decline with age. This relationship between net return and the physical life of an asset is commonly known as profit life (Gransberg et al. 2006).

6.5.2 Life Cycle Costing Process

Life-cycle costing requires that before an asset is acquired or installed, one performs a cost analysis over the life span of the asset. Four sets of costs are generally involved in this process: (1) cost of initial investment, (2) operating costs, (3) maintenance costs, and (4) replacement costs. There are also preliminary costs that an organization will incur before an investment decision is made, which must be included in the cost calculations. This would include costs of planning, information gathering, and training personnel who will be operating the asset, and so forth. If the asset has a residual or salvage value at the end of its useful life it must also be included in the analysis. Like most economic decisions, the process begins with a clear statement of objectives, identifying alternatives (assets), gathering information, determining the life-cycle cost of each alternative, and estimating the payback period.

We can formally express the life-cycle cost of an asset, as follows:

$$LCC = C_0 + [\sum_{t=1}^{T} \frac{OC_t}{(1+i)^t} + \sum_{t=1}^{T} \frac{MC_t}{(1+i)^t} + \sum_{t=1}^{T} \frac{RC_t}{(1+i)^t}] - \frac{SV_T}{(1+i)^T} \tag{6.14}$$

$$= C_0 + \sum_{t=1}^{T} [\frac{OC_t}{(1+i)^t} + \frac{MC_t}{(1+i)^t} + \frac{RC_t}{(!+i)^t}] - \frac{SV_T}{(1+i)^T}$$

where LCC is the life cycle cost, C_0 is the initial cost, OC is the operating cost at time t, MC is the maintenance cost at time t, RC is the replacement cost at time t, SV_T is the salvage value at time T (for t = 1, 2, 3, ..., T), and *i* is the interest rate.

The initial investment costs include the full value of an asset at the time of its acquisition, construction (if it is a physical plant or building), and installation. The level of detail of the costs will depend on the nature of the asset. Obviously, the cost of constructing a building or a physical plant will be different from the cost of purchasing a utility vehicle, a garbage truck, a patrol car, or a large piece of equipment. Some assets may require assistance from a trained personnel or consultant, in which case the cost of consulting should be included in the initial costs of investment. Operating costs, as distinct from maintenance costs, discussed earlier, typically include the costs of utility and personnel such as custodial services. They are also called variable costs because they depend on the volume or quantity used. Ideally, only the costs directly associated with the operation should be included. Indirect costs should be included if it is possible to segregate them by cost items associated with the asset. Since these costs take place over the life span of the asset, it is important to discount them to obtain their present value.

Maintenance costs, which also include repair costs, are those needed for the upkeep of an asset. As noted earlier, well-maintained assets keep the operating costs low and lengthen their useful lives. Examples of maintenance costs are repairing a broken window or door, replacing a tire, repairing a leak in a roof, and so forth. Some maintenance costs are recurring, some are infrequent, and some are difficult to predict. Regular inspection of assets can minimize the likelihood of incurrence of repairs, especially those that are difficult to predict. Since maintenance must be done on a regular basis, they are often treated as annual costs. They can also be treated as fixed costs if an organization contracts out the service to a firm. As with operating costs, all maintenance costs should be discounted to their present value before they are included in the overall cost calculation.

Replacement costs include the costs of replacing an asset or a part of it in the future; they are anticipated expenditures that are required to maintain the operation of an asset. Replacement items usually have a shorter life than the life of the facility where they are installed such as a water heater or a boiler-burner for a heating system. It is expected that these items will fail at some future points in time and need to be replaced to keep the facility operational. As before, all replacement costs must be discounted to their present values before adding them to the life-cycle cost.

Finally, as discussed earlier, the residual or salvage value is the value an asset has at the end of its useful life. Another term that is used interchangeably with residual value is scrap value. Regardless of the term used, they represent the likely value of an asset at the end of its useful life. The value depends on the nature of the asset and the level of detail involved. From an accounting point of view, it depends on how an asset is depreciated.

To give an example, suppose that a government is planning to purchase a dump truck and is seeking bids from two vendors - A and B. Table 6.5 presents the life-cycle costs of the two vehicles. As the table shows, the bid

Table 6.5 Life cycle costs (with and without discounting)

Parameters	*Vendor A (Vehicle 1)*	*Vehicle 1 Discounted*[3,4]	*Vendor B (Vehicle 2)*	*Vehicle 2 Discounted*[5,6]
Bid cost	$90,000	$90,000	$100,000	$100,000
Annual usage	1,800 Hours	---	1,800 Hours	---
Useful life	10 Years	---	10 years	---
Operating costs[1]				
Labor cost	$450,000	$450,000	$450,000	$450,000
Fuel cost	$65,000	$65,000	$55,000	$55,000
Maintenance costs[2]				
Repair and maintenance	$30,000	$16,752[3]	$20,000	$11,168[5]
(Less) Resale value	$15,000	$8,376[4]	$25,000	$13,960[6]
Life-cycle cost	$620,000	$613,376	$600,000	$602,208

[1] Labor and fuel costs are usually not discounted
[2] Assuming a 6% discount rate; DF = 0.55839 (PV = $1/(1 + i)^1$ = $1/(1 + 0.06)^{10}$ = $1/(1.06)^{10}$ = 0.55839)
[3] ($30,000 × DF) = $30,000 × 0.55839 = $16,752
[4] (15,000 × DF) = $15,000 × 0.55839 = $8,376
[5] ($20,000 × DF) = $20,000 × 0.55839 = $11,168
[6] ($25,000 × DF) = ($25,000 × 0.55839 = $13,960

price for vehicle 1 (Vendor A) is $10,000 less than the price for vehicle 2 (Vendor B). Both vehicles have identical life spans of 10 years, and both are expected to operate 1,800 hours a year for each of the 10 years. However, the vehicles vary in terms of their costs of operation and maintenance as well as their resale value. It is these differences in operation and maintenance costs and the resale value that frequently contribute to the differences in life-cycle costs, when comparing multiple bids. The life-cycle cost of the two vehicles, obtained by adding all the costs minus the resale value, is higher for vehicle 1 (vendor A) by $20,000, even though the bid price for the vehicle was less than vehicle 2 (Vendor B). Since the life-cycle cost is much higher for vehicle 1, the government should go with vehicle 2 (Vendor B).

We can also apply Equation 6.11 directly to the example to determine the vendor preference for the government, as shown below:

$$LCC = C_0 + [\sum_{t=1}^{T} \frac{OC_t}{(1+i)^t} + \sum_{t=1}^{T} \frac{MC_t}{(1+i)^t} + \sum_{t=1}^{T} \frac{RC_t}{(1+i)^t}] - \frac{SV_T}{(1+i)^T}$$

$$= \$90,000 + [(\$450,000 + \$65,000) + \$16,752 + 0] - \$8,376$$

$$= (\$90,000 + \$531,752) - \$8,376$$

$$= \$621,752 - \$8,376$$

$$= \$613,376$$

for vendor A, and

$$LCC = C_0 + [\sum_{t=1}^{T} \frac{OC_t}{(1+i)^t} + \sum_{t=1}^{T} \frac{MC_t}{(1+i)^t} + \sum_{t=1}^{T} \frac{RC_t}{(1+i)^t}] - \frac{SV_T}{(1+i)^T}$$

$$= \$100{,}000 + [(\$450{,}000 + \$55{,}000) + \$11{,}168 + 0] - \$13{,}960$$

$$= (\$90{,}000 + \$516{,}168) - \$13{,}960$$

$$= \$621{,}752 - \$8{,}376$$

$$= \$616{,}168 - \$8{,}376$$

$$= \$602{,}208$$

for vendor B.

Note that the labor and fuels costs, which make up the operating costs in the example, were not discounted because these costs usually are not discounted. As before, since it will cost the government \$11,168 more if it goes with vendor A, it should go with vendor B. Keep in mind that ideally the difference should be much larger than what we have in the example to make a sound financial decision, especially if it involves a large, costly item, with a life span of several years.

While life-cycle costing serves as a valuable tool for an organization when making a financial decision, whether to acquire an asset or replace an existing one, it has important requirements that need to be addressed before applying the tool. First and foremost is the data requirement; the organization must have detailed information on all the costs an asset will incur during its life span. Secondly, the costs must be discounted to determine their present value, as we did in the current example. Thirdly, the costs of operation, maintenance over the life span of an asset, and its resale value are essentially estimates, not actual values. Therefore, failing to correctly estimate these costs can have a significant impact on the decision. Finally, in the case of government, since they are required by law to use bids when purchasing or acquiring an asset, the bid process must be carefully observed to ensure full compliance with the legal procedures for vendor selection, opening bids, and awarding contracts.

6.6 Chapter Summary

Good, effective decision making requires that one must compare alternatives to determine the best course of action. There are a wide range of methods that can be used to analyze the costs a decision will produce for an organization. This chapter has presented four methods that are frequently used in cost analysis: differential cost analysis, buy or lease, benefit-cost analysis, and life-cycle costing. Like break-even analysis, differential cost analysis is used to determine an appropriate course of action, based on cost, revenue, and output level of an activity, but the two are not quite the same. The advantage of using differential cost analysis, as opposed to break-even analysis, is that it gives the decision makers an opportunity to evaluate the viability of an alternative decision against the existing condition. As to the decision to buy or lease, much depends on the needs of the organization, the purpose for which an asset will be used, and the savings it will produce for the organization in the long term. The long-term effect of the decision also means that it must consider the time value of money. In addition to the above, the chapter has also presented two other methods frequently used in cost analysis: benefit-cost analysis and life-cycle costing. While both are important as analytical tools for decision making, benefit-cost analysis has a long history of use and has been extensively used in all types of organizations, including government. Finally, life-cycle costing provides useful information about the costs an asset will produce for an organization over its life span.

6.7 Review Questions

6.1 What is differential-cost analysis and how does it differ from break-even analysis? What are some of its advantages and disadvantages?

6.2 Suppose that a large metropolitan government wants to upgrade its convention center so it can hold more activities and attract more visitors to the city. The government projects that its revenue from the upgrade will increase by $1.5 million. The city will incur the following costs to upgrade the center: 1. Direct Labor: $225,000, 2. Direct Materials: $150,000, 3. Overhead: $50,000, 4. Promotion: $25,000, 5. Miscellaneous other expenses: $50,000. What would be the differential cost/revenue for the government?

6.3 Why is it important for a government to weigh the pros and cons of a cost decision before purchasing or acquiring an item? What are the advantages of leasing, as opposed to buying? What role does time value of money play in these decisions?

6.4 A local community hospital needs a state-of-the art X-Ray machine to replace the one it has been using for several years. The hospital has the option to buy or lease the equipment. If the hospital decides to buy the equipment, it will cost $125,000; if it decides to lease, the rental cost will be $15,000 per year. If purchased, there is a salvage value of $25,000 at the end of the asset's productive life. There is also a maintenance cost of $3,000 if the equipment is purchased. The equipment has a useful life of seven years. Calculate the PV of ownership and indicate if the hospital should buy or lease. (Use a discount rate of 5 percent)

6.5 What is a discount rate? What role does it play in benefit-cost analysis? What are the differences between benefit-cost ratio, net present value, and internal rate of return? Under what circumstances would you use one, as opposed to the others? What are some of the limitations of benefit-cost analysis?

6.6 A government is evaluating two investment projects, each with one-time cost of $1 million and a life span of six years. The estimated benefits for the projects are as follows:

Project A	*Project B*
Cost: $1,000,000 (one time)	Cost: $1,000,000 (one time)
Benefit stream:	Benefit stream:
Year 1: $350,000	Year 1: $375,000
Year 2: $425,000	Year 2: $425,000
Year 3: $575,000	Year 3: $530,000
Year 4: $925,000	Year 4: $750,000
Year 5: $850,000	Year 5: $825,000
Year 6: $750,000	Year 6: $950,000

Assuming it will use net present value, which project should the government select? Why? Would the decision be different if it were to use a discounted benefit-cost ratio? (Use a discount rate of 6.0 percent)

6.7 What is accounting rate of return? How does it differ from the conventional discount rate? Would the results be different for Problem 6.6, if we had used an accounting rate of return? How?

6.8 What is a life-cycle cost? How is it different from conventional costs? What are the stages of a life-cycle cost? Discuss with an example.

6.9 Suppose that the Public Works Department of a mid-sized local government is planning to buy an electric motor and receives bids from three vendors. The following provides summary information about the motor features and the bids:

Parameters	*Vendor A (Motor A)*	*Vendor B (Motor B)*	*Vendor C (Motor C)*
Bid Price (Cost)	$1,000	$1,500	$1,200
Duty Cycle Duty Cycle/Year	1,000 Hours	1,000 Hours	1,000 Hours
Life Cycle	10 years	10 Years	10 Years
Energy Consumption/KWh	20 KWh	12 KWh	15 KWh
Cost per KWh	$0.10	$0.10	$0.10

a. Given the information above and assuming no rescale value,

   i. Calculate the energy cost of each motor.
   ii. Calculate the life-cycle cost of each motor.
   iii. Determine the vendor the government should accept the bid from and explain why?

b. Would the decision be different if the motors have the following resale values: Motor A = \$100, Motor B = \$200, and Motor C = \$150? [Hint: the energy cost can be computed in the following way: Energy Consumption/kWh × Energy Cost/kWh x Duty Cycle over the Useful Life = $20 \times \$0.10 \times (1{,}000 \times 10) = \$20{,}000_A$; Life-Cycle Cost = Bid Cost + Energy Cost.

6.10 A county-run hospital that runs several clinics facing a period of low demand and considering closing down three of its clinics temporarily or operate at below capacity. Using hypothetical data, determine the break-even number of patients for each clinic to remain financially viable.

6.11 A State Technology Department needs to equip its field offices with new laptops and tablets for data collection and communication. The state has the choice to buy or lease. Using hypothetical data, determine the best option for the department.

Notes

1 While the present value, PV, measures the current value of a future stream of costs and returns, the future value (FV) measures the value a current investment will produce at some point in time. The calculation of future value (FV) is given by the expression:

$$FV = PV(1+r)^t \tag{1}$$

Thus, if we invest \$95.24 today at a five percent rate of interest (return), it will produce exactly \$100 a year from now; that is, $FV_{t+1} = \$95.24(1 + 0.05)^1 = \$100$, which is the FV of \$95.24 a year from now, t+1. Similarly, if we invest \$90.70 today at 5 percent rate of interest, it will produce \$100 two years from now; that is, $FV_{t+2} = \$90.70(1 + 0.05)^2 = \$90.70(1.1025) \approx \$100$, which is the FV value of \$90.70 two years from now, t = 2, and so forth.

2 If costs are incurred over time (for multiple periods), Equation 6.5 will become

$$NPV = \sum_{t=0}^{T} \frac{B_t}{(1+i)^t} - \sum_{t=0}^{T} \frac{C_t}{(1+i)^t} \tag{2}$$

the same as Equation 6.6. And if there is a Salvage Value (SV) at the end of the useful life of a project, then Equation (2) will become

$$NPV = [\sum_{t=0}^{T} \frac{B_t}{(1+i)^t} - \frac{SV_T}{(1+i)^T}] - \sum_{t=0}^{T} \frac{C_t}{(1+i)^t} \tag{3}$$

3 Several methods can be used for discounting depending on the purpose for which they will be used, such as opportunity cost of capital, marginal rate of time preference, and social rate of time preference, among others. Opportunity cost of capital means the return a given investment would have earned from an alternative (investment), as opposed to the current investment. Marginal rate of time preference means the rate at which the gain one realizes from the consumption or use of a dollar at the margin today is equal to the gain one will realize from a marginal dollar next year, or year after next, and so forth. Social rate of time preference, which is the opposite of marginal rate of time preference in that it measures the valuation society, not an individual, places on its current consumption, as opposed to consumption in the future. For details, see Gramlich (1981).

4 To give an example, suppose that we have two comparable projects, X with a life of 3 three years and Y with a life of 4 years. Together, they produce a common life of 12 years; that is. If Project X is repeated 4 times and Project Y is repeated 3 times, both will produce equal useful lives. Next, we find the NPV for each project and select the one with the higher NPV. The term commonly used to describe this approach is replacement chain method, also known as common-life approach.

References

Aronson, R.J. and Schwartz, E. (1981). Capital budgeting, in R.J. Aronson and E. Schwartz (eds), *Management policies in local government finance*. Washington, DC: ICMA, 433–457.

Cellini, S.R. and Kee, J.E. (2010). Cost-effectiveness and cost-benefit analysis, in J.S. Wholey, H.P. Hatry, and K.E. Newcomer (eds) *Handbook of practical program evaluation*. 3rd Edition. New York: Jossey-Bass, 493–530.

Douglas, J. (1978). Equipment costs by current methods. *Journal of Construction Division, ASCE*, 104(C02): 191–225.

Gramlich, E.M. (1981). *Benefit-cost analysis of government programs*. Englewood Cliffs, NJ: Prentice-Hall.

Gransberg, D., Popescu, R., and Ryan, R. (2006). *Construction equipment management for engineers, estimators, and owners*. Boca Raton, FL: Taylor & Francis.

Khan, A. and Farias, C. (1996). Benefit-cost analysis, in J.M. Shafritz (ed.) *The international encyclopedia of public policy and administration*. New York: Henry-Holt and Company, 173–180.

Lee, R.C. (1996). Life-cycle costing, in J. Rabin et al. (eds) *Budgeting: Formulation and execution*. Athens, GA: Carl Vinson Institute of Government, University of Georgia, Chapter 41: 420–423.

Mikesell, R.F. (1977). *The rate of discount for evaluating public projects*. Washington, DC: American Enterprise Institute for Studies in Public Policy.

Staehr, K. (2006). *Risk and uncertainty in cost-benefit analysis*. Denmark, Copenhagen: Institute for Miljovurdering.

Thompson, M.S. (1982). *Benefit-cost analysis for program evaluation*. Beverly Hills, CA: Sage Publications.

US Department of Transportation. (2002). *Life cycle cost analysis primer*. Office of Asset Management. U.S. Department of Transportation.

US Logistics Management Institute (LMI). (1965). *Life-cycle costing in equipment procurement*. Washington, DC: US Logistics Management Institute.

Part II

Cost Accounting Methods

- Job Costing
- Contract Costing
- Process Costing
- Cost Allocation
- Activity-Based Costing

DOI: 10.4324/9781003486091-8

Part II

Computational Methods

7 Job Costing

7.1 Introduction

All costs boil down to three things: materials, labor, and overhead. A responsible manager must know how to keep track of these costs, as they accumulate.[1] In the private sector, managers keep track of their costs by assigning them to an individual consumer, a cost unit, or to a unit of goods produced. When costs are assigned to an individual consumer, a cost unit, or to a unit of goods produced, it is called unit costing. Unit costing is a useful method when applied to goods that are divisible and there is no free-rider problem such that one can trace the costs to an individual costing unit. Unfortunately, for most public goods, except for those that are provided in a business-like manner, it is difficult to determine the exact quantity of the goods individuals consume. As a result, public organizations often maintain cost information based on a specific job, a good, or a service, rather than on a per capita or per unit basis, although the latter is recognized in cost calculations, where possible. Job costing as well as some of the other costing methods discussed in this and the next few chapters are part of an accounting system that can effectively deal with it.

This chapter begins with a brief discussion of cost accounting, as a system, followed by a detailed discussion of job costing, a method frequently used in cost and managerial accounting in government and non-profit organizations. It also discusses two other methods that are frequently discussed alongside job costing: variable costing, absorption costing. The chapter concludes with a brief discussion of batch costing, as an extension of job costing.

7.2 Cost Accounting System

All organizations have a cost accounting system of one form or another. In a classic work on cost accounting, Thomas Curley, Jr. (1965) emphasized

DOI: 10.4324/9781003486091-9

the need to understand a cost accounting system as the first step before carrying out any accounting activities. Since the activities are interrelated in some fashion, a basic understanding of a cost accounting system can help an organization determine what methods to use, when to use them, and how best to use them. In its bare essence, a cost accounting system deals with methods of keeping track of costs as they accumulate. In other words, it deals with a set of methods organizations can use to track, analyze, and report costs to help improve management operations.

Formally, we can think of a cost accounting system as a process, consisting of a number of distinct but interrelated activities.[2] The activities typically include recording costs, as they accumulate, determining the costs of operation (direct labor, direct materials, and overheads), known as cost measurement, assigning costs to a specific job, activity, or process, and finally allocating them using established methods or some rational basis to ensure control and improve performance. The systems can range from simple rules of thumb approaches to more structured and complex methods. Whether it is simple or complex, to be effective, the system needs to be able to meet the needs of an organization.

Several kinds of methods have been developed over the years, as part of cost accounting systems that can be used depending on the needs of an organization. Two of the methods with a long history of use are job costing and process costing. Other methods that have become part of cost accounting systems in recent years are activity-based costing, target costing, standard costing, and a host of related systems such as variable costing, absorption costing, and so forth. With time, additional systems will be developed, or existing methods will be refined to meet the changing needs of an organization. This chapter focuses primarily on job costing.

7.3 Job Costing

Job costing is an accounting method that traces costs to a specific job, service, or activity. Tracing costs to a specific job makes it possible for an organization to determine the costs it will accumulate separately for materials, labor, and overhead. When materials and labor used in a job can be directly traced to it, as defined earlier, they are called direct materials and direct labor. Indirect materials and labor that cannot be directly traced to a job are generally treated as overheads. Job costing begins when an operating department receives instructions from the authority responsible to begin the work on a job. During this stage, materials are issued, labor is expended, and overheads are incurred. Three things must take place to complete the process: One, a number of source documents must be prepared, two, the information must be entered into a journal, and three, the overhead rate must be determined.

7.3.1 Prepare the Source Documents

Source documents are materials used to accumulate the costs for an individual job. The most frequently used source document is the job cost sheet, prepared primarily to accumulate and summarize cost information on direct materials, direct labor, and overhead. A typical job cost sheet includes the following information: job identification number, job description, beginning and completion dates, and costs of materials, labor, and overhead. The actual entries are made from materials requisition forms, labor cost sheets, and from other evidence of costs. The material requisition form provides a detailed account of the type and quantity of materials that are to be drawn from a central location such as a central warehouse and the job to which the materials are to be charged. The labor cost sheet specifies the number of hours the labor worked, the rate at which the labor was paid, and the total cost of the labor used. Both the requisition form and the labor cost sheet serve as a means for controlling the flow of materials and labor into the job completion process; in particular, for making entries into the job cost sheet.

Table 7.1 presents an example of a simple job cost sheet for street repair for a small local government. According to the table, it cost the government $220,000 in total repair, including $45,000 in direct materials, $125,000 in direct labor, and $50,000 in overheads, of which $17,500 in indirect

Table 7.1 A job cost sheet for street Repair

Summary Information	
Job summary:	
Responsible Department	: Public Works (PW)
Job type/category	: Street repair
Job location	: 19th Street and Flint Avenue
Job/Requisition number	: 037-PW
Related information:	
Job narrative/description	: Requiring asphalt/concrete, and levelling
Date started	January 1, 20XX :
Date completed	January 31, 20XX
Cost Summary (Actual Cost)	
Direct materials	$ 45,000
Direct labor	$125,000
Overhead ($17,500/labor + $32,500 / materials)	$50,000
Total cost:	$220,000

(overhead) labor and $32,500 in indirect (overhead) materials. The table also provides information on the exact nature of the job, the beginning and completion dates, the job requisition number, and the department responsible for the job.

As noted earlier, job costing does not begin until the operating department receives notification that a service order has been issued for the job. Once the direct materials have been issued and the labor costs identified, the operating department makes entries into the job cost sheet charging the job noted on the sheet with the costs of materials and labor used. When the job is completed, the total costs of materials, labor, and the overheads are summarized and presented on the sheet.

7.3.2 Journalize the Information

As the information on materials, labor, and overhead costs becomes available, they are entered into a journal called the book of initial entry. The purpose of journalizing the entries is to show the flow of costs as they accumulate. Several basic transactions are recorded in a journal such as the purchase of materials, issuance of direct and indirect materials, accrual of direct and indirect labor, payment of labor, incurrence of overheads other than materials and labor, and so on. However, before discussing how to journalize the information, let us take a few seconds to discuss what journalizing is and how to journalize. Journalizing is an accounting activity where the accountants, in particular bookkeepers, post (record) the financial transactions in a journal, called the book of initial entry. The procedure commonly used for this purpose is called double-entry accounting.

7.3.2.1 Double-Entry Accounting

One of the oldest systems of accounting, double-entry accounting derives its name from an accounting procedure in which a transaction is recorded as two accounts – a debit account and a credit account. The advantage of using a double-entry accounting system, as opposed to a single-entry accounting system, is that by recording a transaction on both sides, it allows for greater accuracy in recording transactions. The recording typically resembles the letter T because it has two sides, a left side used for the debit account, and a right side used for the credit account. Because of this apparent resemblance with the letter T, the double-entry accounting is often called T-accounting, and the accounts are called T accounts, as shown below:

Debit	Credit
(Left)	(Right)

There is no mathematical justification as to why the debit account should appear on the left and the credit account should appear on the right. It is a convention, more than anything else. In general, when assets are acquired, they are posted on the debit side and liabilities on the credit side of an accounting journal, called the book of initial entry. Since costs in general are considered a liability, any increase in costs is recorded on the credit side. By the same token, any decrease in costs is recorded on the debit side since it represents a decrease in liability.

Convention dictates that when liabilities are incurred by an organization, which should also apply to the government, they should be recognized as such, and vouchers should be issued before paying the liabilities in cash. Therefore, the journal entries must include a recognition of liability when vouchers are issued and a payment of liability when cash payments are made (Lynn and Norville, 1984). The following shows a typical T-account:

Debit	Credit
↑ Asset	↓ Asset

Debit	Credit
↓ Liability	↑ Liability

The greatest advantage of a double-entry accounting system is that the two sides of the account must be equal, meaning that the entries must be balanced. Thus, if a government purchases a vehicle, it will reflect an increase in its asset position; as such, it should be debited. At the same time, it will also increase the liability of the government if it will have to pay for the vehicle using credit or decrease its asset position if it will have to pay using cash, which is an asset and, therefore, it should be credited. If the vehicle is paid-in-full during the accounting period, the two sides should even out. On the other hand, if the payment is not made in full, the difference will appear as "balance" on the liability side of the ledger, known as the book of final entry.

To illustrate how it applies to job costing, let us go back to the street repair problem. Suppose that the central warehouse of the government purchases materials in the amount of \$60,000, which includes \$45,000 in direct and \$15,000 in indirect materials, and pays for them in cash. It is not unusual for a warehouse to have these materials in its inventory, in which case the journal entry would recognize them as a simple inventory account with no outstanding obligation or payment of liability to make.

Assume the scenario that the government does not have the materials in its inventory and that the warehouse had to purchase them. When materials are acquired, they add to the asset position of the government and, as such, will be debited. In government, as in the private sector, all transactions (except for petty cash transactions) require that vouchers be issued before making any payments. Since vouchers are liabilities, any increase in vouchers will increase the liability and will be credited. Likewise, when vouchers are paid, they will decrease the liability position for vouchers and will be debited. Finally, when cash payments are made it will decrease the asset position of the government since cash is an asset and, as such, will be credited.

7.3.2.2 Work-in-Process Account

In general, when materials are issued for a job, they are recorded in an account, called Work-in-Process (WIP), which essentially is an inventory account, indicating the goods and services in the production or delivery process that have not been completed yet.[3] In other words, WIP accounts include materials and partially completed products that are at various stages of production. They do not generally include raw materials at the beginning of a production cycle, or inventory at the end of the production cycle. Indirect materials, on the other hand, are recorded in the overheads account because all costs associated with a job, except for direct materials and labor, are accumulated in this account. It should be worth noting that work-in-process accounts can be prepared at the beginning of a job, or as soon as labor and materials have been issued, or at any time during the accounting period.

The journal entries for the WIP account for direct, as well as for indirect materials (Table 7.1), based on the amount issued and applying the rules for recording transactions in a double-entry or T-accounts, can be presented, as follows:

	Debit	Credit
Beginning WIP, January 1		
1. WIP Materials (Direct)	45,000	
Overhead for Materials (Indirect)	32,500	
Vouchers payable		77,500
•To record purchase of materials		

	Debit	Credit
2. Vouchers Payable for Materials (Direct)	45,000	
Vouchers Payable for Materials (Indirect)	32,500	
Cash		77,500
•To record payment of materials		

Similarly, the direct labor costs accumulated for the job are recorded in the WIP account as debit and the indirect labor costs (Table 7. 1) are debited to the overheads account. As before, to pay for the labor, vouchers must be issued (recognition of liability) and paid out in cash (payment of liability). The entries for the labor cost transactions can thus be shown as

	Debit	Credit
1. WIP Labor (Direct)	125,000	
Overhead for Labor (Indirect)	17,500	
Vouchers payable		142,500
•To record the costs of labor		

	Debit	Credit
2. Vouchers Payable for Labor (Direct)	125,000	
Vouchers Payable for Overhead Labor (Indirect)	17,500	
Cash		142,500
•To record payment of labor		
Ending WIP, January 31		

The process can be continued until every single transaction related to the job is exhausted. Once the journal entries are completed, they are posted onto a ledger (not shown here). A ledger, as noted earlier, is a group of accounts, where the data from the journal entries are recorded and summarized by accounts. In cost accounting, they are commonly known as cost ledgers, which include a principal ledger and a group of subsidiary ledgers. The principal ledger includes general information on various cost accounts, while the subsidiary ledgers include detailed information on these accounts which allows an organization to effectively control its financial information. For instance, in the current example, the job cost sheet will serve as the subsidiary ledger containing the details for the WIP general ledger accounts. It is worth noting that double-entry accounting is not required for cost accounting but has become standard practice because it helps prepare cost journals, as well as ledgers, for reporting purposes, and serves as an instrument for checking reporting errors.

7.3.3 Determine the Overhead Rate

As noted previously, overhead costs are indirect costs that cannot be directly attributed to a specific job. Some overheads, especially those related to utilities, are not always known until the end of a given period. Obviously, once a job is completed, we can easily determine the overhead cost by subtracting the direct cost from the total cost of an operation; that is. TC - DC = OC, where TC is the total cost, DC is the direct cost, and OC is the indirect or overhead cost. For instance, if the total cost of a job is $2.5 million and the costs of direct labor and materials are $2 million, the overhead cost for the operation will be $0.5 million ($2.5 million - $2 million = 0.5 million). And we can repeat the process for overheads for labor and materials.

However, rather than holding the completed job in an inventory until all costs can be traced to it, it may be necessary to develop a system of allocating overhead costs to a job on a predetermined basis. This is where the overhead rate becomes useful, as it can help an organization understand the proportion of overhead costs relative to direct costs. Firms and businesses often use it to determine the efficiency of an operation. In general, the lower the overhead rate, the higher the efficiency. There are different ways to calculate the overhead rate, depending on the purpose for which it is used. The simplest way to calculate the rate is by dividing total overhead costs by an appropriate allocation base such as direct labor hours, direct materials costs, and so forth.

The following provides the expression for calculating a predetermined overhead rate for labor:

$$OR = \frac{TOC}{DLH_i} \tag{7.1}$$

where OR is the overhead rate, TOC is the total overhead cost for the organization, and DLH_i is the direct labor hours for the *i*th job (i = 1,2,3, …, n).

It is worth noting that when the actual data on overhead costs and indirect labor are not available one can use estimates of these costs, using Equation 7.1, where the numerator in Equation 7.1 represents the estimated total overhead costs and the denominator the estimated total direct labor hours. To give an example, suppose that our government in the street repair example has a total overhead cost and total direct labor hours for all street repairs for the year, including the current repair, of $3.5 million and 100,000 hours, respectively. Therefore, its predetermined overhead rate per direct labor hour for the year, based on the expression above, will be $35 an hour, as shown below:

$$OR = \frac{TOC}{DLH}$$

$$= \frac{\$3,500,000}{100,000}$$

$$= \$35$$

We can now use this information to determine the overhead cost of labor for the street repair problem. To do so, let us suppose that our street repair job requires a total of 500 hours of indirect labor, plus indirect expenses such as accidental insurance, support personnel, utility expenses, vehicle insurance, and repair and maintenance. The total overhead cost of labor, based on the overhead rate of \$35 an hour, will be \$17,500; that is, 500 x \$35 = \$17,500 which is what we had for overhead labor (Table 7.1). Next, we need to determine the overhead cost for materials. Let us assume that the overhead rate is based on the total square footage for all repairs for the government, which is \$5.20 per square foot. Assume further that the square footage of the street repair in our example is 6,250. The total overhead cost for materials will therefore be \$32,500; that is, \$6,250 x \$5.20 = \$32,500 (Table 7.1).

Since the selection of a predetermined rate requires that estimates be used for the numerator (total overhead cost), practitioners often use a rule of thumb approach to determine this rate by taking the ratio of an agency budget to the total budget of a government (Kelly, 1984). For instance, if an agency has an annual budget of \$2,382,500 that is approximately 5 percent of the total budget of the government, the overhead rate will also be 5 percent and the overhead allocation for the agency will be \$119,125 (\$2,382,500 × 0.05 = \$119,125). The same procedure can also be used to allocate the overhead costs for every agency operation in the government.

7.3.3.1 Estimating the Overhead Cost

While the rule-of-thumb approach suggested above is simple, there is a problem with it in that if the agency budget constitutes an unusually large (or small) fraction of the total budget, it may over- or underestimate the overhead allocation. Additionally, when money is frequently transferred between funds, or from a higher-level government to a lower-level government, a common practice in government, it may misrepresent the overhead allocation by the amount of the transfer. The alternative would be to remove the effects of interfund transfers before the method can be used, which can be a time-consuming process. The general position taken here for the predetermined rate is that overheads should be allocated on the basis of the factors or activities that cause these costs. In other words, the more an activity causes an overhead, the higher the cost that should be charged to it.

Also, there is a problem with the expressions in Equation 7.1, although it is easier to use, in that we assumed that we have the information on total overhead cost. What if we do not have the overhead rate? In that case, we can directly estimate the cost using the methods we discussed earlier, especially the least square method. The following shows the regression equation for estimating the overhead cost:

$$TOC = a + bX \tag{7.2}$$

where TOC is total overhead cost, a is the estimated fixed overhead cost, b is the estimated variable overhead cost per unit of cost allocation base, which is the direct labor in this case, and X is the total amount of the allocation base (the amount direct labor). Once we have estimated TOC, we can use it to obtain the overhead rate for labor as well as for materials in the same fashion.

7.3.3.2 Multiple Overhead Rates

Organizations often use more than one predetermined overhead rate to apply overhead costs to jobs. For instance, a government may use a different rate for each job. This may be more complex and demanding on time than using a single predetermined rate, but it is more accurate, since it reflects the differences in the nature of jobs that organizations perform. For instance, in the case of a job that is relatively labor intensive, its overhead cost may be based on direct labor hours, as opposed to a job that is more capital intensive and based on machine hours.

7.4 Multiple Jobs

Up to this point, we looked at a single job: a single street repair. In reality, most governments undertake multiple jobs. In other words, instead of a single street repair, there would be multiple street repairs at different parts of the jurisdiction that the government plans to undertake at the same time or at different times of the year. But the process will be the same in that for each job (1) source documents must be prepared, (2) assignments of direct labor, direct materials, and overhead must be journalized, and (3) overhead rates must be determined.

To give an example, let us say that the government in our example plans to undertake three street repair jobs – Repair 1, Repair 2, and Repair 3. Thus, for each job, the government will need to prepare a separate job cost sheet and a final job cost sheet for all three jobs. Figure 7.1 shows the costs, as they accumulate for each job, and a job-cost sheet for all three jobs.

Table 7.2 shows the actual costs of individual jobs as well as the total cost of all three jobs. As the table shows, Job 2 appears to cost more than the other two, since it uses more direct and indirect materials than Jobs 1 and 3, which is normal because jobs can vary in size and resource use

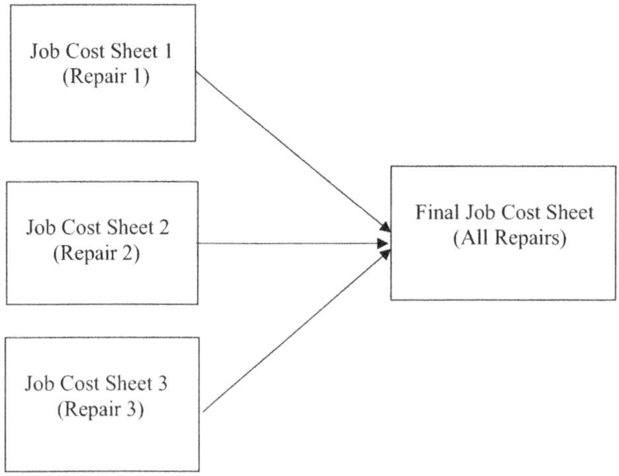

Figure 7.1 Multiple jobs and cost accumulation

Table 7.2 A job-cost sheet for three street repairs

Cost Breakdown	*Job 1 Street Repair 1 ($)*	*Job 2 Street Repair 2 ($)*	*Job 3 Street Repair 3 ($)*
Direct materials	45,000	175,000	50,000
Direct labor	125,000	100,000	170,000
Overhead labor	17,500	25,000	40,000
Overhead materials	32,500	50,000	20,000
Total cost	220,000	350,000	280,000

within the same department or unit of an organization. In accounting terms, one would consider Table 7.2 as the subsidiary ledger since it includes the job cost sheets for all three jobs, showing the costs of direct materials, direct labor, and overheads for each job.

As with the single job, once a decision has been made to undertake the jobs, the process requires that labor, materials, and overhead issued are recorded on a job cost sheet for each job until all the jobs are completed and a final job cost sheet is prepared. Figure 7.2 shows the three jobs in terms of direct labor, direct materials, overheads, and their corresponding WIP accounts, and when the jobs are all completed.

Finally, Table 7.3 shows the WIP accounts for the jobs in process (Jobs 1 and 2) and the job that has been completed (Job 3). In accounting terms,

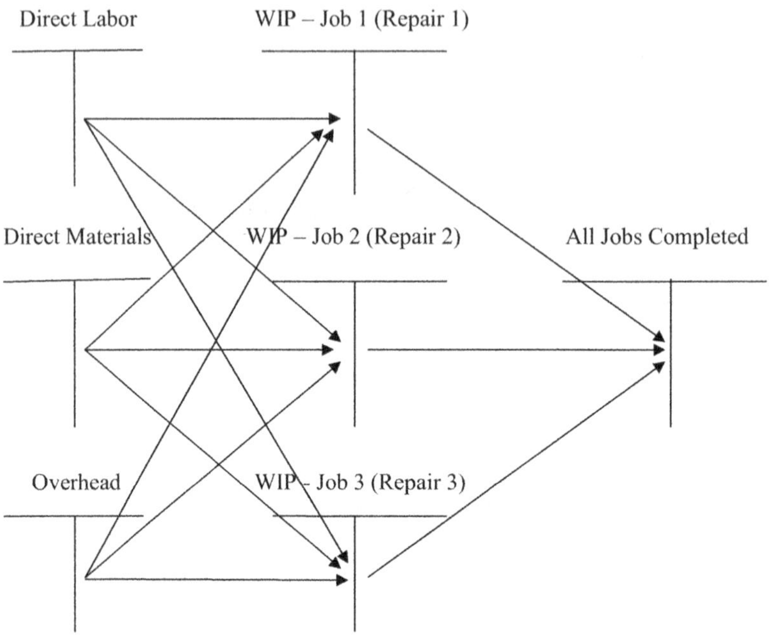

Figure 7.2 Journalizing the cost transactions for multiple jobs

Table 7.3 WIP accounts for the three street repairs

Work-in-Process	*Cost ($)*	*Completed*	*Cost ($)*
Job 1 – Street Repair 1	220,000	Job 3 – Street Repair 3	280,000
Job 2 – Street Repair 3	350,000		
Total cost	570,000		

Table 3 is the general ledger since it summarizes the states of job completion, jobs in process and the job that has been completed. It should be worth noting that journalizing the information for job costing also applies to all cost accounting methods – process costing, activity-based costing, variable costing, absorption costing, and so forth.

7.5 Variable versus Absorption Costing

Early in our discussion of job costing, we treated all costs as product costs, regardless of whether they were fixed or variable. In other words, we treated the cost of a unit of production in terms of direct materials, direct labor, and overhead. No attempt was made to separate fixed costs from variable costs. This process of cost assignment, where no distinction is made between fixed and variable costs, is called absorption costing, or full costing.

Since fixed and variable costs are treated as one in absorption (full) costing, it is not useful for certain types of financial reporting, such as income statements, which may require that some information be provided on contribution margins. As noted previously, a contribution margin is the difference between the price of an item of goods or a service and its variable costs. The margin represents the rate at which the output of an operation contributes to an organization's fixed costs and net income or revenue. The method that clearly recognizes this in preparing a financial statement is variable costing, also known as direct costing.

Variable costing is mostly used for internal reporting since it provides additional information by disaggregating costs into two distinct categories, fixed and variable, whereas absorption costing is primarily used for external reporting, where disaggregation is not always required.

7.5.1 Illustrating the Difference

Let us look at a simple example to illustrate the difference between the two costing methods (variable and absorption) and see if the difference between them can be reconciled. We begin with two simple income statements for an electric utility fund of a local government. Income statements in government are used primarily for proprietary funds, such as water, sewer, electricity, parking meters, and the like, because of their similarity with private sector operations. Table 7.4 presents the two statements, one for absorption costing and the other for variable costing.

According to the table, the net income at the end of the year under absorption costing is obtained by subtracting the operating and the administrative costs of the government from its operating revenue. The operating revenue, in turn, is obtained by multiplying the total units (kilowatt hours) of electricity sold (consumed) by the price of electricity. Note that, for most organizations, operating costs are usually separated from administrative costs to keep proper track of cost assignments. Assume that the government produced 100 million units (kilowatt hours) of electricity last year, of which 80 million units were consumed by the residents at a price of \$0.12 a unit. Accordingly, the operating revenue from the sale of electricity for the government would be $80{,}000{,}000 \times \$0.12 = \$9{,}600{,}00$, as shown in the table.

The operating costs, on the other hand, were obtained by multiplying the total units (of electricity produced) by the cost per unit of

Table 7.4 A simplified income statement: Year ended - December 2XXX

Cost Flow	*Absorption Costing ($)*
Operating Revenue	9,600,000
(-) Operating Costs	8,000,000
Gross Margin	1,600,000
(-) Administrative Costs	1,000,000
= Net income	600,000

Cost Flow	*Variable Costing ($)*
Operating Revenue	9,600,000
(-) Variable (Operating) Costs	5,600,000
(-) Variable (Administrative) Costs	400,000
Contribution Margin	3,600,000
(-) Fixed (Overhead) Costs	3,000,000
(-) Fixed (Administrative) Costs	600,000
= Net Income	0

Reconciliation

Difference in Net Income: $600,000
Reconciliation: [Variable costing income + (Inventory balance x Fixed overhead cost)
= 0 + (100,000,000 - 80,000,000 = 20,000,000 × $0.03) = 0 + $600,000
= $600,000
= Net Income for Variable Costing

electricity. Assume now that the cost of producing one unit (kilowatt hour) of electricity was $0.10, which included $0.04 in direct materials, $0.02 in direct labor, $0.01 in variable overhead, and $0.03 in fixed overhead. The total operating cost for the service, therefore, would be 80,000,000 × $0.10 = $8,000,000, with a gross margin (the difference between operating revenue and operating cost) of $1.6 million; that is, $9,600,000 - $8,000,000 = $1,600,000.

Note that under absorption costing, the net income is obtained by subtracting the administrative costs ($1,000,000) from the gross margin ($1,600,000); that is, $1,600,000 - $1,000,000 = $600,000). The gross margin, in turn, is obtained by taking the difference between operating revenue ($9,600,000) and operating cost ($8,000,000); that is, $9,600,000 - $8,000,000 = $1,600,000. Note also that under absorption costing both fixed and variable costs assigned to the units sold are included in the operating costs, while the administrative costs are treated separately. The reason the administrative costs are treated separately in absorption costing is because they are considered as period costs, meaning that they are not directly related to the production process. As such, they are expensed in the period in which they occur. One can think of them as overheads, but they are different from conventional overheads that are integral to the production or delivery of a good or service.

In contrast, the net income under variable costing is obtained by subtracting the fixed cost of operation (fixed overhead costs + fixed administrative costs = $3,000,000 + $600,000 = $3,600,000) from the contribution margin ($3,600,000); that is, $3,600,000 - $3,600,000 = 0. The contribution margin, on the other hand, is obtained by taking the difference between operating revenue ($9,600,000) and variable costs (variable operating costs + variable administrative costs = $5,600,000 + $400,000 = $6,000,000); that is, $9,600,000 - $6,000,000 = $3,600,000.

Two things are worth noting here: first, the overhead component of the cost is split between fixed overhead and variable overhead, where the latter is subsumed under variable operating costs. The result produces a variable cost that is considerably lower than the operating cost under absorption costs ($5.6 million, as opposed to $8.0 million). The problem can be avoided by constructing a detailed income statement. Second, in calculating fixed overhead costs, consideration is given to the total units of goods and services produced, rather than the total units sold. The reason for this is that since these units were already produced and fixed overhead costs were incurred in producing them, they must be recognized in preparing the income statement.

Another interesting thing to observe in the current example is that net income under absorption costing for the government was $0.6 million, which became 0 under variable costing. In other words, under absorption costing our government had a net income of $0.6 million, which disappeared under variable costing. There is a simple explanation for this: the difference occurred due to the discrepancy between the total output produced and the actual quantity sold or consumed. In general, if the amount of goods and services produced is higher than the amount sold, net income under absorption costing will be higher than net income under variable costing. The opposite is true when the amount produced is lower than the amount sold. If there is no discrepancy (if the amount produced is the same as the amount sold) the net income will be the same for both methods. This explains why the net income was higher under absorption costing in our example.

7.5.2 Reconciling the Difference

A simple way to explain the difference we have just observed in net income between variable and absorption costing is how one expenses the fixed overhead costs under the two methods. For instance, under variable costing the fixed overhead costs are expensed to the total units produced (charged to the period when they were incurred). In contrast, under absorption costing they are expensed to the total units sold (charged to the units when they were sold). The former, as noted earlier, is called period costing, while the latter is known as product costing. It is this difference between the two costing methods, period and product, that produces the difference in net income.

The following shows how the discrepancy occurred as a result of the differences in expensing the fixed overhead costs:

Fixed Overhead Expensed (Variable costing) [100,000,000 × \$0.03]	\$3,000,000
Fixed Overhead Expensed (Absorption costing) [80,000,000 × \$0.03]	\$2,400,000
Discrepancy	\$600,000

According to the information presented above, if the fixed overhead costs were not expensed for the total amount of electricity produced under variable costing, the net income for both methods would have been identical. In other words, if the government had been able to sell 100 percent of the electricity it produced during the accounting period, there would not have been any discrepancy in net income.

Once there is a discrepancy in net income, it may be necessary to find ways in which the difference can be reconciled. We suggest here a simple procedure for reconciliation that will even out the difference in income flow under both methods. For instance, when the number of units sold is less than the total units produced, add the fixed overhead costs for the difference to the variable costing income. When it is more (assuming that there is a carryover from previous periods), do the opposite. Thus, if we multiply the 20 million units of electricity that remain unsold at the end of the year, in our example by the fixed overhead costs of \$0.3 and add this to the net income under variable costing, it will be the same as the net income under absorption costing, as can be seen from the following calculations:

variable costing (net) income + (inventory balance × fixed overhead costs)

= 0 + (20,000,000 × \$0.03)

= 0 + \$600,000

= \$600,000

which is exactly what we had for the net income under absorption costing.

7.6 Batch Costing

When a job is repetitive, it may be useful to complete them in batches, rather than individually, called batch costing. Batch costing is a variation of job costing. In fact, a batch can be treated as a cost unit, as in unit costing.[4] Batch costing is particularly useful in government contracts where cost accounting is used to track and allocate costs for a batch of jobs (Federal Contractor Registry, 2019) Batch costing can also be used in public works, social service delivery, public transportation, application processing, and the like. Determining batch costs is not that complicated once we have information on the total cost of a job, the number of units in a job, the number of batches in a job, and the size of the batch. In fact, it is very similar to job costing, except that batch becomes the cost unit, rather than a job.

We can use a simple expression to determine batch costs, as

$$\text{Batch Cost} = (TC/NU) \times NUB \qquad (7.3)$$

where TC is the total cost of a job, NU is the number of units in a job, NUB is the number of units in a batch, and (TC/NU) is the unit cost. To give an example, suppose that a State Health and Human Services Department processes 5,000 applications a week for a service in a batch of 1,000 applications. The total cost of processing the applications is $75,000, which includes both direct and indirect costs. The batch cost for the applications processed would be $15,000 a batch, with a unit cost of $15. That is, (TC/NU) x NUB) = ($75,000/5,000) x 1,000) = $15 x $1,000 = $15,000.

There are other similarities with job costing that are worth noting. For instance, instead of job cost sheets, one can have batch cost sheets with direct materials, direct labor, and overheads, as in a job cost sheet. However, the process can get complicated when one has to deal with large batches because large batches require significant upfront investments in labor and materials which may tie up resources. Also, batch costing is often misconstrued with another method of cost accounting, called process costing, which takes place in stages, but the two are not the same. While batch costing traces costs for distinct batches of similar jobs, process costing is used when production or delivery is usually continuous and traces costs to each stage of the production or delivery process (discussed later).

7.7 Chapter Summary

Organizations use various methods for accounting for costs. Job costing is one of the methods frequently used in cost accounting. This chapter has provided a general discussion of job costing and its use in government. Although the focus has been on government, job costing and the methods used can be equally applied to nonprofit organizations. The process is the same in that costs are traced to a specific job. By tracing costs to a specific job, an organization can estimate the costs associated with each job accurately. The chapter started with a brief discussion of a cost accounting system, followed by a detailed discussion of job costing. This is followed by a discussion of variable costing, as distinct from absorption or full costing, both of which can be used in conjunction with job costing. However, unlike absorption costing, which treats fixed and variable costs as one, variable costing makes a clear distinction between the two; as such, it is often considered more effective than absorption costing because variable costs tend to have a much greater effect on net income or revenue of an organization than fixed costs. The chapter concluded with a brief discussion of batch costing, which is a variation of job costing.

7.8 Review Questions

7.1 What is a cost accounting system? Why is it important in government? What are some of the methods used in cost accounting systems?

7.2. What is job costing? What are the three important elements of a job costing process? Discuss, with an example of each.

7.3. What is double-entry accounting? What are the advantages of using a double-entry accounting system? Why is it called a T-account?

7.4. What is work-in-process? How does it differ from an inventory account? Given an example of both, showing how the work-in-process account constitutes a sub-account of the inventory account.

7.5 A county government has recently renovated one of its correctional facilities that is largely supported by state funding. It cost the government approximately \$375,000 in direct materials, \$1.2 million in direct labor, and \$350,000 in overheads, of which \$215,000 went to overheads (indirect) labor and the rest to indirect materials. Assume the project used a total of 10,500 hours of indirect labor. Assume further that direct materials were issued by the central warehouse on the day the job started, direct labor was accrued at the time of the journal entry, and overheads were applied at a predetermined rate. The job took approximately six months to complete, from January 1 through June 30, and was assigned the number 057-PB for Plant and Building. Given the information above,

a. Prepare the source document.
b. Journalize the information.
c. Determine the overhead rate.

7.6 What is variable costing? How does it differ from absorption costing? What are the advantages of using variable costing, as opposed to absorption costing?

7.7 Suppose that you have an income statement for a government, with the following information: Operating revenue of $15 million, with (a) operating costs of $12 million, and (2) administrative costs of $2 million. Suppose also that for the same operating revenue of $15 million, it has (1) variable operating costs of $10 million, (2) variable administrative costs of $1 million, (3) fixed overhead costs of $2 million, and (3) fixed administrative costs of $2 million.

Given the information above,

a. Calculate the gross margin and net income for absorption costing.
b. Calculate the contribution margin and net income for variable costing.
c. Explain how you would reconcile the difference.

Notes

1 Cost accumulation is the ascertainment of costs in a structured and systematic fashion. There are two principal approaches to cost accumulation: job costing, discussed in this chapter, and process costing, discussed later.

2 J.R. Martin (2016) provides a good discussion of a cost accounting system. According to Martin, the system should be based on five basic components: One, it should have an input measurement focus based on pure, historical, or standard costing. Two, it should include an inventory evaluation method based on the cost amount that could be traced to an inventory. Three, it should include a cost accumulation method based on how the cost data is collected and identified with respect to jobs (job-order costing), process (process costing), and other methods. Four, it should have a cost flow assumption that refers to how cost flows through an inventory such as weighted average, first-in first-out, or last-in first-out. Five, it should have the capability of recording inventory cost flows at certain intervals, either periodically or permanently.

3 The term Work-in-Process is often used interchangeably with Work-in-Progress. The latter typically includes unfinished goods and services that remain in the inventory that may not be completed or may take a longer time to complete, while the unfinished goods in the inventory account in Work-in-Process will be completed usually within a short period. Inventory accounts, on the other hand, include all goods and materials, as well as work-in-process accounts. In fact,

work-in-process accounts are considered subsets or sub-accounts of inventory accounts.

4 It is a method of calculating the cost to produce a unit of good or service. Unit costing is particularly useful for cost control, performance evaluation, and pricing decisions of a government, among others.

References

Curley, Jr., T.J. (1965). *Essential Elements of a Cost Accounting System.* Paper presented at Management Services Conference of the Missouri Society of Certified Public Accountants, St. Louis, Missouri, October 1965.

Federal Contractor Registry (2019). A look at five types of contracts. *Federal Contractor Registry.* https://federalcontractorregistry.com/a-look-at-5-types-of-government-contracts/September.

Kelly, J.T. *Costing Government Services: A Guide to Decision Making.* (1984). Washington, DC: Government Finance Officers Association.

Lynn, E.S. and Norville, J.W. (1984) *Introduction to Fund Accounting.* Reston, VA: Reston Publishing.

Martin, J.R. (1916). *Management Accounting: Concepts, Techniques, and Controversial Issues.* Management and Accounting Web: http://maaw.info/MAAWTextbookMain.htm

8 Contract Costing

8.1 Introduction

With a few exceptions, as noted previously, governments do not produce goods; they provide them. Governments have a long history of outsourcing or contracting out many of the goods and services that they provide to private providers, for profit as well as non-profit organizations. The term frequently used to describe accounting for outsourcing or contracting out is contract costing. Contract costing is a variation of job costing. The difference between job costing and contract costing is that a contract is much larger in scope than a job. In fact, one can think of job costing as costing for a small job and contract costing as costing for a large job. Occasionally, a contract may include sub-contracts, where a contractor sub-contracts a segment of the job to a sub-contractor, especially if the work is of a special nature that cannot be done internally. Perhaps, more than anything, what makes contract costing important is the sheer amount of money governments spend on contracts each year that run into hundreds of billions of dollars. For instance, federal contracts alone run over several hundred billion dollars a year. Add to this, state and local contracts, the total amount can easily exceed several trillion dollars a year.

This chapter provides an overview of contract costing. It begins with a brief history of government contracts, followed by a discussion of characteristics of contract costing, types of contract costs, contracting process, guidelines and procedure, contract costing standards, contract accounting reports, and contract performance management. The chapter concludes with a brief discussion of government and nonprofit contract relationships, since the nonprofit organizations frequently partner with government to provide goods and services that are beneficial to both.

DOI: 10.4324/9781003486091-10

8.2 Government Contracts

A contract is a legally binding agreement between two or more parties with mutual obligations enforceable by law, where each party is obligated under contract to perform a specific task or a set of tasks and functions. Contracting in government is nothing new. It has a long history that goes back to the late 18th century when the federal government passed the Purveyor of Public Act in 1795 (Federal Contracting Center, 2024), to make it possible for the government to purchase goods and resources it required. Over the next several decades, the government maintained the idea of publicized government procurement activities and passed the Civil Sundry Appropriations Act in 1861 to further expand the use of contracting. The 1900s saw some of the most critical laws surrounding the government contracting since the passage of the Armed Services Procurement Act (ASPA) in 1947. The act made it easier for the Defense Department to buy supplies and services.

In 1994, Congress passed the Federal Acquisition Streamlining Act (FASA), considered to be one of the most significant acts in the history of government contracting. The Act completely transformed the government's contracting activities and made its procurement system easier. For instance, the Act increased the government's use of commercial products and services, increased the bar for verifying value or price, simplified the procurement methods for high-volume and lower value purchases, enhanced small businesses' access to federal contracting opportunities, and enhanced the bidding protest procedure,[1] among others. Two years after FASA, the government passed the Federal Acquisition Reform Act (FARA) to remove obstacles throughout the procurement process. The Act also changed the government's preferred method of purchasing from low bidder offering to the best value. As decades have passed, governments, in particular the federal government, has discovered several flaws and problems with many of the laws, and the legislations have been modified.

At the subnational level, state and local governments have been using service contracts for a long time, which has significantly expanded in the latter half of the 20th century, gaining momentum in the 1970s and 1980s due to the rise of New Public Management (Osborne, 2006; Lane, 2000). The new direction in governance emphasized policies based on efficiency and cost-effectiveness, often pushing for more private sector involvement in government operations (Alford and O'Flynn, 2012). The trend has continued to this day, with various services like waste management, transportation, utility services, and services such as healthcare contracted out to private firms and businesses.

There are two simple explanations why governments outsource or contract out: cost savings and quality. It saves the government money, especially if the government does not have in-house expertise to provide the service. According to a study by Hilke (1992)), contracting out saves governments considerably which can run anywhere from 20 to 50 percent of the total cost of delivery. In a global study on privatization, Savas (2001) found that contracting out saved countries significantly, by as much as 25 percent. Another study by Hodge (1999) found the savings to be much lower at about 15 percent but still considerable. There have been numerous studies in recent years on cost savings the contracts produce for governments. However, the actual amount of savings varies from government to government, depending on the service or job contracted out.

Besides cost savings, governments outsource or contract out for quality. Quality is possible because contractors have the scale to achieve higher quality through standardized processes and economies of scale that a government may not necessarily have. However, to ensure quality governments often include standards or expectations in the contract agreement for delivery on time, and within the budget, and, more importantly, that they meet the specified quality requirements. This minimizes the potential for disagreement at the time of delivery and legal conflicts later (Manion, 2003).

8.3 Characteristics of Contract Costing

As noted earlier, contract costing is an extension of job costing but differs from it in a number of ways such as the size of the job, which is usually larger than a job used in job costing. It also means longer completion time since the jobs are much larger. Other differences include greater susceptibility to cost fluctuations because of longer duration, costs tracked for an entire contract rather than for each job or batch, and job transfer, meaning that it can be subcontracted by the contractor, among others

The following provides a brief summary of the characteristics of a typical contract cost:

1. Contracts are larger in size and scope than a job; as such, they take a much longer time to complete.
2. An organization may receive multiple contracts, depending on contract history and performance, in which case each contract is treated as a cost unit.
3. A separate account is prepared or maintained for each contract.
4. Materials used in a contract are usually direct materials, purchased separately for the contract.
5. Similarly, labor used in a contract is also direct.
6. Most expenses, such as utilities and fringe benefits, are direct.
7. Subcontracts may be used at the discretion of the contractor, if the job is of a special nature that cannot be completed internally.

Several things are worth noting about the characteristics of contract costing, described above. They mostly deal with the costs of labor, materials, machines and equipment as well as sub-contracts used during the contract period. Although they are the primary concerns of the contractors, governments must also take them into consideration in the contract agreement. For instance, contracts should include the costs of labor, and materials used for the job, not the costs of additional materials purchased, or labor acquired. The same applies to machines and equipment, although it is expected that these items are already in the inventory of the contractor. Similarly, if additional work is required to complete the job, which is possible, it should be included in the agreement. Also, when a job is not fully completed during the accounting or contract period, it is important to classify it as a work-in-process inventory account, discussed earlier. Finally, the sub-contracts the contractors use must be of the highest quality to ensure the safety, security, and quality of the job.

8.4 Types of Contracts

All contracts have certain characteristics that are unique to the contracts. For instance, work on contracts is usually carried out at the facility or site of the contractor, and there is a precise time length for completing a contract. If there are multiple contracts, a separate contract is prepared for each to keep track of costs, and to help ascertain costs as they accumulate. From an accounting perspective, each contract is treated as a cost unit. In most instances, as noted earlier, labor costs as well as expenses such as utility, telephone, and insurance, are treated as direct costs. Depending on the contract, it may be necessary to purchase the physical assets, such as vehicles and equipment, for the contract, or lease for the duration of the contract, or include them in the contract costs.

Contracts vary in size and scope. Individual governments determine the types of contracts that would be appropriate for the acquisition and delivery of specific goods and services. For instance, the Federal Contractor Registry (2019)[2, 3] recognizes different types of contracts based on the conditions and time of delivery, seven of which are worth noting. They are fixed-price contracts, cost-reimbursement contracts, cost-plus contracts, time and materials contracts, incentive contracts, indefinite delivery contracts and work-in-process contracts.

8.4.1 *Fixed-Price Contract*

In a fixed-price contract, contractors are asked to submit a bid to complete a project under a predetermined price. They are not subject to any adjustments unless provisions have been included in the original contract.

A good example of a fixed-price contract is when a government contracts a private firm to construct a physical plant, such as a water or sewage treatment plant at a predetermined price, where the contractor assumes the risk of cost overruns, but must deliver the project at the agreed upon price.

8.4.2 Cost-Reimbursement Contract

In a cost-reimbursement contract, contractors are allowed to seek reimbursement of incurred costs up to a prescribed allowance. The allowance is justified because certain costs cannot be predetermined with complete accuracy until the work is in progress or completed. Examples of this type of contract include those used by the Federal Transit Administration, National Weather Services, the US Department of Defense, and Research and Development (R&D). A special case of the cost-reimbursement contract is the cost-sharing contract, where the contractor receives no fee and is reimbursed for the agreed-upon portion of the contractor's allowable costs.

8.4.3 Cost-Plus Contract

The cost-plus contract is essentially a cost-reimbursement contract that provides for the initially negotiated fee to be adjusted later by a formula based on the relationship of total allowable costs to total target costs. The contract specifies a target cost, a target fee, minimum and maximum fees, and a fee adjustment formula. Once the contract has been completed, the fee payable to the contractor is determined in accordance with the formula. The formula provides, within limits, for an increase in the fee above the target fee when total allowable costs are less than the target costs, or a decrease in the fee below the target fee when total allowable costs exceed the target costs. This increase or decrease is intended to provide an incentive for the contractor to manage the contract effectively. As such, another term used for cost-plus contract is cost-plus-incentive-fee contract.

Cost-plus contracts can vary in size and scope, such as cost-plus fixed fee contract, cost-plus fixed percentage contract, and cost-plus guaranteed maximum (or minimum) contract. A good example of a cost-plus fixed fee contract is when a government contracts, say, a facility to be constructed at $20 million, plus a fixed fee of $2 million of the construction cost, to serve as the profit of the contractor. If the profit included in the contract is a percentage of the total cost, such as 10 percent of the construction cost, it is called a cost-plus fixed percentage contract. Finally, the contractor may be paid the actual project cost of $20 million, plus a predetermined fee, with the total not exceeding a set price, say, of $22 million, will be the cost-plus guaranteed maximum contract. If it is set at a minimum, of, say,

$21 million, $1 million above the total cost of construction, it will be a cost-plus guaranteed minimum contract.

8.4.4 Time and Materials Contract

In a time and materials contract, the government, instead of the contractor, is asked to share more of the risk and, as such, the cost burden, especially for projects where it is difficult to predetermine the costs with complete accuracy. A good example of a time and materials contract is when a government contracts, say, an IT specialist to perform complex system maintenance, where the exact scope of the work is uncertain until the specialist has a chance to examine the system and determine the source of the problem, and the government agrees to pay a fixed hourly rate for the service, plus the costs of equipment or parts. There is usually a set price ceiling to prevent excessive costs. The ceiling is typically determined based on the maximum number of hours the specialist will spend on the job, and a fixed percentage or amount for the parts. Thus, if the cost per hour of service is $125, plus 15 percent for parts and materials, not exceeding, say, $2,000, and a maximum of 50 hours for labor, the cost of the contract will be $8,250; that is, $(\$125 \times 50) + \$,2,000 = \$6,250 + \$2,000 = \$8,250$.

8.4.5 Incentive Contract

In an incentive contract, incentives are often used by relating the amount of profit or fee to the contractor's performance and are used in situations where a fixed-price contract is not possible, and the service can be acquired at a lower cost. As noted earlier, incentives are typically used to motivate contractor efforts that might not otherwise be emphasized, and to discourage contractor inefficiency and waste. In fact, both fixed-price and cost reimbursement contracts are categories of incentive contracts. Since it is to the advantage of a government for the contractor to assume substantial cost responsibility and an appropriate share of the cost risk, fixed-price incentive contracts are preferred when contract costs and performance requirements are reasonably certain. On the other hand, cost-reimbursement incentive contracts are subject to the limitations of the government in that the government must have adequate resources to award and manage the contract. The limitations may also include that the contractor's accounting system is adequate for determining costs applicable to the contract, among others.

8.4.5.1 Indefinite-Delivery Contract

Finally, in an indefinite delivery contract, contractors are allowed some flexibility, especially in situations when the exact time and quantity of future deliveries are not known at the time of the contract award. Indefinite-delivery contracts differ from two related contracts: definite-quantity contract, and requirements contract. A definite-quantity contract is used when the exact time and quantity of future deliveries of a definite quantity of specific supplies is known at the time of the contract. The indefinite delivery contract is used when the exact time and quantity of future deliveries of specific supplies is not known at the time or the contract. Also, it may be necessary to use a requirements contract when the government anticipates recurring requirements but cannot pre-determine the precise quantity of supplies. Examples of indefinite-delivery contracts typically include information technology contracts, defense contracts for certain types of defense goods that are at the cutting-edge of technology, and telecommunication contracts.

8.4.5.2 Work-in-Process Contract

When a contract is not completed until the end of the accounting period, the contractor is expected to record the costs in a work-in-process account. It is essentially the work-in-process account, discussed earlier, except that it is prepared by the contractor for internal recording and reporting purposes. Operationally, the procedure used in contract costing is similar to job costing in that each contract is given a distinct number, and a separate account is used for each contract. Like job costing, the contractor is expected to use double-entry accounting for cost reporting and follow some of the same principles for debit and credit used for direct and indirect costs. However, unlike the entries used in job costing, some of the entries in contract costing will be different because the account balance in contract costing is usually profit or loss for the contractor from a contract.

8.5 Contracting Process

All contracts go through a process before the contracts are finally awarded. It is a three-step process: pre-awards, awards, and post-awards. During pre-awards, the process ensures that the government chooses a qualified contractor, preferably with a history of government contracts, and that the agreement is legally binding and mutually beneficial. Government contracts often involve a bidding process, either required by law to ensure that the process is fair and unbiased, or to attract the maximum number of potentials bidders (contractors) to ensure that the process is competitive to keep the contract price low and assure quality. Most governments have standard bidding forms and may require a Request For Proposal (RFP), or a Request For Quote (RFQ) if the goods and services are of a specific nature.

The bids are generally restricted to qualified bidders, preferably with a history of acceptable bid performance, although negotiated contracts are not uncommon, especially for defense contracts with established history. Bid forms are required to include only the related items and specify the terms and conditions of delivery, and any other information as required. Once bids are received, they must be carefully evaluated to narrow the field. Usually, an evaluation team with experience in contract costing and familiarity with the job to be contracted out is put together to evaluate the bids. For most public goods and services, bids are opened in public to maintain the integrity of the process. Exceptions are made for jobs that are highly sensitive.

Before awarding bids and contracts, it may be necessary for the government to put together a cost estimate of the job, especially for large contracts. The estimates are necessary to establish the terms of the contract and negotiate the final contract. If in-house expertise is not available to prepare the estimates, the government may use outside expertise. In fact, the Defense Department frequently uses Independent Government Estimates (IGEs) to find the best estimate of a contract's potential costs. The estimates are usually prepared without any input from the contractor (Department of Defense, 2018).

8.5.1 Contract Guidelines and Procedure

As noted earlier, the amount of money the governments spend each year on contracts runs from hundreds of millions to billions of dollars. Consequently, governments have strict guidelines when awarding contracts to ensure that contract accounting complies with the guidelines fully. Also, before a contract is awarded, it is important to ensure that the contractor has the capabilities to meet the specific requirements of a prospective contract such as an accounting design system that can track financial transactions and financial reports with a large database. Not having a proper accounting design system in place can delay a contract award or may lead to disqualification. Additionally, it is important that the contractor's accounting system meets government specifications, especially at the federal level, which requires that contract accounting follows GAAP to accurately track records and reports associated with a contract (Diene, 2023).

The following provides a broad narrative of what government contract accounting must entail:

Cost identification. The accounting system must be clearly designed to identify all costs either as direct or indirect. Direct costs would include direct materials, direct labor including supervision (assuming it can be tied entirely to the project), and depreciation of plants and machinery (used specifically for the project). Indirect costs, as noted earlier, are those that cannot be attributed to a specific contract but rather incurred to support its operations. Once costs are identified as direct or indirect, they must be accurately recorded in respective ledger accounts (cost ledgers).

Cost allocation. The accounting system must allocate all direct costs as line items or cost objects (such as personnel, materials and supplies, contractual, debt service, and so forth) for which they were incurred. This must appear in a cost ledger. By listing each cost on a separate line, it is easy to monitor how much is being spent on the line items of a project. Table 8.1 presents an example of line items for a cost ledger. As the table shows, the process is similar to the job-cost sheet discussed earlier. This is due in part to the fact that contract costing is an extension of job costing.

Unallowable Costs. Certain items contractors include for cost reimbursement can fail to qualify, termed as unallowable costs. It is important that the guidelines or contract agreements clearly indicate what the items are. If the items included fall outside the contract agreements, the contractors are expected to absorb the costs.

Code of business ethics and conducts. Just like the government, contractors are required to establish written codes of ethics that should be available to employees working for the organizations, especially the contractor. Most organizations that contract with the government provide ethics and compliance training to all participating employees and agents, including contractors and subcontractors. The codes are necessary to

Table 8.1 Simple line items for a cost ledger

Department:	Public Works	
Job Title:	Project X	
Date:	January 1, 20XX	
1.	Line Item	: Payment for direct labor
	Cost account code	: X–05–126
	Cost of labor	: $15,000
	Amount of labor	: Five (Part-time)
2.	Line item	: Purchase of direct materials
	Cost account Code	: X–07–153
	Cost of raw materials	: $2,500
	Quantity	: 100 units

prevent unacceptable conduct. The federal government, in particular, may require reporting of non-compliance to the appropriate government agency.

Sub-Contract. As noted earlier, a contractor may sub-contract a job if the work is of a specialized nature for which facilities are not internally available. Subcontractors are responsible to the primary contractors and the costs of the sub-contract are typically charged to the contract accounts.

Contract modification. On occasion, it may be necessary to modify a contract. Modifications may be bilateral, where both parties must be involved and agree to the changes. However, modifications can be unilateral, in which case only the contacting authority, which is usually the one who can make the changes. Contract violations or not following the rules of contract can lead to termination of contracts.

Finally, before awarding a contract, it is important for the government to conduct an inventory analysis of jobs that are currently under contract as well as those that are not under contract, but are likely to be under contract, along with information on estimated costs, contract costs, and cost savings. Since cost saving, other than quality, is the primary justification for a government to contract out, the inventory analysis can help the government determine which jobs to contract out, and which ones to retain. Table 8.2 presents a simple inventory of contracts and costs associated with each contract. Two sets of jobs are listed in the table: New, a job that has not been contracted out yet, but will be, and existing, meaning that it has already been contracted out.

It should be worth noting that it is not unusual for a government to have a contract that cost it more than initially estimated, in which case it incurs a loss; in other words, there is no cost saving (Rosell, 2003). Job 4, in Table 2, is a good example.

8.6 Contract Costing Standards

Government contracts have standards that all contractors are required to adhere to, called Cost Accounting Standards (CAS), discussed earlier. Standards contain a set of requirements, rules, and conditions that all contractors and subcontractors must follow carefully and thoroughly. The primary objective of these standards is to ensure that they produce cost data that is reliable and consistent with the Generally Accepted Accounting Principles (GAAP). As noted earlier, there are presently 19 standards (numbered 401 to 420), developed at different times since the establishment of CASB, to ensure that all costs related to contracts are

Table 8.2 A simple inventory of job contracts and associated costs

Job, J	*Responsible Department*	*Job Status*	*Current Cost ($M)*	*Contract Cost ($M)*	*Cost Savings ($M)*
J1	D1	New	5[1]	4.5	0.5
J2	D2	Existing	7	6.0	1
J3	D3	Existing	10	8.5	1.5
J4	D4	Existing	8	9	-1
J5	D5	New	4[2]	3.5	0.5
J6	D6	Existing	12	10.5	1.5
---	---	---	---	---	---
J_n	D_m	Existing	6	6	0
Total Cost	---	---	52	48	4[3]

[1,2] Estimated cost, if provided by the government; [3]Net savings. Note: J_n and D_m mean *n* jobs, and *m* departments.

accounted for accurately and fully. Each standard addresses a specific area of cost accounting. For instance, Standard 401 addresses consistency in estimating, accumulating, and reporting costs, Standard 405 on accounting for unallowable costs, Standard 407 on the use of standard costs for direct labor and materials, Standard 409 on depreciation of tangible capital assets, Standard 418 on allocation of direct and indirect costs, and so forth. Taken together, they address six areas of cost accounting that lie at the heart of contract costing: cost accounting concepts, cost allocation methodology, treatment of fixed assets, cost of labor and materials, deferred compensation, and insurance (Annessa and Ivezaj, 2024).

While it is required that the standards must be followed thoroughly, they do not apply across the board for all contracts. Instead, they are based on contract by contract and the coverage the contracts have. Two types of coverage are generally used: moderate coverage and full coverage. Moderate coverage generally is applied to contracts presently under $50 million and full coverage over $50 million. Standards require contractors to disclose in writing their cost accounting practices, while complying with the promulgated cost accounting standards. In the same vein, there are contracts and subcontracts that are exempt from CAS requirements.[4] This includes sealed bid contracts, small businesses, negotiated contracts, and sub-contracts not in excess of the Truth in Negotiation Act (TINA) threshold (which is currently $2 million), acquisition of commercial items, and contracts and sub-contracts with foreign governments, among others (National Archives, 2025).

8.7 Contract Accounting Reports

Contract costing, like all accounting activities, follows a process in that costs have to be traced, assigned, recorded, and finally reported. The result of this process is a set of financial statements, which provide information about an organization's financial position. The statements typically include balance sheet, income, and cash flow statements. The statements constitute the essence of a government or business organization's annual financial report and are used for internal as well as external consumption. Similarly, organizations with government contracts, especially with large contracts, also prepare annual financial reports. The government may have an interest in looking at these statements, especially if the price or cost-flow is based on costs, to see if the cost information included in the report is valid and reliable.

Table 8.3 presents a simple balance sheet for an organization that received a government contract. Balance sheets are prepared using the accounting equation, Assets = Liabilities + Equity. Equity is the difference between assets (what an organization owns) and liabilities (what an organization owes). As the table shows, the two sides must balance, if reported correctly. For instance, if the asset position of the organization increases and there is no change in the liabilities position, then equity must increase to balance the equation. Similarly, if liabilities increase and there is no change in asset position, then equity must decrease to balance the equation, and so forth; hence, the term balance sheet.

The next important financial statement for an organization is the income statement. As the name suggests, an income statement shows all the financial activities of the organization and the results of those activities. Income statements are vital for governments and for-profit organizations. Nonprofit organizations also have income statements. Table 8.4 shows a

Table 8.3 A simple balance sheet of a contracted organization

Assets:		
Cash	$3,000	
Account receivable	3,500	
Fixed asset	8,500	
Total assets	$15,000	
Liabilities:		$7,500
Account payable		2,500
Notes payable		10,000
Total liabilities		
Equity		$5,000

Table 8.4 A simple income statement of a contracted organization

Contract Revenue		$50,000
Contract Costs		
Direct labor	$10,000	
Direct materials	8,000	
Overhead (labor and materials)	12,000	$30,000
Sub-contract	$10,000	
Total costs		$40,000
Gross profit (Gross income)		$10,000
Administrative Expenses	$5,000	$5,000
Net profit (Net income)		$5,000

sample income statement of a nonprofit organization that received a government contract.

As the table shows, the organization had a contract revenue of $50,000, of which $40,000 went to pay for various costs, such as direct labor, direct materials, overhead, and a sub-contract of $10,000. The result produces a gross revenue of $10,000. The organization had administrative expenses of $5,000 related to the contract, which produces a net income of $5,000 for the organization. The third financial statement most organizations produce, which also applies to contract costing, is a cost-flow statement (not shown here), which is important to keep track of cost flows: inflows and outflows, similar to a cash-flow statement for an operating budget (discussed later). As noted earlier, the purpose of these statements is to provide information on the financial position of an organization, including the contracted organizations. The information is frequently used to determine the financial health of an organization.

8.7.1 Contract Costing Audits

Contract accounting reports, like financial reports, are usually followed by audits, called cost accounting standards audits, or CAS audits. While auditing in cost and managerial accounting is mostly ad hoc, compared to financial audits, it is much more specific in contract costing. The objective of CAS auditing is to ensure that the contracts have been in compliance with CAS. The audit process involves a review of the contractor's cost accounting system, procedures, and practices to determine whether they are consistent with the CAS and the contractor's disclosure statements. Three groups of individuals are typically involved in the audit process: internal audit teams, external auditors, and project managers. The results of the audit process included in the audit report identify any deficiencies in the contractor's cost accounting system, the deliverables, and the price structure that may have resulted in the government paying higher costs on covered items, and so forth, plus a host of supporting documents, followed by recommendations for corrective action.

8.7.2 Contract Performance Management

Although contracts include the terms and conditions for delivering goods and services, it is important for government to monitor the performance of the organizations providing them, known as contract performance management. Contract performance management is a process of tracking and analyzing the costs and quality of service provision consistent with the terms and conditions of the delivery by the organization responsible. The goal is to ensure that the contract has been successfully executed.

Contract performance involves a four-step process: tracking, recording, analyzing, and reporting. The process starts with tracking costs associated with a contract between the government and the contracted organization. Once the cost has been traced, it must be recorded by the contractor during the contract period, preferably using a cost ledger. A cost ledger, as noted earlier, records the costs of goods and services as they accumulate, classified by type, expense, and responsible department. All costs have two sides: budgeted and actual. Although it is expected that actual costs will conform to budgeted costs, it is seldom the case. Analyzing costs helps determine the factors that have contributed to the difference and measures to improve them. Finally, preparing the contract accounting report helps determine the profitability or loss from the contract. Managing contract performance is critical to making sure that the steps are carried out successfully with maximum efficiency. In the event the performance fails to produce maximum results, it may be necessary to be proactive and initiate active contract management that would significantly improve contract performance.

8.8 Active Contract Management

Active contract management, also called ACM, deals with a set of strategies that focus on collaborations between government agencies and service providers, especially social services, to improve performance of contracted services. A good example of ACM is the one developed by the Kennedy School of Government (2019) in response to why contract services often fail to achieve their target or expected goals. According to the Kennedy School ACM, there are three simple reasons why contracts fail to achieve their goals: (1) lack of purposeful attempts by government agencies to improve outcomes of contracted services, (2) failure to collect and use meaningful data to improve service delivery, and (3) lack of productive collaboration with service providers. ACM empowers leaders to detect and rapidly respond to problems, make consistent improvements to performance (continuous improvement), and identify opportunities for reengineering (redesigning) service delivery systems (Harvard Kennedy School, 2019).

To achieve maximum efficiency in service provision, ACM suggests a number of strategies based on three basic criteria: One, conduct high-frequency reviews of real time data. Frequently reviewing real-time, operationally meaningful performance data enables agencies and providers to rapidly identify and address service delivery problems before they become ingrained or unfixable. Two, have regular, collaborative meetings between service providers and agencies. Regular collaborative meetings enable service providers and agencies to swiftly troubleshoot problems, solve specific operational challenges, and identify opportunities for broader systems transformation. Three, put together forward-looking performance management roadmaps. Performance management roadmaps help agencies proactively direct in-depth analytical attention toward topics and practices that are critical to success but may not be regularly reported or reviewed.

Similarly, to achieve maximum effectiveness in service provisions, ACM suggests strategies that are straightforward and relatively easy to follow. They include (1) select the right measures to track, (2) use data to drive action, (3) create a collaborative performance management culture, (4) regularly share government administrative data with the providers, and (5) elevate the status of procurement and contract management activities. To what extent the strategies would produce the intended results depend on the ability of the parties to work in close partnership. Collaboration is the essence of ACM. Government too often assumes that responsibility for achieving outcomes rests with providers once a service is contracted out. In practice, the successful outcome of contracted services is a two-way process. Both partners in the contract, the government and the service providers, must work together, in collaboration, to achieve the desired goals.

It should be worth nothing that the strategies suggested in ACM apply primarily to social services. They may not readily apply to all contracts, such as defense contracts, because of the nature of the goods. Defense goods are considerably different from social services, have different objectives, and serve different clientele. The same goes for other services that are not necessarily social services. Nevertheless, as a concept, ACM is useful and can be tailored to meet the challenges of government contracts.

8.9 Nonprofit Contracts

Nonprofit and government organizations have a long history of working together to address social issues and deliver publicly funded programs and services. They often share the same mission and goals and offer each other valuable resources. For instance, government agencies frequently allocate financial resources to nonprofits through contracts and grants that help address local community needs, while nonprofits tend to be more narrowly focused and allow government agencies greater flexibility and reach to address specific issues or target populations (Fyffe, 2015) . Roughly one-third of nonprofit budgets contain funding through government contracts and grants to deliver public programs and services (Pettijohn et al., 2013)

Despite mutual dependence, there are challenges to government nonprofit contracts, especially at the sub-national levels. Many of these challenges are due to bureaucratic and procedural hurdles that can lead to slow and cumbersome dealings. The rigidity of these requirements can constrain an agency's ability to make timely and meaningful changes to the process. A good example is the reporting requirements that are burdensome and often do not accurately reflect the effectiveness of agency contract and grant programs. Reporting is often framed in statutes and generally consists of boilerplate formats containing standard output and outcome measures that are reported at designated intervals (monthly, quarterly, or semiannually) and at the conclusion of the contract or grant. This often leaves little discretion in how state and local agencies and nonprofits report their accomplishments, as these formats for the most part have been developed to comply with federal reporting requirements (Fyffe, 2015). While these are real issues, advances have been made in recent years to bridge the gap and, in all likelihood, will continue in the coming years.

8.10 Chapter Summary

This chapter has presented a broad overview of contract costing. Governments have a long history of outsourcing or contracting out public goods and services to private firms and businesses as well as to non-profit organizations. There are two simple explanations why governments outsource or contract out services instead of providing them directly: cost savings and quality, although there have been questions about the extent of savings and quality outsourcing produces for government. Nevertheless, it is a vitally important function in government that costs governments hundreds of millions to billions of dollars every year. Like job costing, contract costing is a process: It involves tracking, recording, analyzing, and reporting costs, as they accumulate. The chapter provided a broad overview of government contracts; in particular, types of contracts, contract guidelines and procedure, and contract cost reporting. Finally, the chapter concluded with a brief discussion of contract performance management, and nonprofit contracts.

8.11 Review Questions

8.1 What is a contract? Why do governments contract out services? Who are the primary beneficiaries of government contracts?

8.2 What is contract costing? How does contract costing differ from job costing? What are some of the characteristics of contract costing?

8.3 Governments use different types of contracts to achieve specific objectives. Discuss five types of contracts governments use with specific objectives.

8.4 Why is it important to have strict guidelines for government contracts? Discuss the principal guidelines that governments use for contract costing.

8.5 What is a contract accounting report? Discuss the principal elements of a contract accounting report with examples.

8.6 What is contract performance management? How is contract performance monitored? What is active contract management? What strategies are typically used in active contract management?

8.7 What is a contracting process? What is a negotiated contract? Why does a government use negotiated contracts, as opposed to open contracts with competitive bidding?

8.8 A government recently contracted a private firm to construct a bridge at a cost of $7 million that includes $0.5 million for unforeseen problems. It was a fixed-price contract. Unforeseen issues led to an increase in costs, exceeding the contingency by a significant amount. The firm requested an additional payment of $1 million to cover the increased costs, while the government argued that the contractor should absorb the losses due to the fixed-price contract. How should the disagreement be resolved? What should the government do to avoid similar problems in the future?

Notes

1 Although governments do not produce goods in a conventional sense of the term, they provide goods and services for public consumption, commonly referred to as public goods. The goods typically include infrastructure, education, healthcare, public safety, environment, economic insurance, emergency service, disaster relief, and intangible products such as GPS, product safety, legal services, and so forth.

2 A bid protest is a legal challenge to a government contract award. Bidders can protest through the contracting agency, such as the Government Accountability Office (GAO), or the U.S. Court of Federal Claims.

3 The Federal Contractor Registry (FCR, 2019) is a third-party registration service that assists small to large businesses, Fortune 500 companies & state/county/city government agencies with System for Award Management (SAM) registration. SAM is an e-procurement system that collects data from contractors or potential contractors, validates and stores the data, and disseminates the data to various government acquisition agencies.

4 While the standards are required of all contracts, small businesses are often exempt from these standards until they become large enough that will require them to comply with the standards.

References

Alford, J. and O'Flynn, J. (2012). *Rethinking public services: Managing with external providers*. Basingstoke, UK: Palgrave McMillan.

Annessa, J. and Ivezaj, A. (2024). *Overview of cost accounting standards (CAS) for government contractors*. June. www.cbh.com/insights/articles/cost-accounting-standards-cas-government-contractors-guide/#:~:text=Cost%20Accounting%20Standards%20are%20a,taxpayers%20from%20fraud%20and%20abuse

Department of Defense. (2018). Independent Government Cost estimate (IGCE), in *Handbook for services acquisition*. US Department of Defense.

Diene, M. (2023). Importance of proper cost accounting in government contract. www.diener.org/importance-of-proper-cost-accounting-government-contracting/ [Accessed September 14, 2023].

Federal Contracting Center. (2024). *Understanding the past: A history of government contracting*. Washington, DC: Federal Contracting Center. December 17. www.federalcontractingcenter.com/understanding-the-past-a-history-of-government-contracting/

Federal Contractor Registry. (2019). *SAM: The first step in government contracting*. Las Vegas, NV: Federal Contractor Registry.

Fyffe, S.D. (2015). *Nonprofit government contracts and grants: The state agency perspective*. Washington, DC: Urban Institute.

Harvard Kennedy School. (2019). *Active contract management*. Harvard, MA: Harvard Kennedy School of Government Performance Lab.

Hilke, J.C. (1992). *Competition in government-financed services*. New York: Bloomsbury.

Hodge, G.A. (1999). *Privatization: An international review of performance*. New York: Routledge.

Lane, J-E. (2000). *New public management*. New York: Routledge.

Manion, P.W. (2003). (2000). Financing a recycling facility through a public-private partnership, in A. Khan and W.B. Hildreth (eds) *Case studies in public budgeting and financial management*. New York: Marcell Dekker, 763–772.

National Archives. (2025). Code of Federal Regulations: A point in time eCFR system. 9903-201-1 CAS Applicability. January 6. www.ecfr.gov/current/title-48/chapter-99/subchapter-B/part-9903/subpart-9903.2/section-9903.201-1
Osborne, S.P. (2006). The new public governance. *Public Management Review*, 8(3): 377–387.
Pettijohn, S.L., Elizabeth T.B., with De Vita, C.J., and Fyffe, S.D. (2013). *Nonprofit-government contracts and grants: Findings from the 2013 National Survey*. Washington, DC: Urban Institute.
Rosell, E. (2000). The chickens come home to roost: The publicization of private infrastructure, in A. Khan and W.B. Hildreth (eds) *Case studies in public budgeting and financial management*. New York: Marcell Dekker, 773–783.
Savas, E.S. (2001). (. Privatization and the new public management. *Fordham Urban Law Journal*, 28(5): 1731–1737.

9 Process Costing

9.1 Introduction

Goods and services that an organization provides go through a process. A process is a sequence of activities that takes place in stages where each stage typically consists of one or more activities. This simple definition of process also applies to process costing. Structurally, there are some similarities between job costing and process costing in that both track and assign costs to a product, a good or service. But the two are not the same: One focuses on assigning costs to an activity, a job, while the other focuses on assigning costs to a good or service, or product, as it goes through each stage of the production or delivery process. As such, both job costing and process costing belong to a category of costing called product costing. Product costing is the process of determining the total costs of a product, which is usually a good or service. The costs typically include direct labor, direct materials, and overhead. Breaking down costs in terms of direct labor, materials, and overhead helps an organization ascertain the costs precisely and assign them to responsible departments, agencies, or functional units of the organization.[1]

This chapter focuses on process costing. It begins with a brief discussion of process costing versus job costing, followed by a discussion of the stages of process costing, and the methods commonly used in process costing. The chapter concludes with a brief discussion of several topics related to process costing such as joint costing, hybrid costing, and process loss and waste.

9.1 Process Costing versus Job Costing

Formally, we can define process costing as a system of accounting in which costs are assigned equally to all units of a good or service. Since costs are equally assigned to all units of a good or service, it is assumed that the units

DOI: 10.4324/9781003486091-11

produced are homogeneous. As a result, process costing is useful in situations where there is a continuous flow of production such as gas, water, and electricity where product variation is almost nonexistent. However, it can also be applied to situations where the units of production are discrete rather than continuous such as routine citations for traffic infraction, trash collection, vaccines during flu season, and so on, so long as one is able to measure them in distinct units and their essential characteristics remain the same throughout the production or delivery process.

As defined earlier, a process is a series of activities that takes place in stages, usually in sequence, where each stage of the process may consist of one or more jobs. As such, there are some similarities between job costing and process costing in that both have the same goal: to determine the cost of a good or service. a Additionally, both use the same cost flows, double-entry accounting, a predetermined overhead rate, and the basic information used by both to determine the unit cost, which serves as the basis for both. However, there are also significant differences between the two (Seal et al, 2019; Eydman, 2017). For instance, in job costing, costs are ascertained separately for each job, whereas in process costing they are ascertained process-wise. In job costing, costs are assigned when a job is done, whereas in process costing, they are assigned at the end of a specific period, or the end of each sage of a job. However, the most important difference between the two is that in job costing the cost of a job is not transferred to another job, whereas in process costing, the cost of one stage of the process is transferred to the next stage until all the costs have been ascertained.

In addition to those mentioned above, process costing has another important distinguishing characteristic that separates it from job costing. Unlike job costing, process costing assumes a continuous process with homogeneous output, with no product variation. What this means is that one unit of output is essentially identical to another, such as a gallon of milk, a pound of sugar, a cell phone, or a television set, which makes it possible to use physical units as the basis for cost ascertainment. In government, this would apply to situations where there is a continuous flow of output such as a cubic foot of gas, a gallon of water, and a unit or kilowatt hour of electricity, where product variation is also nonexistent. And as noted earlier, it can also be applied to situations where the units of output are discrete rather than continuous, such as routine operations for drug treatments, vaccinations for common diseases, crime investigations, and so on, so long as one is able to measure them in distinct units and their essential characteristics remain the same or do not change much during the production or delivery process.

9.2 Stages of Process Costing

Process costing takes place in stages. Operationally, the stages in process costing are not that complicated, although one may get the impression that they are because they involve multiple stages until the final production or delivery is completed. The simplest way to understand process costing is to think of each stage as a process and each process with an account. The result of the process, which is usually an output quantity, is transferred to the next stage of the process and the process continues until the final good is produced or delivered. Figure 9.1 shows the procedure in process costing.

To give an example, suppose that a state Health and Human Services department has recently introduced a community-wide vaccination program in the state for a health care problem that attacks a certain age group. The number of residents who will receive the vaccine will vary from year to year depending on the severity of the problem. Let us say that the government plans to vaccinate 5,000 residents this year, out of the total population in the age group, based on initial screening. The cost of the program is $1.5 million, but the department will subsidize two-thirds of the cost of vaccination, including supplying the vaccine. The local health department, which will carry out the program, will absorb about a third of the cost estimated to be $480,000. Assume that the program involves a three-stage process: Stage 1– disseminating the information to the respective population group, Stage 2 – initial screening for vaccination, and Stage 3 – vaccinating the desired number. Table 9.1 provides cost information for the three stages.

As the table shows, of the three stages of the program, Process 2 will cost more than the other two because it involves initial screening that requires multiple tests to determine the most vulnerable members within the population group, numbering 5,000. Tables 9.2 – 9.4 show how the cost is transferred from one stage of the process to the next. The last table

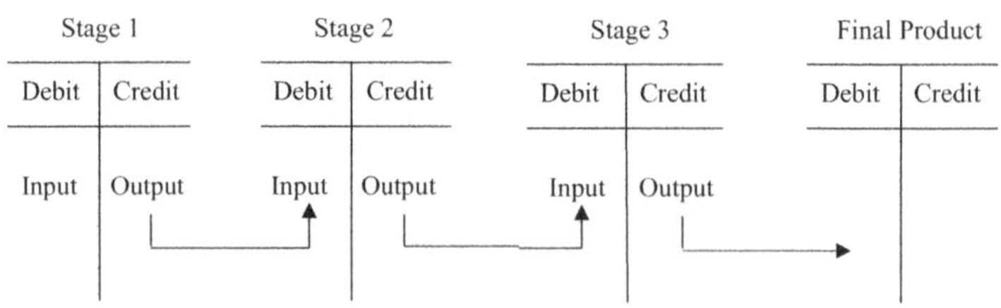

Figure 9.1 Stages of process costing

Table 9.1 Cost of the vaccination program by processes

Cost Category	*Process 1 Cost ($)*	*Process 2 Cost ($)*	*Process 3 Cost ($)*
Direct Materials	20,000	75,000	40,000
Direct Labor	30,000	175,000	60,000
Indirect Materials	4,000	15,000	8,000
Indirect Labor	6,000	35,000	12,000
Total	60,000	300,000	120,000

Indirect costs are assumed at 20% of direct costs

Table 9.2 Cost breakdown for process: Stage 1

Cost Category	*Cost Per Unit ($)*	*Total Cost ($)*		*Cost Per Unit ($)*	*Total Cost[1] ($)*
Direct Materials	4.00	20,000	Cost		
Direct Labor	6.00	30,000	Transferred to		
Indirect Materials	0.80	4,000	Process 2 →	12.00	60,000
Indirect Labor	1.20	6,000			
Total	12.00	60,000		12.00	60,000

[1]N = 5,000

Table 9.3 Cost breakdown for process: Stage 2

Cost Category	*Cost Per Unit ($)*	*Total Cost ($)*		*Cost Per Unit ($)*	*Total Cost[1] ($)*
Transfer to	12.00	60,000	Cost		
Process 1	15.00	75,000	Transferred to		
Direct Materials	35.00	175,000	Process 3 →	72.00	360,000
Direct Labor	3.00	15,000			
Indirect Materials	7.00	35,000			
Indirect Labor					
Total	72.00	360,000		72.00	360,000

[1] N = 5,000

Table 9.4 Cost breakdown for process: Stage 3

Cost Category	*Cost Per Unit ($)*	*Total Cost ($)*		*Cost Per Unit ($)*	*Total Cost[1] ($)*
Transfer to Process 3	72.00	360,000	Cost		
	8.00	40,000	Transferred to		
Direct Materials	12.00	60,000	Final Count →	96.00	480,000
Direct Labor	1.60	8,000			
Indirect Materials	2.40	12,000			
Indirect Labor					
Total	96.00	480,000		96.00	480,000

[1] N = 5,000

Table 9.5 Final process account

	N of Vaccinations	*Cost Per Unit ($)*	*Total Cost[1] ($)*
From Stage 3	5,000	96.00	480,000

[1] Total Cost = $96 × 5,000 = $480,000

in the example, Table 9.5, shows the final accounting of the cost for the program.

9.3 Cost Schedules

To keep the production and delivery process tractable, most organizations use a set of reports, called schedules, similar to job cost sheets but structured differently. Schedules summarize the information resulting from a process costing system. The tables presented above for the vaccination program can be considered as schedules, although typical schedules are much more involved. Three types of schedules are commonly used for this purpose: a schedule of equivalent production, a schedule of cost analysis, and a schedule of cost summary.

9.3.1 Schedule of Equivalent Production

It is common in most organizations that all units of a job that the organizations undertake will be fully completed by the end of an accounting period. If they do, it will make cost ascertainment considerably easy, but that is seldom the case. Frequently, there will be units that will remain incomplete or completed partially; as such, they will appear in an organization's inventory. In traditional costing, when costs are assigned to a good or service, only those units that have been completed are taken into consideration. However, in process costing this would include both completed and partially completed units. Together, these units (completed and partially completed) are called equivalent units. The rationale for including partially completed units in cost ascertainment is that even though they have not been fully completed, the agencies or departments involved in the process did incur some costs (materials, labor, and overhead) for the portion of the job that has been completed; otherwise, it will be underestimated. Therefore, to accurately measure the amount of job in a process (goods produced or service delivered) during a given period one must include both completed as well as partially completed units.

Also, it is important to recognize before the schedules are prepared whether there is any carryover from the previous period. For most new jobs, there will be no carryovers, which means no beginning inventory, but for an existing or a continuing job, there will be carryovers, meaning that there is a beginning inventory. Having a beginning inventory can affect the time it will take to complete the process, the order of completion, and the cost of the process. Two methods are commonly used for calculating the equivalent units, without and with beginning inventory: weighted average method and First-In, First-Out (FIFO) method (Seal et al. 2019). Both methods are simple in concept and can be used together or interchangeably for the same job. There is a third method that is also used, depending on the nature and condition of the job (goods or service), called Last-In, First Out (LIFO).

9.3.1.1 Weighted Average Method

Weighted average is simply the average of a set of observations, which are scaled differently (weighted) based on their importance or contribution to the problem but calculated differently when applied to equivalent units. When applied to equivalent units, they are calculated as the number of units completed during a given period, plus the units that are incomplete multiplied by the percentage of their completion. As noted earlier, equivalent units include both completed and partially completed units.

To give an example, consider the federal Drug Enforcement Agency that deals with the government's Drug Interdiction Program, which is a continuous process of interrupting drug trafficking into the country. The process includes a number of steps (stages) that usually start with queuing (Process 1), followed by detecting (Process 2), sorting (Process 3), monitoring (Process 4), intercepting (Process 5), apprehending (Process 6), and finally prosecuting (Process 7). The steps do not necessarily have to take place in sequence, but for convenience we will assume they take place in sequence and the measures used in each step (stage) are reasonably consistent.

Let us say that the agency has been investigating 125 drug interdiction cases this past year, of which 45 cases were solved completely (prosecuted) by the agency and 80 remain unsolved by the end of the year. Since 45 cases were fully completed, we can safely assume that these cases received 100 percent of materials, labor, and overhead needed to complete them. Of the 80 cases that remain unsolved, assume now that 75 percent were completed as to materials and 60 percent as to direct labor and overhead, called conversion, when the year ended.

To obtain the equivalent units that remain in process, we use a simple expression, given by

$$EU_{\text{Process}} = (UP)(PC) \tag{9.1}$$

where EU_{Process} is the number of equivalent units in process, UP is the number of units remaining in process (to be completed), and PC is the percentage of their completion. The equivalent units for the agency, therefore, will be 60 for materials and 48 for conversion, obtained by applying the expression in Equation 9.1; that is, $UP \times PC = 80 \times 0.75 = 60$ for materials and $UP \times PC = 80 \times 0.60 = 48$ for conversion (direct labor and overhead), respectively.

Since 45 units were fully completed, it is necessary to revise Equation 9.1 so that the new equation will include the units that have already been completed as well as those that remain in process, as shown below:

$$EU_{\text{Total}} = UC + (UP \times PC) \tag{9.2}$$

where EU_{Total} is the total equivalent units, UC is the units completed, and the rest of the terms are the same as before.

Now, applying the revised expression in Equation 9.2 to the problem we can obtain the respective equivalent units, as follows:

$$\begin{aligned} EU_{\text{Total}} &= UC + (UP \times PC) \\ &= 45 + (80 \times 0.75) \\ &= 45 + 60 \\ &= 105 \text{ units} \end{aligned}$$

for materials, and

$$
\begin{aligned}
EU_{Total} &= UC + (UP \times PC) \\
&= 45 + (80 \times 0.60) \\
&= 45 \times 48 \\
&= 93 \text{ units}
\end{aligned}
$$

for conversion.

Table 9.6 shows the total equivalent units for materials and conversion, together with information on the units to be accounted for by the agency. Note that we made an implicit assumption in the example that all 125 cases of interdictions occurred during the accounting period, which means that there were no carryovers (no beginning inventory) from the previous year. As a result, no units appear under the columns for materials and conversion for the beginning inventory. However, if we change the assumption that there were carryovers (a beginning inventory) from the previous year the result would be different. This is where the second method, First-in First-out (FIFO), comes in.

Table 9.6 Schedule of equivalent production

Stages of Completion	*Units to be Completed*	*Equivalent Units*	
		Materials	*Conversion*
I. Without beginning inventory			
Beginning inventory	---	---	---
Units started and completed	45	45	45
Ending inventory	80	---	---
Work-in-process:			
Materials at 75%	---	60	---
Conversion at 60%	---	---	48
Total units	125	105	93
II. With beginning inventory			
Beginning inventory	15	15	15
Units started and completed	30	30	30
Ending inventory	80	---	---
Work-in- process:			
Materials at 75%	---	60	---
Conversion at 60%	---	---	48
Total units	125	105	93

9.3.1.2 First-in First-out Method (FIFO)

While the weighted average method takes into consideration the units that have been completed as well as those that remain in process, it does not take into consideration the units in the beginning inventory, including those that need to be completed first. The FIFO takes into consideration the beginning inventory (the carryovers from previous periods) as well as the units that need to be completed first. This is particularly important in situations such as homicides, drug interdictions, medical treatments, and so forth, where the results (outputs) of a process do not always get completed within a given period and where there are frequent carryovers from previous periods. In other words, there is a continuous flow of output in the production or delivery process where the units remaining in process at the end of one period become the beginning inventory in the next period, and as such, need to be considered first (Figure 9.1).

Thus, in calculating the equivalent units for an organization it is important to take into consideration the units in the beginning inventory. To do so, we need to reformulate the expression in Equation 9.2 for equivalent units by taking into consideration the beginning inventory, so that

$$EU_{\text{Total}} = BI + UC + (UP \times PC) \tag{9.3}$$

where BI represents the beginning inventory and the rest of the terms are the same, as before.

Table 9.6 also shows the equivalent units for the department. According to the table, of the 45 units that were fully completed, let us assume that 15 were in the beginning inventory. That means all 15 units, like the remaining 30 in this group, received full materials, labor, and overhead support needed for their completion. Incidentally, these 15 units, similar to the 30 units, also appear under the materials and conversion columns for the beginning inventory.

As for the 80 units in the ending inventory, for convenience, we assume that 75 percent were completed as to materials and 60 percent were completed with regard to conversion, although we could have used a different percentage for each, thereby producing a total of 105 and 93 equivalent units, for the respective categories, as shown below:

$$\begin{aligned} EU_{\text{Total}} &= BI + UC + (UP \times PC) \\ &= 15 + 30 + (80 \times 0.75) \\ &= 15 + 30 + 60 \\ &= 105 \text{ units} \end{aligned}$$

for materials, and

$$\begin{aligned} EU_{Total} &= BI + UC + (UP \times PC) \\ &= 15 + 30 + (80 \times 0.60) \\ &= 15 + 30 + 48 \\ &= 93 \text{ units.} \end{aligned}$$

for conversion. Note that these results also appear under the materials and the conversion columns in Table 9.6.

It should be worth noting that there is a fundamental difference in application when these methods are used in government, in particular FIFO, as opposed to when they are used in the private sector. For instance, when FIFO is used in the private sector, the units in the beginning inventory are usually completed first, especially if the products are perishable or tend to become obsolete fast, contributing to loss in value the longer they are held in inventory. As such, they need to be transferred out before beginning to work on the current inventory; hence, the term first-in first-out. However, there are situations where the units in the beginning inventory do not necessarily have to be completed before dealing with the units that began in the current period. They can be completed in any sequence but, from an accounting point of view, they must be recognized when calculating the total equivalent units for a given period.

9.3.1.3 Last-in First-out Method (LIFO)

As noted above, in process costing not all units that are in the beginning inventory need to be completed first. It may be necessary sometimes to complete the units that enter the process last, especially in government, before completing those that are already in process, in which case the method that would be appropriate is Last-In First-Out (LIFO). A good example is medical emergencies where patients brought to an emergency room who need to be treated first before other patients waiting in line. Another good example would be criminal investigations where some investigations need to be completed first before other investigations in the process. There are plenty of other situations in government where LIFO would be useful.

However, using LIFO may not be quite as simple in part because ascertaining costs in LIFO can be quite difficult in that it may be necessary to maintain additional record keeping, which can complicate the process. This may partly explain why it is not as widely used in the private sector (Tinkelman, D.P. and Ling, Q, 2022). However, there are situations where it can be helpful. For instance, when the cost of goods increases faster either due to inflation or some other factors it can make the income statement appear higher than it should be.

To give an example, suppose that a firm acquires an inventory at the beginning of the year consisting of 500 units of a good at a cost of $10 a unit, with a total cost of $5,000 ($10 × 500 = $5,000). It sells the good for $13 a unit, producing an income of $6,500 ($13 × 500 = $6,500). Let us say that the cost of the goods increases from $10 a unit to $12 a unit, which will increase the cost of the inventory from the current cost of $5,000 to $6,000 ($12 × 500 = $6,000], while the firm's income statement will show the income of $6,500, assuming the firm is not able to increase the sale price immediately. This means that it will have to pay more in taxes on its income, while its net income decreases by $500 [$6,500 - $6,000 = $500] because of higher cost.

From an income perspective, the firm will be better off selling the last batches or units of the good as fast as possible to minimize the effect on income, since it had to purchase them at a higher price.[2] Theoretically, if price remains the same over time and the inventories are not perishable or do not become obsolete fast it makes very little difference which method is used. Despite its apparent shortcomings, LIFO is used on occasion in the private sector, especially when there is a cost increase because of inflation and other factors, and the goods need to be cleared off the market.

9.3.2 Schedule of Cost Analysis

Once we know the number of equivalent units in an inventory, we can compute the cost of total equivalent units as well as the cost per equivalent unit. The procedure for calculating these costs is quite simple: The former is obtained by simply adding all the costs in an inventory, whereas the latter is obtained by dividing the total cost by the number of equivalent units. The procedure applies equally to all three methods: weighted average, FIFO, and LIFO, especially the first two.

Table 9.7 presents a schedule of cost analysis for the agency with and without the beginning inventory. As the table shows, the total cost of the program for the department, without the beginning inventory, was $6.89 million, which was obtained by adding the costs of units completed ($2,480,000) and the costs of units in WIP ($4,409,6000); that is, $2,480,000 + $4,409,6000 = $6,890,000. To keep the discussion simple, let us assume that we know the costs a priori. When these costs (costs of units completed and units in WIP) are divided by their corresponding equivalent units (from Table 9.6), we have the cost per equivalent unit, which $55,120 ($6,890,000/125 = $55,120). Conversely, if we multiply the equivalent units by the cost per equivalent unit, it will produce the

Table 9.7 Schedule of cost analysis

Cost Description	*Units*	*Costs of units completed ($)*	*Total cost ($)*
I. Without beginning inventory			
Beginning inventory	---	---	---
Units completed	45	2,480,400	2,480,400
Units in WIP	80	2,409,600	4,409,600 -
Cost / Equivalent units	125	55,120	6,890,000
II. With beginning inventory			
Beginning inventory	15	826,800	826,800
Units completed	30	1,653,600	1,653,600
Units in WIP	80	4,409,600	4,409,600
Cost/Equivalent units	125	55,120	6,890,000

total cost of the program. That is, (45 x $55,120) + (80 x $55,120) = $2,480,400 + $4,409,600 = $6,890,000.

Returning to the example, let us assume that the 15 units we have in the beginning inventory will need to be completed first before completing the 30 units in the current period. The total units completed in the current period will remain the same at 45, as before. The process of determining the costs will also be the same, except that the costs of 45 units will be split between units in the beginning inventory and the units in the current period; that is, $826,800 + $1,653,600 = $2,48,400. This is shown in the lower half of Table 9.7.[3]

To see if our calculation is correct, we simply multiply the cost per equivalent unit by the corresponding equivalent units for each cost category and then add them to see if they add up to the total cost of operation for the agency. Since it produces a total cost of $6.89 million, the result appears to be correct, as shown below:

$$\begin{aligned} TC &= (CPU_{Comp} \times EU) + (CPU_{WIP} \times EU) \\ &= [(\$55{,}120 \times 15) + (\$55{,}120 \times 30)] + [(\$55{,}120 \times 80) \\ &= \$826{,}800 + \$1{,}653{,}600 + \$4{,}409{,}600 \\ &= \$6{,}890{,}000 \end{aligned} \tag{9.4}$$

where TC is the total cost, CPU_{Comp} is the cost per unit of completed units, and CPU_{WIP} is the cost per unit of the units remaining in WIP.

9.3.3 Schedule of Cost Summary

The final phase in process costing involves the construction of a schedule of cost summary, showing the costs for both beginning and ending inventories. Information contained in this schedule comes from the schedule of equivalent production and the schedule of cost analysis. Table 9.8 presents the schedule of cost summary for materials and conversion costs.

As shown in the table, the cost of completed units without the beginning inventory is $2,480,400, which is obtained by multiplying the number of completed units by the cost per unit; that is, 45 x $55,120 = $2,480,400. Note that the cost per unit of $55,120 came from Table 9.7, which was obtained by dividing the total cost by the number of equivalent units, completed as well as units in the ending inventory; that is $6,890,000/(45 + 80) = $6,890,000/125 = $55,120. The costs of units in process, on the other hand, were obtained by multiplying the number of units in process as to materials by the cost per unit in WIP, as well as the number of units in process as to conversion by the cost per unit in WIP. That is, (60 x $40,829.63)

Table 9.8 Schedule of cost summary

Cost Description	*Costs of Units Completed ($)*	*Costs of Units in Process ($)*
I. Without beginning inventory		
Beginning inventory	---	---
Units started and		
Completed [45 × $55,120]	2,480,400	---
Ending inventory (WIP)		
Materials: 60 × $40,829.63[1]	---	2,449,778
Conversion: 48 × $40,829.63[2]	- - -	1,959,8222
Total	2,480,000	4,409,600
II. With beginning inventory		
Beginning inventory		
[15 × $55,120]	826,800	---
Units started and completed	1,653,600	
[30 × $55,120]		---
Ending inventory (WIP)		
Materials: 60 × $40,829.63[1]	---	2,449,778
Conversion: 48 × $40,829.63[2]	_ ---	1,959,822
Total	2,480,400	4,409,600

[1,2] $4,409,600/(60 + 48) = $4,409,600/108 = $40,829.63

+ (48 x $40,829.63) = $2,4459,778 + $1,959,822 = $4,409,600. The sum of the two costs, as expected, is equal to the total cost of the program of $6,890,000 ($2,480,400 + $4,409,600 = $6,890,000).

We can repeat the process with the beginning inventory. As shown in Table 9.8, the costs of units completed as well as the costs of units in process with beginning inventory also turn out to be $6.89 million ($2,480,400 + $4,409,600 = $6,890,000), after rounding, as one would expect. A breakdown of these costs will include $826,800 (15 x $55,120 = $826,800) for completed units in beginning inventory and $1,653,600 (30 x $55,120 = $1,653,600) for completed units that began in the current period, with a total cost of $2,480,400 ($826,800 + $1,653,600 = $2,480.400) for completed units. Similarly, a breakdown of costs for the units remaining in process will include $2,449,778 (60 x $40,829.63 = $2,449,778) in material costs and $1,959,822 (48 x $40,829.63 = $1,959,822) in conversion costs, with a combined total of $4,409,600 ($2,449,778 + $1,959,822 = $4,409,600).

It is important to note that so long as there are units remaining in a WIP account, they will automatically become a part of the beginning inventory for the next period. Consequently, one must transfer the costs of completed units out of work-in-process inventory to show the balance at the end of the period. Take the cost for the agency with beginning inventory as a case in point: the total cost of operation for the year was $6.89 million, of which the costs of completed units, including those that appear in the beginning inventory, were $2,284,400; that is, $826,800 + $1,653,600 = $2,284,400. The difference between $6.89 million and $2,284,400, which is approximately $4,409,600, then becomes the costs associated with the beginning inventory, the units completed in the current period, and the units in the inventory account. If the department fails to complete all the units within the accounting period, the balance will become part of next year's beginning inventory, and the process will continue.

9.3.3.1 Modified FIFO

The FIFO method we discussed above is the standard method where the units that are first in are to be completed first before completing the rest in the inventory, usually one unit at a time, which could be time-consuming. The simplest way to address the problem is to take an average of the unit costs of the goods and services transferred within a period called the average method, as used in arithmetic average, or extend the expression in Equation 9.3. The key difference between the two is that modified FIFO uses a single average cost for a period, while standard FIFO tracks the cost of each individual inventory item.

Table 9.9 Schedule of cost summary: The vaccination program

Cost Description	*Stage 1 ($)*	*Stage 2 ($)*	*Stage 3 ($)*	*Cost Summary ($)*
Beginning Inventory	---	---	---	---
Cost of Direct Materials	20,000	75,000	40,000	135,000
Cost of Direct Labor	30,000	175,000	60,000	265,000
Cost of Indirect Materials	4,000	15,000	8,000	27,000
Cost of Indirect Labor	6,000	35,000	12,000	53,000
Work-in-Process	---	---	---	---
Total Cost (w/o Transfer)	60,000	300,000	120,000	480,000
Transfer from Stage 1	---	60,000	---	---
Transfer from Stage 2	---	---	360,000	---
Total Cost (w/Transfer)		360,000	480,000	480,000

9.3.3.1 Returning to the Health Care Problem

Interestingly, we could have constructed similar schedules for the health care problem; it would be much simpler than the ones discussed above. Part of the reason for this is that programs such as vaccinations are one-shot deals in that they do not usually have carryovers from the previous year, and there are also no works that remain in process for next year; as such, they are much easier to construct. This is clearly reflected in cost assignments for each stage of the process. Table 9.9 provides the schedule of cost summary for the program, stage by stage

As can be seen from the table, since there were no carryovers, meaning no beginning inventory, and no work remaining in process inventories, the schedule was relatively easy to construct. Had there been carryovers or work-in-process inventories, the results would have included all three schedules, similar to the Drug Interdiction Program, using the available methods such as weighted average, FIFO, modified FIFO, and so forth.

9.3.4 Process Costing with Multiple Products

In dealing with the drug interdiction problem, we made an assumption that we have a single production unit (the Drug Enforcement Agency) that is responsible for drug interdictions, among others. The drawback of this assumption is that since we were dealing with a single production unit, we needed only one Work-in-Process inventory. In reality, there could be more than one production unit where the output from one department would pass to the next, and eventually to the final inventory account. When more than one unit is involved, the process can be complicated as it would require that the accounting system maintain as many WIP inventory accounts as there are units in the process. This will also require more work, since a separate set of schedules will have to be prepared for each unit and the corresponding work in the process will have to be reconciled in the final account. However, there are situations where the same process may lead to two or more products, in which case the method that is commonly used is joint costing.

9.4 Joint Costing

Joint costing is a special case of process costing. It is primarily used in situations where two or more products emerge from a single process (Fabbozi et al., 2012). While the products may emerge from the same process, they are not separately identifiable until a certain stage is reached in the process. This stage is the split-off point, just like the branches of a tree splitting off from the stem. Costs incurred prior to this point are common costs. There are two main aspects to accounting for joint products: One, how the common process costs should be apportioned between the joint products up to the split-off point. Two, whether the original unit (department or agency) should still be responsible for the costs after the split or allow one or more departments to take over the production or delivery of the products and their costs.

Let us look at the apportion aspect first. We can use the Drug Interdiction Program discussed earlier, as an example. The program has seven stages, from queuing (Stage 1) to prosecuting (Stage 7). Let us say that some of the drug traffickers also have criminal history, including homicides, unrelated to drug trafficking, which the agency did not know until they were apprehended (Stage 6). Stage-6 is the split-off point. Since some of the traffickers had homicide history, the agency decided to forward those cases to the Homicide Department for prosecution. Assume that of the 125 cases, 15 were homicide cases, and it cost the agency $1 million to apprehend the 15 traffickers, excluding prosecution, which is the common cost. In other words, it is the cost the two departments must share since the individuals were involved in both homicides and drug trafficking. As to the exact amount that must be apportioned between the two departments will depend on a variety of factors, including the time the Homicide Department would have spent to apprehend them as well as the costs of labor, materials, and overheads.

With regard to the second aspect, whether the agency will prosecute the remaining 110 cases or forward them to a different department, let us say that the agency will forward them to a different department of the government that prosecutes drug traffickers. The total cost of prosecution, say, is approximately $750,000, which will be split between the Homicide Department and the prosecution department in proportion to the number of cases. It is worth noting that the procedure we used to apportion the cost is called the physical measures (quantity) method since it is based on the physical quantity, the number of drug traffickers and homicide cases which is simple and relatively straightforward. Besides physical measures, there are other methods that can also be used depending on the nature of the products and the stages the products have to go through.

9.5 Hybrid Costing

As the name implies, hybrid costing is a method of costing that combines elements of both job and process costing. It is particularly suitable for products (goods and services) that are specific and standardized, thus allowing for tracking costs at both the individual job level and process level. By combining elements of job-order and process costing, a hybrid system can allocate costs more precisely to individual projects or service areas. For instance, a large government project, such as infrastructure, might use job-order costing to track detailed costs for each phase, while standardized, routine administrative services could be analyzed using process costing. However, implementing a hybrid system can be challenging due to the need to identify which aspects of each costing method are best suited for different government activities and services.

9.6 Process Loss and Waste

Organizations using process costing can easily recognize wastes and losses within various departments and agencies. These may occur for a variety of reasons such as technological gaps, natural causes, and inefficiency. For example, governments frequently experience losses and wastes from inefficiency, overspending, or when resources are spent without precise objectives. This can be due to mismanagement, inexperience, oversight, and duplication of service. Good examples are food stamps, provided under SNAP, to individuals when they do not need them, or when employees misuse overtime, and so forth. In each instance, it costs government money that could be used for other vitally needed goods and services. In fact, the Government Accountability Office (GAO), in its annual audit report, provides details of fraud, wastes, and abuse in various agencies and departments, and the money it costs the government each year (GAO, 2024).

However, losses can also result not necessarily from fraud, waste, and abuse, but from wear and tear, obsolescence, and predictable occurrences during normal operations of the government. These losses are often considered natural, as part of normal operations of the government, and not necessarily related to poor management and inefficiency. From an accounting point of view, the losses, whether they are from normal operations of the government or from unusual circumstances, need to be accounted for to account for the final cost of production and delivery.

9.7 Chapter Summary

Process costing plays a vitally important role in cost accounting, as all goods and services must go through a process before they can be produced or delivered. This chapter has presented a broad overview of process costing, its characteristics, its basic difference from job costing, and the procedure for process costing, including the two most frequently used methods in process costing: weighted average, and First-in and First-out (FIFO). The chapter also focuses on cost schedules typically used for cost reporting in process costing. Process costing is particularly suitable in situations where the products are homogeneous, which makes it possible to assign costs equally to these units. But it can also be applied to situations where the output units are discrete rather than continuous, so long as their essential characteristics remain the same or do not change much during the production or delivery process. The chapter concluded with a brief discussion of several topics related to process costing such as joint costing, hybrid costing, and process loss and wastes.

9.8 Review Questions

9.1 Define process costing. How does it differ from job costing and contract costing?

9.2 What are the three stages of process costing? Give an example of each.

9.3 The IT department of a large metropolitan government processes data that passes through two operating units of the government; we will call them A and B. Unit A collects all the necessary information at the beginning of the process, analyzes them, and prepares the results, while Unit B disburses the information to respective agencies of the government. Both departments use the weighted average method. The work is done uniformly, although the tasks involved are not identical. The following information pertains to Unit A for the month of April:

a. Beginning Work In Process (WIP), February 1: 100,000 pieces of information; 100 percent completed with respect to materials and 40 percent completed with respect to conversion. The costs assigned to the work are as follows:

Materials	$20,000
Labor	10,000
Overhead	30,000

b. Ending Work In Process (WIP), April 30: 50,000 pieces of information; 100 percent completed with respect to materials and 60 percent completed with respect to conversion.
c. Information processed and disbursed: 370,000 pieces [Hint: Units started 320,000]. The following costs were added during the month:

Materials	$211,000
Labor	100,000
Overhead	270,000

Now, using the information above,

i. Prepare a schedule of equivalent units.
ii. Calculate the cost per equivalent unit.

9.4 What is the difference between the weighted average method and FIFO? Under what circumstances would you use one, as opposed to the other?

9.5 A local hospital treated 325 trauma patients last year; 200 of those patients have been completely treated and 125 remain under treatment. Of those who are under treatment, 80 percent were completed with respect to materials (hospital stay) and 40 percent with respect to conversion (direct labor such as nursing care, and overheads) by the time the year ended. Let us suppose that of the 200 patients who were completely treated, 50 were in a queue from the previous year (namely, beginning inventory, meaning that they were already there when the year started).

Given the information above,

a. Prepare a schedule of equivalent units (patients, in our case), using (1) the weighted average method, (2) FIFO, and (3) interpret the results.
b. Prepare a schedule of cost analysis.

c. Prepare a schedule of cost summary.
d. Interpret the results.
[Hint: Use cost data of your choice]

9.6 What is LIFO? How does it differ from FIFO? Give an example where LIFO would be an appropriate method to use in government.

9.7 What is joint costing? How does it differ from a typical process costing.

9.8 What is a split-off point? How are the costs apportioned between pre- and post-split-off point? Give an example.

Notes

1 In cost accounting, it is easy to trace a direct cost, but not so with indirect costs. As such, indirect costs are usually allocated and direct costs are traced; however, cost assignment applies to both direct and indirect costs.

2 To balance out the effect of cost increase for inflation and other factors, firms using LIFO often gives a "tax holiday" to consumers, which lowers their income but also the tax they have to pay on the income.

References

Eydman, M. (2017). Comparison of Job Order and Process Costing. University of the People. www.academia.edu/40840448/Comparison_of_Job_Order_and_Process_Costing.

Fabozzi, F.J., Drake, P.P., and Polimeni, R.S. (2008). (editors) The Complete CFO Handbook: From Accounting to Accountability. New York: John Wiley.

Government Accountability Office. (2024). *GAO overview: Understanding wastes in the federal government.* Washington, DC: Government Accountability Office. www.gao.gov/products/gao-24-107198

Tinkelman, D.P. and Ling, Q. (2022). Rise and decline of LIFO. *Accounting Historians Journal.* 49 (2), 103–120.

10 Cost Allocation

10.1 Introduction

Internally, the functional units of a governments serve two important purposes: those that provide service to other functional units, called service departments, and those that receive or use the service the service departments provide, called user departments. In providing a service, like any service provider, the service departments incur costs that they must allocate to the user departments or to the final users of the service. For instance, a hospital may want to allocate the costs of patient admissions to patient wards or to outpatient services, and eventually to the patients. Similarly, the IT department of a government may want to allocate the costs of its service to the departments that use its service, or a building maintenance department may want to allocate the costs of maintenance to the departments it maintains, and so forth. In general, when a department provides service to other departments, it does not generate any revenue for the organization, since it is internal to the organization, but the provision is essential for the effective functioning of the organization. Although there is no actual transfer of money between the departments, from an accounting point of view, without recognizing the costs the service departments incur and allocating them to respective user departments the total cost of operation of the organization would be seriously undermined.

While cost allocation is relatively simple when it comes to direct costs, indirect costs are much more difficult because they cannot be easily attributed to a single department providing a good or service. However, there are methods, such as activity-based costing, discussed in the next chapter, that can more effectively deal with it. This chapter focuses on cost allocation, with an emphasis on the cost allocation process, followed by a discussion of the methods commonly used in cost allocation.

DOI: 10.4324/9781003486091-12

10.2 Cost Allocation Process

Cost allocation is the process of allocating costs from a service department to one or more user departments for which costs are measured separately. Measuring costs separately makes it possible for an organization to allocate costs properly and, more importantly, to meet legal and reporting requirements, especially where contractual obligations are concerned, a common practice in government. According to Oliver (2000), cost allocation involves a multi-step process. By and large, they include the following: (1) determine the cost object, (2) define the allocation objective, (3) identify the costs, in particular indirect costs since they are more difficult to allocate than direct costs, (4) select the allocation base, which serves as the basis for allocating costs, or a group of costs called a cost pool, to a cost object, (5) calculate the allocation rate which can be easily obtained, for instance, by dividing the total cost by the total quantity, and (6) allocate the costs, using any standard or acceptable methods.

Of the steps mentioned above, the cost allocation base is particularly important because how a base is selected can have a significant effect on the allocation process and, more importantly, on the overall cost management of an organization. Shim and Siegel (1991) suggest several criteria for selecting the base, which can also apply to a government. These include, among others, the cause-and-effect relationship, benefits received, fairness, and ability to pay. The cause-and-effect relationship establishes a logical connection between a cost object and the incurrence of costs. It provides a rationale for allocating costs in that there needs to be a direct relationship between resource consumption and the costs charged to a cost object to justify cost allocation. For instance, if a user department consumes k amount of resources, the cost manager can do a demand analysis to determine what contributed to the level of consumption and its effect on the cost, and how to allocate and control costs if demand changes.

The benefits received criterion is self-explanatory. It simply says that cost should be allocated on the basis of the amount of benefit received by a user department from a service department. To give an example, suppose that a government introduces an organization-wide job training program that will benefit its departments. The government can allocate the costs of the program to all the departments equally, or proportionately based on the number of employees who received training for each department. Thus, if a department sends more of its employees for training it will be charged more; in other words, the more it will absorb the cost.

The fairness criterion implies that the basis of allocation should be fair. Fairness is difficult to define in precise terms, but we can use common sense explanation of what it means. Using the training program as an example, allocating costs based on head counts (number of employees who participated in the program from each department) would be a fair way to allocate the cost than allocating it equally to all the departments so that no one department bears a disproportionate share of the costs. In other words, a department that had no participants, or had the least number of participants in the program does not bear a disproportionate share of the cost.

Finally, the ability to bear criterion indicates that the user departments must have the ability to bear the costs. Again, going back to the training program example, if a user department does not have the ability to bear the cost yet needs the program, the government must find a way to assume the cost or distribute it between the participating departments in some fashion if, in the judgment of the decision makers, the program will benefit all the participating departments vis-a-vis the government, as a whole. In other words, although it may not benefit the departments equally in that some departments may benefit more than others, in the aggregate, the government will be better off from the program.

10.3 Methods of Cost Allocation

Cost allocation is relatively simple if cost flows in one direction from a single service department to one or more user departments, but when several service departments are involved in a process in that when cost flows in multiple directions, allocation can become complex. This section presents three simple but frequently used methods that can deal with different levels of complexity in cost allocation: the direct method, the step-down method, and the reciprocal method.

10.3.1 Direct Method

In a direct method, costs are allocated directly from a service department to one or more user departments. In general, when n-user departments receive service from a service department, the costs are allocated in direct proportion to the amount of service they receive. The proportionality factor, which serves as a basis for cost allocation, is called the cost allocation base. The cost allocation base for a service department reflects the amount of service it provides to other departments. In most instances, the base is selected in such a way that makes it relatively easy to measure. Examples of the cost allocation base will be the number of labor hours, number of machine hours, number of employees, units of goods, and so on.

10.3.1.1 Allocation Based on Total Costs

To give an example, consider a case where the IT department of a government which, for convenience, we will call X, provides service to four user departments within the government, say, D_1, D_2, D_3, and D_4. Let us say that it cost the department \$1.5 million last year to provide the service. The total amount of service provided by the department was 100,000 hours (the cost allocation base) at a cost of \$15 an hour. This included both fixed and variable costs.

We can use a simple expression to determine cost allocation for our service department to the four user departments, based on the total cost of service the department incurred, as shown below:

$$C_j = cQ / m \tag{10.1}$$

where c is the cost per hour of service, Q is the quantity of service, *m* is the number of user departments, and C_j is the cost share of the jth user department (for j = 1, 2, …, m). Therefore, the cost share of each user department for the service the IT department provides is \$375,000; that is, $cQ/m = (\$15 \times 100{,}000)/4 = \$1{,}500{,}000/4 = \$375{,}000$. In other words, $\$375{,}000_1 + \$375{,}000_2 + \$375{,}000_3 + \$375{,}000_4 = \$1{,}500{,}000$, where the subscripts 1, 2, 3, and 4 represent the departments D_1, D_2, D_3, and D_4, respectively.

10.3.1.2 Allocation Based on Proportionality

An important consideration in cost allocation is that it must be fair in that it must be allocated in proportion to the amount of benefit a user department receives. The example presented above assumes that regardless of the quantity of service the user departments received, their cost share would be the same: \$375,000. In reality, very seldom do the user departments consume or receive the same amount of service. In most cases, the amount varies, depending on the size and needs of the user departments. Therefore, we need to use a slightly different expression than the one in Equation 10.1 that would correctly reflect the cost share of the user departments, based on the proportion of service each receives from X.

The following provides a simple expression for allocating costs, based on the proportionality of service the user departments receive:

$$TC_X = \sum_{j=1}^{m} cQ_j \tag{10.2}$$

where TC_X is the total cost of service for department X, c is the cost per unit of service, and Q_j is the quantity or the amount of service the jth department receives (j = 1, 2, 3, …, m). Since c is a constant (remains the same across the board), we can rewrite Equation 10.2 by factoring it out to obtain the cost share of each department, as follows:

$$TC_X = c\sum_{j=1}^{m} Q_j \tag{10.3}$$

Let us now assume that each department consumes or receives a different amount of service from the IT department. For instance, D_1 receives 20,000 hours of service, D_2 receives 30,000 hours, D_3 receives 40,000 hours, and D_4 receives 10,000 hours. Thus, applying the equation above to the amount of service the user departments received, we obtain the following allocation for each of the user departments:

$$\begin{aligned}
TC_X &= c\sum_{j=1}^{4} Q_j \\
&= cQ_1 + cQ_2 + cQ_3 + cQ_4 \\
&= (\$15 \times 20{,}000_1) + (\$15 \times 30{,}000_2) + (\$15 \times 40{,}000_3) \\
&\quad + (\$15 \times 10{,}000_4) \\
&= \$300{,}000_1 + \$450{,}000_2 + \$600{,}000_3 + \$150{,}000_4 \\
&= \$1{,}500{,}000
\end{aligned}$$

where the subscripts 1, 2, 3, and 4 represent respectively the four user departments D_1, D_2, D_3, and D_4, as before.

Table 10.1 shows the cost of service, the allocation base, and the cost share by the four user departments. As the table shows, of the \$1.5 million in total cost the service department incurred, \$300,000 are allocated to D_1, \$450,000 to D_2, \$600,000 to D_3, and \$150,000 to D_4 based on their respective share of the service. In other words, these are the cost shares of the user departments based on the amount of service each received, which are different from the allocation when proportionality was not a factor.

10.3.1.3 Allocation Based on Cost Structure

In the example presented above, we assumed that the constant term c, which is cost per unit of service, included both fixed and variable costs. While the fixed cost remains constant regardless of the quantity, the variable cost, by definition, must vary in relation to the quantity of service the user departments receive. As such, we need to distribute the variable cost among the four departments in proportion to their share of the service so that it does not fall disproportionately on any one department.

Table 10.1 Service cost, allocation base, and cost allocation

Departments	*Cost of Service ($)*	*(Allocation Base)* Hours of Service/Year	*(Allocation Base)* Hours of Service (%)	*Cost Allocation ($)*
Service Department				
Information Technology (X)	1,500,000	---	---	---
User Departments				
Department 1, D_1	---	20,000	20	300,000
Department 2, D_2	---	30,000	30	450,000
Department 3, D_3	---	40,000	40	600,000
Department 4, D_4	---	10,000	10	150,000
Total	1,500,000	100,000	100	1,500,000

The following expression shows the distribution of costs to various user departments with both fixed and variable costs included:

$$TC_X = FC + \sum_{j=1}^{m} VC\left(Q_j\right) \tag{10.4}$$

where TC_X is the total cost, FC is the fixed cost, VC is the variable cost, and Q_j is the quantity of service (hours of service) the jth user department received (j = 1,2, …, m).

Since the Fixed Cost (FC) remains the same regardless of the quantity, each user department must pay the same amount. On the other hand, the Variable Cost (VC) must be allocated among the user departments in proportion to the amount of service received. Equation 10.4 can, therefore, be rewritten to reflect this proportionality factor, as

$$TC_X = FC + VC\sum_{j=1}^{m} Q_j \tag{10.5}$$

Note that VC has been factored out because the variable cost per unit does not change, while the total variable cost will change subject to the quantity of service the user departments receive. Let us suppose that of the $15 per hour cost, $3 or 20 percent is the fixed cost, and $12 or 80 percent is the variable cost per unit of service. This will give us a total of $300,000 in fixed costs; that is, ($15 × 100,000) (0.2) ≈ $1,500,000 × 0.2 = $300,000, to be shared equally among the four user departments. Thus, each department's share of the fixed cost will be $75,000 [$300,000/4 = $75,000]. The remaining $1.2 million ($1,500,000 - $300,000) will then be the variable cost, divided among the user departments in proportion to their share of the service received.

We can now apply the expression in Equation 10.5 to obtain the cost share of each of the four user departments, as follows:

$$
\begin{aligned}
TC_X &= FC + VC\sum_{j=1}^{4} Q_j \\
&= [\text{FC} + \text{VC}(\text{Q}_1)] + [\text{FC} + \text{VC}(\text{Q}_2)] + [\text{FC} + \text{VC}(\text{Q}_3)] + [\text{FC} + \text{VC}(\text{Q}_4)] \\
&= [\$75{,}000 + (\$12 \times 20{,}000_1)] + [\$75{,}000 + (\$12 \times 30{,}000_2)] \\
&\quad + [\$75{,}000 + (\$12 \times 40{,}000_3)] + [\$75{,}000 + (\$12 \times 10{,}000_4)] \\
&= (\$75{,}000 + \$240{,}000_1) + (\$75{,}000 + \$360{,}000_2) + \\
&\quad (\$75{,}000 + \$480{,}000_3) + (\$75{,}000 + \$120{,}000_4) \\
&= \$315{,}000_1 + \$435{,}000_2 + \$555{,}000_3 + \$195{,}000_4 \\
&= \$1{,}500{,}000
\end{aligned}
$$

Interestingly, we could have obtained the same result by directly multiplying the total variable cost by the fraction of service each department received, as shown below:

$$
\begin{aligned}
TC_X &= FC + VC\sum_{j=1}^{4} f_j \\
&= (\text{FC} + \text{VCxf}_1) + (\text{FC} + \text{VCxf}_2) + (\text{FC} + \text{VCxf}_3) + (\text{FC} + \text{VCxf}_4) \\
&= [\$75{,}000_1 + (\$1{,}200{,}000 \text{ x } 0.2_1)] + [\$75{,}000_2 + (\$1{,}200{,}000 \\
&\quad \text{x } 0.3_2)] + [\$75{,}000_3 + (\$1{,}200{,}000 \text{ x } 0.4_3)] + [\$75{,}000_4 + \\
&\quad (\$1{,}200{,}000 \text{ x } 0.1_4)] \\
&= (\$75{,}000_1 + \$240{,}000_1) + (\$75{,}000_2 + \$360{,}000_2) + (\$75{,}000 \\
&\quad + \$480{,}000_3) + (\$75{,}000_4 + \$120{,}000_4) \\
&= \$315{,}000_1 + \$435{,}000_2 + \$555{,}000_3 + \$195{,}000_4 \\
&= \$1{,}500{,}000
\end{aligned}
$$

where f_j is the fraction of service for the jth user department (for j = 1,2,3, and 4), and the rest of the terms are the same, as before.

Table 10.2 shows the distribution of cost share for the four departments. As the table shows, when the variable cost is taken into consideration, the

Table 10.2 Cost allocation based on fixed and variable costs

User Departments	*Fixed Cost ($)*	*Variable Cost ($)*	*Total Cost[1] ($)*	*Total Cost[2] ($)*
D_1	75,000	240,000	315,000	300,000
D_2	75,000	360,000	435,000	450,000
D_3	75,000	480,000	555,000	600,000
D_4	75,000	120,000	195,000	150,000
Total Cost ($)	300,000	1,200,000	1,500,000	1,500,000

[1] Based on cost fixed and variable costs; [2]Based on quantity

cost share of each user department turned out to be different from those observed when no distinction was made between fixed and variable costs (Table 10.1). For instance, the cost share of D_1 increased by $15,000 ($315,000-$300,000) and of D_4 by $45,000 ($195,000-$145,000), while it decreased by $15,000 for D_2 ($435,000-$450,000 = -$15,000) and by $45,000 for D_3 ($555,000-$600,000 = -$45,000). Had the proportionality factor in the variable cost not taken into consideration, D_2 and D_3 would have paid $60,000 more than their share of the cost [($450,000$_2$-$435,000$_2$)+($600,000$_3$-$555,000$_3$ = $15,000$_2$+$45,000$_3$ = $60,000), and D_1 and D_4 would have paid $60,000 less than their share of the cost [($300,000$_1$-$315,000$_1$)-($150,000$_4$-$195,000$_4$) = (-$15,000$_1$)+(-$45,000$_4$) = -$60,000].

10.3.2 Step-Down Method

While it is simple to use, the direct method has a major weakness in that it does not take into consideration the reciprocal services, where a service department is both a user and a provider. In other words, it can provide as well as receive service. This is where the step-down method, also known as the hierarchical method, becomes useful in that it takes into account the reciprocal provision without which it may leave some of the costs unallocated, making the allocation process inefficient. Operationally, it provides a more accurate distribution of costs to ensure that resources are allocated in a manner that is consistent with the structure of an organization and its objectives. As such, it is much more efficient than the direct method, but one needs to be careful how the order is selected.

10.3.2.1 Order of Selection

The way the method works is that a service department is selected first, and a pro-rata share of its costs allocated to the departments that receive the service. Next, a second department is selected and its costs, including those allocated from the first department, are then allocated to all the departments it services except for the one allocated first. What this means is that the allocations are made in such a way that the departments whose costs have been previously allocated do not absorb any costs of the departments being allocated. This makes it possible to avoid problems, such as double counting for reciprocity, that may result from the allocation process. The process continues until all service costs have been fully allocated.

Since order plays an important role in the step-down method, there are different ways in which the order can be determined. For instance, select the department that provides the maximum amount of service to other service departments, either in absolute terms or as a percentage of total amount of service, followed by the department that provides the second most, the department that provides the third most, and so forth, until the order of all the service departments has been exhausted. Another approach would be to randomly select a service department which makes it easier to allocate.

Given a choice between the two approaches, the first approach is more frequently used because it takes into consideration the actual amount of service provided by a service department rather than the number of departments receiving the service; as such, it meets the basic criteria for cost allocation, discussed earlier. However, it is possible to select the departments randomly rather than using a specific order, which makes it easier to allocate, but this is recommended only in situations where the percentage or fraction of services provided by the departments is relatively evenly distributed. Therefore, it makes very little difference as to which department is selected first.

10.4 Returning to the Example

To illustrate the cost allocation process for reciprocal services, let us return to the example we used for the direct method with one service and four user departments. Assume now that we have four departments (D_1, D_2, D_3, and D_4), and no X, of which three are service departments (D_1, D_2, and D_3) and the fourth department, D_4', is the user department (we used a prime to distinguish it from the service departments), meaning that it does not provide any service to the other departments. In other words, the three service departments provide services to each other as well as to the user department, D_4', while the user department uses the services of the three departments but does not provide any service, in return (Figure 10.1).

From the point of view of allocation, when a service department provides a service to other departments, it needs to indicate the amount of

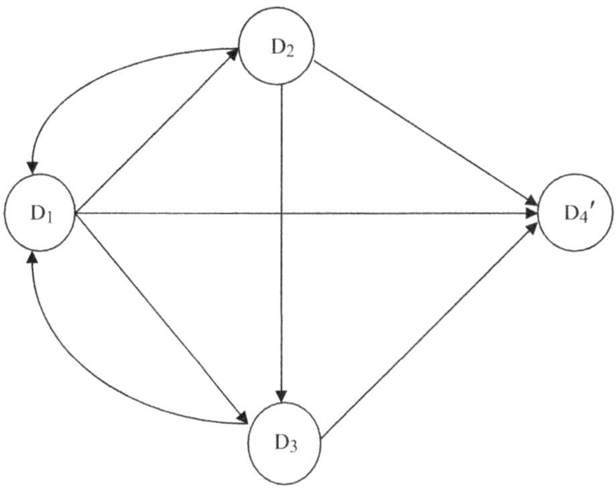

Figure 10.1 Reciprocal services for the four departments

service it provides and the corresponding cost it needs to allocate. It does not include the cost it incurs itself; as such, it will appear as 0 in the principal diagonals of the allocation table. We need to keep in mind that the cost we are allocating is the cost the service department incurs in providing service to other departments as well as the service it receives from other departments.

Table 10.3 shows the amounts of service provided by the three departments to each other as well as to the user department, and their corresponding costs. For instance, department D_1 provides 20,000 hours of service to D_2, 30,000 hours to D_3, and 15,000 hours to D_4'. In other words, D_2 receives 20,000 hours of service from D_1, D_3 receives 30,000 hours of service from D_1, and D_4' receives 15,000 hours of service from D_1. Similarly, department D_2 provides 25,000 hours of service to D_1, 45,000 hours to D_3, and 30,000 hours to D_4'. Conversely, D_1 receives 25,000 hours of service from D_2, D_3 receives 45,000 hours of service from D_2. Finally, D_3 provides 20,000 hours of service to D_1, none to D_2, and 25,000 hours to D'_4, which means that D_1 receives 20,000 hours of service and D'_4 25,000 hours of service from D_3.

As for costs, let us assume that we have the following service costs for the four departments: \$450,000 for D_1, \$550,000 for D_2, \$750,000 for D_3, and \$700,000 for D_4', with a total cost of service of \$2,450,000. These are the costs of service prior to allocation that must be allocated among the service departments as well as to D_4', which only receives service but does not provide any service (Table 10.3).

Table 10.3 Service cost and allocation base

Service/User Departments	*Allocation Base Hours of Service Provided (in 1,000)*			*Costs Prior To Allocation ($1,000)*
	D_1	D_2	D_3	
D_1	0	25	20	450
D_2	20	0	0	550
D_3	30	45	0	750
D_4'	15	30	25	700
Total:	65	100	45	2,450

Table 10.4 Allocation of service costs: Direct method

	Cost Allocation by Department ($1,000)			D_4' *($1,000)*
	D_1	D_2	D_3	
Costs prior to allocation	450	550	750	700
Allocation:				
$D_1(15/15)$[1]	(450.00)			450
$D_2(30/30)$[2]		(550.00)		550
$D_3\ (25/25)$[3]			(750.00)	750
Total:	0	0	0	2,450

[1,2,3] Based on Table 10.3

10.4.1 Direct Method

Table 10.4 shows the cost allocation by the three service departments to D_4'. As the table shows, since the service flows in one direction from the service departments to the user department, D_4', it will absorb 100 percent of their service costs, which is $1,750,000 of service costs to each other ($450,000 + $550,000 + $750,000), plus the costs of service it receives from the service departments of $700,000.

However, the problem with the direct method is that the allocation undermines the cost of service by the service departments to each other and, as a result, the final allocation is not entirely based on the degree of causation. For instance, the $450,000 service costs D_1 incurred include the costs of service it provided to D_2 and D_3, which is ignored under the direct method, and the full cost of \$450,000 is allocated to D_4'. In other words, D_4' absorbs the full cost of D_1's service to D_2 and D_3, plus the cost of service it received from D_1. The same for the service costs of D_2 and D_3. The step-down method tries to address the problem by taking this into consideration.

10.4.2 Step-Down Method

We can now apply the step-down method to the allocation problem, discussed above. Our first goal is to select the order of the departments. Let us say that we use the first approach. Thus, based on the largest amount of service provided by a service department to other service departments, we select order D_1, D_2, and D_3, since (20,000 + 30,000) / 65,000 = 0.77 for D_1 > (25,000 + 45,000) / 100,000 = 0.70 for D_2 > (20,000/45,000) = 0.44 for D_3 (Table 10.3). This means that D_1 provides more service to other departments than D_2 (77 percent as opposed 70 percent for D_2), which provides more service than D_3 (70 percent as opposed to 40 percent for D_3). Accordingly, all three departments (D_2, D_3 and D_4') utilizing D_1's service shared its costs of \$450,000.

The distribution of D_1's cost to the three departments (D_2, D_3 and D_4') are \$138,460 for D_2, \$207,690 for D_3, and \$103,850 for D_4', obtained in the following way: \$450,000 × (20/65) = \$450,000 × 0.30769 = \$138,460 for D_2, \$450,000 × (30/65) = \$450,000 × 0.46154 = \$207,693 for D_3, and \$450,000 × (15/65) = \$450,000 × 0.23077 = \$103,846 for D_4'. This is shown in Table 10.5 To see if our allocations are correct, we can add these costs to see if they equal D_1's service cost of \$450,000, which turns

Table 10.5 Allocation of service costs: Step-down method

	Cost Allocation by Department (\$1,000)			*D_4' (\$1,000)*
	D_1	*D_2*	*D_3*	
Costs prior to allocation	450	550	750	700
Allocation:				
D_1(20/65, 30/65,15/65)[1]	(450.00)	138.46	207.69	103.85
D_2(45/75, 30/75)[2]	0	(688.46)	413.08	275.38
D_3(25/25)[3]	0	0	(1,370.77)	1,370.77
Total:	0	0	0	2,450.00

[1,2,3] Based on Table 10.3

out to be the case; that is, \$138,460 + \$207,693 + \$103,846 = \$449,999 ≈ \$450,000, meaning that our allocations were correct.

Similarly, the departments utilizing D_2's service (D_3 and D'_4) shared its costs of \$688,460 which includes the original cost of \$550,000 before allocation, plus the \$138,460 that came from D_1 [\$550,000 + \$138,460 = \$688,460]. As before, the distribution of the costs of \$688,460 to D_3 and D_4', are \$413,080 for D_3 and \$275,380 for D_4', obtained in the following way: \$688,460 × (45/75) = \$688,460 × 0.6 = \$413,076 for D_3, and \$688,460 × (30/75) = \$688,460 × 0.4 = \$275,384 for D_4', which when added together come out to be \$688,460 [\$413,076 + \$275,384 = \$688,460], indicating that our allocations were correct. Note that D_1 was excluded from D_2's cost allocation, as discussed earlier.

Finally, both D_1 and D_2 were excluded in D_3's allocation of \$1,370,770 (Table 10.6), which includes the original cost of \$750,000 before allocation, plus the costs that came from D_1 and D_2 [\$750,000 + (\$207,690 + \$41 3,080) = \$1,370,770]. To see if our allocations were correct, we add all the service costs, including the cost prior to the allocation of \$700,000 for D_4', which come out to be \$2,450,000 [\$700,000 + \$103.85 + \$275.38 + \$1,37 0.77 = \$2,450,000], indicating that our allocations were correct. Note that if we had another service department, say, D_5, then D_1, D_2, and D_3 would be excluded from D_5's allocation, and so forth.

This is an important weakness in the step-down method in that, while it recognizes the service a service department provides to other service departments and the cost it incurs, it does not take into consideration the service the department receives from the other departments. What this means is that once a service department's cost has been allocated, no further costs are allocated back to it. This leaves 0's under the service department columns (Table 10.6). In other words, it does not fully account for reciprocity. This is where the reciprocal method becomes useful in that it captures the full picture of how the service departments use each other's services, which leads to a more accurate allocation of costs.

10.4.3 Reciprocal Method

The reciprocal method, in contrast, takes explicitly into consideration the reciprocal provision between the service departments, as well as reciprocal allocation of costs. It recognizes that a service department not only provides service to other departments but also receives services from other departments, which is reflected in cost allocation. This leads to a more accurate allocation of costs, as the costs are distributed between the departments based on the actual use of service.

However, there is one important difference with the step-down method in that the reciprocal method can be analytically more complex than the step-down method. The complexity comes from the fact that since the method considers all the service departments together, based on the services they provide to each other as well receive, it may be necessary to present the problem in terms of a system of simultaneous equations. The purpose of these equations is to find solutions for the cost of individual service departments. Once the solutions to the equations have been found, they can be used for allocating costs of each department independently to all user departments, including the department itself.

To illustrate how the method is used, let us go back to the problem again. We start with the three service departments, D_1, D_2, and D_3, as before. To be consistent with our earlier discussion, we begin with D_1, although it does not make much difference which department we start with, since the order is not important under the reciprocal method. Our objective is to set up an equation for D_1 that will include its original costs of \$450,000, plus a share of the costs of D_2 and D_3. As shown in Table 10.3, across the rows, D_1 should absorb 25 percent of D_2's cost [25,000/100,000 = 0.25], and 44 percent of D_3's [20,000/45,000 = 0.44]. Therefore, the equation for D_1 will be

$$D_1 = 450{,}000 + 0.25D_2 + 0.44D_3 \tag{10.6}$$

Similarly, D_2 should absorb 31 percent of D_1's cost [20,000/65,000 = 0.31], and D_3 should absorb 46 percent of D_1's cost [30,000/65,000 = 0.46] and 45 percent of D_2's cost [45,000/100,000 = 0.45]. The equations for D_2 and D_3 will, therefore, be

$$D_2 = 550{,}000 + 0.31D_1 \tag{10.7}$$

$$D_3 = 750{,}000 + 0.46D_1 + 0.45D_2 \tag{10.8}$$

We can now solve these equations simultaneously to find the costs for each service department by substituting Equations 10.7 and 10.8 into Equation 10.6, first for D_1, as shown below:

$$\begin{aligned}D_1 &= 450{,}000 + 0.25D_2 + 0.44D_3\\ &= 450{,}000 + 0.25\ (550{,}000 + 0.31D_1) + 0.44\\ &\quad (750{,}000 + 0.46D_1 + 0.45D_2)\\ &= 450{,}000 + 137{,}500 + 0.0775D_1 + 330{,}000 + 0.202D_1 + 0.198D_2\\ &= 917{,}500 + 0.28D_1 + 0.198D_2\end{aligned}$$

Next, substituting Equation 10.7 for D_2 into the right-hand side of the solved equation above, we get

$$
\begin{aligned}
D_1 &= 917{,}500 + 0.28D_1 + 0.198D_2 \\
&= 917{,}500 + 0.28D_1 + 0.198\ (550{,}000 + 0.31D_1) \\
&= 917{,}500 + 0.28D_1 + 108{,}900 + 0.061D_1 \\
&= 1{,}026{,}400 + 0.341D_1
\end{aligned}
$$

With slight algebraic manipulation, D_1 can be reduced to

$$
\begin{aligned}
D_1 - 0.341D_1 &= 1{,}026{,}400 \\
0.659D_1 &= 1{,}026{,}400 \\
\therefore\ D_1 &= \$1{,}557{,}511.38 \approx \$1{,}557{,}511
\end{aligned}
$$

As before, substituting the above result into Equation 10.7, we obtain the solution for D_2:

$$
\begin{aligned}
D_2 &= 550{,}000 + 0.31D_1 \\
&= 550{,}000 + 0.31(1{,}557{,}511.38) \\
&= 550{,}000 + 482{,}828.53 \\
&= \$1{,}032{,}828.53 \approx \$1{,}032{,}829
\end{aligned}
$$

Finally, substituting the values of D_1 and D_2 into Equation 10.8, we get the following value for D_3:

$$
\begin{aligned}
D_3 &= 750{,}000 + 0.46D_1 + 0.45D_2 \\
&= 750{,}000 + 0.46(1{,}557{,}511.38) + 0.45(1{,}032{,}828.53) \\
&= 750{,}000 + 716{,}455.23 + 464{,}772.84 \\
&= \$1{,}931{,}228.07 \approx \$1{,}931{,}228
\end{aligned}
$$

The results obtained from solving the simultaneous equations for D_1, D_2, and D_3 thus represent the amounts for each of the departments after allocations have been made. Put simply, these are the amounts that are to be allocated to respective departments in proportion to the services they have received from other service departments. Table 10.6 shows the reciprocal allocations.

As the table shows, of the \$1,557,511 (1,557.511) obtained for D_1, \$482,829 (1,557.511 x 0.31 = 482.829) are allocated to D_2, \$716,455 (1,557.511 x 0.46 = 716.455) allocated to D_3, and \$358,288 (1,557.511 x 0.23 = 358.228) to D_4'. Similarly, of the \$1,032,829 (1,032.829) obtained for D_2, \$258,207 (1,032.829 x 0.25 = 258.207) are allocated to D_1, \$464,773 (1,032.829 x 0.45 = 464.773) allocated to D_3, and \$309,849 (1,032.829 x 0.30 = 309.849) to D_4'. The process is repeated for D_3 to show

Table 10.6 Allocation of service costs: Reciprocal method

	Cost Allocation by Department ($1,000)			*D'$_4$ ($1,000)*
	D_1	*D_2*	*D_3*	
Costs prior to allocation	450	550	750	700
Allocation:				
D_1(.31, .46, .23)[1]	(1,557.511)	482.289	716.455	358.228
D_2(.25, .45, .30)[2]	258.207	(1,032.829)	464.773	309.849
D_3(.44, .00, .56)[3]	849.927	0	(1,931.653)	1,081.726
Total:	0	0	0	2,449.803

[1] 1,557.511 x (20/65) = 1,557,511 x 0.31 = 482.289 for D_2; similarly, for D_3 and D_4 (Based on Table 10.3)

[2] 1,032.829 x (25/100) = 1,032.829 x 0.25 = 258,207 for D_1; similarly, for D_3 and D_4 (Based on Table 10.3)

[3] 1,931.653 x (20/45) = 1,931.653 x 0.44 = 849.927 for D_1; similarly, for D_4 (Based on Table 10.3)

similar allocation of service costs; that is, of the $1,931.653 (1,931.653 obtained for D_3, $849,927 (1,931.653 x 0.44 = 849.927) are allocated to D_1, and $1,081,726 (1,931.653 x 0.56 = 1,081.726) allocated to D_4'. Also, as can be seen from the table, unlike the step-down method, the reciprocal method shows the cost share of the individual service departments, based on the services they provide as well as receive.

10.4.3.1 Reciprocal Allocation by Matrix Inversion z

The procedure we used to solve the system of equations above is called the substitution method, which works fine as long as the number of equations to be solved remains small. When the number increases in size; in other words, when there are many more service departments with complex reciprocal relationships, it becomes difficult to use the method because of the number of substitutions that will be required. The alternative is to use matrix algebra; in particular, matrix inversion (Gere and Weaver, 1965). Appendix C shows the reciprocal allocation by matrix inversion for the four departments.

10.4.3.2 Which Method to Use

For many practical problems, the differences between the step-down and the reciprocal method are relatively small, in which case the step-down method can be considered acceptable. However, when there are significant interdependencies between service departments, the reciprocal method provides a more accurate allocation. On the other hand, the reciprocal method can be analytically demanding, requiring knowledge of mathematics such as matrix algebra, if the number of service departments increases considerably. If the differences are minimal, the step-down method would suffice in most instances.

10.5 Cost Allocation and Normal Operating Costs

A common assumption in cost allocation is that the cost the service department incurs is strictly for the service the department provides to the user departments, and there is no cost overlap with the department's own current operating costs. In other words, these costs do not include the service department's own operating costs. But what if the costs were not separated, in which case they must be separated prior to allocation. The simplest way to deal with this is to subtract the current operating costs of the service department, before the service provision, from the cost of service to the user departments. For instance, if the cost of a service department is \$2 million for its service to the user departments, and its current operating cost is \$0.5 million, before the service provision, then the service cost of the department will be \$1.5 million (\$2 million - \$0.5 million), which are to be allocated to the user departments, using any of the methods discussed above.

Since we do not know the normal operating costs of each of the three service departments, D_1 , D_2, and D_3, no attempt was made to separate them from the service costs. However, if we assume that 10 percent of the costs of the service departments include current operating costs, before the service provision, then we will need to subtract that amount from the service cost of each of the three departments. This will lower the service costs to \$405,000 for D_1 [\$450,000 - (\$450,000 × 0.1) = \$450,000 - \$45,000 = \$405,000], \$495,000 for D_2 [\$550,000 - (\$550,000 × 0.1) = \$550,000 - \$55,000 = \$495,000], and \$675,000 for D_3 [\$750,000 - (\$750,000 × 0.1) = \$750,000 - \$75,000 = \$675,000], which is what we will need to allocate to the user departments, instead of the service costs we allocated.

Also, in the example we used, we assumed one user department, D_4', but there may be more than one user department, D_{41}', D_{42}', D_{43}', ..., D_{4m}', which is rather common for most organizations, including government. Regardless, the process of allocation will be the same, except that we will have more user departments that receive service but do not provide any service in return.

10.6 Dealing with Indirect Costs

It should be worth noting that in our example we assumed that the costs the service department allocates to the user departments include both direct and indirect costs, and no attempt was made to separate them. A real challenge in cost allocation is how to allocate indirect costs, since it is easier to allocate direct costs than indirect costs. The traditional approach to allocating indirect costs is to use a predetermined (overhead) rate, based on volumes such as direct labor hours, direct labor costs, direct machine hours or units of production, as we did for job costing. The traditional approach works well in situations where the focus is on volumes, but in situations where volumes are not necessarily the sole determining factor in cost allocation, or in situations where indirect costs have not been clearly identified, it tends to produce less than accurate results.

Abe Livchitz (2021) suggests a simple three-step process for indirect cost allocation: (1) identify the indirect costs, (2) create a cost pool, and (3) select an allocation method. As noted earlier, indirect costs are costs that cannot be precisely attributed to a cost object because of their inherent jointness characteristics. This would typically include rent, utilities, depreciation of facilities, such as plants and buildings, repair and maintenance of vehicles and equipment, if they are used for multiple purposes. It may also include management operations such as supervision. Once the indirect costs have been identified, the allocation is relatively straightforward in that one simply needs to group the costs into one or more cost pools, depending on the characteristics of the costs and the purpose of allocation, then select an appropriate method for cost allocation (Lohrey, 2021). This is where methods such as Activity-Based Costing (ABC), discussed in the next chapter, become useful.

10.7 Chapter Summary

Cost allocation deals with the allocation of costs to a department, an agency, or to any other responsibility center of an organization. Cost allocation is an important component of the cost accounting system, discussed briefly in the previous chapter. This chapter has provided a detailed discussion of cost allocation, with a brief introduction to the cost allocation process, followed by a detailed discussion of three of the commonly used methods in cost allocation: direct, step-down, and reciprocal. Of the three methods, the direct method is much simpler to use, but it does not take into consideration the service the departments provide to other departments, or the service they receive in return, called reciprocal allocation, which is common in most organizations. The step-down method addresses both, but, the reciprocal method addresses the latter much better. However, the reciprocal method can be demanding analytically, especially if the number of departments, service as well as user, become large. The chapter concluded with a brief discussion of cost allocation with normal operating costs, and also when indirect costs are involved.

10.8 Review Questions

10.1 Define cost allocation. What are some of the important underlying considerations in cost allocation? What would happen if you relaxed some of those considerations?

10.2 What is a cost allocation process? What criteria are commonly used in cost allocation?

10.3 What is a cost allocation base and why is it important in the cost allocation process? What criteria are commonly used to determine this base?

10.4 What methods are commonly used in cost allocation? Discuss any two methods with examples.

10.5 Suppose that we have the following information on the services a city-operated electric utility enterprise that provided electricity to three departments of the city last year, other than itself: Public Works (D2), Public Safety (D3), and General Administration (D4). We will call the departments user departments and the utility enterprise the service department, D1. The amount of service provided by D1 to D2, D3, and D4 for the year, respectively, were 1.2 million units, 1.3 million, and 0.75 million units. It cost the utility company $100,000 in fixed cost and $0.05 in variable cost per unit to provide the service. What was the total cost of service provision to D1? What would be the cost share (total, fixed, and variable) for the recipient departments? [Hint: Use the direct method]

10.6 Suppose now that for the problem above, we selected the four departments at random, three of which (D1, D2, and D3) are service/user departments and one (D4) is purely a user department. The following shows the amount of service provided by the service departments and their corresponding cost:

Departments	*D1 (Units of Service)*	*D2 (Units of Service)*	*D3 (Units of Service)*	*Total cost ($)*
D1	---	1,500	25	350,000
D2	150	---	50	50,000
D3	100	2,000	---	450,000
D4′	200	2,500	75	650,000
Total:	400	6,000	150	1,500,000

Given the information above,

a. Allocate costs to the user departments using the direct method
b. Allocate costs to the user departments using the step-down (sequential) method
c. Allocate costs to the user departments using the reciprocal method
d. Interpret the results

[Hint: Use the substitution method for (c)]

References

Gere, J.M. and Weaver, W., Jr. (1965). *Matrix algebra for engineers*. New York: D. Van Nostrand Company.

Livschitz, A. (2021). *Indirect cost allocation – Finding your true bottom line*. Abbott, Springham & Lynch. www.aslcpa.com/newsletters/indirect-cost-allocation-finding-true-bottom-line/ [Accessed March 25, 2021].

Lohrey, J. (2021). What are some ways to allocate indirect costs? *Chron*. https://smallbusiness.chron.com/ways-allocate-indirect-cost-73462.html [Retrieved May 7, 2021].

Oliver, L. (2000). *The cost management toolbox: A manager's guide to controlling cost and boosting profits*. New York: American Management Association.

Shim, J.K. and Siegel, J.G. (1991). *Modern cost management and analysis*. Hauppauge, NY: Barron's Foundation Series.

11 Activity-Based Costing

11.1 Introduction

A real challenge in cost allocation is how to allocate indirect costs, since it is easier to allocate direct costs than indirect costs. In traditional costing, indirect costs are allocated using a predetermined rate, based on the rate for the entire organization, which is easy to determine, as we saw in job costing. Traditional costing works well for indirect costs in situations where the focus is on volume such as amounts of labor hours, amounts of materials, and so forth. But in situations where volumes are not necessarily the sole determining factor in cost allocation, or in situations where indirect costs have not been clearly identified, it tends to produce less than satisfactory results. Indirect costs, as noted previously, are costs that cannot be precisely attributed to a cost object because of their inherent jointness characteristics. This would typically include rent, utilities, depreciation for facilities such as plants and buildings, repair and maintenance of vehicles, equipment, and so forth, as well as management operations such as supervision, if the responsibility overlaps multiple jobs or activities. Once the indirect costs have been identified, the allocation is relatively straightforward. This is where methods such as Activity-Based Costing (ABC), which was specifically designed for allocating indirect costs, become useful.

This chapter provides a broad discussion of activity-based costing for single as well as multiple jobs, followed by a brief discussion of two related topics, time-driven activity-based costing and performance-based activity-based costing. The chapter concludes with a brief discussion of performance-based management.

11.2 Background Discussion

Activity-based Costing (ABC) was introduced in the early 1980s as an alternative to the traditional costing method with substantial indirect costs (Greico and Pilachowski, 1994). In traditional costing, costs usually go into

DOI: 10.4324/9781003486091-13

a cost pool and from there they are allocated to cost objects. A cost pool is simply a group of costs put together in a pool from which allocations are made, while cost objects are items or activities for which costs are measured. Theoretically, a cost object could be anything, a department, a program, a job, a good "a service, as well as an activity or a group of activities for which costs are ascertained.

However, the process of allocating indirect costs using the traditional method, while useful, does not provide an accurate picture of cost allocation because it does not include activities that are important in cost measurement. ABC corrects the problem by including activities as the building blocks, which makes it easier to allocate costs. An activity is a task, or a unit of work, with a specified objective such as producing a good or delivering a service. Activities are essentially processes that consume substantial resources to carry out the tasks of an organization. The rationale for using activities as the basis for cost allocation is simple: if one can think of an organization carrying out a number of distinct activities, and assigning costs to activities, then allocating them from the activities to cost objects, based on a common denominator, makes better sense than allocating them directly to cost objects (Lohrey, 2021). The common denominator, called cost allocation base, typically includes measures such as the number of labor hours, number of machine hours, amount of vehicle miles, and so forth, and serves as the foundation for allocating costs. This is consistent with the basic structure of a government, where it is organized by departments, functions, programs, activities, and process.

An important advantage of using ABC, as opposed to traditional costing, is that since the costs are allocated directly from a cost pool to activities, and finally to cost objects, it is possible to turn some of the indirect costs into direct costs (Cokins, 2006; Michel, 2004; Weiss, 1997).[1] Structurally, the activities in ABC are similar to costs in a cost pool in traditional costing, except that they are organized by activities, called an activity pool. But, unlike traditional costing, the costs in ABC flow from the activity pool to cost objects (Figure 11.1). However, the direct costs remain the same under both traditional costing and ABC; it is the indirect costs that are allocated directly from the activities to the cost objects that make ABC an attractive alternative to the traditional costing method.

Operationally, allocating indirect costs in ABC is quite simple once one is able to identify the activities and create an activity cost pool. In fact, we can easily expand the steps we discussed for indirect cost allocation in the previous chapter to include an activity cost pool: (1) define the activities, (2) create an activity cost pool, and (3) select an allocation method to allocate the costs from the activity pool to cost objects. The process, as noted earlier, is the same for both, except that in the case of ABC, costs are allocated from a cost pool to activity pool, and from there to cost

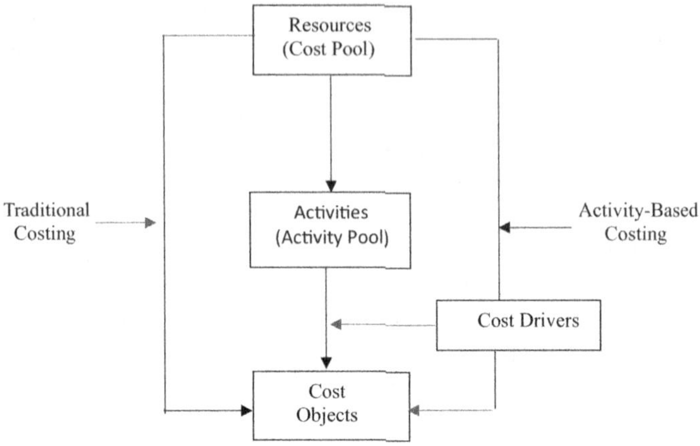

Figure 11.1 Traditional Costing and ABC

objects, based on cost drivers, rather than directly from the cost pool to cost objects (Figure 11.1).

11.3 ABC Process

Developing ABC for an organization, especially in government and non-profit organizations, is not complicated, except that it may require some changes in the management process because of the nature of the activities and the use of an activity pool. For instance, before implementing ABC, it may be necessary for the management to conduct a thorough analysis of the strengths and weaknesses of the decision and, if possible, do a cost-benefit analysis to ensure that the long-term benefits of implementing ABC will outweigh its costs. Once a decision has been made to implement, the process should begin with a number of clearly defined steps that are easy to follow. In some cases, it may be useful to conduct a pilot study, similar to pre-testing in statistical studies, to a segment of the organization where the method will be applied before implementing it for the entire organization. This will allow the organization to work out any obstacles that may impede the successful implementation of the system.

The following steps are typically used in developing ABC for an organization:

1. Prepare a list of activities by functional areas.
2. Classify each activity using some established criteria.
3. Identify the appropriate cost driver for each activity.

4. Determine the cost-driver level for each activity.
5. Calculate the cost-driver rate for each activity.
6. Calculate the total cost of the activities.
7. Allocate costs

Several things are worth noting in the process described above; in particular, how the activities are identified, how they are classified, how the cost drivers and their levels are determined and, finally, how the cost driver rates are calculated. Activities are generally identified by a process known as tracing that determines how much of each activity is consumed by the final user which, for the government, will be the public. For nonprofits, they will be individuals needing the service. Tracing costs to the final user serves two important purposes: One, it allows us to understand the cost structure and, two, it helps us determine if an alternative activity is superior to the current activity (Brimson and Antos, 1994).

11.3.1 Cost Hierarchy

There are no hard and fast rules for classifying activity costs. However, the convention is to use a cost hierarchy that organizes various activity costs into different levels based on their relationship with cost objects. The classification of costs into different levels can help improve our understanding of cost structure and help define them accurately. This makes it easy to identify and eliminate unnecessary and wasteful costs. More importantly, the classification can help identify cost allocation bases that can serve as cost drivers of the activity cost pools. Four levels of cost hierarchy are generally used in ABC: unit level, batch level, service level, and facility level (Horngren et al., 2016).

The unit-level costs, the lowest level in the hierarchy, are the costs of activities performed on each unit of a good or service. Examples of unit-level costs are direct materials, direct labor, and machine and equipment-related costs such as repair and maintenance. The batch-level costs, next in the hierarchy, are the costs of activities performed on a group of units rather than on an individual unit of a good or service. Examples of batch-level costs are setup costs, inspection costs, and ordering costs. The third level in the hierarchy, the service or product-level costs, takes into consideration the costs of activities for a service rather than individual units or groups of units of the service. Examples of service-level costs are design costs, engineering costs, and marketing costs, especially for a new good or service an organization plans to offer. Finally, the facility-level costs, the highest level in the hierarchy, include the costs of activities that support an entire functional area rather than goods and services. Examples of facility-level costs are rent, utilities, administration, and depreciation. In general, facility-level costs are used in situations where the activities cannot be easily traced to a specific cost object. On the other hand, where goods are divisible and it is possible to trace the costs of activities to a specific cost object, the unit level makes the most sense.

Activities can also be classified based on whether they are recurring or non-recurring, or if they are primary or secondary. In general, primary activities are those that contribute directly to the mission of an organization, while the secondary activities are those that support the primary activities. In using the secondary activities, it is important to make sure that redundant activities are not included in the process. One way to determine that is to ascertain the degree of their influence in the primary activities; in other words, the mission of the organization.

11.3.2 Cost Driver, Cost-Driver Level, and Cost-Driver Rate

Three terms are critical to activity-based costing and how they are used in practice: Cost driver, cost-driver level, and cost-driver rate. Cost drivers serve as the link between the activities in an activity pool and the cost objects; they are what drive the costs of an operation. For instance, if an operating department of a government needs a machine to remain in place for a certain number of hours (machine hours), and employees to work for a certain number of hours (labor hours) for an activity, then the amount of machine and labor hours will serve as the cost drivers. In fact, there is a cause-and-effect relationship between a job or activity and cost drivers.

Formally, we can express this relationship between the cost of an operation, or activity, and its corresponding cost drivers, as

$$C = f(X) \tag{11.1}$$

where C is the cost of an operation or activity, and X is the explanatory variable, in this case, the cost driver.

If multiple explanatory variables (cost drivers) are involved in the operation, say *n*, then the expression in 11.1 can be extended to include multiple explanatory variables (cost drivers). That is,

$$C = f(X_1, X_2, X_3, \ldots, X_n) \tag{11.2}$$

In fact, we can easily extend the expression in Equation 11.2 to show the amount of contribution the cost drivers would make toward the cost using a simple linear regression model (cause-and-effect relationship) we discussed earlier, as shown below:

$$C = \alpha + \beta_1 X_1 + \beta_2 X_2 + \ldots + \beta_n X_n + e \tag{11.3}$$

where α and βs are the respective intercept and slopes of the cost-driver model. To ensure that the drivers can be operationalized, they are frequently expressed in numerical terms such as number of months, number of years, number of miles, number of purchase orders, square feet of physical space, and so forth.

Cost-driver levels are what operationalize the cost drivers. They represent the actual quantity such as number of machine hours per month, number of labor hours per quarter, number of months a facility has been in operation, and so forth. Finally, the cost driver rate (the cost per unit of activity that changes with the volume or quantity) is obtained by dividing the cost of an activity by the appropriate cost driver level, and can be expressed as

$$\text{CDR} = \text{Activity cost}/\text{CDL} \tag{11.4}$$

where CDR is the cost-driver rate and CDL is the cost-driver level.

For instance, to obtain the cost-driver rate for insurance coverage for a government department, say, Public Works, that operates three vehicles, we divide the cost of vehicle insurance (activity cost) by the cost-driver level, which will be the number of miles the vehicles will be driven during a year. Let us say the insurance cost is \$15,000 a year and the cost-driver level for all three vehicles is 10,000 miles per year. Therefore, to obtain the cost-driver rate, we divide the insurance cost of \$15,000 by the cost-driver level of 10,000 miles, which will produce a cost-driver rate of \$1.50 per vehicle mile for the year; that is, \$15,000/10,000 = \$1.50.

11.3.3 Application of ABC

To illustrate how the method is used, let us go back to the street repair problem we introduced at the beginning of the chapter under job costing. We conduct it in two stages: First, using the traditional costing method, and then using ABC. Our cost object is street repair for the Public Works department of a small local government. Table 11.1 shows cost allocation for the street repair problem under traditional costing. As the table shows, the total cost of street repair was \$220,000. It is possible to have different overhead costs under the two methods, because the indirect cost allocation is different under the two systems. The difference is due to the differences in the ways in which the indirect costs are allocated. In traditional costing, the indirect costs are generally allocated based on a predetermined rate for the entire government, whereas under ABC they are allocated based on the level of activities. The direct costs under both methods, on the other hand, remain the same.

Let us now apply ABC to the problem (Table 11.2). As with the traditional method, we proceed in three stages: First, determine the direct costs

Table 11.1 Street repair: Traditional method

I. Direct Costs				
		N of Hours	Rate/Hour	Cost ($)
Direct labor		3,125	$40.00/hour	125,000.00
		Amount/SF/ Fuel	Rate/SF/Fuel	Cost ($)
Direct materials		6,250/SF 6,250 Gallons	$4.80/SF $2.40/Gallon	30,000.000 15,000.000
Total direct cost				170,000.00
II. Indirect Costs (Overhead)				
Indirect labor		N of Hours	Overhead Rate[1]	Cost ($)
		500	$35/hour	17,500.00
Indirect materials		Amount (SF)	Rate/SF	
		6,250 SF	$5.20/SF	32,500.00
Total Indirect cost				50,000.00
III. Total cost of repair				220,000.00

[1] Based on a predetermined overhead rate for the government. Note: SF = Square foot

of labor and materials, which are similar to costs in traditional costing such as the size of the crew, the types of materials used, and so forth. Next, determine the activities, which for indirect costs would be insurance coverage for the crew, support personnel, utility expenses, vehicle insurance, and vehicle repair and maintenance. Finally, determine the cost drivers, cost driver levels, and cost driver rates for each activity. According to the table, the cost drivers are the number of months, hours, and miles associated with each activity. Cost-driver levels are given by the actual numbers, such as the number of crew members, number of months, hours, and miles for each activity for the duration of the job. And the cost driver rates are obtained by dividing the cost of each activity by the associated cost-driver level.

Once we have the details on cost drivers, cost driver levels, and cost-driver rate, determining the cost of each activity is relatively straightforward: simply multiply the cost driver level by the corresponding cost

Table 11.2 Street repair: ABC (single repair)

I. Direct Costs				
Direct Labor (Cost Allocation Base)		N of Hours	Rate/Hour	Cost ($)
Six-member crew[1]		3,125	$40.00/Hour	125,000.00
Direct Materials (Cost Allocation Base)				
Material types		Amount	Rate	Cost ($)
Asphalt		6,250 SF	$3.60/SF	22,500.00
Other materials		6,250 SF	$1.20/SF	7,500.00
Fuel		6,250 Gallons	$2.40/Gallon	15,000.00
Total materials				45,000.00
Total direct cost				170,000.00
II. Indirect Costs (Overhead)				
(Activity)	Cost driver	Cost-driver level	Cost-driver rate[3]	Cost ($)
Insurance coverage[2]	N of months	One month	$1,833.33/member	11,000.00
Support personnel	N of hours	500 hours	$35.00/hour	17,500.00
Utility expenses	N of months	One month	$1,500/month	1,500.00
Vehicle insurance (4)	N of miles	10,000 miles	$0.75/mile	7,500.00
Vehicle R&M (4)[4]	N of miles	10,000 miles	$1.25/mile	12,500.00
Total indirect cost				50,000.00
Total Cost				220,000.00

1 Assumes non-salaried members (salaried personnel are typically full-time, including supervision and other support services, which appear under support personnel)
2 For each member of the crew for a month
3 Cost divided by the cost driver level: $11,000/6 = $1,833.33. Alternatively, $1,833.33 x 6 = $11,000.00
4 R&M represents repair and maintenance

driver rate. For instance, if the cost-driver level for indirect labor is 100 hours, and the cost-driver rate is $15 per hour, the cost of indirect labor will be $1,500 ($15 × 100). Alternatively, if we do not know the cost-driver rate but have information on the cost of an activity, we can obtain the rate by dividing the cost by the cost driver level, discussed earlier. Thus, to obtain the cost-driver rate for insurance coverage, we divided the cost of insurance coverage by the cost-driver level, which produced a rate of $1,833.33; that is, $25,000/12 = $1,833.33/month. We do the

Table 11.3 Street repair: ABC (multiple repairs)

	Repair 1	*Repair 2*	*Repair 3*	*All 3 Repairs*
Cost Breakdown	Cost ($)	Cost ($)	Cost ($)	Total Cost ($)
Direct labor	125,000.00	150,000.00	100,000.00	375,000.00
Direct materials	45,000.00	50,000.00	40,000.00	135,000.00
Overhead (Indirect Cost)	50,000.00	64,000.00	38,000.00	152,000.00
Total cost	220,000.00	264,000.00	178,000.00	662,000.00
Repair 1				
(Activity)	Cost driver	Cost driver level	Cost-driver rate	Cost ($)
Insurance coverage	N of months	One month	$1,833.33/member	11,000.00[1]
Support personnel	N of hours	500 hours	$35.00/hour	17,500.00
Utility expenses	N of months	One month	$1,500/month	1,500.00
Vehicle insurance (4)	N of miles	10,000 miles	$0.75/mile	7,500.00
Vehicle R&M (4)	N of miles	10,000 miles	$1.25/gallon	12,500.00
Six-member crew			Total indirect cost	50,000.00
Repair 2				
(Activity)	Cost driver	Cost-driver level	Cost-driver rate	Cost ($)
Insurance coverage	N of months	Two months	$1,875/member	30,000.00[2]
Support personnel	N of hours	600 hours	$20/hour	12,000.00
Utility expenses	N of months	Two months	$1,000/month	2,000.00
Vehicle insurance (5)	N of miles	10,000 miles	$0.75/mile	7,500.00
Vehicle R&M (5)	N of miles	10,000 miles	$1.25/gallon	12,500.00
Eight-member crew			Total indirect cost	64,000.00
Repair 3				
(Activity)	Cost driver	Cost driver level	Cost-driver rate	Cost ($)
Insurance coverage	N of months	One month	$1,800/month	9,000.00[3]
Support personnel	N of hours	350 hours	$21.43/hour	7,500.00
Utility expenses	N of months	One month	$1,500/month	1,500.00
Vehicle insurance (3)	N of miles	10,000 miles	$0.75/mile	7,500.00
Vehicle R&M (3)	N of miles	10,000 miles	$0.125/gallon	12,500.00
Five-member crew			Total indirect cost	38,000.00

[1] $1,833.33 × 6 × 1 = $11,000; [2]$1,875 × 8 × 2 = $30,000; [3]$1,800 × 5 × 1 = $9,000

same to obtain the remaining rates for our street repair problem. In the event the cost information is not available, we can always use the rate for the entire government and use the traditional method, but it will not be ABC.

The example we presented above is simple since it deals with a single cost object, but the process can be easily expanded to include multiple cost objects. In each case, the cost drivers, cost driver levels, and cost driver rates will be different, depending on the activities. The steps will be essentially the same. To illustrate how ABC is applied to multiple cost objects, let us consider two additional street repairs the Public Works Department completed in different parts of the city. In practice, the number of street repairs can run into dozens each year for most local governments. For convenience, we will call them repairs 1, 2 and 3, the repair 1 being the example we discussed. Table 11.3 shows the activity costs for the three repairs.

The information can be further summarized for the three repairs to provide an overall picture of how much the repairs cost in terms of direct labor, direct materials, and overhead (Table 11.3). As the table shows, it cost the government $375,000 in direct labor, $135,000 in direct materials, and $152,000 in overheads (indirect costs), with a total of $662,000.

11.4 Time-Driven Activity-Based Costing

While ABC has been extensively used in a wide variety of situations, including surveys and feedback response studies that frequently rely on internally generated data. This can be a time-consuming process, especially for the latter, that can affect cost determination. To correct the problem, Kaplan and Anderson (2007) suggested an alternative approach to the traditional ABC method, using time as an important determining factor. It is based on how time data are collected, processed, and used for calculating activity costs, and is called time-driven Activity-Based Costing (TDABC).

The strength of TDABC comes from the fact it simplifies the costing approach by eliminating the need to interview and survey tasks of ABC. It does so by applying simple time equations that directly assign resource costs to the activities performed and transactions processed. According to the authors, only two parameters are needed to estimate costs: One, the capacity cost rate for the service, and two, the capacity usage for each activity, which, when added, produces the total service time, both of which are relatively simple and easy to calculate.

The following expressions are used to determine the capacity cost rate and the capacity usage:

1. Capacity-Cost Rate (CCR) = Total Cost/Total Service Time (11.5)

2. Capacity Usage (CU) $= \sum_{j=1}^{m} \left(UT_j\right)\left(CDL_j\right)$ (11.6)

where CCR is the capacity-cost rate (cost-driver rate), CU is the capacity usage (total time), UT_j is the time unit for jth activity, CDL_j is the cost-driver level for jth activity (j = 1, 2, ..., m).

Since the total service time is usually the same as capacity usage in TDABC, we can substitute it for total service time in Equation 11.5, so that the new expression will be

Capacity-Cost Rate (CCR) = Total Cost/Capacity Usage (11.7)

Once we have information on the capacity usage, we can estimate the total cost of service based on the cost of capacity usage, as shown below:

Total Cost of Service = Cost of Used Capacity + Cost of Unused Capacity (11.8)

We can formally express the cost of used capacity as the sum of rate per minute times the cost driver level, and the cost of unused capacity as the difference between the total cost of service and the cost of used capacity, as shown below:

$$CUC = \sum_{j=1}^{m} (CCR_j)\left(CDL_j\right) \quad (11.9)$$

$$CUUC = \text{Total Cost of Service} - \text{Cost of Used Capacity} \quad (11.10)$$

where CUC is the cost of used capacity, CCR_j is the rate per unit time for jth activity and CDL_j is the cost driver level for jth activity (for j = 1, 2, ..., m), and CUUC is the cost of unused capacity.

We can now add the two expressions in Equations 11.9 and 11.10 to obtain the total cost of service, so that

$$\begin{aligned}\text{Total Cost of Service} &= \text{Cost of Used Capacity} + \text{Cost of Unused Capacity} \\ &= \sum_{j=1}^{m} (CCR_j)\left(CDL_j\right) + CUUC \quad (11.11)\end{aligned}$$

where CCR, CDL, and CUUC are the same, as before.

Finally, from the expression in Equation 11.11, we can easily determine the cost savings for the time-driven model by subtracting the cost of unused capacity from the total cost of service, or capacity usage. That is,

$$\text{Cost Savings} = \text{Total Cost of Service} - \text{Cost of Used Capacity} \quad (11.12)$$

which is essentially the cost of unused capacity.

11.4.1 Application of TDABC

To illustrate how the method is used, let us look at the operating cost of running the Public Relations Department of a mid-sized local government, which most governments maintain these days, although the size of the department will vary for different governments. Let us suppose that it cost the government $320,000 last year to operate the department, which includes service personnel, a supervisor, and technology, including machines and equipment. The department performs three activities: (1) receive and respond to public inquiries, in particular complaints about government services, (2) process the complaints, and (3) gather general information about the individuals making the complaints. On average, the department spends 30% of its time on receiving and responding to complaints, 60% of its time on processing the complaints, and 10% on gathering personal information.

Let us further suppose that the following information was available from the department for the three activities last year: the number of complaints received and responded – 2.500; the number of complaints processed, based on the merits of inquiries – 1,500, and the number of personal information gathered – 2,000, which is less than the number of complaints, since some individuals may not be willing to provide personal information. These are essentially the cost driver levels for each activity. The cost breakdowns for the activities, as provided by the department, are as follows: Activity 1 - $75,000; Activity 2 - $225,000, and Activity 3 - $20,000, with a total cost of $320,000. The total amount of time the department spent last year on these activities was 100,000 minutes, which is the capacity usage or total service time for all three activities. Table 11.4 shows the ABC process for our service department.

According to the table, the cost driver rates were obtained by dividing the cost allocation for each activity by the corresponding cost driver level, which produced the following results: $30 for activity 1, $150 for activity 2, and $10 for activity 3. We can now compare these results with those obtained for TDABC to see the amount of savings it can produce for the government, since an important objective of TDABC is the cost savings it generates for an organization from savings on capacity usage. Table 11.5 shows the results of the TDABC process.

Table 11.4 ABC process for cost allocation

Activities[1,2,3]	*Time Spent (%)*	*Cost Allocation ($)*	*Cost-Driver Level*	*Cost-Driver Rate ($)*
Activity 1	30	75,000	2,500	30.00 per inquiry
Activity 2	60	225,000	1,500	150.00 per processing
Activity 3	10	20,000	2,000	10.00 per information
Total		$320,000		

[1] N of complaints received and responded; [2]N of complaints processed; [3]N of information gathered

Table 11.5 TDABC process for cost allocation

Activities	*Unit Time (Minutes)*[1]	*Capacity Cost*[2] *(CCR = $3.20/ minute)*	*Cost-driver Level (CDL)*	*Total Time (Minutes)*[3]	*Total Cost ($)*[4]
Activity 1	10	32.00	2,500	25,000	80,000
Activity 2	30	96.00	1,500	45,000	144,000
Activity 3	5	16.00	2,000	10,000	32,000
Used capacity				80,000	256,000
Unused capacity (20%)				20,000	64,000
Total				100,000	320,000

[1] Average time for each activity;
[2] Capacity-cost = UT × CRR (e.g., 10 × $3.20 = $32.00)
[3] Total time (usage) = Unit time (UT) × Capacity usage (e.g., 10 × 2,500 = 25,000 for Activity 1)
[4] Total cost = Capacity-cost rate (CRR) × Total time (e.g., $3.20 × 25,000 = $80,000 for Activity 1)

The following explains how some of the results in Table 11.5 were obtained:

1. Capacity-Cost Rate (CCR) = Total Cost/Total Service Time
   = $320,000/100,000
   = $3.20

$$2.\ \text{Capacity Usage (CU)} = \sum_{j=1}^{m}\left(UT_j\right)\left(CDL_j\right)$$
$$= (10\times 2{,}500) + (30\times 1{,}500) + (5\times 2{,}000)$$
$$= 25{,}000 + 45{,}000 + 10{,}000$$
$$= 100{,}000$$

$$3.\ \text{Total Cost of Service} = \text{CUC} + \text{CUUC}$$
$$= \sum_{j=1}^{m}\left(CCR_j\right)(CDL_j) + CUUC$$
$$=[(\$3.20\times 25{,}000) + (\$3.20\times 45{,}000) + (\$3.20\times 10{,}000)] + (\$3.20\times 20{,}000)$$
$$= [(\$80{,}000 + \$144{,}000 + \$32{,}000] + \$64{,}000$$
$$= \$256{,}000 + \$64{,}000$$
$$= \$320{,}000$$

$$4.\ \text{Cost Savings} = \text{Total Cost of Service} - \text{Cost of Used Capacity}$$
$$= \$320{,}000 - \$256{,}000$$
$$= \$64{,}000$$

A couple of things are worth noting in the table: One, both ABC and TDABC use the cost-driver rates to estimate the costs of activities. However, in the case of TDABC, the rate is calculated differently, based on time (the rate per minute) in that it converts everything in terms of time to estimate the total time spent on an activity and uses that information to determine the cost of the activity. This is important because the real savings come from the differences between the two rates. As can be seen from the table, the cost-driver rate for TDABC on average was lower than the rate for ABC, which produced a saving of $64,000 for the department. In other words, had the department used TDABC, it would have generated net savings of $64,000 for the department. Two, the authors suggest that since all the data in TDABC are converted into time before calculating the final costs, it is possible to create a database that is consistent and can be used for forecasting the future costs of an operation for an organization, so long as no changes are made in the activities. This adds a new dimension to the conventional ABC, thereby making it more dynamic in character.

11.5 Performance-Based Activity-Based Costing

An important concern in all organizations is how well the organizations are performing and how to account for them. There is a third variation of activity-based costing, called Performance-Based Activity-Based Costing (PBABC), which focuses on performance that is not addressed in either method. It does so by combining elements of both activity-based and time-driven activity-based costing (Carroll and Lord, 2016). Performance measurement plays an important role in all government activities, including cost accounting. Two measures are commonly used in performance measurement: efficiency and effectiveness. Efficiency deals with productivity to determine how efficiently an organization is utilizing its resources, in particular labor and materials, based on an input-output relationship, while effectiveness measures the extent to which the organization has been able to achieve its goals and objectives. The measure commonly used in performance evaluation is variance analysis. PFABC uses variance analysis to evaluate the performance of an organization in terms of its efficiency and effectiveness. In general, the smaller the variance, the greater the efficiency and effectiveness.

Measuring performance in activity-based costing can be arduous, as it involves multiple stages of cost and activity measurement. Several alternatives have been suggested in recent years. This section discusses an approach that uses elements of both ABC and TDABC. It is a nine-step process that is detailed and analytical (Namazi, 2009).

The following provides a summary of the steps:

1. Identify the major activities, which are the same as ABC.
2. Determine the amounts of resources spent on each activity such as time (similar to TDABC).
3. Determine the rate of each resource activity, the same as cost driver rate in ABC.
4. Determine the cost of each activity, using an appropriate method.
5. Calculate each activity's standard rate, which is a predetermined rate.
6. Calculate activity price variance.
7. Calculate the costs of applied activities.
8. Calculate activity quantity variance.
9. Calculate the productivity of each activity.

Two things are worth noting in the steps suggested above: One, the standard rate, which separates it from conventional ABC and TDABC, is the baseline for measuring actual costs and, more importantly, serves as the benchmark for measuring performance. It can be based on historical costs, or the rates for comparable activities, or expected costs. For instance, if the actual costs are lower than the standard costs at the end of the accounting period, then the organization is considered to have a favorable variance. Conversely, if the actual costs are higher than the standard costs at the end of the accounting period, then the organization is considered to have an unfavorable variance. Two, there are different methods that one can use to determine the cost of an activity. Important among the methods are flexible cost assignment method (which includes committed costs, such as costs of machinery, rent, and IT), cost-driver assignment method (used typically in ABC), weighted average method (based on the weights assigned to each activity in terms of how much resources the activities consume, time required to perform an activity, and so forth), net realizable value method (if the goal of the organization is to maintain high positive return), and multicriteria decision models (where the cost drivers are both quantitative and qualitative), and the list goes on. Each method has its strengths and limitations. As such, which method one would use depends on the purpose for which it will be used.

11.5.1 Application of PBABC

Let us look at a simple example to illustrate how the method is used. We will use the example we used for TDABC. We will start with the three activities of the government Public Relations Department: (1) receive and respond to complaints about government services, (2) process the complaints, and (3) gather general information about the individuals making the complaints. The time the department spends on each activity on average is the same as TDABC. The cost-driver rates as well as cost-driver levels are also the same as those used in TDABC. We will apply the method in two stages: First, we will measure performance in terms of quantity and cost variance based on comparison between actual and standard time, since we are using the TDABC data (Table 11.5). Next, we will measure performance under three alternative costing methods: standard, budgeted, and target (Table 11.6). For both sets of measures, we will use the cost-driver assignment method used in ABC and also used in TDABC for comparison.

A cursory look at Table 11.6 would show that the department has both favorable and unfavorable variances. This is because the standard time can be higher or lower than the actual time. We assumed, for convenience, the standard time is based on recent surveys of similar governments and the actual time is based on the time department used for each activity. As the table shows, it has 5,000 and 2,000 minutes of unfavorable variance, and 3,000 minutes of favorable variance, meaning that the actual time the department takes to receive and respond to complaints as well as the time it takes to gather information is hgher than the standard time (Activities 1 and 3). Translated into cost terms, it indicates an unfavorable cost variance of

Table 11.6 PBABC process for performance measurement: quantity-cost variance

	Unit Time (Minutes)	*Unit Time (Minutes)*	*Cost-Driver Level (CDL)*	*Total Time (Total Usage)*	*Total Time (Total Usage)*	*Quantity Variance*	*Cost Variance ($)*[1]
	Actual	*Standard*	*No Change*	*Actual*	*Standard*	*Efficiency*	*Efficiency*[2]
Activity 1	10	8	2,500	25,000	20,000	5,000 (U)	16,000 (U)
Activity 2	30	32	1,500	45,000	48,000	3,000 (F)	9,600 (F)
Activity 3	5	4	2,000	10,000	8,000	2,000 (U)	6,400 (U)

[1] With CCR at $3.20/minute; [2]F = Favorable; U = Unfavorable; None = No change

$16,000 and $6,400, respectively, for the two activities, since the standard times in both cases are lower than the actual time. The favorable quantity variance of 3,000 minutes and the corresponding cost variance of $9,600, on the other hand, are due to the lower complaints processing time for the department than the standard processing time (Activity 2).

Next, to determine the overall performance (efficiency) of the three activities for the department, which is an important component of PBABC analysis, we subtract the favorable variance from the unfavorable variance, which produces a quantity variance of 4,000 minutes; that is, [(5,000 + 2,000) - (3,000) = 7,000 - 3,000 = 4,000)]. In other words, the overall efficiency of the department is negative (unfavorable). In terms of cost variance, the overall performance (efficiency) of the department turns out to be negative at $12,800; that is, [($16,000 + $6,400) - ($9,600) = $22,400 - $9,600 = $12,800)]. In common sense terms, the government is not doing a good job so far as the actual and standard time and costs of public relations activities are concerned.

Let us now look at the cost performance of the department against the performance of the three measures mentioned earlier: standard, budgeted, and target. For convenience, we will keep the unit time and capacity cost the same for all three measures as actual but change the rate. This is normal in cost analysis, when studying how different methods would compare under different price and cost conditions. For instance, standard cost, like standard time, as we noticed, can be equal to, higher than, or lower than the actual cost, depending on the rate. Budgeted costs are what a government typically uses to budget for a department and its activities before the actual fiscal year begins. Like the standard cost, it can be equal, higher, or lower than the actual cost, based on the rate used. Finally, the target cost is what a government, and organizations in general, set as the goal for their functional units to achieve within a specified time. Since they are targets, target cost understandably will be different from the rest. Table 11.7 presents the efficiency of all four measures, including the actual (current).

It should be worth noting that for the purpose of comparison, we changed the capacity-cost rates (cost-driver rates) for all three measures, but no changes were made to the capacity usage (cost-driver levels). The capacity-cost rates used are $3.10/minute for standard, $3.30/minute for budgeted, and $3.00/minute for target. As one would expect, the scenarios would invariably change when we change the CCR. As the table shows, since the standard rate is lower than the actual rate (conversely, the actual rate is higher than the standard rate), it produces an unfavorable variance for the department for all three activities. The scenario reverses for budgeted since the rate is higher than the actual rate (conversely, the actual rate is lower than the budgeted rate), producing a favorable variance for

Table 11.7 PBABC process for performance measurement: alternative costings

	Unit Time (Minutes)	*Capacity Cost ($)*	*Capacity Cost ($)*	*Capacity Usage*	*Total Cost ($)*	*Total Cost ($)*	*Variance ($)*
	Actual	*Actual*[1]	*Standard*[2]	*No Change*	*Actual*	*Standard*	*Efficiency*
Activity 1	10	32.00	31.00	2,500	80,000	77,500	2,500 (U)
Activity 2	30	96.00	93.00	1,500	144,000	139,000	5,000 (U)
Activity 3	5	16.00	15.50	2,000	32,000	31,000	1,000 (U)
	Standard	*Standard*	*Budgeted*[3]	*No Change*	*Actual*	*Budgeted*	*Efficiency*
Activity 1	10	32.00	33.00	2,500	80,000	82,500	2,500 (F)
Activity 2	30	96.00	105.00	1,500	144,000	157,500	13,500 (F)
Activity 3	5	16.00	17.50	2,000	32,000	35,000	3,000 (F)
	Target	*Actual*	*Target*[4]	*Target*	*Actual*	*Target*	*Efficiency*
Activity 1	10	32.00	30.00	2,500	80,000	75,000	5,000 (U)
Activity 2	30	96.00	90.00	1,500	144,000	135,000	9,000 (U)
Activity 3	5	16.00	15.00	2,000	32,000	30,000	2,000 (U)

[1] CCR at $3.20 (actual); [2]CCR at $3.10 (standard); [3]CCR at $3.30 (budgeted); [4]CCR at $3.00 (targeted)

the three activities. Finally, the scenario changes again when the target rate is set lower than both the standard and actual rates (conversely, the actual rate as well as the standard rate much higher than the target rate), it produces an unfavorable balance for the department for all three activities, as one would expect. In fact, we could have used a variable rate for each activity under each measure, instead of a fixed rate, which in all likelihood would produce a combination of favorable and unfavorable variances for the three activities.

While PBABC has obvious advantages over conventional ABC and TDABC in that it is more flexible, as it allows different cost drivers when allocating costs to different activities, it can be time consuming. Also, one has to be careful how the resources are used to optimize, especially input resources (labor, materials, and overheads), so as not to use more resources than are necessary for optimal production and delivery of goods and services.

11.6 Activity-Based Management

In addition to the methods discussed above, there are other methods that also use ABC as a basis for cost measurement, the most notable among these is Activity-Based Management (ABM). Growing out of the work of the Texas-based Consortium for the Advanced Manufacturing-International (CAM-I), ABM extends the use of activity-based costing as a management tool to reduce costs and improve the decision process (Miller, 1996). The way ABM works is that it breaks down all activities into two distinct categories: those that add value to the goods or services an organization provides such as extending local library hours or upgrading a community recreation center, and those that do not add any value such as moving a cost item before installing it that serves no purpose. Removing cost items from the process that do not add value allows the decision makers to better understand the cost structure and can help reduce the cost of production and delivery.

Operationally, both ABC and ABM follow the same process, at least during the initial stage: (1) identify the activities, (2) calculate the cost of each activity, and (3) determine the cost drivers. In that regard, ABC can be treated as a precursor to ABM. The difference between the two is that ABC is cost oriented, while ABM is more management focused. As such, the information ABC produces can serve as the basis for ABM. But ABM can also improve the performance of ABC by removing cost items or activities that do not add any value from cost calculation and, therefore, making ABC more effective as a cost allocation tool. Formally, we can write it as:

$$\text{Actual cost} = \text{Initial costs} - \text{Nonvalue-added costs} \tag{11.13}$$

To give an example, suppose that the total cost of a government service, say, X, is \$2.5 million, which includes items that add value to the service and items that do not. Suppose further that the cost of the items that do not necessarily add any value to the service is \$0.2 million, including both direct and indirect costs; as such, subtracting the costs of nonvalue-added items from the total cost would reduce the actual cost of the service to \$2.3 million. Of \$2.3 million, let us say that the direct cost is \$1.8 million, and the indirect cost is \$0.5 million. We can now apply ABC to allocate indirect costs, which would produce a more accurate picture of cost allocation than when the service included value-added and nonvalue-added cost items. The real challenge, however, is how to eliminate the nonvalue-added cost items. This typically requires an initial cost analysis that includes all possible cost items, then systematically eliminating the items that do not add any value to the good or service provision. There are a host of methods that can be used for this purpose such as value engineering, lean-manufacturing principles, total quality management, and so forth.

The development of ABM, along with a host of other related methods that have been developed over time are parts of a process known as continuous improvement. Continuous improvement deals with on-going efforts by firms and businesses, as well as government and non-profit organizations, to continuously improve goods, services, and processes. It does so by removing unnecessary activities, as in ABM, thereby reducing costs, and improving organizational capability, efficiency, and quality over time (Albright and Lam, 2006). The underlying rationale is that improvements in general take time, but continuous improvement can bring about improvements incrementally. (a little at a time).

11.6.1 Strengths and Limitations of ABC and ABM

The greatest advantage of using ABC for cost allocation, as opposed to traditional costing, is its ability to deal with indirect costs by breaking them down into distinct activities. This reduces the problem of overestimation as well as underestimation when indirect costs are allocated based on organization-wide overhead rate. It also produces results that are far more accurate than traditional costing because it is based on a cause-and-effect relationship in cost incurrence. This brings in objectivity to the cost allocation process. However, it is not without its limitations. For instance, not all costs can be defined in terms of activities or cost drivers that are precise and unambiguous. Also, ABC is a complex system that increases with the number of activities, requiring more time and resources. Additionally, the implementation of ABC requires specialized skills that may not be readily available in all organizations.

As for ABM, since it is an extension of ABC, it carries with it some of the same strengths and limitations of ABC. While it can definitely produce cost savings for an organization by removing items that do not add much value to the production or delivery process, ABM can be time-consuming. For instance, the time it requires to collect information on every single cost item, tangible as well as non-tangible, using an appropriate method to determine which ones do not add value, could be enormous and also costly. Additionally, some costs may be difficult to assign to a specific activity that can lead to subjective cost allocation, which is also a concern with ABC. Furthermore, especially from a management perspective, since continuous improvement constitutes an important component of ABM, employees may resist it if they perceive it as an additional burden or may be reluctant to change. Despite this, for both methods, strengths outweigh their limitations.

11.7 Chapter Summary

A common concern with cost allocation is how to allocate indirect costs. The traditional costing method, while useful and simple to use, does not quite address the problem. Activity-based costing was particularly designed to deal with indirect costs. Unlike traditional costing, where costs flow from a cost pool to cost objects, in activity-based costing costs flow from a cost pool to an activity pool, and from there through a set of cost drives to cost objects, which makes indirect cost allocation much easier. This chapter has presented a broad discussion of activity-based costing, as distinct from traditional costing. It also presented a brief discussion of Time-Driven Activity-Based Costing (TDABC) that was developed to provide a dynamic foundation to conventional Activity-Based Costing (ABC). The chapter further presented a second variation of activity-based costing, called Performance-Based Activity-Based Costing (PBABC). Finally, the chapter concluded with a brief introduction to Activity-Based Management (ABM), as an extension of Activity-Based Costing (ABC) that focuses on management, especially for improving managerial decision making.

11.8 Review Questions

11.1 What is activity-based costing? How does it differ from the traditional costing method?

11.2 What is a cost hierarchy? How is the hierarchy used to classify activity costs?

11.3 Define and distinguish between cost driver, cost-driver level, and cost-driver rate.

11.4 What are the steps in an activity-based costing; more importantly, what specific measures would you take to implement an activity-based costing system in government? Explain.

11.5 Suppose that you are working as an intern for ABC City and have been asked by the city administration to estimate the cost of street cleaning for the year.

You have the following information for the service:

1. Activities: vehicle maintenance, vehicle insurance, utility usage, facility maintenance, and payroll processing.
2. Total cost for the year for the city (by activity): Vehicle maintenance – \$375,000; Vehicle insurance – \$225,000; Utility usage – \$8,500; Facility maintenance – \$25,600; Payroll processing – \$83,500.
3. Cost driver for the city (by activity): Vehicle maintenance – Garage labor hours; Vehicle insurance – Mileage/year; Utility usage – Square feet occupied; Facility maintenance – Square feet occupied; and Payroll processing – Number of employees.
4. Cost driver level for the city (by activity): Vehicle maintenance – 1,500 hours; Vehicle insurance – 1,215,000 miles; Utility usage – 4,500 sq. ft.; Facility maintenance – 4,500 sq. ft.; and Payroll processing – 350 employees.
5. Cost driver level for street cleaning (by activity): Vehicle maintenance – 25 hours; Vehicle insurance – 121,500 miles; Utility usage – 375 sq. ft.; Facility maintenance – 375 sq. ft.; and Payroll processing – 5 employees.

In addition to the above, you also have information on direct labor and material costs for street cleaning, as follows:

1. Labor (Driver) – 1,750 hours @ \$10.50 an hour
2. Material (Fuel) – 3,000 gallons @ \$3.50 a gallon

Now, using the information above, calculate

a. the cost of direct labor.
b. the cost of direct materials.
c. the cost of driver rate.
d. the indirect (support) cost for each activity, and
e. the total cost of street cleaning (using activity-based costing).
f. the total cost of the service for the government.

11.6 What is time-driven activity-based costing? How does it differ from a typical activity-based costing system? Give an example.

11.7 What is performance-based activity-based costing? How does it differ from time-driven activity-based costing? Give an example.

Note

1 There are different ways to turn indirect costs to direct costs. The simplest is to divide the total cost (direct + indirect) by 1 + (total cost – indirect cost). For instance, if the total cost of an activity is $50,000, of which direct cost is $30,000, which is 60 percent of total cost and indirect costs is $20,000, which is 40 percent of total cost, then the conversion will produce a direct cost of $50,000 / 1.60 = $31,250.

References

Albright, T. and Lam, M. (2006). Managerial accounting and continuous improvement initiatives: A retrospective and framework. *Journal of Managerial Issues*, XVIII (2), Summer: 157–174.

Brimson, J.A. and Antos, J. (1994). *Activity-based management*. New York: John Wiley.

Carroll, N. and Lord, J.C. (2016). The growing importance of cost accounting in hospitals. *Journal of Health Care Finance*, 43(2): 172–185.

Cokins, G. (2006). *Activity-based cost management in government*. Tysons Corner, VA: Management Concepts.

Greico, Jr. P.L. and Pilachowski, M. (1994). *Activity-based costing: The key to world class performance*. New York: PT Publications.

Horngren, C.T., Datar, S.M., Rajan, M.V., Beaubien, L., and Graham, C. (2016). *Cost accounting: Managerial emphasis*. Seventh Canadian Edition. Toronto: Pearson.

Kaplan, R. and Anderson, S.R. (2007). *Time-driven activity-based costing*. Boston, MA: Harvard Business School.

Lohrey, J. (2021). What are some ways to allocate indirect costs? *Chron*. https://smallbusiness.chron.com/ways-allocate-indirect-cost-73462.html

Michel, R.G. (2004). *Cost Analysis and activity-based costing for government*. Chicago, IL: Government Finance Officers Association.

Miller, J.A. (1996). *Implementing activity-based management in daily operations*. New York: John Wiley.

Namazi, M. (2009). Performance-Focused ABC: a third generation of activity-based costing system. *Cost Management*, 23(5), 34–47.

Weiss, B. (1997). *Activity-based costing and management: Issues and practices in local government*. Chicago, IL: Government Finance Officers Association.

Part III

Cost Management and Control

- Standard Costing, Variance Analysis, and Cost Internal Control
- Quality Control and Related Measures
- Budgeting for Planning and Control
- Emerging Trends

DOI: 10.4324/9781003486091-14

12 Standard Costing, Variance Analysis, and Cost Internal Control

12.1 Introduction

Perhaps the single most critical element for an organization, especially from a cost management perspective, is cost control. Cost control is the process of ensuring that the cost of operation for an organization does not exceed its target cost and that there are no cost overruns. Ideally, the more an organization can control its costs without lowering the quality or quantity of goods and services it provides, the more efficient the organization is. While occasional cost overruns are not unlikely because of events and circumstances over which an organization may not have sufficient control, it is important that all organizations, large or small, adopt measures that would ensure cost control as part of their normal operation. There is a diverse array of these measures, ranging from cybernetics which deals with the study of all forms of control, to simple variance and ratio analysis, to cost internal control, to decision tools such as those used in operations research that one can use.

This chapter presents a brief discussion of the need for cost control, followed by a detailed discussion of the measures commonly used in cost control. This includes standard costing, variance analysis, ratio analysis, and cost internal control.

12.2 The Need for Cost Control

For an organization to operate efficiently, it must perform two vitally important functions. First, it must plan, in that it must make a systematic effort to undertake those activities that would help it achieve the goals of the organization. Second, it must undertake measures that would help control costs without significantly affecting the quality or quantity of goods and services it provides. The greatest advantage of using control measures is that they can help an organization evaluate its performance by comparing actual performance against planned, standard or target

DOI: 10.4324/9781003486091-15

performance; as such, creating opportunities for determining where the problems have occurred and how to correct them. The result of the process would be reduced cost of operation and greater efficiency for the organization.

According to Clark and Lorenzoni (1998), a well-developed cost control system serves several important purposes for an organization. At a minimum, it can help focus an organization's attention on potential trouble areas by determining how its performance compares with planned or target performance. It can also help create a cost-conscious work environment that would allow the individuals working in an organization to appreciate the impact their work has on the cost of operation and make the efforts necessary to minimize the cost of operation; thereby, producing substantial savings for the organization.

12.3 Standard Costing

Most discussions on cost control start with a measure that provides the basis for an organization to compare the actual costs of its operation against those planned or targeted called standard costing. The term "standard" means benchmark against which current measures and practices are compared to evaluate the performance of an organization and make informed decisions. When applied to cost accounting, it means a predetermined cost based on quantitative and other measures to determine how efficiently and effectively an organization has been able to carry out its activities. Besides evaluating performance, it can also be used for other activities that are important in effective functioning of an organization such as predicting future costs, setting targets, analyzing budget decisions, and managing costs, among others.

Three steps are commonly used in standard costing: (1) setting cost standards, (2) determining the standard costs, and (3) revising standards, if necessary.

12.3.1 Setting Cost Standards

Setting standards generally means determining a target or benchmark against which current and future measures can be compared to improve organizational performance. From a cost management perspective, it means setting predetermined or expected costs to serve as a benchmark against which to compare actual costs to determine any deviations from the standards and use the information for better cost management. However, there are no hard and fast rules for determining the standards one would use for cost measurement. Different types of standards are used depending on the purpose for which the information will be used, but for convenience, we will look at five that are frequently used in standard costing: basic, current, normal, expected, and ideal.

Basic Standards. These standards remain unchanged for a long time in that they do not reflect the changes in cost, price, and other variables that affect the quality of an item of goods or a service; as such, they do not have much value in cost control. Since these standards tend to remain in place for a long time, they are usually set on a long-term basis.

Current Standards. These standards reflect what an organization expects the actual costs will be in the current period. The standards are periodically adjusted to reflect the actual change, which is a common occurrence in most organizations resulting from changes in the factors of production or delivery, such as costs of labor, materials, and overhead. As such, they are considered more useful in cost control than basic standards.

Normal Standards. Unlike the basic or current standards, these standards reflect standards under normal operating conditions. Since the standards are based on normal or routine operating conditions of an organization, they often serve as the baseline for measuring performance. They are realistic and achievable, with rooms for periodic adjustments for normal fluctuations that one would expect in an organization.

Expected Standards. These standards are expectations of what an organization may experience at some future points in time, based on beliefs, assumptions, and past experiences. Since they are based on expectations, it is likely that the standards will contain some uncertainties.

Ideal Standards. These standards are based on what can be achieved under the most desirable conditions. For instance, what would be the output or final product if all the factors of production are working at their fullest capacity with no underperformance of labor, or less than optimal use of machines, tools, and equipment. Unfortunately, while desirable, they are difficult to attain; hence, the term ideal.

There is a further category of standards we can add to the above, called historical standards, based on the averages of the past. While more realistic than the ideal standard, there is an inherent weakness in historical standards since they can include past inefficiencies which can be easily passed on to new standards. As such, they are not considered as useful as current or expected standards. Nevertheless, they can serve as a good starting point.

12.3.2 Determining the Standard Costs

Determining standard costs follows a number of steps. The first and foremost is to establish cost centers to define the line of responsibility, followed by a classification of accounts, identifying the types of standards one would use, and finally, selecting the standards for analysis and measurement. Cost centers, as defined earlier, are those for which the costs are ascertained such as a department, an agency, a cost item, and a group of items. Accounts are usually classified under different headings using symbols and codes, based on different items of expenses. A detailed list of these accounts can be easily found in the financial statements organizations prepare throughout the accounting cycle and present as a formal report at the end of the year called Annual Comprehensive Financial Report (ACFR). For cost accounting, they will be expenses or costs related to labor, materials, and overheads.

Once the type of standard an organization wants to use for cost measurement and control has been determined, the next step in the process is to set the standards to be used. The responsibility for setting standards usually falls on a committee or a group of individuals with good knowledge of accounting process, planning and budgeting, performance auditing, and organizational responsibility, among others. Standards are set both in terms of physical quantity, such as units or hours, and monetary terms, such as price, rate, or cost.

Standard costs are generally expressed in terms of individual elements of a cost structure, such as those we discussed earlier. They are direct material cost, direct labor cost, and overhead. The following provides a brief discussion of each:

Direct Material Cost (DMC). Direct material cost is the cost of materials that directly go into the production or delivery of an item of goods or a service. It has two component elements: Standard Material Quantity (SMQ), which is usually the industry standard, and Standard Material Price (SMP). which is obtained by multiplying the standard quantity by the standard price; that is, DMC = SMQ × SMP. For instance, if the standard quantity to be used in the production of a good is 10 units and the standard price for each unit is \$5, the direct material cost for the good will be \$50 (\$5 × 10).

Direct Labor Cost (DLC). Direct labor cost is the cost of labor that is directly involved in the production or delivery of good or service. Like direct materials cost, it also has two component elements: Standard Time (ST) to complete a job within a prescribed or pre-determined time, and Standard Rate (SR) at which labor is paid, and is obtained by multiplying the standard time by the standard rate; that is, DLC = ST × SR. Thus, if it takes 25 hours to complete a job and the price of labor is \$20 an hour, both of which are standards for the job, the direct labor cost will be \$250 (\$20 × 25).

Standard Overhead Cost (SOC). Standard overhead cost, which is usually predetermined, also has two component elements: a Fixed Overhead Rate (FOR) and a Variable Overhead Rate (VOR). The fixed overhead rate is obtained by dividing the standard overhead for a given period, usually the budgeted period, by budgeted units or budgeted hours, while the variable overhead rate is obtained by dividing the variable overhead by budgeted units or budgeted hours.

12.3.3 Revising Standards

An interesting aspect of standard costing is that standards are flexible in that they can be established for any amount of time and there are no set rules for setting a time frame. The rule of thumb is that if they are set for a short period, frequent revisions may be necessary which could be time consuming and costly. On the other hand, if they are set for a long period, they may not be useful because of changes in conditions such as changes in inflation, technology, material and labor rates which could make the standards obsolete or redundant. This means that standards have to be revised from time to time to take into consideration the changing circumstances that have a direct bearing on the goods and services an organization provides.

Standards may also need to be revised to reflect any permanent changes in the methods of production and delivery process, changes in physical capacity to deliver the goods and services, and if there exists a large variation between standard and actual. The point is that revision in standards is necessary to facilitate control over costs and improve the overall functioning of the organization.

12.4 Variance Analysis

Once the standards to be used for cost performance have been determined, the next step is to compare them against the actual cost to determine the variance between the two, and the method that is used for this purpose is variance analysis. As the name implies, variance analysis deals with the difference between actual and standard costs. Standard costs, as defined earlier, are predetermined costs based on what production or delivery costs should be under efficient conditions.

Efficient conditions generally mean that all the factors that go into the production or delivery of a good or service for an organization to work at their optimum or fullest capacity. It is a desirable choice for an organization, but very few organizations perform at their fullest capacity and, as such, serve as a standard for comparing observations on costs and performance. Therefore, standards can be construed as reference points against which one would expect the actual costs to perform. If variances are a normal occurrence, which they are for most organizations, then performance should be acceptable so long as the variance is kept to a minimum, or so long as it is within some intervals around the standard (as in interval estimation, discussed earlier).

Since a variance is the difference between actual and standard cost or price, we can use a generic expression to define it as

$$\text{Variance} = \text{Actual} - \text{Standard} \tag{12.1}$$

If it is for cost, then it will be actual cost minus standard cost, and the variance will be cost variance. And if it is for price, then it will be actual price minus standard price, and the variance will be price variance, and so forth. w

Two things are necessary to perform a successful variance analysis, called conditions for variance analysis. One, it must be tied to a specific activity so that one is able to collect relevant data. Two, the data collected must be reliable; that is, it must be consistent so that the same results can be obtained from repeated applications. The latter is necessary to ensure that any deviation a variance analysis produces is not due to unreliable data or error in data collection. Theoretically, one could calculate as many types of variances as data would permit; however, for the purpose of illustration here, we will focus on five that are frequently used in variance analysis: price variance, usage variance, efficiency variance, overhead variance, and budget variance.

12.4.1 Price Variance

Price variance, as noted above, is the difference between actual and standard or market price. Two types of price variances are commonly used in variance analysis: one related to materials used in the production or delivery of an item of goods or a service, called material price variance, and the other related to the price an organization charges for the goods and services it provides called the service price variance. Cost control is primarily concerned with the former.

Material price variance is obtained by comparing the actual price of materials with their market price. The assumption here is that the market price of materials reflects a competitive price, excluding any distortions in the marketplace. If such distortions are present in a marketplace, the convention is to use the average price for materials and use that as a surrogate or proxy for the market price. To give an example, consider a federal agency that purchased 500 units of a certain item, say, screw drivers, at a cost of $7,625. The price the agency paid for each unit is $15.25, while the market price is $12.50 per unit. At this price, the market cost of the units purchased will be $6,250. Therefore, the material price variance for the agency is $1,375, obtained by taking the difference between the actual and the market price. That is,

$$\begin{aligned} MPV &= AP\text{-}MP \\ &= \$7{,}625 - \$6{,}250 \\ &= \$1{,}375 \end{aligned} \tag{12.2}$$

where MPV is the material price variance, AP is the actual price paid for materials, and MP is the market price of materials. Assume for the sake of argument that the market price is the standard price, the difference between the two would indicate the amount the agency has overpaid, which is $1,375.

12.4.2 Usage Variance

Usage variance is the difference between the actual and the standard usage of materials. When the usage variance is multiplied by the price of the materials used, it produces the cost of overutilization (or underutilization) of materials. To give an example, suppose that the health and human services department of a government recently purchased 100 units of an item for a job that requires 80 units. The department used 95 units to complete the job, thereby producing a usage variance of 95 - 80 = 15. Note that the five units that remain unused (100 – 95 = 5) become part of the inventory to be used later (assuming that it will not become obsolete or lose its use value).

Assume further that the department spent $45 for each unit, with a total cost of $4,500 for the 100 units purchased. Since the department spent 15 units more than what is considered standard for the job, the cost of overutilization to the department would be $675.00. That is,

$$\begin{aligned} CO &= (p \times UU) - (p \times UR) \\ &= (\$45 \times 95) - (\$45 \times 80) \\ &= \$4{,}275 - \$3{,}600 \\ &= \$675 \end{aligned} \tag{12.3}$$

where CO is the cost of overutilization, UR is the units required, UU is the units used, and p is the price per unit. Interestingly, we could have also obtained the same result by simply multiplying the price per unit by the number of units overutilized; that is, $\$45 \times 15 = \$675$.

12.4.3 Efficiency Variance

This is really an extension of usage variance involving the usage of labor time. It is called efficiency variance because it compares actual labor time with planned or standard labor time. As with usage variance, multiplying the observed variance by the price of labor will produce the cost of over or underutilization of labor. To give an example, consider a local government that takes an average of 25 minutes to dispose of one ton of solid waste. Suppose that the government spent 2,000 hours of labor time last year to dispose of 25,000 tons of waste which, based on the available standard time, would have taken 1,875 hours. The result produces an efficiency variance of 2,000 - 1,875 = 125 hours.

Assume now that the government paid $14.50 an hour for labor time, with a total labor cost of $29,000. Therefore, the total loss to the government due to overutilization of labor would be $1,812.50. That is,

$$\begin{aligned} LGO &= TCL - SCL \qquad (12.4) \\ &= (\$14.50 \times 2{,}000) - (\$14.50 \times 1{,}875) \\ &= \$29{,}000.00 - \$27{,}187.50 \\ &= \$1{,}812.50 \end{aligned}$$

where LGO is the loss to the government due to overutilization, TPL is the total cost of labor, and SCL is the standard cost of labor. As before, we could have obtained the same result by multiplying the price of labor per hour by the number of hours overused by the government; that is, $14.50 x 125 = $1,812.50.

12.4.4 Overhead Variance

Overhead variance is the difference between actual and standard overhead costs. The computation of this variance is somewhat more involved than any of the other variances we discussed in that it includes both fixed and variable overhead costs. Take, for instance, a government that spent $25,500 in variable and $74,500 in fixed overhead costs for a recreation service, with a total overhead cost of $100,000 ($25,500 + $74,500). Let us say that it cost the government 750 hours in indirect labor to provide the service. The standard price of labor is $18.50 an hour. The overhead variance, based on the above information, therefore, will be $11,625. That is,

$$\begin{aligned} OV &= AOC - SOC \qquad (12.5) \\ &= \$100{,}000.00 - [(\$18.50 \times 750) + \$74{,}500)] \\ &= \$100{,}000 - \$88{,}375 \\ &= \$11{,}625 \end{aligned}$$

where OV is the overhead variance, AOC is the actual overhead cost, and SOC is the standard overhead cost. It is the amount the government has overpaid in overhead costs for the service.

Note that we left the fixed overhead cost unchanged because it is likely that it will be the same under both conditions. In the event it is different, we can always adjust it by following the same procedure as the one we used for variable overhead.

12.4.5 Budget Variance

Budget variance is the difference between the budgeted and the actual cost of an operation. Budget variance is a common occurrence in most organizations, especially in government where budgeting is a recurring exercise. Several factors contribute to this variance such as poor cost estimates, fluctuations in the economy, cost overruns due to unforeseen events, and so on. To give an example, suppose that it cost a government $1.925 million to run a program last year that was initially budgeted for $1.682 million. The budget variance for the government, obtained by taking the difference between the two, therefore, will be $0.243 million; that is, $1.925 million - $1.682 million = $0.243 million.

Although budget variance in cost accounting generally focuses on the cost side of an operation, it can also deal with the revenue or income side, in which case it is called an income (revenue) variance. Income variance occurs when there is a deviation between budgeted income and actual income. For instance, consider a government that had expected to earn $8.375 million in revenue from an operation last year, but instead earned $7.986 million. The resultant variance in income for the government would be $0.389 million; that is, $8.375 million - $7.986 million = $0.389 million.

12.4.6 Decision Involving Variance Analysis

All variance analysis serves two important purposes: One, they help us determine if a problem has occurred in the course of providing a good or service. Two, they also help us trace the cost-effect that the problem will have on an organization. Therefore, a properly conducted variance analysis can not only identify where in the process a problem has occurred but can also save money for an organization by determining the cost effect the problem will have on its operations.

Performing variance analysis involving real world data costs time and money. However, most of these costs entail the costs of labor and materials one would incur in collecting, refining, and analyzing cost and related data for these analyses. Although data requirements for individual analysis are usually low, they can be quite substantial as the number of analyses to be done increases. This raises an interesting question: at what point should an organization decide to do a variance analysis? Since cost is the primary factor in this case, the answer will depend on the cost of doing an analysis, as opposed to not doing an analysis. In general, if the expected cost of doing an analysis is less than the cost of not doing an analysis, it should be worth undertaking.

We can formally express this relationship as

$$pC + (1-p)(C+V) < (1-p)D \tag{12.6}$$

where p is the probability that a serious problem has occurred, C is the cost of doing an analysis, V is the cost of correcting a problem (if it is discovered from variance information that a problem has occurred that needs to be fixed), D is the cost of not correcting the problem, and $(1-p)$ is the probability that a serious problem has not occurred. Note that $(1-p)$ is the complementary probability of p; therefore, the sum of p and $(1-p)$ must be equal to 1; that is, $p+(1-p) = 1$.

Suppose now that we have the following information for an agency that wants to do a variance analysis: C = \$750, V = \$2,500, and D = \$5,000. Assume that we do not have any information on p. Since we do not have any information on p, we can make a conservative assumption that it is 0.50 (there is only a fifty percent chance that no problem has occurred). This is an acceptable assumption in statistical analysis if it can be argued that the agency concerned is basically doing a good job. Therefore, substituting these values into the expression in Equation 12.6, we can determine if the expected costs of doing the analysis will be lower than not doing the analysis. That is,

$$pC + (1-p)(C+V) < (1-p)D$$
$$\text{or } (0.5)(\$750) + (1 \times 0.50)(\$750 + \$2{,}500) < (1-0.50)(\$5{,}000)$$
$$\text{or } \$375 + \$1{,}625 < \$2{,}500$$
$$\text{or } \$2{,}000 < \$2{,}500$$

where \$2,000 is the cost of doing the analysis and \$2,500 is the cost of not doing the analysis. Since the expected cost of doing the analysis is less than the cost of not doing the analysis, the analysis is justified. It should be worth noting that there are cases or situations, especially in government, where an analysis is justified even if it costs more to do the analysis.

12.5 Ratio Analysis

Like variance analysis, ratio analysis can be used to determine the discrepancy between actual and standard performance, and the cost effect the deviation will have on an organization. A ratio is a simple mathematical relationship between two quantities. Ratio analysis has been extensively used in finance, going back to the 1920s when it was first applied to DuPont Corporation and has since been used in other areas, including accounting.[1] As in variance analysis, there is a wide range of ratios that can be used, but, for convenience, we will discusses three that are simple and easy to use: efficiency ratio, capacity ratio, and activity ratio.

12.5.1 Efficiency Ratio

Efficiency ratios are used for both labor and materials usage. An efficiency ratio for labor usage shows the relationship between actual labor hours and standard labor hours, and is given by the expression

$$ER = \left(\frac{Actual\,time}{Standard\,time}\right) \tag{12.7}$$

where ER stands for efficiency ratio.

To give an example, consider a government that has used 3,500 hours of labor for an activity, say Z, where the standard for the activity is 3,000 hours, which gives us a ratio of 1.1667. That is,

$$ER = \left(\frac{3,500}{3,000}\right)$$
$$= 1.1667$$

In general, the ratio must be equal to or less than 1, or 100 percent, to be efficient. It is possible that in the current example the ratio could be less than 1, which is not unlikely, if, for instance, the labor brings a skills set that was not available previously for similar jobs. Since the observed ratio in our example is 1.1667 (1.1667 - 1.0000 = 0.1667), which is 16.67% ($0.1667 \times 100 = 16.67$) above the acceptable level of efficiency, it indicates inefficiency in labor use by the government by that amount. Keep in mind that much depends on how the ratios are set up; in other words, what goes in the numerator and the denominator. In general, the variable we are interested in should be in the numerator and the variable we are comparing against should be in the denominator.

Assume now that the standard cost of labor for the activity is \$12.50 an hour, then based on the total labor hours used the government has spent \$6,250 more than it should have; that is, $(3,500 - 3,000) \times \$12.50 = 500 \text{ x } \$12.50 = \$6,250$.

12.5.2 Capacity Ratio

Capacity ratio, on the other hand, shows the relationship between the actual time spent on an activity and the budgeted time. Since the comparison is based on labor hours, it is also called labor capacity ratio, and is given by the expression

$$CR = \left(\frac{Actual\,time}{Budgeted\,time} \right) \tag{12.8}$$

where CR is the capacity ratio.

To give an example, let us go back to the problem we have just discussed. Assume that the budgeted time for the activity is 3,300 hours, which may not be the same as standard time, gives us a ratio of 1.06. That is,

$$CR = \left(\frac{3,500}{3,300} \right)$$

$$= 1.0606$$

Like the efficiency ratio, to be efficient the ratio must be equal to or less than 1, or 100 percent. This is because we are using actual time (hours) against the budgeted time, which means that we expect the actual time not to exceed the budgeted time. Budgeted times are usually based on past experiences of an organization and are often used in efficiency calculation when standard time is not available or when an organization wants to set its own targets. Since the observed ratio in our example is 1.0606, which is 6% [(1.0606 - 1.00) × 100 = 0.0606 × 100 = 6.06] above the acceptable level of efficiency, it indicates an inefficiency in labor use by the government by that amount. In other words, it has used 6 percent more labor to complete the activity than allocated. Translated into dollar terms, it means that the government has spent $2,500 more on labor cost than it should have, if it had strictly gone by the budgeted time; that is, (3,500 - 3,300) × $12.50 = 200 x $12.50 = $2,500.

12.5.3 Activity Ratio

When an organization plans to undertake an activity, it is quite likely that its budgeted time or cost will not correspond to standard time or cost. This is due to the fact that organizations vary in their capacity when utilizing resources; in particular, labor. The activity ratio shows this relationship by comparing the budgeted time against the standard time (or cost), and is given by the expression

$$AR = \left(\frac{Budgeted\ tme}{Standard\ Time} \right) \tag{12.9}$$

where AR is the activity ratio. Since it does not directly deal with actual time or cost, the activity ratio merely sets the limit for the budgeted time (or cost), which can be used for calculating capacity and other ratios.

To give an example, let us go back to the same problem and use the same information we have used for calculating the efficiency and the capacity ratios. The result produces an activity ratio of 1.10 or 110%. That is, (3,300 / 3,000) x 100 = 1.10 x 100 = 1.10.

$$AR = \left(\frac{3,300}{3,000} \right)$$
$$= 1.10$$
$$(1.10 - 1 \times 100 = 0.10 \times 100 = 10\%).$$

As before, to be efficient the ratio must be less than equal to 1, or 100 percent, What this means is that the government's allocation of time for the activity is 10 percent (110-100) above the standard time. In cost terms, it means that the government's estimate of the budgeted cost exceeds the standard cost by \$3,750; that is, $(3{,}300 - 3{,}000) \times \$12.50 = \$3{,}750$.

Although we have discussed three ratios, it is possible to construct as many ratios as may be necessary. Variance and ratio analyses have been extensively used in the private sector, but not much in government. As can be seen from the preceding examples, they are simple to construct yet extremely useful for measuring cost performance, in particular those related to materials, labor, and overhead. Perhaps the greatest advantage of using these measures is their low data requirements. The fact that these measures require a limited amount of information means that the costs of doing the analysis are relatively low.

12.5.4 Cost-Effectiveness Ratio

Considerably different in structure from the ratios discussed above, the Cost-Effectiveness ratio (C:E) is similar to Benefit-cost Ratio (B:C), discussed earlier, except that the focus is on effectiveness. The method is particularly suitable for projects and programs where the benefits cannot be readily expressed in dollar terms, which is a common problem in benefit-cost analysis. As such, it is obtained by comparing the monetary effects of a project with its non-monetary effects, and is expressed as

$$C:E = \frac{C}{NME} \tag{12.10}$$

where C:E is the cost-effectiveness ratio, C is the cost or monetary effects, and NME is the non-monetary effect.

As can be seen from the expression in Equation 12.10, there are some similarities between the cost-effectiveness ratio and benefit-cost ratio in that both measure the level of return from resource use. In benefit-cost ratio, the focus is on efficiency, while in cost-effectiveness ratio it is on effectiveness. In other words, to what extent has a project or activity achieved its intended objective. To give an example, suppose that a government wants to build a neighborhood recreation center to reduce juvenile crimes. It will cost the government approximately $250,000 to build the facility but will reduce crime by 65 percent in the next five years. The cost-effectiveness ratio for the project will be $250,000/65.0 = $3,846.15. What this means is that it will cost the government on average $3,846.15 to reduce the crime rate by one percent. Put simply, it is the cost per one percent reduction in crime for the neighborhood recreation center.

While the example above deals with a single project, the method can be easily extended to compare multiple projects, programs, and activities. When multiple projects are involved, the decision rule is similar to B:C. Namely, select the project that produces the highest cost-effectiveness ratio, assuming the projects are comparable. If they are not comparable, they can be grouped into distinct categories based either on project characteristics or their aggregate costs. Consider a case where a State Education Agency introduced a magnet program in several underperforming schools in the state to improve student math and science performance. Similar programs have been established in other parts of the country. The agency recently tested 1,000 high school students from five different schools (A, B, C, D, and E), with the newly introduced program that produced varying results.

Table 12.1 shows a three-year test result (average), including the most recent year, on a scale of 0 to 100 for five schools, randomly selected, that have similar programs along with their costs which include, among others, costs of equipment, instruction, operation, and maintenance. According to the table, School A has the lowest cost-effectiveness ratio with a value of $15,466.67, which means that it will cost the district on average $15,466.67 for each successful point or score on a scale of 1 to 100. In other words, it is the cost per achievement score for School A. Similarly, it is $31,944.44 for School B, $21,500.00 for School C, and so forth.

Table 12.1 Cost-effectiveness analysis of a state education program

Participating Schools	*Cost Per 1,000 Students ($)*	*Effectiveness Measure (Performance Score)*[1]	*C:E ($/Score)*
A	1,160,000	75	15,466.67
B	2,875,000	90	31,944.44
C	1,720,000	80	21,500.00
D	4,395,000	95	46,263.16
E	1,380,000	85	16,235.29

[1] On a scale of 1 to 100

The evaluation produces interesting results: The school that produced the best result, which is D, is also the costliest school. It cost almost $15,000 more for each additional score than School B, which has the second-best performance. On the other hand, School E produced a reasonably good result (3rd highest) at a cost that is a little more than one-third the cost of School D. From a decision-making point of view, if the Agency wants to introduce the program in all the schools in the state in the future, the results could serve as an important guidepost for what it would need to do to further improve student performance, especially in schools that are lagging behind in math and science.

While much simpler than benefit-cost analysis, an important concern in cost-effectiveness analysis, as in benefit-cost analysis, is how to calculate the present value of cost-effectiveness since the benefits in most instances are intangible. This was not a problem in the current example because the results (performance scores) are measurable in terms that do not have a time-dimension in the sense that the value of a test score increases or decreases relative to time, as monetary benefits or returns often do. If the returns were expressed in terms of the change in value over time it would pose a real challenge for the decision makers. The alternative would be to discount them the same way as one would discount a stream of benefits and costs. However, discounting a stream of intangible benefits could pose additional problems because of the difficulty in selecting a discount rate that would be appropriate.

12.6 Cost-Performance Index

A measure frequently used for evaluating cost performance that has some similarities with ratio analysis is the Cost Performance Index (CPI), which is different from the consumer price index we discussed earlier. It is essentially a ratio, given by the expression, CPI = EV/AC, where EV is the earned value, defined as the monetary value of the amount of work completed against the amount budgeted, and AC is the actual cost of the amount of work completed. It ranges between greater than, equal to, and less than 1. Thus, an index of 1 means the project is on target, greater than 1 means it is over the budget, and less than 1 means it is under the budget.

To give an example, suppose that a nonprofit organization operates a service program with a budget of $250,000 for six months, and will serve at least 200 individuals . The program has been in operation for three months, which is the half-way point through its schedule. At the halfway point, let us say that 100 individuals have been served at a cost of $125,000, which is 50 percent of the budget; that is, $\$250{,}000 \times 0.50 = \$125{,}000$. It is the Earned Value (EV) of the program at the halfway point. We can now use this information to obtain the Cost Performance Index for the program. To obtain the index, we simply divide the earned value, which is $125,000, by the actual cost at the half-way point, which is $125,000. This would give us a CPI of 1, indicating that the program is on target.

Let us now suppose that the program is halfway through its schedule, but the organization has already spent $200,000, serving 100 individuals, which is 50 percent of the number it is supposed to serve. The result would produce an index of 1.2 ($150,000/$125,000), indicating that the program is 20 percent over the budget; that is, $(\$150{,}000/\$125{,}000) - 1.0) \times 100 = (1.2 - 1.0) \times 100 = 0.20 \times 100 \approx 20$ percent. On the other hand, if the program had spent $100,000 at the halfway point, instead of $125,000, while serving the same number of individuals, it would produce an index of 0.8 ($110,000/$125,000), indicating that the program is 20 percent under the budget; that is, $[1 - (\$150{,}000/\$125{,}000)] \times 100 = (1 - 1.2) \times 100 = -0.20 \times 100 = -20$ percent. which is an indication of efficiency. In other words, the organization is doing a good job of running the program efficiently, assuming no change or reduction in service quality.

12.7 Cost Status Report

It is not unusual to find a flaw or defect in a project or program after the initial phase of project completion, requiring the government to abandon the project. This invariably would cost the government time and resources that are irreversible, known as a sunk cost, discussed earlier. Since sunk costs are irreversible in that they cannot be recovered, in most instances, the government has no choice but to absorb the cost. On the other hand, if the job is outsourced or contracted out to a private firm, then it is the responsibility of the firm to bear the cost of the defective portion of the project cost. However, much will also depend on the conditions of the contract or the nature of the agreement between the government and the outsourced firm.

Table 12.2 Example of a cost status report

Factor	*Budgeted Cost ($)*	*Estimated Cost ($)*	*Cost Commitment ($)*	*Cost Exposure ($)*	*Cost to Date ($)*	*Over or Under ($)*
Labor	750,000	825,000	400,000	---	425,000	75,000
Materials	175,000	200,000	100,000	100,000	---	25,000
Contractual	3,250,000	3,250,000	2,175,000	850,000	225,000	0
Equipment	350,000	375,000	200,000	---	175,000	25,000
Other	75,000	100,000	75,000	---	25,000	25,000
Total	4,600,000	4,750,000	2,950,000	950,000	850,000	150,000

One way to avoid the problem, such as the one discussed above, is to prepare a cost status report as the project goes through different stages of completion. Several categories of costs are generally recorded in a cost status report such as budgeted cost, estimated cost based on progress since the initial budget decision, cost commitment based on the progress made, cost exposure based on estimated (additional) cost, cost to date, and cost over or under. Table 12.2 presents an example of a cost status report for a facility construction.

As the table shows, there is an estimated cost overrun of $150,000, with 18.48 percent of the projected budgeted cost incurring to date [$850,000/$4,600,000)×100 = 18.48%]. When problems such as cost overruns take place, the government needs to pay careful attention to the factors that have contributed to the problem. Cost overruns can take place for a variety of reasons, some of which the government may not have any control over. But, for those over which the government has control, it must take all possible measures to address them. Even for those over which the government may not have much control, it is important to develop a set of contingencies to deal with the problems when they occur.

12.8 Cost Internal Control

Cost internal control deals with a set of measures that are important for an organization to ensure that its resources are used for intended purposes and that there are no cost overruns. These measures are essentially the same for all organizations, although their application may vary. They serve as important first steps toward cost management and control. Some of these measures are simple, requiring very little effort and resources, while others are exhaustive requiring detailed and careful analysis throughout the process. This section presents here six such measures that are frequently used in cost control: responsibility assignment, expenditure control, cash control, fraud and waste control, performance auditing, and information management.

12.8.1 Responsibility Assignment

Responsibility assignment deals with the allocation of responsibilities to individuals to carry out the diverse tasks of an organization. Assigning responsibilities allows an organization to keep track of its activities consistent with its goals and objectives. This, in turn, makes it possible to hold individuals, in particular those who have been entrusted with such responsibilities, accountable when deviations occur. In a typical organization, the responsibilities follow the chain of authorities with appropriate separation of tasks. For instance, the accounting and finance functions of a government are vested in the finance department, usually headed by a director. For large organizations, the two functions are usually performed by different units, where the accounting functions are headed by a controller, followed by a treasurer, accountants, and bookkeepers.

In general, the tasks individuals perform in an organization should be non-overlapping to avoid any potential problem of duplication. For instance, the responsibility of a treasurer in a government is to manage its cash and other credit activities, including cash-flow analysis, credit rating, and portfolio management. Similarly, the responsibility of a controller is to plan and control the financial activities, which would include, among others, identifying deviations from planned and efficient performance, financial reporting, auditing, administering government taxes, managing assets, and providing consulting services to the administration. The separation of responsibilities not only reduces redundancy in operation but also cuts costs and makes coordination among various units of an organization and their activities much easier.

12.8.2 Expenditure Control

Expenditure control is the first and foremost financial measure an organization uses to bring its expenditure within the limits of its resource capabilities. Expenditure control, especially in government, takes place in two ways: through regulating timing of obligations and expenditures, and publishing financial and accounting reports on a regular basis (Lynch, 1995). Regulating timing ensures that funds are obligated for intended purposes and that their misuse is kept to a minimum. Most organizations use variance analysis, similar to the ones discussed earlier, to show the amount of funds an agency has received and the actual amount it has spent on a specific activity within a given period. Similarly, publishing financial and accounting reports is essential to show what kinds of expenditure an organization has incurred and how they compare with those intended. These reports, which should be published on a quarterly, if not on a weekly or monthly basis, can also serve as principal source documents for the annual financial report that most financial organizations, including government, are required to publish at the end of each fiscal or calendar year.

12.8.3 Cash Control

Cash control is the means by which an organization controls its cash (cash receipts and cash disbursements). Cash control is extremely important in government, especially at the local level, where a government receives the bulk of its revenue, such as revenue from property taxes, during certain times of the year, while its expenditure takes place consistently throughout the year. This creates two operational problems: a cash surplus when more revenue is received than expenditure incurred, and a cash shortage when expenditure exceeds revenues received. Cash control helps a government maintain a balance between the two by ensuring that it has enough cash to carry out its normal day-to-day operation, while making sure that any surplus that is generated in the process does not remain idle. When surpluses are accumulated, they are usually invested in securities earning additional revenue for the government.

12.8.4 Fraud and Waste Control

Every year governments lose billions of dollars from fraud, waste and abuse at all three levels of government, but more so at the federal level. In fact, the Government Accountability Office (GAO), in its annual report, provides a detailed listing of government programs and activities where waste, fraud and abuse have taken place during the fiscal year costing the government billions of dollars. Although the government has undertaken measures to control the problem, unfortunately, it remains a serious concern. However, from a cost management perspective, organizations can control fraud, waste and abuse by taking measures that would eliminate waste such as by clearly identifying where the problem has occurred, increasing the speed of response to minimize time, improving quality, and reducing costs. These measures constitute the essence of a procedure called Lean Operating System (LOS).

12.8.5 Performance Auditing

Auditing is a process of investigating the accuracy of the information a government provides on its financial, accounting, and other activities for a fiscal or accounting year. There are three specific objectives an auditing process serves for an organization: (1) determine the extent to which it has been fair and accurate in presenting its financial position;(2) determine whether or not it has complied with the stated laws, regulations, and mandates that influence its financial transactions; and (3) determine the extent to which it has been able to achieve its stated goals and objectives. The first two objectives together are called financial auditing, while the third is called performance auditing.

Financial auditing is based on a set of standards by which one can measure and evaluate the financial position of a government, while performance auditing is much broader in scope. There are no set standards that can accurately guide and measure the performance of an organization. However, by focusing on goals and objectives, performance auditing can address the broader question of efficiency and effectiveness; in particular, how an organization carries out its operations and the manner in which it utilizes its resources in achieving those goals and objectives (Brown, 1982). In other words, by placing emphasis on goals and objectives and their achievement, performance auditing attempts to measure an organization's bottom-line performance.

Since performance auditing is primarily concerned with efficiency, it tends to pay more attention to the internal operations of an organization. This is where cost accounting becomes useful. As noted earlier, cost accounting produces cost and related information that is essential for an organization to carry out its day-to-day operations. Therefore, by producing accurate, objective, and reliable information, cost accounting can significantly ease the tasks of performance auditing.

12.8.6 Information Management

All organizations need to have a good information system in place in order to maintain quality internal control. Without good, reliable, and quality information and its management, most organizations will find it difficult to make effective decisions. Information management deals with the management of data that has been processed and analyzed to meet the specific needs of an organization. There is a difference between information management and a term interchangeably used with it called data management. Data management refers to the management of raw, unprocessed facts and figures that are gathered by an organization as part of its normal, everyday operation. As organizations increase in size and complexity, their information requirement also increases; thereby, placing additional demands on information management.

With an abundance of information and computing facilities these days, more organizations are focusing on what is known as intelligent use of information. By intelligent use of information, we mean cutting through redundant and useless information to obtain those that have a direct bearing on the functioning of an organization. To make intelligent use of information, one requires a clear understanding of the critical needs of an organization and developing an information base to meet those needs.

12.9 Chapter Summary

An important function of cost accounting is cost management and controlling costs. Cost management and control deal with monitoring, analyzing, and controlling costs in an organization. In controlling costs, organizations use various methods to monitor and evaluate cost performance and, eventually, to control costs. The range of methods that can be used for this purpose has increased considerably over the years. This chapter has briefly discussed four such measures: standard costing, variance analysis, ratio analysis, and cost internal control. Most of the measures used for cost control are within the purview of the government, especially those used for cost internal control. These include responsibility assignments, expenditure control, cash control, fraud and waste control, performance auditing, and information management. The chapter concluded with a brief discussion of each.

12.10 Review Questions

12.1 What is cost control? What role do cost standards play in controlling costs?

12.2 What is standard costing? What steps are typically used in standard costing? Define and distinguish between (a) basic standards, (b) current standards, (c) normal standards, (d) expected standards, and (e) ideal standards.

12.3 What is variance analysis? What are the conditions for variance analysis? Discuss the decision rule, with example, for determining whether to conduct a variance analysis.

12.4 Define and distinguish between (a) price variance, (b) usage variance, (c) efficiency variance, (d) overhead variance, and (e) budget variance.

12.5 A local community hospital does 315 X-rays a week. The standard costs per unit of material, labor, and overhead for X-rays are as follows:

1. Direct materials: 315 films (assuming an average of 2.5 X-rays per patient) ×$12 (per film) = $3,780.
2. Direct labor: 5 minutes (per X-ray) ×$35 (per hour) = $2.92.

3. Indirect labor: 2 minutes of labor time (per X-ray) ×$20 (per hour) = $0.67, and
4. Indirect materials: 2 minutes of machine time (per X-ray) ×$10 (per hour) = $0.33.

The hospital costs for materials, labor, and overheads (variable as well as fixed) for the year were as follows:

1. Direct materials: $235,872.
2. Direct labor: $78,275.
3. Variable overhead: $15,340, and
4. Fixed overhead: $6,875.

Now, using this information, calculate the following:

a. Total variance.
b. Material variance.
c. Labor variance.
d. Variable overhead variance, and
e. Fixed overhead variance.

12.6 What is a ratio? How is ratio analysis used in measuring cost performance? Define and distinguish between (a) efficiency ratio, (b) capacity ratio, and (c) cost-effectiveness ratio?

12.7 What is a Cost Performance index? Give an example of how you would use the index to measure cost performance.

12.8 What is a cost status report? What are the elements of the report? How would you use the report to determine cost-overrun? Give an example.

12.9 What is cost-internal control? What measures are commonly used in cost internal control? Give an example of each.

Note

1 The objective of DuPont analysis is to break down a firm's return on equity (ROE) into a set of ratios such as net profit margin, asset turnover, and financial leverage. The ratios provide a comprehensive view of the firm's financial performance.

References

Brown, R.E. (1982) *Auditing performance in government; Concepts and cases.* New York: John Wiley.

Clark, F. and Lorenzoni, A.B. (1998). *Applied cost engineering.* New York: CRC Press.

Kerzner, H. (2009). *Project management: A systems approach to planning, scheduling and control.* New York,: John Wiley.

Khan, A. (1996). Cash management: Basic principles and guidelines, in J. Rabin et al. (eds) *Budgeting: Formulation and execution*. Athens, GA: Carl Vinson Institute of Government, The University of Georgia, 313–322.

Lynch, T.D. (1995). *Public budgeting in America*. Englewood Cliffs, NJ: Prentice Hall.

Ziegenfuss, Jr., J.T. and Bentley, J.M. (2000). Implementing cost control in health care: Strategies driven by organizational systems approach. *Practice and Systems Research*, 13(4): 453–474.

13 Quality Control and Related Measures

13.1 Introduction

Quality is critical to effective management of an organization. There has been a significant interest in quality control in government in recent years resulting from two interrelated developments: an increase in public demand for lean and efficient government, and an increase in public expectation that the goods and services they receive from government in return for their tax dollars are of the highest quality. Quality control deals with various methods, tools, and approaches for diagnosing the lack of quality, defined commonly as nonconformity of standards in materials, machines, and processes. In government, as in the private sector as well as in non-profit organizations, quality control remains a major concern. Quality control can ensure both; in particular, the latter by maintaining quality specifications throughout the production and delivery process (from the acquisition of materials, supplies and equipment to the final delivery of the goods and services).

This chapter focuses on quality control and related measures. It begins with an introduction to quality control and variations in quality, followed by a detailed discussion of a couple of commonly used control charts, and an aspect of quality control that lies at the heart of most control activities, called process capability (Ott and Schilling, 1990). It also briefly touches base on measures such as quality engineering, quality assurance, and costs in quality control. The chapter concludes with a brief discussion of total quality management.

13.2 Defining Quality

Defining quality is not as simple as it may seem. Quality is fundamentally relational; there is no universal definition of quality, but intuitively, as well as in practice, we know what the term means when, for instance, we purchase a good or use a service. However, based on the purpose for which

DOI: 10.4324/9781003486091-16

the term is used, there are different ways to define quality. For instance, from an economic point of view, we can define quality as the value for price we pay for the utility we derive from the goods and services we consume. From a production or manufacturing point of view, quality can be defined as suitability of a product for use without any defect in that it will not easily break down or produce adverse effects during its use (Juran and Gryna, Jr., 1980). From a measurement point of view, quality can be defined as conformance to standards, similar to what we discussed under standard costing, which simply means how well a good or service meets the target, and its tolerance limits (Crosby, 1979).

Since deviations from standards are relatively easy to measure, quality control studies frequently use conformance of standards as the principle guiding tool for quality measurement. However, quality is not always related to a good or service; it can also apply to an organization and its performance such as how well an organization has performed in reducing the crime rates for a community or a healthcare organization in increasing the accessibility of health care services for the poor and the needy. Interestingly, the two are not necessarily mutually exclusive. According to Deming (1982), both are necessary in quality control – quality of conformance, based on standards or specifications, and quality of performance, based on an analysis of how well the goods and services had performed when consumed or used.

Regardless of how quality is defined, the primary objective of any organization is to ensure that the goods and services it provides are of the highest quality and that they conform to standards (specifications) and that they perform well when used. To make sure that quality is maintained throughout the process, one needs to understand the factors that affect quality and take appropriate measures to control them. This is generally known as process control. For any organization, process is the most important element that determines how successful or effective an organization is in carrying out its activities. Everything revolves around process. If the process is inoperative or not managed efficiently, it will produce ineffective results. A process is simply a series of activities that transform input into output. Inputs generally include factors such as materials (data, raw materials, and information), machines (instruments, tools, and equipment), labor (experience, skill, and training), and management (organizational structure, style, and relationship), and outputs are the amounts of goods produced, or services delivered.

13.3 Variations in Quality

A necessary condition for quality control is that the factors described above must be of the highest quality to ensure quality results. For example, when quality materials are used in a production or delivery process they will reduce waste, increase performance, and lengthen the life of a good or service. Similarly, quality machines will reduce frequent breakdowns, minimize wear and tear, and smooth out the production or delivery process. Likewise, quality labor will ensure the skills an organization needs to increase its performance and maintain quality throughout the process. Finally, quality management will ensure better working conditions for its labor and guarantee a work environment that will be conducive to productivity.

So long as there are no variations in the conditions during a production or delivery process described above, organizations should not have any difficulty in maintaining quality control. However, variations do occur, and in some cases, they are inevitable even for services that are repetitive. Two types of factors frequently contribute to these variations: chance factors and assignable factors. The presence of chance factors in a process means that certain variations are bound to occur in an organization due to causes such as sudden changes in weather that behave in an unpredictable fashion. They are often beyond human control and, as such, cannot be prevented in most instances. Consequently, one must allow for these variations when providing goods and services. Variations of this nature are called allowable variations.

The assignable variation, on the other hand, is caused by nonrandom factors such as defective materials, poor handling of machines, incorrect work procedure, and so on. As such, they are manageable, meaning that they can be identified and corrected before they can cause any major damage to the process. Variations due to these factors are called preventable variation. Since one does not have much control over the random causes of variation, the most one can do in quality control is identify the assignable causes of variation and make every effort to keep the variation under control. Most of the tools used in quality control, including the ones discussed here, are essentially geared toward that.

13.4 Use of Control Charts

Perhaps the single most important tool used in quality control, especially for analyzing variations in a process is a control chart. A control chart is an effective means for discovering and correcting the assignable causes of variation outside the pattern of random causes. Developed originally by Shewart in 1924, and subsequently popularized by Deming (1950; Kilian, 1992) when he applied them to management, they are essentially pictorial devices used for detecting unnatural patterns of variation, defined as lack of control in data resulting from repetitive processes. Since control charts are mostly pictures (figures), they are simple to construct and easy to interpret. Furthermore, they can tell us whether a process is in control by visually comparing the location of quality characteristics on a chart.

13.4.1 Steps in a Control Chart

Constructing a control chart is quite simple. However, it requires that several conditions are satisfied before the charts can be constructed. These conditions typically include (1) checking for errors in the instruments used, (2) selecting a set of subsamples from the population from which data are collected for analysis, (3) calculating the relevant statistics for each subsample, (4) setting the control limits, and (5) constructing the control chart. Each of these steps is briefly discussed next.

13.4.2 Checking for Errors

The construction of a control chart begins with measurement; in particular, measurement in handling machines and tools, in designing instruments, in reading data, and so forth. For any production or delivery problem, errors can always enter the measurement process due to faulty use of machines and tools, a lack of clear knowledge in dealing with these tools, or a lack of clear understanding of quality characteristics. Since the conclusions drawn from control charts depend on the variability of the quality being measured, it is important that the mistakes in reading data or handling tools are kept to a minimum so that one can draw valid and reliable conclusions from these charts.

13.4.3 Selecting Subsamples

The rationale for using subsamples in a control chart is to make comparisons of performance statistics possible. A subsample is a fraction of a sample drawn from a given population. There are no hard and fast rules for determining how many subsamples one must select in a quality control study and how many units each subsample must contain. However, the rule of thumb is to have between 4 to 5 units in each subsample, with the number of subsamples not exceeding 25. The idea behind restricting the number of subsamples to 25 is that it should not be too few such that there is not enough information in a data set and that it should not be too many such that it will include the entire data set. The latter could be costly as well as time-consuming. In reality, the number can vary depending on the process being analyzed but the number of units to be included in a subsample always remains fixed.

13.4.4 Calculating Relevant Statistics

Once the sample size and the number of subsamples to be included in a study have been determined, the calculation of actual statistics for various charts can begin. This is not a difficult exercise since the statistics used in quality control are relatively simple. What is important, however, is the need to understand the distribution of the population from which these subsamples have been drawn. There are two simple explanations for this: First, the knowledge of population distribution which makes it possible to know a priori what statistics to use in a study. Second, especially where control charts are involved, it can provide clear guidance regarding how to use those statistics to set the limits for a chart. The latter is particularly important in quality control because without these limits it will be difficult to determine the extent to which a process is in control. Control limits lie at the heart of quality control. As noted earlier, these limits set the boundaries against which quality measures are compared to see whether a process is out of control.

13.4.5 Setting the Control Limits

All control charts have one characteristic in common: They consist of three horizontal lines; a central line to indicate the desired level of the process; a line above the central line called the upper limit or boundary of control; and a line below the central line called the lower limit or boundary of control. Together, the upper and lower boundaries determine the control limits within which one can expect to find most sample points (observations) in a data set. In general, when the points lie inside these limits, the process is said to be in control and when they lie outside the limits, it is said to be lacking control. Figure 13.1 shows a typical control chart.

For most control charts, the central line represents the average or mean of the distribution of data points. Therefore, any point that lies outside the control line represents a deviation from the mean. In a typical control chart, the deviations are given by $\pm 3\sigma$, where $+3\sigma$ represents the Upper Control Limit (UCL) and -3σ represents the Lower Control Limit (LCL), as one would find in a typical standard normal distribution covering over 99 percent of the area under the curve. However, having all the data points within the control limits, while it may indicate that the process is not statistically out of control, it may still indicate the potential for a problem. For instance, if a large number of data points lie, say, on one side of the central line, it may indicate that an assignable cause of shift in the quality may have occurred. Also, it may be necessary to check, from time to time, if any gradual shift has taken place in the movement of the data points over time and determine what is contributing to it.

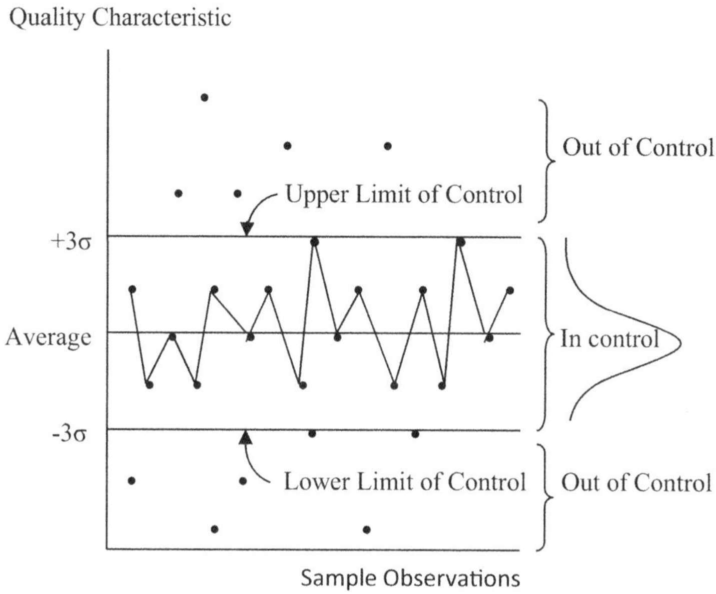

Figure 13.1 A typical control chart

13.4.6 Constructing the Charts

Finally, as shown in Figure 13.1, the control charts are plotted on a rectangular coordinate axis, with the vertical scale representing the statistical measures or quality characteristics, such as $\overline{X}$ (sample mean), and the horizontal scale representing the sample observations (numbers). As noted earlier, for a process to work successfully, points on a given chart should always lie between the control limits. When the points do not lie inside these limits, it means the process is out of control. From a decision-making point of view, it then becomes important for the decision makers to know why the process is out of control; in particular, what has caused it. In general, when a point resides outside the control limits it is an indication that assignable causes, rather than random factors, have contributed to the problem. Although in principle that is the case, in reality one needs to look at the distribution of all the data points, even those which are within the limits, to make certain that there is no unusual pattern that could tell us otherwise.

13.5 Types of Control Charts

There is a wide range of control charts one can use, depending on the characteristics one is trying to measure and analyze for quality control. They fall into two broad categories: variable control charts and attribute control charts. Variable control charts deal with variables whose values are continuous such as income, height, weight, distance, and so forth. Attribute control charts, on the other hand, deal with variables whose values are discrete such as success-failure, conformity-nonconformity, pass-fail, taste, color, and the like. Since the variables used in variable control charts are continuous, the methods commonly used for these charts are measures of central tendency and dispersion such as mean, standard deviation, and range. In contrast, since the variables used in attribute control charts are discrete and not continuous, the measures of central tendency and dispersion used for these charts are based mostly on proportions and frequencies (number of occurrences of a given attribute of a variable in a data set). There is a range of charts one can use for quality control. This section discusses two control charts that are frequently used in quality control: $\bar{X}$ and R charts.[1]

13.5.1 $\bar{X}$ and R Charts

As noted earlier, the purpose of quality control is to detect the assignable causes of variation in a process. The control limits on the X-bar and R charts are placed in such a way that they reveal the presence or absence of these causes of variation based on several statistical measures such as the mean ($\bar{X}$), range (R), and standard deviation (s). In general, the $\bar{X}$ chart is used to measure the variability in the location, such as the mean (average) of the process, and the R chart is used to measure the range of control in the process.

13.5.1.1 Calculation of $\bar{X}$ and R Statistics

The calculation of $\bar{X}$ and R charts begins with the calculation of a set of means, ranges, and standard deviations for each sample or subsample. The procedures for determining these statistics are quite simple. For instance, let X_{ij} ($i = 1, 2, 3, \ldots, n$) be the measurements on the jth sample ($j = 1, 2, 3, \ldots, m$), then the mean $\bar{X}$, the range R, and the standard deviation s for the jth sample can be expressed as

$$\bar{X}_j = \sum_{i=1}^{n} X_{ij} / n \qquad (13.1)$$

$$s_j = \sqrt{\sum_{i=1}^{n} (X_{ij} - \bar{X})^2 / n - 1} \tag{13.2}$$

$$R_j = \max<i> Xij - \min<i> Xij \tag{13.3}$$

for j = 1, 2, 3, ..., m and i = l, 2, 3, ..., n.

From the above, one can obtain a new set of means for $\bar{X}$, R, and s called the aggregate means. Aggregate means serve a useful purpose in quality control by providing a base against which individual statistics (mean, range, standard deviation, and so on) can be compared to determine if a process is out of control.

Equations 13.4–13.6 explain how these new means are constructed for $\bar{X}$, R, and s, as shown below:

$$\begin{aligned}\bar{\bar{X}} &= \sum_{j=1}^{m} \bar{X}_j / m \\ &= (\bar{X}_1 + \bar{X}_2 + \bar{X}_3 + \ldots\ldots\ldots + \bar{X}_m) / m\end{aligned} \tag{13.4}$$

$$\begin{aligned}\bar{R} &= \sum_{j=1}^{m} R_j / m \\ &= (R_1 + R_2 + R_3 + \ldots\ldots\ldots + R_m) / m\end{aligned} \tag{13.5}$$

$$\begin{aligned}\bar{s} &= \sum_{j=1}^{m} s_j / m \\ &= (s_1 + s_2 + s_3 + \ldots\ldots\ldots + s_m) / m\end{aligned} \tag{13.6}$$

where$\bar{\bar{X}}$, $\bar{R}$, and $\bar{s}$represent the new means; that is, the mean of means, the mean of ranges, and the mean of standard deviations, respectively.

13.5.1.2 Additional Measures

Setting the control charts for $\bar{X}$ and R charts depends on two additional measures: standard error of $\bar{X}$ and the sampling distribution of R. A standard error is simply the standard deviation of a sampling statistic such as the sampling mean (the mean of the means of a sampling distribution, based on repeated samples). For instance, if σ is the process standard deviation (the standard deviation of the population), the standard error of the sampling mean is given by $\sigma / \sqrt{n}$. That is,

$$SE(\bar{X}_j) = \sigma / \sqrt{n} \tag{13.7}$$

where SE is the standard error of the mean $\bar{X}$ for the jth sample, σ is the corresponding standard deviation, and n is the sample size.

The sampling distribution of the range R, on the other hand, is given by the expected value, which can be written as a function of a constant that changes with the sample size. That is,

$$E(R) = k\sigma \tag{13.8}$$

where E(R) is the expected value of R, k is a constant that changes with sample size n, and the σ is the same as before.

13.5.1.3 Setting the Control Limits for $\bar{X}$ Chart

As noted earlier, setting the control limits for any chart, including the $\bar{X}$ and R charts, also requires that we state in advance whether we know the population parameters, u (population mean) and σ (population standard deviation). If we know the population parameters, it is understandable that we set the limits based on the known parameters meaning that we do not have to estimate them; we can simply plug them in. If we do not know them a priori, then we must first obtain the estimates of the parameters from the observed data before setting the limits.

We start with the assumption that we know the population parameter u, and its corresponding standard deviation, σ. The 3σ control limits for the $\bar{X}$ chart, based on our earlier discussion of setting the control limits, can be written as

$$UCL_{\bar{X}} = \mu' + A\sigma' \tag{13.9}$$

$$LCL_{\bar{X}} = \mu' - A\sigma' \tag{13.10}$$

where UCL and LCL are the upper and lower limits of control, respectively, μ' is the known population mean, σ' is the known population standard deviation, and A is a constant, similar to k, representing $3 / \sqrt{n}$ that changes with sample size n.[2] In reality, information on the constant terms can be obtained directly from published sources such as a quality control table which can be easily plugged into the equations to determine the limits.[3]

If we do not know the population parameters, we can use the sample range as an estimate of the variability of the process to construct the control limits. We know from our knowledge of measures of dispersion that range (R) is simply the difference between the highest and the lowest value in a sample (Equation 13.3). The advantage of using range is that it can provide useful information about the variability of the data. In general, the higher the range, the greater the variability in the data is, and vice versa. Accordingly, the control limits for the $\overline{X}$ chart can be written as

$$UCL_{\overline{X}} = \overline{\overline{X}} + A_2\overline{R} \tag{13.11}$$

$$LCL_{\overline{X}} = \overline{\overline{X}} - A_2\overline{R} \tag{13.12}$$

where $\overline{R}$ is the mean of ranges, A_2 is a constant representing 3 standard deviations of range that changes with sample size n, similar to k, and the rest of the terms are the same as before.[4] Interestingly, the values of the constant terms such as A_2 for different samples can be obtained directly from a quality control table, as one would find in a standard t or z table.

13.5.1.4 Setting the Control Limits for R Chart

The R chart, like the $\overline{X}$ chart, plays an important role in quality control; it measures the variability of a process. While the $\overline{X}$ chart measures the central tendency, the R chart measures the dispersion of the process, but the methods for developing and using the R chart are essentially the same as the $\overline{X}$ chart. The central line represents the mean range, $\overline{R}$, and $\pm 3\sigma$ represent the upper and the lower limits of control.

Like the control limits for $\overline{X}$ chart, the 3σ control limits for the R chart can be presented in the following way:

$$UCL_R = D_4\overline{R} \tag{13.13}$$

$$LCL_R = D_3\overline{R} \tag{13.14}$$

where D_3 and D_4 are constants that change with the sample size *n*.

As before, information on D_3 and D_4 can be obtained from any standard table for control charts such as the one produced by the American Society for Testing Materials (ASTM, 1951; Neubauer, 2010), similar to statistical

Table 13.1 Values corresponding to constants for selected control charts

n	A_2	A_3	D_2	D_3	D_4
2	1.880	2.659	1.128	0	3.267
3	1.023	1.954	1.693	0	2.574
4	0.729	1.628	2.059	0	2.282
5	0.577	1.427	2.326	0	2.114
6	0.483	1.287	2.534	0	2.004
7	0.419	1.182	2.704	0.076	1.924
8	0.373	1.099	2.847	0.136	1.864
9	0.337	1.032	2.970	0.184	1.816
10	0.308	0.975	3.078	0.223	1.777

For $\bar{X}$ charts (A_2 and A_3), for estimating σ (D_2), and for R charts (D_3 and D_4).

tables one would find in any standard statistics textbook. They can also be tabulated by hand for different values of n, but the process will be cumbersome and time consuming. Table 13.1 presents the information commonly used for constructing a control chart for a small number of observations.

13.5.1.5 $\bar{X}$ and R Charts Together

Although the $\bar{X}$ and R charts use different variables in quality control, both variables play an important role in explaining the variation in quality; as such, it is important to take both measures into consideration when constructing a control chart. Let us look at a simple example to illustrate this. Suppose that the Human Resource Department of a State Government wants to investigate the absentee problem that has become a major concern for several of the departments in recent months. Let us say that the government allows its employees two weeks of paid vacation and two weeks of unpaid leave of absence during the year. The absentee problem is over and above of what the employees are entitled. Table 13.2 presents the data for a sample of 10 departments for each of the 5 working days for an entire year. The table also presents information on the corresponding mean, range, and standard deviation for each department.

To determine if the process is in control, we can now apply the Equations 13.11–13.12 for the $\bar{X}$ chart and Equations 13.13–13.14 for R charts, as shown below:

$$UCL_{\bar{X}} = \bar{\bar{X}} + A_2\bar{R} = 42.7 + (0.557)(19.7) = 53.673$$

$$LCL_{\bar{X}} = \bar{\bar{X}} - A_2\bar{R} = 42.7 - (0.557)(19.7) = 31.727$$

Table 13.2 Absentee data and related statistics for quality control (in hours)

Dept.	*M*	*T*	*W*	*R*	*F*	*Total*	*Sample Mean*	*Sample Range*	*Standard Deviation*
1	60	55	57	50	72	294	58.8	22	8.23
2	58	47	40	45	53	243	48.6	18	7.02
3	32	30	30	28	45	165	33.0	15	6.86
4	45	44	40	37	60	226	45.2	23	8.87
5	47	45	38	32	48	210	42.0	16	6.82
6	27	25	25	28	35	140	28.0	10	4.12
7	34	30	22	20	48	154	30.8	28	11.19
8	43	38	32	34	55	202	40.4	23	9.18
9	56	47	45	42	68	258	51.6	26	10.55
10	53	48	48	39	55	243	48.6	16	6.19

n = 10; $\bar{\bar{X}} = 42.7$; $\bar{R} = 19.7$; $A_2 = 0.557$; $D_3 = 0$; $D_4 = 2.114$; $\bar{s} = 7.90$

For the $\bar{X}$ chart, and

$$UCL_R = D_4\bar{R} = (2.114)(19.7) = 41.646$$

$$LCL_R = D_3\bar{R} = (0.00)(19.7) = 0$$

for the R chart.

As the results of the control limits show, the process is out of control for one of the ten departments (Department 1) for the $\bar{X}$ chart since it lies outside the control limits. However, the same conclusion cannot be drawn for the distribution of the range for the R chart since all the data points lie within the control limits. Note that although we have not constructed the actual charts, we can still identify the departments (namely, the sample units) that are out of control by visually comparing the statistics we have obtained for our sample with the upper and lower limits of control for a given chart.

Additionally, the results produced by the two charts create an interesting dilemma for the decision makers since no definitive conclusions emerge from the charts. In reality, when one is faced with a situation where a clear-cut picture does not emerge from the charts, the convention is to construct the R chart first. If the chart indicates that the process is out of control, there is no need to construct the $\bar{X}$ chart until the process is brought under control. The $\bar{X}$ chart then serves as a checking device to ensure that the process is in control.

It should be worth noting that it is not necessary to use both standard deviation and range at the same time because for small samples the standard deviation, s, and its corresponding range, R, behave identically.

In statistical terms, this means that they move in the same direction; that is, if s is small, R is likely to be small, and vice versa. However, for large samples an extreme outlier in either direction can have a significantly large effect on range, while its effect on the standard deviation will be much less. What this means is that for analyzing variability involving small samples, the range can be used as a substitute for standard deviation with little loss of efficiency. Since range is almost as efficient as standard deviation in small samples, it is preferred to standard deviation in quality control.

13.5.2 Errors in Control Charts

Once we have estimated the values of the population parameters (population characteristics), based on a sample drawn from the same population, we ask ourselves if the estimated parameters were obtained by error (chance) and conduct specific tests to ensure that the estimates are reliable, so that we can draw the conclusion with a certain degree of confidence that they there were not obtained by chance. Similarly, we can ask ourselves if the statistics we observed for various control charts such as mean, range, standard deviation, proportion, and so forth were obtained by error and conduct appropriate tests (namely, hypothesis tests) to determine with a certain degree of confidence that they were not obtained by error.

From a statistical point of view, if we draw the wrong conclusion we will be in error. Two types of errors are commonly associated with statistical tests that also apply to control charts: Type I and Type II. The Type I error occurs when a process thought to be out of control is, in fact, not out of control. Likewise, the Type II error occurs when a process thought not to be in control is, in fact, out of control (Table 13.1).

To give an example, suppose that we are conducting a hypothesis test for an $\bar{X}$ chart for process control, with a population mean (μ) of 50. The null hypothesis for the test is that the process is in control if μ is equal to 50 and out of control if it is not equal to 50, which is a standard two-tailed test (because the rejection region lies on both sides of the tail in a normal distribution). We know from our elementary knowledge of inferential statistics that a null hypothesis is a statistical statement that we reject on the empirical grounds that it is not true, so we will not be in error. In other words, we will not commit a Type I error by incorrectly rejecting

Table 13.3 Errors in quality control

	Process	In Control	Out of Control
Hypothesis (Null)	In Control Out of Control	No Error Error – Type I	Error – Type II No Error

the hypothesis when it is true. Put differently, when we correctly reject the hypothesis, by default, we accept the alternative hypothesis, which is what we are trying to establish.

To test the hypothesis that μ ≠ 50, meaning that it could be higher or lower than 50, we follow a number of steps called hypothesis testing procedures: (1) set a significance level called the α level (namely, the probability of rejecting a null hypothesis when it is true, which is set before the test is conducted, usually at 0.05 or 0.01), (2) collect data from a sample and calculate the relevant statistics, which in this case will be mean (sample mean, $\bar{X}$) and its corresponding standard error,$s/\sqrt{n-1}$), where n-1 is the degrees of freedom, (3) find the observed t (z) value, depending on the size of the sample (namely, t-value, if the sample size is ≤ 30; z-value, if otherwise), (4) compare the observed t (z) against its critical (theoretical) value from a standard t (z) table, and (5) draw the relevant statistical conclusion; that is, reject the null hypothesis if the observed t (z) is greater than or less than the critical value for a two-tailed test, greater than for a right-tailed test, and less than for a left-tailed test.

Let us say that we have collected data on 10 observations and have calculated their mean and standard deviation, which came out to be $\bar{X}$ = 56 and s = 5. We set the α level at 0.05 and follow the test procedures in sequence, starting with the null and alternative hypotheses:

1. H_0: = 50
   H_1: μ ≠ 50
2. α = 0.05
3. $t = \dfrac{\bar{X}-\mu}{s/\sqrt{n-1}}$

$$= \frac{56-50}{5/\sqrt{10-1}}$$

$$= \frac{6}{1.67}$$

$$= 3.5928 \approx 3.60$$

Having calculated the *t* statistic, we now compare it against its critical value that can be found in the t table in any standard statistics textbook. Since the observed t = 3.60 is higher than the critical t* = 2.262 with 9 degrees of freedom (n-1 = 10-1 = 9) for a two-tailed test for α = 0.05 (α/2 = 0.05/2 = 0.025), we can reject the null hypothesis that the process mean is 50 with 95 percent degree of confidence (1-0.05 = 0.95) and accept, by default, the alternative hypothesis that it is not 50.

While being able to reject the null hypothesis at a given level of α, it does not necessarily guarantee that our observed t was not due to error.

For the latter, we need to find the *p* value – the probability associated with the critical t (the probability that the observed t did not occur by chance). With 9 degrees of freedom (n - 1 = 10 - 1 = 9) and t = 3.60, the probability that the observed t did not occur by chance is between 0.01 and 0.005 $(0.005 > p(t) > 0.01)$ which can be obtained from any standard t table. For a one-tailed test; that is, if we were to conduct a right or left-tailed test, it would be between 0.005 and 0.0025, and in both cases the results would be statistically significant.

13.6 Process Capability

An important aspect of quality control is to be able to evaluate if the process is in control. The control charts we have discussed so far help us determine that, but they do not tell us if the process has met the specifications we set a priori. Most organizations, public as well as private and nonprofit, have certain specifications that they want the process to meet when providing a good or service. Specifications are tolerances or limits of quality characteristics that we are willing to accept. When a process meets the specifications, or even exceeds, it is called process capability. For instance, say, a local school district sets a target graduation rate for high school students at 85 percent with a standard deviation of ±5, which means that the acceptable range or limits of graduation for the district will be between 80 and 90 percent (85 ± 5). For most organizations, the acceptable limits are based on past experiences, quality of personnel, use of technology, resource base, and so forth. To ensure that the service provision has met the acceptable limits, process variation must not exceed process specification, as set by the decision makers.

While the control charts provide an effective means for monitoring a process, unfortunately, they do not ensure process capability. For an organization to be able to provide a good or service that is acceptable in that it falls within the acceptable limits, the process must be capable and in control before its provision can take place. To determine whether the process has met the expectations, one needs to use measures other than the control charts that can provide a precise knowledge of process capability. Two measures are commonly used for this purpose: Process Capability Ratio, C_p, and Process Capability Index, $C_{pk.}$ The former is called Six-Sigma (6σ) and the latter Three-Sigma (3σ), because the sigma (σ) provides the width or range of acceptable limits for measuring process capability. The rationale for using 6σ, as opposed to 3σ, is that most measurement processes lie within $\pm 3\sigma$ with a total of 6σ's that cover over 99 percent of the area under the normal curve, which is almost the entire curve.

13.6.1 Process Capability Ratio, C_p

The process capability ratio shows how well a good or service meets the range specified by the design limits. In general, if the design limits are larger in that they exceed expectations than the limits specified in the process, the average of the process can be allowed to be flexible. In other words, it can move in either direction from the center. The capability ratio is obtained by taking the ratio of specification range to process range. The specification range shows the difference between the Upper Specification Limit (USL) and the Lower Specification Limit (LSL), while the process range shows the limits given by the sigma, which in this case is 6, as shown below:

$$C_p = \frac{USL - LSL}{6\sigma} \tag{13.15}$$

where C_p is the capability ratio, USL and LSL are the upper and lower specification limits, and 6σ is the process limit.

Three possible ranges of values are commonly used in process capability ratio that can help us interpret the results: 1. $C_p = 1$: the process has met the specifications; 2. $C_p \geq 1$: the process has exceeded the specifications; and 3. $C_p \leq 1$: the process is not capable of meeting the specifications. The first indicates that the process is minimally capable; the second, it exceeds the minimal capability; and the third, it is below the minimal capability.

13.6.2 Process Capability Index, C_{pk}

Like the process capability ratio, the process capability index also tells us how well a good or service meets the range specified by the design limits. While the capability ratio is useful in measuring process capability, it has an inherent weakness in that it assumes that the variability in a process lies entirely on the specification, which may not always be the case. This is where the capability index is considered a better measure in that it provides two options and selects the one that produces the minimum value of the two to explain the variability.

The capability index is given by the expression, as shown below:

$$C_{pk} = \min[\frac{USL - \mu}{3\sigma}; \frac{\mu - LSL}{3\sigma}] \tag{13.16}$$

where μ and σ are, respectively, the mean and standard deviation of the process and the rest of the terms are the same, as before.

Let us look at a simple example to illustrate the two indices. Suppose that the average time it takes to complete the blood work for a county run hospital laboratory is 28 minutes ($\mu = 30$), with a standard deviation of 2 minutes ($\sigma = 2$). The standard time for the work is 27 with an upper specification limit of 30 minutes (USL = 30) and a lower specification limit of 24 minutes (LSL = 24). The administration wants to know if the laboratory can meet the performance standard.

We can now apply the information to both measures, starting with the capability ratio first:

$$C_p = \frac{USL - LSL}{6\sigma}$$

$$= \frac{30 - 24}{(6)(2)}$$

$$= 0.50 \text{ Minutes}$$

which is less than 1. Since the ratio is less than 1, it does not meet the target specification. In other words, the process is below the minimum capability.

Next, we apply the information to the capability index:

$$C_{pk} = \min[\frac{USL - \mu}{3\sigma}; \frac{\mu - LSL}{3\sigma}]$$

$$= \min[\frac{30 - 28}{(3)(2)}; \frac{28 - 24}{(3)(2)}]$$

$$= \min[0.333; 0.67]$$

$$= 0.333 \text{ Minutes}$$

which is the lower of the two. Since there are two choices, the rule of thumb is to consider the lower (min) value. Unfortunately, both choices came out to be less than 1, indicating that it does not meet the target specification. In other words, it is below the minimum capability. Interestingly, both measures, C_p and C_{pk}, indicate that the process fails to meet the minimum expectations of quality.

13.7 Other Measures of Quality Control

In addition to the control charts discussed above, there are other measures that one can also use to ensure quality control in an organization. The number of these measures has been steadily increasing over the years; in particular, with recent interests in quality control as a means for increasing productivity. To go over the entire breadth of these measures developed to date is beyond the scope of this chapter. However, a number of these measures, although less analytical in nature than those discussed here, are worth mentioning because of their increasing popularity with the practitioners. Important among them are check sheets, histograms, flow charts, Pareto charts, cause-and-effect diagram, scatterplots, six sigma, and balanced scorecard, which, together with the control charts, constitute the basic tools of quality control (Montgomery, 2005; Tague, 2004).

The following provides a brief description of each:

Check sheets. Check sheets are simply charts used for gathering both quantitative and qualitative data. The idea is to start with an exhaustive set of data and gradually eliminating through a descriptive process the ones that are not relevant to the problem. With easy availability of computers, the check sheets can be easily maintained electronically and updated periodically to ensure thoroughness of the process. Since the data is checked against sources, manner of collection, its relevance to the problem, and so forth, it is often called tally sheets.

Histograms. Histograms provide a visual picture of the characteristics of a population based on a sample drawn from the same population. They are essentially frequency distributions of the data, presented in graphical forms. Besides providing a visual picture of the characteristics of the variables being measured, they can also tell us if the distribution of the data approximates a bell (normal) curve, if it is positively or negatively skewed, the nature of the outliers, and so forth.

Flow Charts. Flow charts break down a problem into its constituent components, for instance, a process into a set of sub-processes in a sequential manner. Breaking down a process into a sequence of sub-processes makes it possible to analyze the sub-processes in greater detail, as well as to help us understand the causes of the problem and find appropriate solutions for a sub-process that causes the problem. Construction of flowcharts involves using symbols such as an oval or circle (to indicate a beginning or end), an arrow (to indicate the direction of flow), a square or rectangle (to indicate a process), a diamond (to indicate an indecision), and so forth.

Pareto Charts. Named after the famous 19th century Italian economist and sociologist Valfredo Pareto, these charts are constructed using both bars and line graphs. The bars represent frequencies of data such as cost or income, while the lines represent the cumulative total. The bars are presented in descending order, with the tallest on the left and the shortest on the right, so that one is able to make a visual comparison of the factors that are more important than others, as one moves from the left to the right. The construction of the charts is based on a principle called the Pareto principle, which says that one only needs to look at a small percentage of sources to determine the cause of the problem. For instance, we can look at 20 percent of the data or sources to determine that they cause 80 percent of the problem, instead of looking at the entire population.

Cause-and-Effect Diagram. Also called the fishbone chart, it was developed by Kuoru Ishikawa in 1943 to determine the cause-and-effect relationship in a problem. It is called a fishbone diagram because it resembles a fish skeleton with a head, a backbone, and bones (branches) connected to the backbone. The method for using the diagram is simple: define the goal or problem to be solved at the head, then fill in the branches with factors that cause the problem through a process of brainstorming until the best possible solution is found to address the problem. The factors typically include labor, materials, equipment, and procedures.

Scatterplots. These are primarily used to show the cause-and-effect relationship between two variables, an independent variable (cause) and a dependent variable (effect), on a two-dimensional plane. The relationship is presented as a set of coordinates on the plane, with the dependent variable on the vertical axis and the independent variable on the horizontal axis. While the scatterplots are extremely useful in providing an initial impression of the cause-and-effect relationship, they do not provide a precise measure of the relationship. For the latter, one needs to use methods such as correlation, regression, and other statistical measures.

Six Sigma (6σ). Described earlier under process capability, six sigma is extremely useful in improving the performance capability of an organization by minimizing the process variation. Developed by William Smith, an engineer at Motorola in 1986, six sigma has been extensively used in a wide range of business and industrial organizations but has also been receiving attention in government (Villanova University, 2020; Maleyeff, 2007). Its objective is to find errors and identify areas that need improvement to enhance the quality of a product, a good or service. It does so with the help of a variety of tools and statistics, such as those discussed earlier, to determine where the problem has occurred, how to fix it, and continue to monitor it to avoid the potential for future problems in the process.

Balanced Scorecard. Governments have been using various methods for measuring performance for a long time, especially for measuring efficiency, effectiveness, and economy. Most of these methods are results-based and can produce mixed results (Mayne, 2007). A good example is performance measurement. One way to address the problem is to use 'balanced scorecard,' a holistic approach that provides a framework for balancing short- and long-term measures, financial and non-financial measures, and internal and external perspectives. Originally developed by Kaplan and Norton (1992), it has been extensively used in business organizations and, of late, in government. It is based on four performance metrics that also apply to government and non-profit organizations: learning and growth, internal processes, finance, and customer, which in the context of government will be public. It allows organizations to pool information in a single report, providing information on service quality, financial performance, and improving efficiency.

In addition to those mentioned above, there are other measures that can also be used in quality control such as quality circle (volunteer groups of workers doing similar jobs to meet regularly during work hours under the leadership of their supervisors to identify, analyze, and find ways to solve problems they encounter on the job), stratification (breaking down a whole category into smaller, related subgroups to identify possible causes of a problem), benchmarking (adopting the best practice in order to excel in a given job or activity), reengineering (redesigning an existing process to improve the service costs and quality attributes), and gap analysis (developing an understanding of goods and services provided from multiple perspectives), to name just a few, and the list continues to grow. Interestingly, Kuoru Ishikawa in 1968 formally introduced many of these charts and diagrams to solve problems involving large-scale industries, referred to as the basic tools of quality control.

13.8 Quality Assurance

A term that frequently appears alongside and at times interchangeably with quality control is quality assurance, but the two are not quite the same. We can think of them as pre- and post. Quality assurance usually takes place before the production or delivery process begins to make sure that the system and the procedures are in place that can prevent defects during the process. Quality control checks for defects and issues toward the end but before the final production or delivery process. Although some of the measures used in quality assurance and quality control overlap, the measures used in quality assurance primarily focus on developing quality standards, implementing process controls, developing quality procedures, training employees on quality procedures, and developing procedural manuals and guidelines, among others.

13.9 Quality Engineering

While the measures suggested above have been quite effective in assuring quality, there have been numerous efforts in recent years to develop measures that would further ensure quality. Quality engineering is one such measure that has received considerable attention. The difference between quality assurance and quality engineering is where the emphasis is placed. In quality assurance, the emphasis is placed on the finished product, good or service. In quality engineering, on the other hand, the emphasis is placed on each stage of the process. As such, it is much more encompassing than quality assurance. The driving force behind quality engineering is the application of recently developed technologies, such as artificial intelligence, automation and other developments in concert with some of the existing measures to provide a comprehensive approach that is more dynamic than the conventional quality assurance (Boog, 2020). Since the focus in quality engineering is on the process, it is particularly useful when applied to continuous production or delivery process.

Interestingly, when the focus of analysis in quality control is on quality engineering, rather than on quality assurance, the process that is used to assess quality is called engineering process control. Most control studies use statistical process control, discussed earlier. However, unlike the statistical process control, engineering process control uses a combination of techniques, including some that are statistical in nature to manipulate the adjustable variable so as to bring the output of the process close to the target value. The way the approach works is that it, first, forecasts the output deviation from the target, assuming no quality control, and then takes the necessary action to cancel out the deviation. The control is achieved using appropriate feedback, or feed-forward control that indicates when and by how much the process should be adjusted to achieve the target (Misra, 2008)

13.10 Costs in Quality Control

Costs remain at heart of all control measures, including quality control. As noted earlier, the primary objective of quality control in any organization, public, private, or nonprofit, is to reduce the costs of operation. If control efforts do not lead to any savings in costs or cost reductions then, in principle, there is no need for quality control. However, for most control activities, cost savings are real, and they remain a principal objective of quality control for most organizations.

Three types of costs are generally associated with quality control: assessment costs, prevention costs, and nonconformance costs. Assessment costs are what an organization incurs in terms of measuring quality characteristics to ensure that they conform to quality standards. These costs typically include the costs of inspection, labor as well as materials, costs of approval or certification when organizations meet quality standards, and so on. Prevention costs involve costs when organizations take measures to prevent poor quality of products or performance. Examples of prevention costs would include the costs associated with quality planning, design, and development of quality measurement instruments, quality training, and so on. Since the assessment and prevention costs are incurred by an organization to assure, or conform to quality, they are often called conformance costs. Finally, nonconformance costs, also called failure costs, occur when an organization fails to meet quality standards. This may be due to poor quality of labor, materials, and overheads (namely, expenses accumulated for a service up to the point when nonconformities are detected).

Although exact statistics are not available, nonconformance costs constitute the lion's share of quality costs for an organization. A rule of thumb breakdown would put these at about 50 percent and the rest divided between assessment and prevention costs. In general, there is an inverse relationship between prevention costs and the costs of assessment and failure: when prevention costs increase, they lead to better quality conformance which, in turn, reduces assessment costs. With lower assessment costs, the costs of nonconformance are also expected to decrease. Figure 13.2 shows a diagrammatic presentation of how improvements in quality can reduce the overall cost and that reduction is optimal at the point where the conformance and non-conformance costs intersect.

Interestingly, when both conformance and nonconformance costs are present in goods and services provisions, the optimal or minimum cost will be at the lowest point on the total quality cost curve, obtained by vertically adding the non-conformance and conformance cost curves.

13.10.1 Measures of Quality Costs

Decision makers are often interested in comparing quality costs of one time period with that of another time period to assess the overall quality of a good or service. Since the services provided vary both in costs and quantity over time, it is not always possible to compare quality costs in absolute dollar terms. Consequently, one needs to relate the cost data for a given period to a base that measures the degree of activity for that period similar to the indirect cost allocation method, discussed earlier.

To illustrate the point above, think of a situation where the cost of direct labor is proportional to the quantity of goods produced or service provided. Let us say that 25 units of direct labor are used to produce 75 units of a good, say X, 40 units of direct labor used to produce 120 units

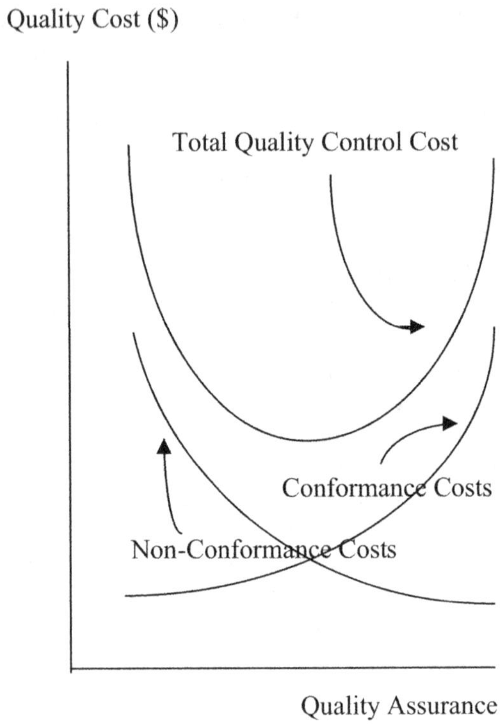

Figure 13.2 Optimal quality cost

of a good, say, Y, and so on. Thus, using direct labor as a base, quality costs can be expressed as a percentage of direct labor. The advantage of using direct labor as a base is that by treating quality costs as a percentage of the base, it can avoid the effect the variation in quantity could have on the quality cost measure.

Since the base one uses is critical to cost comparisons, it is important that it responds to changes in quantity and is not impacted by extraneous factors. To give an example, consider a situation where for two time periods, t1 and t2, quality costs and the quantity of a service provided by a government remain the same, say, $200 of quality costs for 150 units of the service provided for each of the two time periods. Assume that direct labor is the base, and it costs the government $5,000 in direct labor at time t_1, and $7,500 at time t_2. Therefore, based on the percentage of direct labor as a measure, quality cost will be 4 percent [$200/$5,000) × 100 = 4.0] at time t_1, and 2.67 percent [$200/$7,500) × 100 = 2.67] at time t_2. The difference in quality costs between the two time periods can thus be attributed to some extraneous factors that may have affected the base that did not exist at time t1. If the extraneous factors did not intervene, the labor costs would have been the same for both time periods.

The use of direct labor as a base raises an interesting question: why not use the units of goods and service as the base instead of direct labor? The problem with this is that it can unnecessarily complicate the process. Complication arises due to the fact that when one evaluates the performance of an organization at the end of an accounting period, one must not only take into consideration the units of goods produced or the amount of service provided throughout the year, but also the units that are partially completed. In other words, one must consider both to have a true measure of the cost involved: completed as well as partially completed units. This, in turn, makes cost calculations somewhat difficult, as we have seen in the chapter on on job costing. The calculation becomes even more complicated if product mixes are involved in the production or delivery process. The use of direct labor as a base avoids some of these problems.

Although direct labor is considered useful as a base, there are other types of bases that can also be used as a quality-cost measure such as cost per equivalent unit, cost as a percentage of total revenue, and so on. In reality, what is important to remember is that whatever one uses as a base, it must be consistent, be able to produce results that are comparable both over time and across space, and that it is free of biases that can result from variations in cost and quality. One way to ensure that the bases one uses are comparable and that they will produce consistent results is to plot them on a two-dimensional plane, with quality costs on the vertical axis and time on the horizontal axis. If the plots produce parallel lines for the bases being compared (if they move in the same direction), it is an indication that they are comparable and will produce results that will be consistent over time.

13.10.2 Opportunity Costs in Quality Control

In addition to those discussed above, there is a category of cost that deserves some attention, especially when dealing with quality costs. It is called the cost of lost income or revenue resulting from poor perception in the market of the goods and services an organization provides. For instance, when a government provides a service such as recreation or health care that is of much lower quality than what is available in the market, it will affect the perception of the public and, therefore, of the quantity consumed even though the price at which it is sold or delivered may be lower than the price of its competitors (assuming that price is not a factor). This type of cost is generally known as opportunity cost, mentioned earlier. Although important as a cost concept, there is a problem in calculating the opportunity costs due to poor consumer or public perception. No one quite knows how to accurately measure the amount of revenue or income lost based on "what if the perception had been different." In other words, it is almost impossible to find data based on estimates of "what could have been" that will be reliable enough to draw accurate conclusions on lost revenue.

Several other factors also add to this complication, including some that are directly related to current accounting practices. For instance, conventional accounting practice does not provide enough guidance regarding how to account for lost benefits of added market share (where a government has to compete with the private sector to provide good or" service) or the value of added quantity in moving an organization further along the learning curve. Despite this difficulty, the organization must have some knowledge of the costs it would incur, however rudimentary that knowledge may be, due to lost revenue from poor perception. One way to deal with the problem is to develop some changes in the current accounting practices consistent with changing conditions in the market, or the economy in general.

13.11 Total Quality Management

A term that frequently appears alongside quality control is total quality management, or TQM, in short. In fact, TQM is the culmination of the quality control movement that started with the work of Walter Shewart in the 1920s, mentioned earlier. It was subsequently expanded by Deming in the 1940s, Juran (1961) in the fifties, Feigenbaum (1961) in the 1950s and 1960s, Teguchi (1962) Ishikawa (1968) in the 1960s, and Crosby (1979) in the 1970s, although their works received more attention in the 1970s, 1980s and 1990s.

Deming's work is particularly noteworthy because it recognized for the first time that management should be an integral part of quality control, not just the workers who were traditionally held responsible for poor quality, suggesting that about 15 percent or so of the error can be attributed to workers and the rest to the system and process variation. Deming outlined his philosophy on quality in his famous "14 points" that, to this day, serve as the guidelines for quality improvement. These include, among others, consistency of purpose, frequent inspection, continuous improvement, on the job training, supervision and leadership, interaction within the organization and recognition for hard work.

Expanding on the works of Shewart and Deming, Juran introduced his famous quality trilogy: quality planning, quality control, and quality improvement. He also emphasized the importance of quality costs.

Feigenbaum's work deserves considerable attention because he introduced the concept of total quality control which became the foundation for total quality management. Crosby's approach to quality control was more on rigor and precision, suggesting that the job must be done right the first time and that there is no room for error, calling it "zero defect" policy. Besides developing the cause-and-effect diagrams, we mentioned earlier, Ishikawa is also credited with developing the concept of total quality control. Finally, Teguchi's work added a robust dimension to quality control by suggesting that a product must be able to withstand varying work conditions. Like Juran, his work also emphasized the importance of quality costs.

TQM attempts to integrate the various dimensions into a coherent process within an organization to ensure continuous improvement in the quality of goods and services an organization provides. The end result of TQM is customer satisfaction, which, from the perspective of government, is the public whose opinion on how satisfied they are with the services they receive determines how well a government is performing.

13.12 Chapter Summary

Quality control deals with methods, tools, and approaches to diagnose the level of quality, or lack thereof, in a process. Although it is difficult to determine precisely what quality means for many of the goods and services a government provides, it is possible to identify specific areas of service operation where one could use control measures to assure quality. There is a wide range of measures that one can use for this purpose. The most frequently used measure is a control chart. This chapter has provided the essential characteristics of two charts, $\bar{X}$and R, that are frequently used in quality control, in particular, those related to process control. Most of these charts are simple enough that one should not have much difficulty in constructing them. The chapter also provides a detailed discussion of an aspect of quality control that lies at the heart of most control activities, called process capability, followed by an overview of measures such as quality engineering, quality assurance, and costs in quality control. The chapter concluded with a brief discussion of total quality management.

13.13 Review Questions

13.1 Define quality. Why is quality control important in government? Give examples of service provision where quality control would be highly effective.

13.2 What is process control? What contributes to variations in quality?

13.3 What is a control chart? What roles do control charts play in quality control? What are the properties of a control chart? Discuss the steps in preparing a control chart.

13.4 Suppose that several government agencies (federal, state, and local) are looking into the performance of a number of industries, their products, as well as services provided by various government agencies. You have been asked to help them with their investigations. Here is what they are planning to do:

1. The Food and Drug Administration (FDA) will investigate several new drugs introduced into the market recently on their effectiveness on lung-cancer patients.
2. The Department of Transportation (DoT) will investigate whether passenger safety has been violated by the major airlines in recent months.
3. A State Parole Board will investigate early paroles for repeat offenders at several prison facilities in the state in recent months.
4. A city council will investigate traffic accidents for malfunctions of newly installed cameras on major intersections in several communities in the city in recent months.

Given the information above,

a. Explain how you will use the control charts you will use in each case, and why.
b. Collect relevant data from a hypothetical population group in each case, calculate the relevant statistics, and construct the charts.
c. Show which ones are out of control and explain why.

13.5 A healthcare administrator recently visited several local health care clinics to determine the percentage of people within a mandatory age group were vaccinated in four consecutive weeks, following a major virus outbreak:

Clinic	*Week 1 (%)*	*Week 2 (%)*	*Week 3 (%)*	*Week 4 (%)*
1	50	55	62	57
2	55	58	60	54
3	57	60	60	58
4	60	65	75	60
5	58	57	62	58

Given the information above,

a. Calculate the$\bar{\bar{X}}$ and R of the age group vaccinated.
b. Calculate the$X$ and $\bar{R}$ of the age group vaccinated.
c. Calculate the upper and lower control limits of $\bar{X}$, R, and explain if the vaccination effort is in control or out of control and interpret the results.
d. Construct the$\bar{X}$, R, and explain if the vaccination effort is in control or out of control and interpret the result.

13.6 Define process capability, as it applies to quality control. How would you distinguish between process capability ratio and process capability index? Give an example of each from an organization you are familiar with.

13.7 Suppose that the average (μ) response time to a 911 call for a medium size local government is 10 minutes, with a standard deviation (σ) of two minutes. Suppose also that the standard response time for a community of similar size is eight minutes, with an upper specification limit (UCL) of 12 minutes and lower specification of limit (LCL) of five minutes. Calculate the process capability ratio and process capability index for 911 calls for the government and interpret the results.

13.8 What is quality cost? What measures are commonly used in quality costs? Give an example from a community you are familiar with of how it would measure quality costs of providing a service (a) over a period of three years (t_1, t_2, and t_3) and (b) in comparison with three communities of similar size (C_1, C_2, and C_3) where t and C stand for time and community, respectively.

13.9 What is quality engineering? How does it differ from quality assurance? Give an example of each.

Notes

1 Besides X and R charts, there are other types of charts that are also used, such as p, d, c, and s charts. The p-chart is primarily used for determining the proportion (fraction) of nonconformities in a process, while d chart (also known as np chart) is used for determining the actual number of nonconformities, and c chart (also called count chart) is used to determine the number of nonconformities or defects in a sample that provides data for inspection or investigation. Although not required in the same sample, when the sample size is small, s charts are often used as an alternative to R charts when the sample size increases.

2 The 3σ control limits for the $\bar{X}$ chart can be formally expressed as

$$E(\bar{X}) \pm 3SE(\bar{X}) = \mu \pm 3\sigma / \sqrt{n} = \mu' \pm k\sigma' \quad (1)$$

where $E(\bar{X})$ is the expected value of X-bar (i.e., the mean of $\bar{X}$, $\bar{\bar{X}}$), $SE(\bar{X})$ is the standard error of X-bar, $\sigma / \sqrt{n}$ (standard deviation of a sampling statistic such as the sampling mean, which is the mean of a sampling distribution based on repeated samples), k is a constant representing $3/\sqrt{n}$ that changes with sample size n, and μ and σ are population parameters (population mean and standard deviation).

3 In fact, the American Society for Testing Materials (ASTM) published one of the most authoritative tables in 1951 that provides information on various factors used in quality control analysis with different samples that to this day remains the industry standard.

4 When we do not know the population parameters μ and σ, we can use the estimates of μ and σ from observed data to determine the control limits for the $\bar{X}$chart. That is,

$$\bar{X} \pm \left(3\frac{\bar{R}}{d_2}\right)\frac{1}{\sqrt{n}} \tag{2}$$

$$= \bar{X} \pm \left(\frac{3}{d_2\sqrt{n}}\right)^{\bar{R}}$$

$$= \bar{X} \pm A_2\bar{R}$$

where Equation (2) is an estimate of $\hat{\mu} \pm 3\hat{\sigma}/\sqrt{n}$, with $\bar{X}$ representing the estimate of$\hat{\mu}$, $\bar{R}/d_2$representing the estimate of $\hat{\sigma}$, d_2 is a constant that changes with sample size n, and A_2 is a constant representing $3/d_2\sqrt{n}$. Since d_2 changes with the sample size, A_2 also changes with the sample size.

References

ASTM. (1951). *Manual on quality control of materials*. Philadelphia, PA: American Society for Testing Materials (ASTM).

Boog, J. (2020). Quality engineering vs. quality assurance: Everything you need to know. *QA Lead*, October 19, 2020, https://theqalead.com/general/quality-engineering-vs-quality-assurance/ [Retrieved January 15, 2021].

Crosby, P.B. (1979). *Quality is free*. New York: New American Library.

Deming, W.E. (1950). *Elementary principles of statistical control of quality*. Tokyo, Japan: Nippon Kagaku Gijutsu Renmei.

Deming, W.E. (1982). *Quality, productivity and competitive position*. Cambridge, MA: Center for Advanced Engineering Study, MIT.

Feigenbaum, A.V. (1961). *Total quality control*. New York: McGraw-Hill.

Hitoshi, K. (1985), *Statistical methods for quality improvement*. Tokyo, Japan: The Association for Overseas Technical Scholarship.

Ishikawa. K. (1968). *Guide to quality control*. Tokyo, Japan: JUSE.

Juran, J.M. (1961). *Quality control handbook*. New York: McGraw-Hill.

Juran, J.M. and Gryna, Jr., F.M. (1980). *Quality planning and analysis*. Second Edition. New York: McGraw-Hill.

Kaplan, R.S. and Norton, D.P. (1992). The balanced scorecard: Measures that drive performance. *Harvard Business Review*, 70(1), January–February: 71–79.

Kilian, C.S. (1992). *The world of Edwards Deming*. Knoxville, TN: SPC Press.

Maleyeff, J. (2007). *Improving service delivery with lean six sigma*. Strategy and Transformation Series. Hartford, CT: IBM Center for the Business of Government.

Mayne, J. (2007). *Challenges and lessons in implementing results-based management. Harvard Evaluation*, 13(1): 87–109.

Misra, K.B. (2008). Quality engineering and management, in M.K.B. Misra (ed.) *Handbook of performability engineering*. London, England: Springer-Verlog London, 157–170.

Montgomery, D. (2005). *Introduction to statistical quality control*. Hoboken. NJ: John Wiley.

Neubauer, D.M. (ed.). (2010). *Manual on presentation of data and control chart analysis*. West Conshohocken, PA: ASTM International.

Ott, E.R. and Schilling, E.G. (1990). *Process quality control*. Milwaukee, WI: Quality Press.

Taguchi, G. (1962). *Studies on mathematical statistics for quality control*. Doctoral dissertation, Kushu University, Japan.

Tague, N.R. (2004). *Seven basic quality tools. The quality toolbox*. Milwaukee, WI: American Society for Quality.

Villanova University. (2020). *Six sigma in government*. Villanova University, March 12, 2020. www.villanovau.com/resources/six-sigma/six-sigma-government/ [Accessed July 31, 2020].

14 Budgeting for Planning and Control

14.1 Introduction

Budgeting plays a vitally important role in the functioning of an organization – public, private, and nonprofit, but more so in government. It involves a set of activities that take place throughout the year that are detailed, structured, and time-consuming. There is a direct relationship between planning, budgeting, and costs. Costs refer to expenses the activities incur, while budgeting deals with the process that deals with how to plan, allocate, manage, and control costs of these activities within a defined time frame. More specifically, to understand the role budgeting plays in all this, it is important to understand the essential elements of a budget that include, among others, the budget process, types of budgets, budget forecasts, budget structure, and the development of the budget – operating as well as capital. The elements are common in both government and nonprofit organizations, except that they are much more detailed and involved in government.

This chapter provides a brief discussion of each, with an emphasis on government budget. This is not difficult to understand, considering the size of a government budget that runs from a few million dollars for a small local government, to hundreds of millions, to billions of dollars for a large government. The chapter, in particular, focuses on both operating and capital budget, and concludes with a brief discussion of the impact a capital budget has on the operating budget.

14.2 Planning and Budgeting

There is a direct relationship between planning and budgeting. Planning deals with mission, goals, and objectives of an organization and the development of plans to achieve them. An important component of planning is the development and execution of a budget. A budget is a financial plan for carrying out the routine and non-routine activities of an organization

DOI: 10.4324/9781003486091-17

within a defined time frame. As a plan, it helps an organization coordinate these activities to ensure that they are carried out in an orderly and timely manner within the available resources, as determined by the decision makers; in particular, by the legislature for a government, and the board for a nonprofit organization.

Two types of budgets are generally prepared by most organizations: an operating budget and a capital budget. The operating budget, which is prepared on an annual basis, deals with the routine day-to-day operations of an organization. As such, it is concerned with materials, labor, overhead, expenditure, revenue, cash, and other routine activities. The capital budget, on the other hand, deals with non-routine activities of an organization that are long-term in nature such as roads, bridges, highways, buildings, and so on. The two, however, are integrated by a process where the operating budget includes a capital component that deals with the capital expenditure for the budget year plus any other expenditure that is carried over from previous years called capital outlay. What makes this integration possible is the fact that the capital budget which is prepared for several years into the future, usually five to six, is divided into annual segments so that capital outlay for any given year can be easily incorporated into the operating budget for that year.

In addition to being a planning instrument, a budget is extremely useful as a control device. For instance, once a budget has been approved and funds have been allocated for execution, they must be followed through. This may appear somewhat rigid to those who may not be familiar with public budgeting, but there is a rationale for this apparent inflexibility. In the private sector, competitive market forces serve as a vehicle to ensure that the resources of an organization are efficiently managed and utilized. In other words, when a private firm or business becomes inefficient, it will not make enough profit to stay in business and will eventually be forced out of the market. Since no such conditions exist in government, nonmarket mechanisms such as laws, regulations, mandates, and various compliance requirements are necessary to achieve the goals and objectives of the government.

Additionally, governments are often required either by law or by established procedure to prepare their budgets according to a formal structure called the budget systems. The systems, which vary between governments, provide specific guidelines regarding how a budget should be prepared, including setting goals, objectives, programs, and activities. This is important because without this structure it will be difficult to carry out the budgetary activities of a government. More importantly, it will be difficult to achieve the goals and objectives of the government in a planned and coherent manner.

14.3 Budget Process

All budgets, whether they are prepared annually or biennially, go through a process called the budget cycle. The cycle consists of four distinct, but interrelated phases: preparation, appropriation, implementation, and evaluation, and each phase consists of a number of activities. The process is time-consuming, detailed, and involved in that a budget has to be prepared, it has to be appropriated, it has to be implemented and, finally, it has to be evaluated. Interestingly, the process is similar for all three levels of government (federal, state, and local) but varies in complexity depending on the size of the budget and the level of government.

The cycle begins when the various agencies and departments receive instructions from the chief executive and the central budget office to prepare their budget requests for the upcoming budget year. Instructions are detailed and clear to avoid the potential for any ambiguity, as the agencies put together their requests. At a minimum, it is expected that the requests would include the following: (1) mission, goals, and objectives of the agency, consistent with the larger mission and goals of the government, (2) budget assumptions, including any changes in service provision, explanations for change and their effects on the budget and the government, (3) details of the service provision in quantitative terms, including performance measures, (4) expense calculations by line items as well as funding sources, and (5) putting together the budget as a coherent document that is thorough, interspersed with numbers yet easy to understand.

The budget of a government is essentially a proposal. It does not automatically guarantee the funding requests made in the proposed budget: appropriations must be made. Appropriation is a legislative decision on how the government spends money on various functions and activities, and it is where the greatest political battle takes place. Legislative consideration of the budget begins immediately, as soon as the budget is submitted to the legislature. Like the preparation phase, the process is very similar at all three levels (federal, state, and local), except that it becomes more complex at the federal level because of the sheer size of the budget, and the number of programs needing appropriation decisions that run into hundreds,

The implementation of the budget begins when the agencies and the departments receive authority to incur obligations that will result in immediate or future government expenditures called budget authority. Three types of authority are commonly used during this process: contract authority, spending authority, and borrowing authority. In a contract authority, agencies are allowed to enter into a contract agreement with a private firm (vendor) or another government to acquire goods and services within a specified time up to an established level, as determined under the appropriation guidelines. In a spending authority, the agencies are allowed to undertake expenditures from a specific fund (governmental funds, proprietary funds, and so forth) for a specific purpose within a specified time up to an established level, as determined under the appropriation guidelines. Finally, agencies are also allowed to borrow from another fund or from the treasury to incur obligations, called borrowing authority. Table 14.1 presents the timetable of activities for a local budget, called the budget calendar.

Table 14.1 Timetable for a local budget process

Timetable[1]	*Specific Activity*
First week in January	• Chief Administrative Officer (CAO) meets with the Budget Director (BD) and others to review current year spending
Second week in January	• CAO and BD meet with the Mayor and Council to review the current year budget and discuss policies and priorities for the upcoming budget year
Last week in January	• BD distributes worksheets for departmental budget preparation, including the budget calendar
First week in February	• Departments begin budget preparation (estimation)
Second week in February	• BD makes the initial revenue projection and discusses with CAO and the Mayor
Third week in February	• CAO, along with BD, provides additional budgetary information to the departments in light of the projections (for example, budget cuts, salary increase, and the like.)
First week in March	• Budget requests are submitted by the departments
Second week in March	• Internal hearings are held with the department heads
Third week in March	• Public hearings (open to the public) are held
Last week in March	• BD asks the departments to make revisions and resubmit the budget requests
Second week in April	• Departments resubmit the requests
First week in May	• CAO and the Mayor, with the assistance of BD, put together the proposed budget and send it to the Council
Second week in May	• Council (local legislature) holds open budget meeting, deliberates key issues, and makes final budgetary decision on the budget
First week in June	• Council adopts the budget
July 1	• Fiscal year begins

[1] Dates are approximate

The cycle ends with an audit of government finances, including the budget, and evaluation of various programs carried out during the fiscal year. The objectives of these activities are to ascertain the extent to which the government (1) has complied with the spending requirements, (2) presented the results of its financial operations and reported its financial position in accordance with the Generally Accepted Accounting Principles (GAAP), and (3) the extent to which the completed programs have achieved their stated goals and objectives. The first two together are called the financial audit, and the third is called the performance audit.

While financial audits are based on a set of accepted standards, such as GAAP, by which one can measure and evaluate the financial position of a government, performance audits are much broader in scope. There are no set standards that can accurately guide and measure the performance of an organization. However, by focusing on goals and objectives, the performance audit can address the broader question of efficiency and effectiveness; in particular, how an organization carried out its operations and the efficiency with which it utilized its resources (allocated funds) in achieving those goals and objectives. In other words, by placing emphasis on goals and objectives, and their achievement, the performance audit can measure an organization's bottom-line performance.

14.3.1 Nonprofit Budget Process

The process is similar for a nonprofit organization in that a budget has to be prepared for programs consistent with the goals and objectives of the organization (National Council of Nonprofits, 2024). Preparation involves estimation of income and expenses for the upcoming budget year and presented to the board (the decision-making body of the organization) for approval before it can be implemented. Like government, implementation involves a monthly or quarterly cash-flow analysis of income and expenses (discussed later in the chapter), followed by evaluation at the end of the budget year for performance and goal achievement.

As for auditing, nonprofit organizations are also required to complete a financial audit, depending on the size of the organization. In particular, the organizations that receive federal funding or federal funding passed through the state are required to have an audit, if the funding exceeds a certain amount. Some grant providers may require nonprofits to conduct audits to ensure that their financial systems are transparent to justify future funding. Even if granting institutions do not require an audit, it is important for the organizations to conduct an annual audit for transparency and to ensure that the funds are well-managed.

Interestingly, the accounting and auditing standards nonprofit organizations use are similar to those used by for-profit organizations, established by the Financial Accounting Standards Board (FASB), while governments, particularly state and local governments, use standards established by the Governmental Accounting Standards Board (GASB). The federal government, on the other hand, uses standards established by the Government Accountability Office (GAO), not GASB, which are contained in a guidebook called the Yellow Book. For internal operations, it follows the standards outlined in a similar book, called the Green Book. However, like government, GAAP serves as the foundational accounting principles for nonprofit organizations.

14.4 Budget Forecasts

Budgets are essentially estimates; estimates of revenue and expenditure. The preparation of the budget requires a basic knowledge of the forecasting process and forecasting methods. Most budgets are prepared using methods that range from simple calculations such as arithmetic average to advanced methods that are highly sophisticated, such as econometric and advanced multivariate time-series models. Interestingly, simple methods such as arithmetic average or simple moving average, such as those used in cash budgeting, can often produce as good and reliable forecasts as advanced sophisticated methods.

14.4.1 Revenue Forecasts

Forecasting in general is a demanding exercise, but much more so for revenue forecasts because of the nature of the revenue sources (variables) that vary in range and characteristics such as income tax, sales tax, user fees and charges, intergovernmental revenue, and so forth. Besides the range, there are also uncertainties with many of these variables, even during normal economic times, as to how much revenue a government would collect because of the presence of factors over which the government does not have much control. On the other hand, forecasting revenue for variables such as property tax is relatively uncomplicated because it is primarily based on the assessed value of property and the rate at which the property will be assessed for the forecasting period, both of which are within the purview of the government.

Given the demanding nature of budget forecasts, especially revenue forecasts, the responsibility for developing revenue forecasts often falls on multiple entities. For instance, for the federal government, the responsibility falls on the Department of Treasury, along with the Council of Economic Advisors on the economic outlook, and the Congressional

Budget Office; the latter, on the budget aggregates. At the state level, the responsibility typically falls on the Comptroller of Accounts, along with the governor's budget office, while at the local level it falls on the central budget office and the finance department. Ideally, forecasting should be done in-house, but in the event that in-house expertise is not available, governments often engage outside expertise, consultants, and firms.

14.4.1.1 Nonprofit Revenue Forecasts

Forecasting is equally important for nonprofit organizations. Although the conventional methods used for forecasting government revenues can be used for nonprofit organizations, there are methods that nonprofit organizations often use that are simple and less demanding on data. Two of these methods are the discount method and the cutoff method (Jitasa, 2023). In a discount method, the forecaster identifies the dollar amount an organization expects to receive from each fundraising source and then multiplies that dollar amount by the fundraising probability. For example, if the organization is applying for a \$25,000 grant and has a 75% probability of receiving the grant, the forecasted revenue would be discounted to \$18,750 (\$25,000 × 0.75 = \$18,750) to be on the conservative side, although it may end up receiving the full amount of the grant.

Under the cutoff method, the forecaster identifies the total amount of predicted fundraising revenue, then multiplies the amount by the overall probability estimation. For instance, if the organization had a successful history in fundraising and there is an 80 percent chance of success in receiving, say, \$100,000 of revenue, then the forecasted revenue would be \$80,000 (\$100,000 × 0.8 = \$80,000). Interestingly, while both methods use probability of success, the first method relies on expectations and the second method on history.

14.4.2 Expenditure Forecasts

Unlike revenue forecasts, expenditure forecasts are much less complicated because the government has a good knowledge of the activities it plans to undertake in the coming years. As such, the responsibility for preparing the expenditure budget, in particular the expenditure forecasts, typically falls on the respective agencies and departments. This is due to the fact that they are directly responsible for providing the goods and services and, as such, have a much better knowledge of the costs the provisions will entail. The forecasts are generally prepared by object classification such as personal services (salaries and wages, including benefits), materials and supplies, debt service, contract obligations, capital outlay, and miscellaneous other costs.

The simplest way to forecast a government budget, in particular expenditures, is to assume that next year's budget will be the same as the current year, which means that there will be no change in demand or the cost of providing government services and, consequently, no change in the level of revenue that will be needed to provide them. These are known as naïve forecasts. Since naïve forecasts assume the current conditions to be the same as last year, they can serve as an initial decision tool from which to make the appropriate changes in the budget.

We can use a simple expression to describe it, as shown below:

$$\hat{Y}_{t+1} = Y_t \tag{14.1}$$

where $\hat{Y}_{t+1}$ is the value of Y at time t + 1, and Y_t is the current value of Y.

To give an example, suppose that a mid-sized local government wants to forecast its General Fund budget (expenditure) for various line items (cost objects) for next year. The government starts with an initial assumption that next year's budget, t + 1, will be the same as the current year, t, which will serve as its base. Table 14.2 shows the naïve forecasts for the General Fund (GF) budget of a government for next year, t + 1.

Assume that the budget for our government will change, say, increase by a constant amount across the board next year. The constant could be the inflation rate or any other measure the forecaster may find useful to define the change. We can then plug the constant term into the expression in Equation 14.1 to show the change in next year's budget, so that the new expression will be

$$\hat{Y}_{t+1} = cY_t + Y_t \tag{14.2}$$

Table 14.2 General fund budget: Expenditure forecasts by line items

Expenditure by Object Classification	*FY_t Current year ($1,000)*	*FY_{t+1} Unadjusted ($,1000)*	*FY_{t+1} Adjusted[1] ($1,000)*	*FY_{t+1} Partially adjusted[2] ($1,000)*
Personnel services	650,000	650,000	669,500	669,500[2]
Materials and supplies	15,000	15,000	15,450	15,450[2]
Contractual	120,000	120,000	123,600	120,000
Insurance	25,000	25,000	25,750	25,750[2]
Capital outlay	75,000	75,000	77,250	75,000
Miscellaneous	10,000	10,000	10,300	10,000
Total:	$895,000	$895,000	$921,850	$915,700

[1,2] Assuming a 3% increase due to inflation

where c is the constant and the rest of the terms are the same, as before.

Assume further that the government has decided to increase next year's budget by three percent across the board for all line items, based on the projected inflation rate for next year. This will increase the budget from \$895 million this year, t, to \$921.85 million, next year, t+1. The table shows both the current year and next year's budget. Suppose now that instead of increasing the budget across the board for all line items, the government has decided to increase it for three of the line items (personal services, materials and supplies, and insurance), while keeping the rest constant. The new budget will therefore be \$915.7 million, a little less than the across-the-board increase, and we can repeat the process for year 2, t+2. In fact, we can repeat the process for any number of years and line items (cost objects) to produce the desired changes in the forecast. However, the end-product will no longer be a naïve forecast because once a change has been made in the original forecast the results will no longer be the same as the current year; that is, $\hat{Y}_{t+i} \neq \hat{Y}_t$ (i^{th} year).

It should be worth noting that the assumption underlying a naïve forecast is that past relationships will continue unchanged but that is seldom the case. Even if it were to remain the same, it is unlikely that the factors that affect a government budget such as the cost of labor, materials, and supplies will remain constant over time. On the other hand, if a forecaster has past information on the changes in any of these factors, the information can be used to develop simple expressions to produce suitable forecasts.

In the example presented above, we assumed that all the information needed to develop an expenditure budget is available a priori, but when the information is not readily available one needs to estimate the budget using forecasting methods that can vary in complexity. However, for both revenue and expenditure forecasts, there is a wide range of methods that can be used but which method or combination of methods will be used depends on the availability of data, knowledge and skill of the forecaster, and the time frame within which the forecasts need to be completed. Also, as noted earlier, forecasts are not actual revenues and expenditure; they are estimates of actual revenues and expenditure. As such, they need to be constantly updated as new information becomes available to ensure the accuracy of the forecasts.

14.4.2.1 Nonprofit Expense Forecasts

Forecasting expenses for nonprofit organizations, similar to forecasting government expenditures, is simple and uncomplicated. In general, expenses are broken down into distinct categories such as fundraising, administrative, and programs. The combination of fundraising and administrative expenses that is necessary to operate a nonprofit organization makes up its overhead, which typically includes rent, utilities, and insurance. In other words, those expenses that are not directly tied to program activities. While there is no cut-and-dried rule for an organization's expense budget, the rule of thumb is to spend roughly 35 percent of their funding on overhead expenses and 65 percent on their programs (Jitasa, 2023). The best way to estimate the expenses of a nonprofit organization is to examine what the organization has spent in the past, then adjusting it for new expenses, similar to naïve forecasts.

14.5 Operating Budget

The operating budget, as noted earlier, is one of the two budgets the governments at all three levels (federal, state, and local) prepare on a regular basis. It deals with everyday operations of a government and is prepared for the next fiscal year. Most fiscal years are twelve months long, which is a reasonable length of time to execute the budget. There are a handful of state and local governments that deviate from this practice. Most of these governments use a biennial budget, prepared for execution over a two-year period, as opposed to twelve months.[1] The process is the same for both in that the budget has to be prepared, it has to be appropriated, it has to be implemented, and finally evaluated.

Governments prepare their budgets by funds, by functions, and by programs, together with the details of the expenditure activities. Most governments maintain multiple funds, divided into three broad categories:[2] Governmental funds, proprietary funds, and fiduciary funds. Examples of Governmental funds would be General fund, capital projects fund, debt service fund; for proprietary funds they would be enterprise funds, and for fiduciary funds they would be trust and agency funds. Trust and agency funds are not usually included in the document, unless a specific function or program is funded out of trust funds. A typical operating budget includes all four (funds, functions, programs, and expenditure) and is prepared in a manner that is easy for the public to understand and the practitioners to carry out the operations of the government. An important requirement in preparing a budget, especially the operating budget, is that it has be balanced.[3] Likewise, non-profit organizations are also expected to balance their operating budget to ensure that their expenses stay within the budget (match their income).

Operationally, all budgets have two sides: a revenue side, called the revenue budget, and an expenditure side, called the expenditure budget. The revenue budget typically includes all sources of revenue from which a government collects its revenues, tax as well as non-tax, such as income tax, sales tax, property tax, franchise tax, user fees and charges, fines and forfeitures, and intergovernmental revenue. The expenditure budget similarly includes a detailed list of expenditure on various programs and activities that a government plans to undertake, from public safety to health care, to education, to transportation, environment, and economic development, among others.

For nonprofit organizations, the revenue budget typically includes individual donations, contributions from corporations (including sponsorships), grants from private foundations and government agencies, membership fees, fundraising campaigns, in-kind donations, and earned income from sale of goods or services related to their mission. The expenditure budget, on the other hand, includes expenditure on various programs and activities, which, unlike the government, is different for different organizations. However, expenses for both government and nonprofit organizations are quite similar in that they typically include salaries and wages, rent, administrative costs, travel expenses, program-related costs, and utilities.

Preparing the budget for both government and nonprofit organizations is a two-way process; one for revenue and one for expenditure, but both must be considered simultaneously to determine the final budget. The process requires a clear understanding of the organizations' economic and revenue base, their current and past budget history, the needs of the public (for government) and the beneficiaries (for nonprofits), and the political process (for government) that would shape the budget outcome.

14.5.1 Budget Structure

As noted earlier, budgets are prepared using a formal structure that ties the various elements of a budget into a coherent document. The structure provides the foundation that guides the development of the budget, which, for convenience, can be defined as budget management systems or budget systems, in short. Although terms such as budget formats, budget approaches, and budget types are often used, "budget system" seems more appropriate because, like any system, all budgets have a formal structure with interrelated components that are tied together in a coherent fashion to achieve the goals and objectives of an organization.[4]

Understanding the systems and their structure is important to understand how budget decisions are made and the results those decisions have for individual departments and agencies, as well as for the public at large. Understanding the systems and their structure is also important to understand the management structure of a government, beginning with the chief administrative officer, all the way down to the unit managers dealing with various components of the budget. A number of budget systems have been developed over the years, from line-item, to program, to performance, to zero-based, to strategic, to outcome-based, and so forth. Of these, the line-item budget serves as the core budget, since all other systems are built on it. This section briefly discusses a cost-based budget, which is a variation of performance budgeting system, with a program structure that resembles a program budget, based on line items that serve as the foundation.

14.5.1.1 Cost-Based Budget: An Illustration

All budgets have a line-item structure, showing how the money will be spent on various line items or cost objects. The items typically include personal (salaries and wages), materials and supplies, contractual, debt services, capital outlay, and other miscellaneous items. Each of these items can be further divided into a subset of items. For instance, personal services can be divided into full-time, part-time, overtime, retirement benefits, health insurance, worker's compensation, and so forth. Similarly, materials and supplies can be divided into office supplies, general supplies, printing, and so on. However, the allocation does not show for what purpose the money will be used or the goals and objectives the allocated funds will achieve, which is an important weakness of a line-item budget. This is typically addressed in a program budget.

Program Budgeting Structure. In a program budget, allocations are made for expenditure on specific programs rather than on specific cost or line items, although line itemization remains an integral part of the budget. Programs are generally targets for action by individual functional units such as public works, public safety, education, transportation, health and human services, parks and recreation, and so forth. The difference between a line-item and a program budget is that in a program budget the focus is on specific programs and activities and not on specific line items or cost objects, which makes it possible to tie the allocation decisions to program goals and objectives. In other words, in a program budget, allocation decisions are made in such a way as to ensure that there is congruence between budget allocation and program goals and objectives of the organization, although line itemization remains central to the system.

Operationally, a program budget has three key elements: One, the establishment of program goals and objectives for individual departments or agencies, two, the development of plans to achieve the goals and objectives within a specified time frame, and three, the determination of resources that will be required to achieve the goals and objectives. Preparing a program budget, like a line-item budget, is quite simple.

Since it is structurally similar to a line-item budget, all one needs to do is describe the goals and objectives for individual programs, then develop a list of cost or line items for the programs consistent with program goals and objectives. Given that most government programs are repetitive in nature, the recent history of budget allocation, including the current allocation, can serve as a valuable guide for determining the dollar amount to be spent on each program, next year, with appropriate adjustments for inflation, discretionary changes, and so forth.

Cost-Based Budget. An interesting aspect of program budgeting is that, like line items, a program structure can be built into any budget system. Table 14.3 presents a simple cost-based budget for a local government with a program structure and line items. The program is Solid Waste Collection for residential units and is operated by the Water and Sewer Department. The division responsible for the program is Sewage, which performs a number of other functions, besides solid waste collection, such as wastewater treatment, hazardous waste disposal, recycling, and so forth. As shown in the table, the program goal is to collect solid waste in a timely manner to prevent health hazards. The program objective is to collect solid waste, say, twice a week throughout the year, including holidays. In reality, a program can have multiple goals and objectives, but, for convenience, we will use a single goal and a single objective.

Structurally, a cost-budget is based on traditional program structure that divides costs into two basic categories: fixed and variable. As discussed earlier, fixed costs are costs that do not change, regardless of the quantity produced, whereas variable costs change with changes in the quantity produced. Thus, in the current example, the total cost of the program for next year will be the sum of the fixed and the variable costs. The fixed costs would include the costs of leasing (if the government has to lease a space, a building, or a vehicle), debt service, the portion of personal service that is salaried, supplemental retirement, benefits, including paid leave, since these costs will remain unchanged during the budget year. The variable costs, on the other hand, would include materials and supplies, capital outlay, the portion of personal service that is based on hourly wages, and overtime, since these costs would vary depending on the amount of labor and materials used. As shown in the table, the sum of the fixed and variable costs makes up the total budget for next year, which is \$1,700,000 (\$1,345,000 + \$355,000 = \$1,700,000).

Costs can also be classified as direct and indirect. Direct costs are costs that can be directly attributed to an activity, whereas the indirect costs cannot; as such, the term that is frequently used to define them is overhead. Overhead costs for individual activities are often difficult to determine. As a result, most organizations use overhead cost as a fixed

Table 14.3 A simple cost-based budget

Department: Water and Sewer
Functional Unit (Division): Sewage
Expenditure Budget
Fiscal Year: 2XXX–2XXX

Program: Solid Waste Collection
Program Goal: To pick up solid waste in a timely manner to prevent health hazards
Program Objective: To pick up solid waste twice a week throughout the year, including holidays

Cost Categories	*Cost ($)*
07–02–01–000[1]	
I. Fixed Costs	
Personal Services	
Salaries (Full-time)	$680,000
Supplemental Retirement	45,000
Workman's Compensation	35,000
Supervision (Fixed)	90,000
Benefit (including Leave)	110,000
Total Personal (Fixed)	$960,000
Contractual/Lease	125,000
Debt Service	45,000
Miscellaneous	215,000
Total Fixed Cost	$1,345,000
II. Variable Costs	
Personal Services	
Wages (Part-time)	$60,000
Overtime (Salaried)	40,000
Total Personal (Variable)	$100,000
Materials and Supplies	130,000
Capital Outlay	25,000
Vehicle Use	85,000
Miscellaneous	15,000
Total Variable Cost	$355,000
III. Total Cost of Operation (incl. overhead) ($1,345,000 + $355,000)	$1,700,000

[2] Fund and account information

percentage of the total cost of operation for the entire organization and use it as the overhead for the respective activity. Let us suppose that the overhead cost of operation for the government in our example is 12.65%. We can then use it to determine the overhead cost for solid waste collection, which will be \$215,000 (\$1,700,000 × 0.1265). The remaining \$1,485,000 will then go toward direct costs (direct labor and direct materials). The total cost of solid waste collection for next year, t + 1, will therefore be the sum of two costs: Direct cost + Indirect cost (overhead); that is, \$1,485,000 + \$215,000 = \$1,700,000. The process can be further extended by breaking down direct costs into different types of direct labor, direct materials, and so forth. Overhead, on the other hand, is usually treated as an all-inclusive category.

14.6 Implementation Measures

The budget comes full circle once it is ready for implementation by various agencies and departments since it is the agencies and departments which initiated the process by putting together their budget requests. Once the implementation process begins, it is important for a government to prepare two documents: a cash budget to keep track of cash flows (inflows and outflows), and a cash accounting report to keep track of cash position. This is frequently associated with a process of monitoring and control called budgetary accounting. Preparing the documents is relatively uncomplicated since most of the information is available to the government, although preparing the cash budget requires a basic knowledge of forecasting.

14.6.1 Cash Budget

A cash budget deals with expected cash receipts (inflows) and cash disbursements (outflows). A good starting point for a cash budget is a cash-flow analysis, which is prepared using three simple pieces of information: cash inflow, cash outflow, and net flow (the difference between inflows, namely, the flow of funds from all revenue sources, and outflows, that is, disbursements for all expenditures). The analysis serves an important purpose by identifying in advance the cash position of an orgnaization and, more importantly, how to deal with a potential problem such as cash shortage.

Cash budgets can be prepared on a weekly, monthly, or quarterly basis, but usually on a weekly or monthly basis. Daily cash budgets are not uncommon, depending on the availability of information and the interest of the government. The following steps are typically used in preparing a cash budget: cash balance at the beginning of the reporting period called the beginning balance, cash receipts (inflows), cash disbursements (outflows), and changes in cash balance at the end of the period, called the ending balance. Table 14.4 presents a simple cash budget of a local government based on monthly receipts and disbursements for a three-month period.

Table 14.4 A monthly cash budget

Cash Flows	*Monthly Flow ((\$ (\$1,000)*		
	January	*February*	*March*
Beginning Balance (BB)			
Cash Receipts (Inflow)			
Tax revenue	---	(147)	395
Property tax	27,238	28,165	28,956
(Local) Sales tax	6,285	5,987	5,823
(Local) Franchise tax	7,347	7,549	7,450
Non-tax revenue			
Charges and fees	2,455	2,138	2,107
Fines and forfeitures	1,570	1,296	1,325
Intergovernmental revenue	5,216	6,295	6,794
Miscellaneous	1,079	1,512	1,928
Total Inflows (Excl. BB):	51,190	52,942	54,383
Cash Disbursements (Outflow)			
Salaries and wages	31,514	32,925	32,975
Materials and supplies	3,295	2,764	2,516
Debt service	5,760	5,760	5,760
Benefit payments	2,127	2,479	2,863
Capital outlay	7,295	7,387	7,956
Miscellaneous	1,346	1,085	1,215
Total Outflows:	51,337	52,400	53,285
Changes in Cash Balance			
= Net cash flow	(147)	542	1,098
+ Beginning balance	----	(147)	395
= Ending balance (EB)	(147)	395	1,493

According to the table, the net flow for the government at the end of the first period, which is the month of January, is -\$147,000; this then becomes the beginning balance for the next period, which is February. In general, if the ending balance (the balance at the end of a period) is positive, it adds to the total revenue for the next period and the converse is true, when it is negative. The process can be repeated for as many time periods as one would like. In reality, a cash flow analysis for more than six months may not be useful because of the likelihood of errors that increases with time in forecasting future flows, although theoretically it can be prepared for any number of months. It should be worth noting that the forecasts presented in the table were not actual forecasts, but used here for illustrative purposes, although one could use any standard forecasting methods, especially those suitable for short-term forecasts such as simple moving average.

14.6.2 Cash Accounting Report

A cash accounting report, on the other hand, is prepared to keep track of cash position at the end of an accounting period. Like a cash budget, the reports are usually prepared on a daily, weekly, monthly, and quarterly basis. Preparing the report beyond the daily report is not complicated, since one only needs to add the daily balances to get the weekly balance, add the weekly balances to get the monthly balance, and so forth, but always keeping the same reporting structure. Table 14.5 presents a simple daily cash accounting report for a government; it includes two funds and five accounts but can be easily extended to include additional funds and accounts.

Ideally, two sets of cash accounting reports should be prepared: one for the government, and one separately for each fund that produces an income or revenue for the government. This would include both Governmental Funds, such as the General Fund, and Proprietary Funds such as the water fund, sewer fund, electric utility fund, parking meter fund, and so forth. As the table shows, all five accounts, with the exception of parks and recreation, had a positive beginning balance. The position appears to remain the same at the end of the week.

There is a similarity between a cash accounting report and a cash budget in that both start with a beginning balance and conclude with an ending balance, with one difference: while the cash accounting reports are prepared at the end of the accounting period, the cash budgets are prepared at the beginning of the accounting period. This makes sense because a cash budget, like any other budget, is about current, as well as about future cash flows – cash inflows and cash outflows. Having the budget prepared

Table 14.5 A daily cash accounting report

Account No.	*Fund Name*[1]	*Beginning Balance ($000)*	*Receipts ($000)*	*Disbursements ($)*	*Ending Balance ($)*
000-00	General Fund				
001-01	General Govt.	1,150	125	250	1,025
001-05	Parks & Recreation	(15)	20	10	(5)
002-00	Enterprise Funds				
002-01	Water	375	140	135	380
002-02	Electric Utility	450	175	200	425
002-03	Parking Meter	150	15	25	140
	Total:	2,110	475	625	1,965

[1] By funds

at the beginning of the accounting period allows the government to know in advance about any potential problems such as cash shortage, so it can take appropriate measures to deal with the problem when it occurs.

14.6.3 Budgetary Accounting

A system that is often used to monitor and control government expenditure, especially during the implementation phase of the budget process, is budgetary accounting. The primary purpose of budgetary accounting is to monitor and control government spendings by the agencies and departments to ensure that they do not exceed the appropriations and that they are spent for the purpose for which they were appropriated. In that sense, budgetary accounting serves more as a management tool than as a control device.

Three types of accounts are typically used in budgetary accounting: Appropriations, allotments, and encumbrances. Appropriations are authorizations given by the legislature to make expenditure commitments and incur obligations for specific programs. Allotments are a portion of the appropriation currently available for expenditure or to incur obligations. And encumbrances are a portion of the appropriation reserved or set aside for expenditures at some future points in time and that the funds will be available when the expenditure takes place. One other account that is important in budgetary accounting is estimated revenues. As noted earlier, estimated revenues are what a government is likely to collect in the coming years, including the proposed budget year, and serve as the guidelines for appropriation. We can use a simple expression to show the relationship between the three accounts, as given below:

$$\text{Appropriations} - \text{Encumbrances} - \text{Allotments} = \text{Unencumbered Balance} \quad (14.3)$$

$$\text{Alternatively, Appropriation} - (\text{Encumbrances} + \text{Allotments}) = \text{Unencumbered Balance}$$

Let us look at a simple example to illustrate. Suppose that a government has \$50 million in appropriations for expenditure by the Public Works Department: \$35 million for salaries and wages, \$2 million for materials and supplies, \$5 million for professional and contract services, \$3 million for other operating expenditures, \$5 for capital outlay, and \$2 million in encumbrances. Suppose now that the department received \$10 million in allotment for salaries and wages, \$0.5 million for materials and supplies, \$1 million for professional and contractual services, \$0.5 million for other operating expenditures, and \$2 million for capital outlay in the first quarter. The unencumbered balance for the quarter will, therefore, be \$34M. That is,

$$\text{Appropriations} - (\text{Encumbrances} + \text{Allotments}) = \text{Unencumbered Balance}$$

$$= [(\$35M + \$2M + \$5M + \$3M + \$5) - [\$2m + (\$10M + \$0.5M + \$1M + \$0.5M + \$2M)]$$

$$= \$50M - (\$2M + \$14M)$$

$$= \$34M$$

Looking at the result, as allotments are made for expenditure by the department, they are adjusted (subtracted) from the appropriations to obtain the unencumbered balance, which in our example would be \$34 million. Assume that the allotments are made in quarterly installments and that adjustments are made accordingly, by the end of the fourth quarter, the unencumbered balance should be 0. Keep in mind that negative balances are not allowed in government, especially state and local governments, since, by law, these governments are required to maintain a balanced budget, which also applies to budgetary accounting. The process is a simple yet effective way to monitor and control government expenditures against appropriations, thus making sure that they stay within the appropriation limits. It should be worth noting that we could have also presented this information in a table (not shown here), showing how the appropriation balance would decrease, as allotments continued to be made until the end of the fiscal year, producing a 0 unencumbered balance to balance the equation.

14.7 Capital Budget

Capital budgeting plays a vitally important role in the overall budgetary activities of a government. In some ways, it can be considered much more important than the routine operations of a government because of the impact these activities have on long-term economic growth and development of a government. The activities, commonly referred to as capital improvement activities, involve investments in physical assets such as roads, bridges, highways, land, buildings, vehicles, equipment, physical plants, and so forth. The level and quality of capital assets in a government and how well they are maintained indicate how well its economy is performing. In general, the better the condition of capital assets, the stronger the economy.

A capital budget has several distinguishing characteristics that separate it from an operating budget. First and foremost, it deals with expenditures that involve investments in physical assets that are non-recurring and have a life span of several years.[5] Second, although the expenditures are non-recurring in that the construction or acquisition of assets involves one-time expenditure, the use of the assets requires recurring operating expenditures. What this means is that while the budget is prepared for five or six years, it is updated annually, which establishes a direct linkage with the operating budget where they appear as annual capital outlays. Third, expenditure on capital assets involve large commitments of resources, which, depending on the assets, can run into hundreds of millions of dollars. Fourth, and as noted earlier, investments in capital assets are vitally important for long-term economic growth and development of an economy. A strong and vibrant economy needs well-developed and maintained capital infrastructure to sustain its pace of economic growth and development. Fifth, but not least, once constructed or acquired, the assets remain in place for a long time, which makes it difficult to reverse or change the decision once they have been put in place.

Like government, most nonprofit organizations also maintain a separate capital budget that varies in scope and size of the organization, and their essential characteristics are the same as those for government: They include non-recurring expenditure on physical assets that typically have a life span of more than a year. The assets are usually segmented in terms of how long the assets are generally expected to last before needing replacement. The longer period categories are reserved for purchases that will last for many years into the future such as adding a pavement, a parking lot, or expanding a facility such as renovating a college or hospital to accommodate new programs or specialized services.

14.7.1 Selecting Capital Projects

Governments often receive more requests for capital projects and improvement programs from their agencies and departments than the available resources can permit. This makes it necessary to prioritize, in other words, rank the projects in order, based on some criteria, for selection. Prioritization helps a government determine the projects that are more important, gives it the lead time for effective decision making and, more importantly, brings objectivity into the decision process. Unfortunately, there are no precise measures for developing criteria by which to prioritize, but most would agree that the criteria must be consistent with the goals and objectives of an organization (Hatry, 1988). Since projects vary in size and scope, a simple approach would be to select criteria that make good common sense and have an appeal to the public such as essential to maintaining community health and safety, maintaining the existing levels of service, meeting emergency needs, and so forth. If a community has a strong political orientation, one could also add political consideration such as strengthening public support or community interest.

There is a wide range of methods that can be used for this purpose, ranging from simple rule of thumb that relies on subjective judgment, to the use of measurement scales, such as ordinal, interval, or ratio, as well as methods commonly used in financial decision making such as benefit-cost ratio or net present value that relies on time value of money, and so forth. This section focuses on measurement scales, in particular ordinal, that can be used for prioritizing capital projects, especially where multiple projects are involved with different goals and objectives. Ordinal scale is a quantitative measure that takes into consideration the degree of difference in the characteristics of a variable, which in this case will be the projects. The scale can range anywhere from 1 to 5, to 50, or to 100 points, depending on how fine the shades of difference the decision makers would prefer. The end-product of a rating system is usually a matrix or table.

To illustrate, let us look at a simple example with seven projects for downtown redevelopment, six criteria, on a five-point ordinal scale, five being the highest and one being the lowest. For convenience, we will call the projects P1, P2, P3, P4, P5, P6, and P7. Ideally, when one is dealing with a large number of projects, it is important that the projects are grouped or organized by size or any other characteristics to allow the decision makers the opportunity to get a good sense of the projects being considered for ranking. To rank a project, all one needs to do is assign a score to a project, using the scale against a criterion, and add the scores to determine the final ranking of the projects. Table 14.6 shows the ranking of the projects.

As the table shows, Project P5 ranks the highest in priority order, followed by P1, P6, P2, and so forth. While the structure of the rank order appears simple and easy to follow, the problem with conventional scoring

Table 14.6 A two-dimensional rating matrix for capital projects

Project Criteria	*P1 Rating Score*	*P2 Rating Score*	*P3 Rating Score*	*P4 Rating Score*	*P5 Rating Score*	*P6 Rating Score*	*P7 Rating Score*
1 Safety/Health	4	5	5	3	4	4	3
2 Economic Growth	4	3	3	4	5	3	4
3 Community Need	5	5	5	5	5	5	5
4 Funding Availability	4	3	3	2	5	4	2
5 Operating Cost	4	3	2	3	4	4	2
6 Sustainability	4	4	4	4	4	4	4
Total Score (Rank)	25(2)	23(4)	22(5)	21(6)	27(1)	24(3)	20(7)

systems, in particular the use of an ordinal or interval scale, is that while they generate scores that can be easily aggregated to produce the overall ranking of a project, they do not readily allow for project comparison. Comparison allows the decision makers to determine the relative importance of a project to the overall goal of an organization. In other words, a project that ranks high must be superior to all other projects in comparison, given the goals and objectives of an organization and the criteria used for project ranking. Determining the relative importance is critical in project prioritization, especially when one is dealing with limited resources.

As for nonprofit organizations, electing capital projects for nonprofits is relatively simple because the choices are often limited as to the number of projects nonprofit organizations deal with. However, like government, they can vary in size and structure. Also, what would be considered a capital project can vary, depending on the mission of the organization. For instance, for a small nonprofit organization a project costing several thousand dollars can be considered a capital project, while for a large nonprofit organization it can run into several million dollars. Alternatively, individual organizations can define what they would consider a capital project.

14.7.2 *Capital Budgeting with Budget Constraints*

Governments, like most organizations, operate under budget constraints. Conventional measurement scales, such as ordinal, interval or ratio, used for ranking capital projects, while easy to use, do not readily allow for dealing with budget constraints. However, there are methods such as mathematical programming that can be used to deal with budget constraints, but the process is complex and analytically demanding. Alternatively, one can use methods such as benefit-cost ratio or net present value, discussed earlier, to determine a cut-off level for budget constraints.

To give an example, consider the example we used in the preceding section, where a government is looking into seven relatively small projects for downtown redevelopment. Let us say that we have the following information on the costs and benefits, respectively, for each project: P1 – \$1.350 million and \$1.450 million, P2 – \$1.460 million and \$3.750 million, P3 – \$5.325 million and \$6.825 million; P4 – \$2.175 million and \$1.650 million; P5 – \$2.350 million and \$4.740 million, P6 – \$1.540 million and \$2.540 million, and P7 – \$3.450 million and \$2.795 million, where the first term represents costs and the second term represents benefits. Table 14.7 shows the costs, benefits, and the benefit cost ratio (B:C) for each project, along with their rankings, based on the ratio, and the cumulative costs of the projects. Note that all seven projects cost a total of \$17.650 million.

Table 14.7 Ranking capital projects: B:C

Project	*Project Cost ($)*	*Project Benefit ($)*	*B:C*[1]	*Project Ranking*	*Project Cost ($)*	*Cumulative Cost ($)*
P1	1,350,000	1,450,000	1.07	P2 (R1)	1,460,000	1,460,000
P2	1,460,000	3,750,000	2.57	P5 (R2)	2,350,000	3,810,000
P3	5,325,000	6,825,000	1.28	P6 (R3)	1,540,000	5,350,000
P4	2,175,000	1,650,000	0.76	P3 (R4)	5,325,000	10,675,000
P5	2,350,000	4,740,000	2.01	P1 (R5)	1,350,000	12,025,000
P6	1,540,000	2,540,000	1.65	P4 (R6)	2,175,000	14,200,000
P7	3,450,000	1,795,000	0.52	P7 (R7)	3,450,000	17,650,000

[1] B:C = $\Sigma B / \Sigma C$

As can be seen from the table, five of the seven projects (P1, P2, P3, P5, and P6), except for Projects P4 and P7, are acceptable since their B:C ratios are greater than 1. Let us assume that there is no budget constraint, which means that the government can undertake all five projects. Projects P4 and P7 are not considered since their B:C < 1. Ideally, a government can undertake all projects for consideration if it does not have any budget constraint, so long as their B:C > 1. Let us assume that the government has a budget constraint of $10 million, in which case it can fully undertake four projects, P2, P5, P6, and P1, since their cumulative costs of $6.7 million ($1.46M + $2.35M + $1.54M + $1.35M = $6.7 million) are less than $10 million, plus a significant portion of P3 ($5.325M), if fractional projects are acceptable, because accepting it fully will exceed the budget constraint ($6.7 million + $5.325 million = $12.025 million > $10 million). If not, the government will either have to abandon P3 or have to ask for additional funding so that all five projects can be undertaken. Incidentally, it will still leave P4 and P7 out because their B:C ratios are less than 1.

It should be worth noting that the project benefits and costs were not discounted in the current example for the time value of money because time was not considered a factor in this case, meaning that all seven projects would be completed in one year or less and the benefits would not extend over multiple years. However, most capital projects produce costs and benefits that extend over multiple years, in which case the cost as well as benefit streams will need to be discounted for time value of money using an appropriate discount rate, assuming the cost and benefits can be measured in precise monetary terms. In the event they cannot be measured in precise monetary terms, the convention is to use surrogates or proxy variables that can provide a good sense of the monetary values of the projects.

14.7.3 Impact on the Operating Budget

No discussion of capital budgeting is complete without some discussion of the impact the capital budget has on the operating budget. This stems from the fact that since a government has limited funds to spend on both operating and the capital budget, it needs to make careful decisions on how best to allocate the funds between the two. In other words, any decision to spend money on capital projects will have a direct impact on the operating budget, and vice versa, although the degree of impact will be different for different governments depending on the size of the projects, how the funds are generated to finance the projects, and the way the costs are distributed over time. For instance, if the projects are financed using debt, then the amount of debt that can be potentially supported by the government, especially if there is an existing debt, will determine the amount of debt the government can issue.

Another impact the capital budget has on the operating budget is the cost of operation and maintenance. Capital expenditure involving construction and acquisition of assets will add to the costs of operation and maintenance. Most governments are concerned that the costs do not exceed the ability of the operating budget to support the normal operations of the government. In some cases, a government may decide to restrict the debt service to a fixed percentage of the operating budget to ensure that the debt service payments do not overburden the operating revenues of the government.

However, the impact of capital expenditure on the operating budget can also be positive in that, if executed properly, it can lead to substantial cost savings for the government. For instance, if infrastructure maintenance such as road repair can be funded through the capital budget, it can produce considerable cost savings for the operating budget by eliminating an important cost commitment from the operating budget. Also, maintaining capital assets in good working conditions can prevent frequent breakdowns and potential loss of service, thereby saving the government considerable sums of money over time.

From an operational perspective, understanding the impact of the capital budget on the operating budget is important to have a sense of the effect the capital expenditures will have on current and future operations of the government and the time it will take for the operating budget to make the necessary adjustments. In general, the greatest impact occurs with new projects, as opposed to existing projects requiring normal operation and maintenance. For instance, in a study of forty-eight largest US cities, Bland and Nunn (1992) found that labor intensive services such as police and fire protection are more sensitive to capital expenditures than most other services. Their findings further noted that since the operating and the capital budgets are often prepared independently, there is a need for close coordination between the two budget cycles, especially in those cases where the impact on the operating budget is clear and positive.

14.8 Chapter Summary

Budgeting plays a vitally important role in government as well as in nonprofit organizations. It is the instrument a government uses to allocate its limited resources to meet the competing needs of society vis-à-vis the public. Similarly, for nonprofit organizations, it is the means by which the organizations allocate their contributed funds on various programs and activities. For both government and nonprofit organizations, budgeting is an ongoing exercise that takes place throughout the year. It is a time-consuming process, especially for the government, since all government budgets have to go through a range of activities that are rigorous, from budget preparation until they are formally adopted and implemented. This chapter started with a brief discussion of the relationship between planning and budgeting, followed by a detailed discussion of the budget process, budget forecasts, operating budget, budget structure, implementation measures, and capital budget. The chapter concluded with a brief discussion of the impact of a capital budget on the operating budget.

14.9 Review Questions

14.1 What is a budget? What is the difference between an operating and a capital budget? Discuss the relationship between budgeting and planning.

14.2 What is a budget process? Discuss the stages of the budget process and explain the role they play in budget decision making.

14.3 Select the annual operating budget of a government or nonprofit organization of your choice and go over the section on budget process. Briefly summarize the steps of the process, including post-adoption amendment. Also, highlight the fund structure used in the budget.

14.4 Why is forecasting important in public budgeting? What role does forecasting play in the budget process? Why is it more difficult to forecast government revenues than expenditure? Give an example of how you would estimate a personnel budget.

14.5 What is a naïve forecast? Write the equation for a naïve forecast. Look at the example of a naïve forecast in the chapter. Redo the forecast for next year using 2.5 percent inflation rate (1) for some of the cost items, and (2) all the items.

14.6 What is a budget system? What role does a budget system play in the budget process?
14.7 What is a program budget? What are the strengths and limitations of a program budget? Give an example of a program budget.
14.8 Looking at the budget you have selected in 14.3, indicate the budget system or systems it is using to develop the budget. How effectively is the government or the organization using the system? Would you suggest a different system? Why?
14.9 Looking at the budget in 14.3, does it include budget forecasts? What method or methods does it use for forecasts? What do the forecasts tell you about the direction of growth in revenue and expenditure?
14.10 What is a cash budget? How does it differ from a cash accounting report? What are the steps in preparing both? Give an example of each.
14.11 What is budgetary accounting? How does it monitor and control compliance with budget appropriations. Give an example.
14.12 Why is capital budgeting important in government? What are the characteristics of a capital budget and what role does it play in the economic growth and development of a government?
14.13 Why is it necessary to prioritize capital projects? What are the advantages of using a ratio scale as opposed to an interval scale, when prioritizing? Discuss, with reference to the methods suggested in the chapter.
14.14 Returning to the budget of the government or nonprofit organization in 14.3, does it have a capital budget? If so, indicate the types of projects it is considering for development. Explain the methods it is using to finance the projects. Also explain the impact the capital expenditures have on the operating budget.
14.15 What are the differences between benefit-cost ratio, net present value, and internal rate of return? Given a choice, which one would you use? Discuss, with an example, how benefit-cost ratio can be used in capital budgeting under budget constraints.

Notes

1 Interestingly, 44 states used biennial budgeting in 1940; today, less than two dozen states do. Since 1968, some 18 states have changed their budget cycles – 15 from biennial to annual, and 3 from annual to biennial (Kogan et al, 2012).

2 A fund is an accounting entity with its own set of self-balancing accounts. Unlike a for-profit organization, which operates as a single accounting entity because its revenue comes from a single source, vis-a-vis the price individuals pay for the goods and services they consume, a government collects its revenues

from multiple different sources, segregated into multiple funds and accounts. The segregation of accounts by funds allows the government to carry out specific functions and activities, as determined by legal and other requirements.

3 The state and local governments are required by law to balance their budgets, but not the capital budget, which means the capital expenditures of the government can be debt financed, as they often do. Incidentally, the federal government is not required to balance its budget.

4 A system is a collection of elements, connected in an organized way. The elements of a system can be concepts (language), objects (a machine consisting of component parts), and subjects (a man-machine system consisting of concepts, objects, and subjects). A system may exist in nature as a natural aggregation of component elements found in nature, called natural system, or it may be contrived by man as an aggregation of elements that are related and constituted as a system, called man-made system (Checkland, 1976).

5 When discussing the life span of an asset it may be necessary to make a distinction between types of lives such as economic life, ownership life, physical life, and useful life. Economic life is the time (usually expressed in years) over which an asset is expected to operate with minimum cost to its owner. The ownership life will vary depending on how long an asset is held by the owner. Physical life is the time when an asset is acquired to the time when it is no longer able to produce goods and services. If an asset is managed properly with due care, the chances are that the physical life of an asset will coincide with the time of its acquisition to the time it is abandoned or replaced. Finally, useful life is the time when an asset is kept in productive use with normal repair and maintenance.

References

Bland, R.L. and Nunn, S. (1992). The impact of capital spending on municipal operating budgets. *Public Budgeting & Finance*, 12(2): 32–47.

Checkland, P.B. (1976). Toward a system-based methodology for real-world problem solving, in J. Beishon and G. Peters (eds) *Systems behavior*. New York: Harper & Row (for Open University Press), 51–77.

Hatry, H.P. (1988). *Guide to setting priorities for capital investment*. Washington, DC: Urban Institute Press.

Jitasa. (2023). *Nonprofit budgeting: Understand the basics*. Jitasa Group. June 20. www.jitasagroup.com/jitasa_nonprofit_blog/nonprofit-budgeting-understand-the-basics/

Kogan, R., Greenstein, R., and Horney, J.R. (2012). *Biennial budgeting: Do the drawbacks outweigh the advantages?* Washington, DC: Center on Budget and Policy Priorities. www.cbpp.org

15 Emerging Trends

15.1 Introduction

Organizations are not static or monolithic entities, as they were once perceived. They are constantly changing, making it necessary to change and adopt measures to keep up with the changes, as they occur. Increasing demand for goods and services, changing technologies, and rising expectations are placing additional demands on the management to become more responsible as well as responsive to those they serve. In government, where changes take place more gradually than in the private sector, one can expect to see the same kind of demand placed regularly on the decision makers to plan to keep up with the changes. This also applies to cost and managerial accounting in government. Although it has a long history of use in government, especially at the federal level, much of the focus has been on contract costing, which is understandable since the government at all three levels (federal, state, and local) contracts out many of the goods and services they provide to private firms and businesses, including nonprofit organizations. The preceding chapters were an attempt to illustrate how it can be used in all areas of government, not just contract costing.

Cost and managerial accounting is an evolving field. As it continues to evolve, it will place new demands and challenges on government, nonprofit organizations, as well as other users. Although the fundamentals of the field will not change, there are areas that are likely to experience challenges in the coming years that will also apply to government. This concluding chapter briefly discusses some of these challenges and directions of change.

15.2 Organizational Dynamics

As organizations grow and become complex, the need for increased reliance on cost and related information for management operations will also increase. At the same time, more advanced tools and techniques will

DOI: 10.4324/9781003486091-18

emerge to replace the existing ones. Combined with new advancements in computer technology and scientific know-how, the emerging tools and techniques will provide the decision makers with more opportunities to deal with complex problems with greater ease.

Two factors are more than likely to speed up this evolution process: One, the future decision makers, bureaucrats and public administrators will be better trained than their predecessors, thereby making it easy for them to implement changes. Their awareness and increasing familiarity with methods, tools, techniques, and technology will allow them to accept the changes more easily. Two, the availability of high-speed computers with enormous capabilities to process data (many of which are already available), together with artificial intelligence, machine language, and other developments will make it even more possible to solve complex problems, especially those that are large and unstructured, with relative ease.

However, these scenarios of optimism would become feasible only if the organizations concerned are willing to make the necessary changes that will become incumbent upon them, as time progresses. As a necessary condition, the organizations must be willing to make sure that internal conditions, especially those that have a direct bearing on those who make decisions and those who carry them out, are in place to serve the larger goals of the organization.

15.3 Emerging Trends

Like all fields of study, cost and managerial accounting will continue to evolve in the coming years, as it did in the past, which will be reflected on how government, nonprofit, and other organizations use them to meet their growing needs. Several areas are likely to experience growth and change in the coming years. This chapter discusses five changes that are likely to stand out: digital transformation, predictive costing, integrated reporting, constrained optimization, and continuous improvement.

15.3.1 Digital Transformation

Digital transformation integrates technologies such as artificial intelligence and machine language with on-going practices that can enhance cost and managerial accounting, especially accounting processes. Among the many benefits, digital transformation will increase accuracy and efficiency of routine operations of government (Harrison, 2023; Eom and Leo, 2022). More specifically, tools such as data analytics will help improve data-driven decision-making to identify trends and patterns, for instance, in crime investigation, medical procedures, improved performance in service delivery and evidence-based policy decisions. Another area where digital transformation can further improve government operations is e-government to allow better access to government services. With digital transformation, government employees can better access systems, applications, and data remotely from any location (US General Services Administration, 2023).

15.3.2 Predictive Costing

A second area that is likely to see major changes is predictive costing, which is essentially forecasting future costs based on historical data. We have briefly discussed forecasting under cost behavior and estimation. There has been tremendous growth in forecasting methodologies over the years, and recent advancements in artificial intelligence and machine language software will produce further growth in the coming years with enormous ability to analyze a large amount of cost data to predict future trends. Management accountants have been using predictive analytics to develop budgets, both operating and capital, but with advanced forecasting knowledge and application they will be able to assess risks and uncertainty with greater accuracy and make better informed and strategic decisions.

15.3.3 Integrated Accounting and Reporting

Cost reporting remains one of the areas that is likely to see major changes in the coming years. There has been a growing emphasis on integrating financial and non-financial information in cost reports. Combined with automation and technological development, this will be useful in automatic cost tracking, allocation, and reporting. This will further improve decision making and compliance with real-time project cost insights. Additionally, there has been emphasis on integrating cost accounting with financial management, and budgeting. For instance, in 1995, Congress expanded the Chief Financial Officers' act of 1990 (US Chief Information Officers Council, 1995) to create the Office of the Federal Financial Management (OFFM) within the Office of Management and Budget (OMB). Integrating cost accounting with the financial management system and budgeting will better allow the government to develop, monitor, and report cost information, and improve financial execution of the government, especially at the agency level. The process will further improve financial management staff capabilities, and with proper care, is likely to deter fraud, waste, and abuse of government resources, which has been a consistent problem in government for a long time.

15.3.4 Constrained Optimization

All organizations, government, for profit, and nonprofit, operate under constraints: resources, time, and technology. Constraints add to the costs of production and delivery. The goal of an organization, therefore, is to optimize the production and delivery process at the lowest cost, without affecting quantity or quality. Traditional cost and managerial accounting literature recognized early on that every system has one process, called a bottleneck or constraint with the least production capacity, that determines the output of the entire system. The result obviously is inefficient. In the mid-1980s, Goldratt and Cox (1986) suggested a theory, called the Theory of Constraints, to deal with the problem by recognizing an entire production process or delivery system around the constraint, since, according to the authors, the system could not produce or work faster than the rate of the constraint. The constraint would indicate when to release the materials for production or delivery, and the output would be optimum, subject to the constraint. The problem with the theory of constraints is that it recognizes a single (major) constraint, but in reality, there could be multiple different constraints, all affecting the process. The question then is how to deal with multiple constraints.

While methods such as lean manufacturing (to eliminate waste and improve efficiency), six sigma (to reduce variability and improve quality), or just-in-time (to produce goods sufficient to meet demand and reduce inventory), are one way to address the problem. They can be effective if they could all be used together as one model, rather than individually, to address the problem. Since each method has a specific goal or objective, the best alternative would be to use models that can deal with multiple goals and constraints yet produce optimum results. Multiple objective optimizations models, such as goal programming, which has been extensively used in operations research to deal with optimization problems with multiple goals, is a good example. There are other methods that are less demanding analytically, such as multi-attribute analysis, which could be easily integrated into the accounting process. Network analysis, which has been receiving some attention in recent years in cost and managerial accounting literature, would be another good example.

15.3.5 Continuous Improvement

Continuous improvement has a long history that goes back to the 1970s, following the two major oil crises that shook the world, followed by slow industrial production, economic growth and recession that continued into the 1980s. The result was a proliferation of initiatives that became the hallmark of growth and productivity, such as Just-In-Time (JIT), Total Quality Management (TQM), Statistical Process Control (SPC), Target Costing (TC), benchmarking, Theory of Constraint (TOC), Activity-Based Management (ABM), six sigma (6σ), Balanced ScoreCard (BSC), and reengineering (RR), among others. a. The interesting thing about these initiatives is that, while each addresses a specific area of concern, they are not mutually exclusive. Perhaps, more than anything, these developments changed the dynamics of cost and managerial accounting, from traditional measurement and reporting of business activities to working in groups or teams from multiple disciplines, from finance to marketing and economics, to operations research and industrial engineering, to statistics. In other words, the multidisciplinary framework in contemporary cost and managerial accounting is dynamic in that it serves both as its strength and provides a solid foundation for continuous improvement to keep pace with the changing conditions.

15.4 Likely Challenges

All changes, large or small, come with challenges that need to be overcome before the changes can be fully integrated into the core discipline. The emerging trends highlighted above, including others that have not, have analytical content. This is because the technological changes that will be integral to this process require greater appreciation for analytical skills. At the same time, to be effective, these developments will require a good grounding in organizational dynamics, clear digital success metrics such as adoption of technology and organizational performance and, more importantly, a human-centered design that will pay attention to human needs and requirements.

There will be other challenges, mundane and conventional, that will also need to be addressed. This will include timeliness and reliability of data, globalization, and dealing with diverse regulatory environments, and cyber security from increasing reliance on digital platforms that can easily expose cost accounting systems to cyber threats. Incorporating environmental costs and sustainability metrics into cost reporting would pose a real challenge since it is a relatively new concept. In the interim, there could be a real shortage of skilled personnel that may slow down the change.

15.5 Other Considerations

Finally, for an organization to be able to able accept new ideas, concepts, tools and approaches, and implement them for improved performance requires time, cost money, and use of resources that are often scarce. Even simple and everyday concepts such as buy or lease, managing inventory, and assuring quality in service provision require skill to design, time to analyze, and money to support the process that will eventually utilize them. However, time, skill, and money are scarce resources that must be carefully utilized to realize the goals of an organization. Successful implementation requires that one must fully understand and evaluate the costs and benefits of implementation. In other words, where possible, one must perform formal analysis using methods such as benefit-cost analysis, cost-effectiveness analysis, and the like to determine if the benefits of implementation outweigh the costs of implementation (Boardman et al., 2001). Clearly, for many of the topics discussed throughout the text, including those that have not been discussed, the return must be greater than the cost to justify their use in dealing with a specific problem before they could be formally implemented.

15.6 Chapter Summary

As organizations become increasingly complex, their functions also become complex and processes more exhaustive. The issues the decision makers are concerned with will also become more diverse. Along with efficiency and productivity, decision makers will be expected to deal with every conceivable aspect of development and change that will shape the future of cost and managerial accounting. This chapter has briefly discussed several trends and challenges that will shape the future of cost and managerial accounting, most of which are based on technological developments. Management issues that are integral to the decision process in an organization are also integral to this process. They are multidimensional in nature, from simple economics to ethical, to legal concerns. Additionally, there are other areas of management that are also important in effective functioning of an organization, particularly in government such as employee motivation, conflict resolution inside bureaucracy, leadership role, and so forth. Although organizations may not fully utilize many of the developments and tools discussed in the text, the familiarity with them can significantly affect the way in which the management makes decisions and the manner in which they try to implement them.

15.7 Review Questions

15.1 What is organizational dynamics? What are the two important factors that are likely to change organizational dynamics as it relates to cost and managerial accounting?

15.2 What changes are likely to shape the future of cost and managerial accounting? What role will technology play in this?

15.3 What challenges cost and managerial accounting, as a field of study, are likely to encounter to realize the emerging trends? What measures should an organization take to deal with these challenges?

References

Eom, S-J. and Leo, J. (2022). Digital Government transformation in turbulent time: Responses, challenges, and future direction. *Government Information Quarterly*, 39(2), March. https://pmc.ncbi.nlm.nih.gov/articles/PMC8914696/

Goldbratt, E.M. and Cox, J. (1986). *A process of ongoing improvement*. Great Barrington, MA: North River Press.

Harrison, K. (2023). 13 benefits of digital transformation for local governments. *GovPilot*. www.govpilot.com/blog/benefits-of-digital-transformation-for-local-governments. [Accessed December 15, 2023].

US Chief Information Officers Council. (1995). Chief Financial Officers Act, 1990, in *Information Technology Laws*. Washington, DC: Chief Information Officers Council.

US General Services Administration. (2023). *Digital strategy*. Washington, DC: GSA. Public Law 115–336, "21st Century Integrated Digital Experience Act." Annual Report. www.gsa.gov/technology/government-it-initiatives/digital-strategy

Appendix A

Least Square Method

The least squares criterion serves a very important purpose in regression analysis in that it allows us to estimate the parameters directly from it. The only requirement is that they must be estimated in such a way as to ensure that they are efficient (they have the minimum variance). To illustrate this, let us recall Equation 4.12 for the two-variables case, X and Y, and the equation $Y = \hat{a} + \hat{b}X + \hat{e}$ which, with slight reorganization, can be written as

$$\hat{e} = Y - \hat{Y} \tag{1}$$

$$= Y - (\hat{a} + \hat{b}X)$$

$$= Y - \hat{a} - \hat{b}X$$

Our objective is to find the estimates of a and b in such a way as to ensure that the sum of the squared errors, $\Sigma(\hat{e}^2)$. where $\hat{e}$ which is the estimated error (variance), will be a minimum (Equation 4.15). That is,

$$\text{Minimize} \sum \hat{e}^2 = \sum (Y - \hat{a} - \hat{b}X)^2 \tag{2}$$

with respect to $\hat{a}$ and $\hat{b}$.

To obtain the estimates of a and b such that the sum of the squared deviations will be minimum, we take the partial derivative of $\sum (\hat{e})^2$ with respect to $\hat{a}$ and $\hat{b}$, and set them equal to 0. That is,

$$\frac{\partial \sum \hat{e}^2}{\partial \hat{a}} = \frac{\partial \sum (Y - \hat{a} - \hat{b}X)^2}{\partial \hat{a}} = 0$$

$$2\sum (Y - \hat{a} - \hat{b}X)(-1) = 0$$

$$-2\sum Y + 2n\hat{a} + 2\hat{b}\sum X = 0 \tag{3}$$

for $\hat{a}$.

Similarly,

$$\frac{\partial \sum \hat{e}^2}{\partial \hat{b}} = \frac{\partial \sum (Y - \hat{a} - \hat{b}X)^2}{\partial \hat{b}}$$
$$2\sum (Y - \hat{a} - \hat{b}X)(-X) = 0$$

$$-2\sum XY + 2\hat{a}\sum X + 2\hat{b}\sum X^2 = 0 \tag{4}$$

for $\hat{b}$.

We can simplify these expressions by dividing them through by -2, so that we have

$$\sum Y - n\hat{a} - \hat{b}\sum X = 0 \tag{5}$$

$$\sum XY - \hat{a}\sum X - \hat{b}\sum X^2 = 0 \tag{6}$$

With slight rearrangement, Equations 5 and 6 can be written as

$$\sum Y = n\hat{a} + \hat{b}\sum X \tag{7}$$

$$\sum XY = \hat{a}\sum X + \hat{b}\sum X^2 \tag{8}$$

The new equations (7 and 8) are called the normal equations.

From these two equations (7 and 8), we can easily obtain the values of $\hat{a}$ and $\hat{b}$ by solving them simultaneously, so that

$$\hat{a} = \frac{\sum Y}{n} - \frac{\hat{b}\sum X}{n} \tag{9}$$

$$\hat{b} = \frac{n\sum XY - \sum X \sum Y}{n\sum X^2 - (\sum X)^2} \tag{10}$$

Appendix B

Finding the t-Values

In general, the t values are computed by taking the ratio of the estimated parameters to their corresponding standard errors. That is,

$$t_{\hat{a}} = \frac{\hat{a}}{S_{\hat{a}}} \tag{1}$$

$$t_{\hat{b}} = \frac{\hat{b}}{S_{\hat{b}}} \tag{2}$$

The standard errors are essentially the standard deviations of the estimated parameters and are given by the square roots of their variances. The following expressions are commonly used for the standard errors of $\hat{a}$ and $\hat{b}$, as shown below:

$$S_{\hat{a}} = \sqrt{VAR(\hat{a})} \tag{3a}$$

$$= \sqrt{\frac{[(\sigma_E^2)(\sum x^2)]}{n\sum(X - \bar{X})^2}} \tag{3b}$$

for $S(\hat{a})$, and

$$S_{\hat{b}} = \sqrt{VAR(\hat{b})} \tag{4a}$$

$$= \sqrt{\frac{\sigma_e^2}{\sum(X - \bar{X})^2}} \tag{4b}$$

for $S(\hat{b})$, where $\sigma^2 = \sum \hat{e}^2 / (n-k)$, with k as the number of parameters in our regression model, and n as the sample size (namely, the number of observations in our data set). As noted earlier, $\hat{e}^2$is the error variance, indicating the squared difference between the observed and estimated values of the dependent variable Y, $(Y-Y)^2$; that is, $e^2 = [Y-(\hat{a}+bX)]^2 = (Y-Y)^2$. Obviously, the closer the estimated values to the observed values the better is the model (namely, the greater is the fit).

Now, to obtain the t values for our estimated parameters we simply substitute the values from Tables 4.3 and Table 4.5 into the respective terms in Equations 3b and 4b, so that

$$t_{\hat{a}} = \frac{\hat{a}}{\sqrt{\frac{[(\sigma_e^2)(\sum X^2)]}{n\sum (X-\bar{X})^2}}}$$

$$= \frac{20,357.11}{\sqrt{\frac{(2,645,508.34)(32,590,000.00)}{(12)(1,549,166.68)}}}$$

$$= \frac{20,357.11}{2,153.56}$$

$$= 9.4528$$

is the observed t corresponding to $\hat{a}$, and

$$t_{\hat{b}} = \frac{\hat{b}}{\sqrt{\frac{\sigma_e^2}{\sum (X-\bar{X})^2}}}$$

$$= \frac{17.757}{\sqrt{\frac{2,645,508.34}{1,549,166.68}}}$$

$$= \frac{17.757}{1.307}$$

$$= 13.5861$$

is the observed t corresponding to $\hat{b}$.

Appendix C

Reciprocal Allocation by Matrix Inversion

Matrix inversion is a process in which a square matrix (one in which the number of rows is equal to the number of columns), when inverted and subsequently multiplied by the original matrix, produces an identity matrix (one in which the principal diagonals are all 1's and the off-diagonal elements are all 0's). To see how the method applies to reciprocal allocation, we begin with the equations for the three service departments and present them in terms of a system of simultaneous equations, as shown below:

$$D_1 = 450{,}000 + 0.25D_2 + 0.44D_3 \qquad (1)$$
$$D_2 = 550{,}000 + 0.31D_1 + 0.00D_3 \qquad (2)$$
$$D_3 = 750{,}000 + 0.46D_1 + 0.45D_2 \qquad (3)$$

With slight reorganization, the equations can be written a

$$1.00D_1 - 0.25D_2 - 0.44D_3 = 450{,}000 \qquad (4)$$
$$-0.31D_1 - 1.00D_2 - 0.00D_3 = 550{,}000 \qquad (5)$$
$$-0.46D_1 - 0.45D_2 + 1.00D_3 = 750{,}000 \qquad (6)$$

Using the standard matrix notations, the equations can be further written as

$$AD = C \qquad (7)$$

where A is the matrix of coefficients, D is a column vector of service departments, and C is a column vector of costs corresponding to each of these departments.

Expanding the terms of the expression in Equation 6.21, we can write it in full as

$$\begin{bmatrix} 1.00 & -0.25 & -0.44 \\ -0.31 & 1.00 & 0.00 \\ -0.46 & -0.45 & 1.00 \end{bmatrix} \begin{bmatrix} D1 \\ D2 \\ D3 \end{bmatrix} = \begin{bmatrix} 450{,}000 \\ 550{,}000 \\ 750{,}000 \end{bmatrix}$$

Now, to obtain the inverse of the matrix A we do the following: first, find a matrix of cofactors (submatrices with plus and minus signs), A^c, which are obtained by taking the determinants (single values or scalars found only in square matrices) of the submatrices by removing a row and a column corresponding to an element of the matrix, each time a determinant is calculated for one of the submatrices. Thus, for a 3×3 matrix, there will be nine determinants corresponding to nine submatrices.

The following shows the cofactor matrix for the allocation problem, A^C:

$$A^C = \begin{bmatrix} 1.0000 & 0.3100 & 0.5995 \\ 0.4480 & 0.7976 & 0.5650 \\ 0.4400 & 0.1364 & 0.9225 \end{bmatrix}$$

Second, we take the transpose of this matrix by changing the rows into columns called an adjoint matrix, $(A^c)^T$. That is,

$$\left(A^C\right)^T = \begin{bmatrix} 1.0000 & 0.4400 & 0.4400 \\ 0.3100 & 0.7976 & 0.1364 \\ 0.5995 & 0.5650 & 0.9225 \end{bmatrix}$$

Third, and finally, we divide the adjoint matrix by the determinant of the original matrix, $|A|$, to obtain the inverse matrix, which turns out to be 0.6587.[3] Therefore, dividing the adjoint matrix, $(A^c)^T$, by 0.6587 (the determinant of A) will produce the inverse matrix for the problem, as shown below:

$$\left(A^C\right)^T / |A| = \begin{bmatrix} 1.5181 & 0.6803 & 0.6680 \\ 0.4706 & 1.2109 & 0.2071 \\ 0.9101 & 0.8578 & 1.4005 \end{bmatrix} = A^{-1}$$

Next, to obtain the value of the column vector C (i.e., the cost of each service department), we multiply the inverse matrix by C. That is

$$A^{-1}C = \begin{bmatrix} 1.5181 & 0.6803 & 0.6680 \\ 0.4706 & 1.2109 & 0.2071 \\ 0.9101 & 0.8578 & 1.4005 \end{bmatrix} \begin{bmatrix} 450{,}000 \\ 550{,}000 \\ 750{,}000 \end{bmatrix}$$

$$= \begin{bmatrix} 1{,}558{,}310 \\ 1{,}033{,}090 \\ 1{,}931{,}710 \end{bmatrix} = \begin{bmatrix} D1 \\ D2 \\ D3 \end{bmatrix}$$

The result shows the costs associated with each service department which, respectively, are \$1,558.310 for D_1, \$1,033,090 for D_2, and \$1,931,710 for D_3. As expected, the results came out to be close to those obtained by the substitution method (Table 10.6), except for rounding-off errors.

Note that for a 3×3 matrix, the determinant can be obtained by the expression (Gere and Weaver, 1965), as shown below:

$$|A| = A_{11}A_{22}A_{33} + A_{12}A_{23}A_{31} + A_{13}A_{21}A_{32} - A_{13}A_{22}A_{31} - A_{11}A_{23}A_{32} - A_{12}A_{21}A_{33}$$

where the terms of the expression represent the coefficients of the original matrix, A. Substituting the respective values into the terms of the expression, taking their products, and adding them will produce the determinant of A, which turns out to be 0.6587.

Bibliography

AGA-CPAG. (2009). *Managerial cost accounting in federal government: Providing useful information for decision making*. Washington, DC: AGA-CPAG Research Series, Report No. 22.

AICPA. (2019). *Audit and accounting guide: Healthcare entities*. Durham, NC: American Institute of Certified Public Accountants.

Aguila, P.R., Jr. and Petersen, J.E. (1991). Leasing and service contracts, in J.E. Petersen and D.R. Strachota (eds) *Local government finance*. Chicago, IL: Government Finance Officers Association (GFOA), 321–338.

Albright, T. and Lam, M. (2006). Managerial accounting and continuous improvement initiatives: A Retrospective and Framework. *Journal of Managerial Issues*, XVIII (2), Summer: 157–174.

Alford, J. and O'Flynn, J. (2012). *Rethinking public services: Managing with external providers*. Basingstoke, UK: Palgrave McMillan.

Ammons, D.N. (1991). *Administrative analysis for local government: Practical application of selected techniques*. Athens, GA: Carl Vinson Institute of Government, University of Georgia.

Anderson, L.G. (1977). *Benefit-cost analysis: A practical guide*. Lexington, MA: Lexington Books.

Anderson, L.K. (1992). *Managerial accounting*. Cincinnati, OH: Southwestern Publishing.

Annessa, J. and Ivezaj, A. (2024). Overview of Cost Accounting Standards (CAS) for Government Contractors. June. www.cbh.com/insights/articles/cost accounting-standards-cas-government-contractors-guide/#:~:text=Cost%20Accounting%20Standards%20are%20a,taxpayers%20from%20fraud%20and%20abuse

Apostolou, N.G. et al. (1992). Research and trends in governmental accounting and reporting. *International Journal of Public Administration*, 15(5): 1121–1150.

Archibald, R.D. (1976). *Managing high technology programs and projects*. New York: John Wiley.

Aronson, R.J. and Schwartz, E. (1981). Capital budgeting, in R.J. Aronson and E. Schwartz (eds) *Management policies in local government finance*. Washington, DC: ICMA, 433–457.

ASTM. (1951). *Manual on quality control of materials.* Philadelphia, PA: American Society for Testing Materials (ASTM). For a more direct use of information contained in the table, especially as they relate to specific charts, see Neubauer, D.M. (ed.) (2010). *Manual on presentation of data and control chart analysis.* West Conshohocken, PA: ASTM International.

Bails, D.G. and Peppers, L.C. (1982). *Business forecasting: Forecasting techniques and application.* Englewood Cliffs, NJ: Prentice-Hall.

Baumol, W.J. (1952). The transaction demand for cash: An inventory theoretic approach. *Quarterly Journal of Economics*, 66: 546–556.

Bingham, R.D. (ed.). (1991). *Managing local government: Public administration in practice.* Thousand Oaks, CA: Sage.

Bland, R.L. and Nunn, S. (1992). The impact of capital spending on municipal operating Budgets. *Public Budgeting & Finance*, 12 (2), June: 32-47

Boardman, A., Greenberg, D., Vining, A., and Weimer, D. (2001). *Cost-benefit Analysis: Concepts and practice.* Upper Saddle River, NJ: Prentice Hall.

Boog, J. (2020). Quality engineering vs. quality assurance: Everything you need to know. *QA Lead*, October 19, 2020, https://theqalead.com/general/quality-engineering-vs-quality-assurance/ [Retrieved: January 15, 2021].

Box, G.E.P. and Jenkins, G.M. (1976). *Time series analysis: Forecasting and control.* San Francisco, CA: Holden-Day.

Brackner, J.W. (1992). Consensus values should be taught. *Management Accounting*, August, p. 19.

Brimson, J.A. and Antos, J. (1994). *Activity-based management.* New York: John Wiley.

Briers, M.S. and Hirst, M. (1990). The role of budgeting information in performance evaluation. *Accounting, Organization and Society*, 15(4): 373–398.

Brown, D.S. (1983). The managerial ethic and productivity improvement. *Public Administration Review*, 36 (September): 223–250.

Brown, K.W. (1993). The 10-point test of Financial condition: Toward an easy to use assessment tool for smaller cities. *Government Financial Review*, 9(6): 21–26.

Brown, R. (1905). *History of accounting and accountants.* London: Ballantyne, Hanson & Company.

Brown, R.E. and Sprohge, H-D. (1987). Governmental managerial accounting: What and where is it? *Public Budgeting & Finance*, 7(3), January: 35–46.

Brown, R.E. et al. (1982). *Auditing performance in government.* New York: John Wiley.

Brown, R.E., Myring, M., and Gard, C.G. (1999). Activity-based costing in government: Possibilities and pitfalls. *Public Budgeting & Finance*, 19, June: 3–21.

Brooks, R.C. and Pariser, D.B. (1996). Local government accounting and the need for audit follow up, in J. Rabin, et al. (eds) *Budgeting: Formulation and execution.* Athens, GA: Carl Vinson Institute of Government, The University of Georgia, 525–531.

Busch, D.M. (1991). *The New critical path method: The state-of-the-art modeling and time-reserve management.* Chicago, IL: Probus Publishing.

Business Week. (2014). Thinking machines. *Business Week Online.* www.businessweek.com/archives/2000/b3693096.arc.htm [Retrieved August 7, 2014].

Carr, D.K. and Litterman, I. (1993). *Excellence in government: Total quality management in the 1990's*. Arlington, VA: Coopers and Lybrant.

Carroll, N. and Lord, J.C. (2016). The Growing Importance of Cost Accounting in Hospitals. *Journal of Health Care Finance*, 43(2): 172–185.

Carter, M.W. and Price, C.C. (2000). *Operations research: A practical introduction*. New York: CRC Press.

Cellini, S.R. and Kee, J.E. (2010). Cost-effectiveness and cost-benefit analysis, in J.S. Wholey, H.P. Hatry, and K.E. Newcomer (eds) *Handbook of practical program evaluation*. 3rd Edition. New York: Jossey-Bass, 493–530.

Chan, J.C. (1981). Standards and issues in governmental accounting and financial reporting. *Public Budgeting & Finance*, 1, Spring: 55–66.

Chappels, T.M. (1999). *Financially focused quality*. Boca Raton, FL: St. Lucie Press.

Charnes, A., Cooper, W.W., and Rhodes, E. (1978). Measuring the efficiency of decision-making units. *European Journal of Operations Research*, 2(6): 429–444.

Chaurasia, P.K. and Shankar, G. (2012). *Some applications of GERT analysis in quality control*. Sunnyvale, CA: Lambert Academic Publishing.

Checkland, P.B. (1976). Toward a System-Based Methodology for Real-World Problem Solving, in J. Beishon and G. Peters (eds) *Systems Behavior*. New York: Harper & Row (for Open University Press), 51–77.

Christopher, W.F. and Thor, C.G. (1995). *The 16-point strategy for productivity and total quality*. Portland, OR: Productivity Press.

Choudhury, G. (2011). The dynamics of organizational climate: An exploration. *Management Insight*, 7(2), December: 111–116.

Clark, F. and Lorenzoni, A.B. (1998). *Applied cost engineering*. New York: CRC Press.

Cokins, G. (2006). *Activity-based cost management in government*. Tysons Corner, VA: Management Concepts.

Cooper, R. (1997). *Target costing and value engineering*. Portland, OR: Productivity Press.

Coltman, M.M. (1987). *Hospitality management accounting*. New York: Van Nostrand Reinhold.

Corporate Finance Institute (2021). *Depreciation methods: The four main types*. https://corporatefinanceinstitute.com/resources/knowledge/accounting/types-depreciation-methods/ [Retrieved March 15, 2021].

Cory, R.C. and Rosenberg, P. (1984). Costing municipal services, in J. Metzer (ed.) *Practical financial management*. Washington, DC: International City Management Association (ICMA), 50–62.

Crosby, P.B. (1979). *Quality is free*. New York: New American Library.

Crosson, S.V. and Needles, B.E. (2008). *Managerial accounting*. Boston, MA: Houghton-Mifflin

Cullins, J.G. (1998). *Public finance and public choice*. Oxford, England: Oxford University Press.

Curley, Jr., T.J. (1965). *Essential elements of a cost accounting system*. Paper presented at Management Services Conference of the Missouri Society of Certified Public Accountants, St. Louis, Missouri, October 1965.

Daellenbach, H.G. et al. (1983). *Introduction to operations research techniques*. Boston, MA: Allyn and Bacon.

Davis, O.A. and Whinston, A.B. (1967). On the distinction between public and private goods. *American Economic Review*, 57 (2): 360–373.

DeGroot, M.H. (1975). *Probability and statistics*. Reading, MA: Addison-Wesley Publishing, 349–355.

Deming, W.E. (1982). *Quality, productivity and competitive position*. Cambridge, MA: Center for Advanced Engineering Study, MIT.

Deloitte. (2024). *AICPA audit and accounting guide: Not-for-profit entities*. https://dart.deloitte.com/USDART/home/auditing/aicpa/audit-accounting-guides-audit-risk-alerts/aicpa-audit-accounting-guide-not-for

Deming, W.E. (1950). *Elementary principles of statistical control of quality*. Tokyo, Japan: Nippon Kagaku Gijutsu Renmei.

Deming, W.E. (1982). *Quality, productivity and competitive position*. Cambridge, MA: Center for Advanced Engineering Study, MIT.

Department of Defense. (2018). Independent Government Cost estimate (IGCE). In *Handbook for services acquisition*. US Department of Defense.

Diene, M. (2023). Importance of proper cost accounting in government contract. www.diener.org/importance-of-proper-cost-accounting-government-contracting/ [Accessed September 14, 2023].

Douglas, J. (1978). Equipment costs by current methods. *Journal of Construction Division, ASCE*, 104(C02): 191–225.

Droms, W.O. (1986). *Finance and accounting for non-financial managers*. Reading, MA: Addison-Wesley.

Easterly, W. and Levine, R. (2001). It's not a factor accumulation: Stylized facts and growth models. *The World Bank Economic Review*, 15(1): 177–219.

Enders, W. (2014). *Applied econometric time series*. New York: John Wiley.

Eom, S-J. and Leo, J. (2022). Digital Government transformation in turbulent time: Responses, challenges, and future direction. *Government Information Quarterly*, 39(2), March. https://pmc.ncbi.nlm.nih.gov/articles/PMC8914696/

Fallou, C. (1971). *Value analysis to improve productivity*. New York: Wiley Interscience.

Farnum, N.R. (1994). *Modern statistical quality control and improvement*. Belmont, CA: Duxbury Press.

Federal Contracting Center. (2024). *Understanding the Past: A History of Government Contracting*. Washington, DC: Federal Contracting Center, December 17. www.federalcontractingcenter.com/understanding-the-past-a-history-of-government-contracting/

Federal Contractor Registry. (2019). A look at five types of contracts. *Federal Contractor Registry*. https://federalcontractorregistry.com/a-look-at-5-types-of-government-contracts/

Feigenbaum, A.V. (1991). *Total quality control*. New York: McGraw-Hill.

Finkler, S.A., Ward, D.M., and Baker, J.J. (2007). *Essentials of cost accounting for health care organizations*. Boston, MA: Jones and Bartlett Publishers.

Fishman, T.C. (2020). America's next crisis is already here. *The Atlantic*. May 21, 2020. www.google.com/search?q=state+and+local+governments+in+financial+troubles&ie=utf-8&oe=utf-8&client=firefox-b-1

Forrest, E. (1996). *Activity-based management: A comprehensive implementation guide*. New York: McGraw-Hill.

Foster, S. (2020). The state and local budget crisis is already here – and your finances could take a big hit. *The Federal Reserve*. September 4, 2020. www.bankrate.com/banking/federal-reserve/how-state-local-budget-crisis-could-hit-finances-taxes-layoffs/ [Retrieved: September 15, 2020].

Fountain, J.R., Jr. (1990). Future changes in financial reporting: A primer on GASB. *Intergovernmental Perspective*, Fall: 35–37.

Fowler, T.C. (1990). *Value analysis and design*. New York: Van Nostrand Reinhold.

Freeman, R.J. et al. (1988). *Governmental and non-profit accounting: Theory and practice*. Englewood Cliffs, NJ: Prentice-Hall.

Friedman, M. (1996). Calculating compensation costs, in J. Rabin, et al. (eds) *Budgeting: Formulation and execution*. Athens, GA: Carl Vinson Institute of Government, University of Georgia, 265–275.

Fyffe, S.D. (2015). *Nonprofit government contracts and grants: The state agency perspective*. Washington, DC: Urban Institute.

Garner, C.W. (1991). *Accounting and budgeting in public and non-profit organizations*. San Francisco, CA: Jossey Bass Publishing.

Garner, S.P. (1954). *Evolution of cost account to 1925*. Tuscaloosa, AL: The University of Alabama Press.

Geiger, D.R. (2010). *Cost management and control in government: Fighting the cost war through leadership driven management*. New York: Business Expert Press, LLC.

Gere, J.M. and Weaver, W., Jr. (1965). *Matrix algebra for engineers*. New York: D. Van Nostrand Company.

GFOA. (2010). Inflationary indices in budgeting. *GFOA Best Practices*. Chicago, IL: Government Finance Officers Association. www.gfoa.org/materials/inflation ary-indices-in-budgeting

GFOA. (2019). *Code of ethics*. Chicago, IL: Government Finance Officers Association (GFOA).

Goldbratt, E.M. and Cox, J. (1986). *A process of ongoing improvement*. Great Barrington, MA: North River Press.

Gilchrist, W. (1976). *Statistical forecasting*. New York: John Wiley.

Gransberg, D., Popescu, R., and Ryan, R. (2006). *Construction equipment management for engineers, estimators, and owners*. Boca Raton, FL: Taylor & Francis.

Grant, E.L. and Leavenworth, R.S. (1996). *Statistical quality control*. New York: McGraw-Hall.

Glick, P.E. (1990). *A public manager's guide to governmental accounting and financial reporting*. Financial Reporting Series, No. 10. Chicago, IL: Government Finance Officers Association (GFOA).

Gore, A.J. (1993). *Creating a government that works better and costs less*. Washington, DC: U.S. Government Printing Office.

Gortner, H.J. (1981). *Administration in the public sector*. New York: John Wiley, 69–94.

Gramlich, E.M. (1981). *Benefit-cost analysis of government programs*. Englewood Cliffs, NJ: Prentice-Hall.

Gransberg, D., Popescu, R., and Ryan, R. (2006). *Construction equipment management for engineers, estimators, and owners*. Boca Raton, FL: Taylor & Francis.

Green, W.H. (2003). *Econometrics*. New York: Prentice Hall.

Greico, Jr. P.L. and Pilachowski, M. (1994). *Activity-based costing: The key to world class performance*. New York: PT Publications.

Gupta, S.K. and Cozzolino, J.M. (1975). *Foundations of operations research for management*. San Francisco, CA: Holden-Day.

Hackbart, M.H. and Ramsey, J.R. (1993). Public cash management: Issues and practices, in T.D. Lynch and L. Martin (eds) *Handbook of comparative public budgeting and financial management*. New York: Marcel-Dekker, 293–312.

Halachmi, A. (ed.). (1999). *Performance & quality measurement in government: Issues and experiences*. Burke, VA: Chateline Press.

Hammel, F.C (1988). *Breakeven analysis: A decision-making tool* (wilh P.G. Goulet). Washington, DC: US Small Business Administration, Office of Business Development.

Harrison, K. (2023). 13 benefits of digital transformation for local governments. *GovPilot*. www.govpilot.com/blog/benefits-of-digital-transformation-for-local-governments [Accessed December 15, 2023].

Hart, D.J. (1990). How activity accounting works in government. *Management Accounting*. September:36–40.

Harvard Kennedy School. (2019). *Active Contract Management*. Harvard, MA: Harvard Kennedy School of Government Performance Lab.

Harvey, N. (2007). Use of heuristics: Insights from forecasting research. *Thinking and Reasoning*, 13(1): 5–24.

Hatry, H.P. (1981). *Practical program evaluation for state and local governments*. Washington, DC: The Urban Institute.

Hatry, H.P. (1988). *Guide to setting priorities for capital investment*. Washington, DC: Urban Institute Press.

Havens, H. (1983). Integrating evaluation and budgeting. *Public Budgeting & Finance*, 3(2): 102–113.

Hay, L.E. and Engstorm, J.H. (1993). *Essentials of accounting for governmental and Not-for-profit organizations*. Homewood, IL: Irwin.

Henry, N. (1999). *Public administration and public affairs*. Upper Saddle River, NJ: Prentice-Hall, 457–474.

Herbert, L. Killough, L.N., and Steiss, A.W. (1984). *Governmental accounting and control*. Monterey, CA: Brooks/Cole Publishing.

Herzlinger, R.E. and Nitterhouse, D. (1994). *Financial accounting and management control for non-profit organizations*. Cincinnati, OH: Southwestern Publishing.

Hey, J.D. (1991). *Experiments in economics*. Cambridge, MA: Blackwell.

Hilke, J.C. (1992). *Competition in government – financed services*. New York: Bloomsbury.

Hillier, F.S. and Lieberman, G.J. (1986). *Introduction to operations research*. Third Edition. San Francisco, CA: Holden Day.

Hillier, F.S., Lieberman, G.J., Nag, B., and Basu, P. (2017). *An introduction to operations research*. New Delhi, India: McGraw-Hill.

Hitoshi, K. (1985). *Statistical methods for quality improvement*. Tokyo, Japan: The Association for Overseas Technical Scholarship.

Hodge, G.A. (1999). *Privatization: An international review of performance*. New York: Routledge.

Holm, L. (2018). *Cost accounting and financial management for construction project managers*. New York: Routledge.

Hood, C. (1995). The new public management in the 1980's: Variations on a theme. *Accounting, Organizations and Society*, 20: 93–109.

Horngren, C.T. (1996). *Introduction to management accounting*. Upper Saddle River, NJ: Prentice-Hall.

Horngren, C.T., Datar, S.M., Rajan, M.V., Beaubien, L., and Graham. C. 2016. *Cost Accounting: Managerial Emphasis*. Seventh Canadian Edition. Toronto: Pearson.

Hyde, A.C. (1991). The development of budgeting and budget theory: The threads of budget reform, in Hyde, A.C. (ed.) *Government budgeting: Theory, process, and politics*. Pacific Grove, CA: Brooks/Cole Publishing, 1–6.

Hyndman, R.J. and Athanasopoulos, G. (2018). *Forecasting principles and practice*. New York: Texts. Online, Open-Access Textbooks

Ignizio, J.P. (1976). *Goal programming and extensions*. Lexington, MA: Lexington Books.

Ingram, R.W. et al. (1991). *Accounting and financial reporting for governmental and nonprofit organizations: Basic concepts*. New York: McGraw-Hill.

Ives, M. (1992). 25 years of state and local government financial reporting: An accounting standards perspective. *Government Accounting Journal*, Fall: 1–5.

Ives, M., Patton, T.K., and Patton, S.R. (2013). *Introduction to governmental and Not-for-profit accounting*. New York: Pearson.

Ishikawa, K. (1968). *Guide to quality control*. Tokyo, Japan: JUSE.

Jitasa. (2023). *Nonprofit budgeting: Understand the basics*. Jitasa Group. June 20. www.jitasagroup.com/jitasa_nonprofit_blog/nonprofit-budgeting underst and-the-basics/

Johnson, J.M. (1982). *Handbook of depreciation methods, formulas and tables*. New York: Prentice-Hall.

Juran, J.M. (1951). *Quality control handbook*. New York: McGraw-Hill.

Juran, J.M. and Gryna, Jr., F.M. (1980). *Quality planning and analysis*. Second Edition. New York: McGraw-Hill.

Kalfayan, F.G. (2012). *Mastering depreciation*. New York: American Institute of Professional Bookkeepers (AIPB).

Kaplan, R. and Anderson, S.R. (2007). *Time-driven activity-based costing*. Boston, MA: Harvard Business School Publication Corporation.

Kasozi, E. (2013). *Cost accounting management*. Munich, Germany: GRIN Verlag.

Kelley, J.T. (1984). *Costing government services: Guide for decision making*. Washington, DC: Government Finance Officers Association (GFOA).

Kerzner, H. (2009). *Project management: A systems approach to planning, scheduling and control.* New York: John Wiley.

Keynes, J.M. (1921). *A treatise in probabilities.* London: McMillan (Referred to by Keynes in the book, was developed originally by Bernoulli and subsequently expanded by Laplace and others).

Khan, A. (1989). Forecasting a local government budget with time-series analysis. *Stale and Local Government Review*, 21, Fall: 123–129.

Khan, A. (1996). Cash management: Basic principles and guidelines, in J. Rabin, et al. (eds) *Budgeting: Formulation and execution.* Athens, GA: Carl Vinson Institute of Government, The University of Georgia, 313–322.

Khan, A. (1997). Capital rationing, priority setting, and budget decisions: An analytical guide for public managers, in R.T. Golembiewski and J. Rabin (eds) *Public budgeting and finance.* New York: Marcel-Dekker, 963–974.

Khan, A. and Farias, C. (1996). Benefit-cost analysis, in J.M. Shafritz (ed.) *The international encyclopedia of public policy and administration.* New York: Henry-Holt, 173–180.

Kilian, C.S. (1992). *The world of Edwards Deming.* Knoxville, TN: SPC Press.

Kogan, R., Greenstein, R., and Horney, J.R. (2012). *Biennial budgeting: Do the drawbacks outweigh the advantages?* Washington, DC: Center on Budget and Policy Priorities. www.cbpp.org

Kriens, J., van Lieshout, J.T., and Verheyen, R.P. (1983). Management accounting and operations research. *European Journal of Operations Research*, 13(4): 339–352.

Lanzillotti, R., Dirlam, J.B., and Kaplan, A.D.H. (1958). *Pricing in big business.* Washington, DC: Brookings Institution.

Lapsley, I. and Mitchell, F. (eds) (1996). *Accounting and performance measurement.* London, England: Paul Chapman Publishing.

Lane, J-E. (2000). *New public management.* New York: Routledge.

Lanen, W., Anderson S., and Maher, M. (2020). *Fundamentals of cost accounting.* New York: McGraw Hill Education.

Lapsley, I. and Mitchell, F. (eds) (1996). *Accounting and performance measurement.* London, England: Paul Chapman Publishing.

Lanzillotti, R., Dirlam, J.B., and Kaplan, A.D.H. (1958). *Pricing in big business.* Washington, DC: Brookings Institution.

Lee, D.R. (1982). On the pricing of public goods. *Southern Economic Journal*, 49(1), July: 99–105.

Lee, R.C. (1996). Life-cycle costing, in J. Rabin et al. (eds) *Budgeting: Formulation and execution.* Athens, GA: Carl Vinson Institute of Government, University of Georgia, Chapter 41: 420–423.

Levin, H.M. (1983). *Cost-effectiveness: A primer.* Beverly Hills, CA: Sage.

Li, S. (1996). *Analyzing efficiency and managerial performance using sensitivity scores of DEA models.* New York: Garland Publishers.

Livschitz, A. (2021). *Indirect cost allocation – Finding your true bottom line.* Abbott, Springham & Lynch; https://www.saltmarshcpa.com/cpa-news/blog/indirect-cost-allocation58-finding-your-true-bottom-line.asp

Lohrey, J. (2021). What are some ways to allocate indirect costs? *Chron*. https://smallbusiness.chron.com/ways-allocate-indirect-cost-73462.html [Retrieved May 7, 2021].

Lynch, T.D. (1995). *Public budgeting in America*. Englewood Cliffs, NJ: Prentice Hall.

Lynn, E.S. and Norville, J.W. (1984). *Introduction to fund accounting*. Reston, VA: Reston Publishing.

Makridakis, S.G., Wheelwright, S.C. and Hyndman, R.J. (1998). *Forecasting: Methods and applications*. New York: John Wiley.

Maleyeff, J. (2007). *Improving service delivery with lean six sigma*. Strategy and Transformation Series. Hartford, CT: IBM Center for the Business of Government.

Manos, K.L. (ed.) (2020). *Government contract costs and pricing handbook*. Washington, DC: Thomson West.

Marburger, D. (2013). *Economic decision-making using cost data*. New York: Business Expert Press.

Martin, J.R. (1916). *Management accounting: Concepts, techniques, and controversial issues*. Management and Accounting Web, http://maaw.info/MAAWTextbookMain.htm (undated).

Martino, R.L. (1970). *Critical path networks*. New York: McGraw-Hill.

Mayne, J. (2007). *Challenges and lessons in implementing results-based management*. Sage.

Mazmanian, D.A. and Sabatier, P.A. (1981). *Effective policy implementation*. Lexington, KY: Lexington Books.

Mckenna, C.K. (1980). *Quantitative methods for public decision making*. New York: McGraw-Hill.

Mead, D.M. (2006). A manageable system of economic analysis for governments, in H.A. Frank (ed.) *Public financial management*. New York: Taylor & Francis, 383–419.

Mead, D.M. (2018). *An Analyst's Guide to Government Financial Statements*. Norwalk, CT: Government Accounting Standards Board.

Mears, P. (1995). *Quality improvement tools & techniques*. New York: McGrawHill.

Metcalf, H. (1885). *Cost of Manufactures*. New York: John Wiley.

Montgomery, D. (2005). *Introduction to statistical quality control*. Hoboken, NJ: John Wiley.

Michel, R.G. (2004). *Cost analysis and activity-based costing for government*. Chicago, IL: Government Finance Officers Association.

Mikesell, J.C. (2014). *Fiscal administration: Analysis and application for the public sector*. Belmont, CA: Wadsworth Publishing.

Mikesell, R.F. (1977). *The rate of discount for evaluating public projects*. Washington, DC: American Enterprise Institute for Studies in Public Policy.

Miller, A.D.G., et al. (2009). *Managerial cost accounting in federal government: Providing useful information for decision making*. Washington, DC: AGA CPAG Research series, Report No. 22, September.

Miller, D.W. and Starr, M.K. (1960). *Executive decisions and operations research*. Englewood Cliffs, NJ: Prentice-Hall. (For a discussion on Wald's criterion).

Miller, G.J. (1993). Cost-benefit analysis, in M. Holzer (ed.) *Public productivity handbook*. New York: Marcel- Dekker, 253–279.

Miller, J.A. (1996). *Implementing activity-based management in daily operations*. New York: John Wiley.

Mishan, E.J. (1982). *Cost-benefit analysis*. London, England: George Allen and Irwin.

Mislick, G.K. and Nussbaum, D.A. (2015). *Cost estimation: Methods and tools*. New York: John Wiley.

Misra, K.B. (2008). Quality engineering and management, in M.K.B. Misra (ed.) *Handbook of performability engineering*. London, England: Springer-Verlog London, 157–170.

Montgomery, D.C. (1996). *Introduction to statistical quality control*. New York: John Wiley.

Montgomery, D.C. and Johnson, L.A. (1976). *Forecasting time-series analysis*. New York: McGraw- Hill.

Mudge, A.E. (1971). *Value engineering: A systematic approach*. New York: McGraw Hill.

Mundel, M.E. (1978). *Motion and time study: Principles and practices*. Englewood Cliffs, NJ: Prentice-Hall.

Mushkin, S. (ed.) (1972). *Public prices for public profits*. Washington, DC: Urban Institute Press.

Nahmias, S. (1993). *Production and operations analysis*. Homewood, IL: Irwin.

Nash, S.G. (1996). *Linear and Non-Linear Programming*. New York: McGraw-Hill.

National Archives. (2025). Code of Federal Regulations: A point in time eCFR system. 9903-201-1 CAS Applicability. January 6. www.ecfr.gov/current/title-48/chapter-99/subchapter-B/part-9903/subpart-9903.2/section-9903.201-1

National Council of Nonprofits (2024). *Budgeting for Nonprofits*. www.councilofnonprofits.org/running-nonprofit/administration-and-financial-management/budgeting-nonprofits [Accessed November 28, 2024].

Nayyar-Stone, R. and Hatry, H.P. (2010). *Using survey information to provide evaluative citizen feedback for public service decisions*. Washington, DC: The Urban Institute.

Neubauer, D.M. (ed.). (2010). *Manual on presentation of data and control chart analysis*. West Conshohocken, PA: ASTM International.

Oakland, J.S., Turner, M., and Oakland, R. (2014). *Total quality management and operations excellence: Text with cases*. New York: Routledge.

Oliver, L. (2000). *The cost management toolbox: A manager's guide to controlling costs and boosting profits*. New York: American Management Association.

Oracle-Public Sector. (2010). *Federal government managerial cost accounting*. Oracle White Paper. Washington, DC: Oracle.

Osborne, S.P. (2006). The new public governance. *Public Management Review*, 8(3): 377–387.

Ott, E.R. and Schilling, E.G. (1990). *Process quality control*. Milwaukee, WI: Quality Press.

Patton, T., Patton, S., and Ives, M. (2019). *Accounting for governmental & nonprofit organizations*. Cambridge, England: Cambridge University Probusiness Publishers.

Pearce, D.W. (1983). *Cost-benefit analysis*. New York: St. Martin's Press.

Pettijohn, S.L., Elizabeth, T.B., with De Vita, C.J., and Fyffe, S.D. (2013). *Nonprofit-Government Contracts and Grants: Findings from the 2013 National Survey*. Washington, DC: Urban Institute.

Pierce, L.W. and Rust, K.I. (1991). Government Enterprises, in J.E. Peterson and D.R. Strachota (eds). *Local government finance*. Chicago, IL: Government Finance Officers Association (GFOA), 393–416.

Pindyck, R.S. and Rubinfeld, D.L. (1991). *Econometric models and economic forecasts*. New York: McGraw-Hill.

Points, R. (1990). Recent developments in accounting and financial management in the United States, in A. Premchnd (ed.) *Government financial management*. Washington, DC: International Monetary Fund, 334–336.

Poister, T.H. and Streib, G. (1994). Municipal management tools from 1976 to 1992: An interview and update. *Public Productivity Review*, 18(2), Winter:115–126.

Prichard, R.E. (1980). *The lease/buy decision*. New York: AMACOM.

Raiffa, H. (1968). *Decision Analysis*. Reading, MA: Addision-Wesley.

Rautenstrausch, W. (1939). *Economics of business enterprise*. New York: John Wiley.

Rayburn, L.G. (1996). *Cost accounting: Using a cost management approach*. Chicago, IL: Irwin.

Rayburn, F.R. (1996). Cost Accounting Standards Board (1970–1980; 1988-), in M. Chatfield and R. Vangermeersch (eds) *History of accounting: An international encyclopedia*. New York: Garland Publishing, 170–180.

Rao, T.N. (2018). Validation of analytical methods. *Intechopen*. www.intechopen.com/books/calibration-and-validation-of-analytical-methods-a-sampling-of-current-approaches/validation-of-analytical-methods

Reed, B.J. (1997). *Public finance administration*. Thousand Oaks, CA: Sage.

Richardson, K. (1998). The effect of public vs. private decision environment on the use of the net present value investment criteria. *Journal of Public Budgeting, Accounting, and Financial Management*, 10(1), Spring: 21–52.

Rivenbark, W.C. (2005). A historical overview of cost accounting in local government. *State and Local Government Review*, 37(3): 217–227.

Rivera, G. (2016). *Forecasting for economics and business*. New York: Routledge.

Robinson, M. (1998). Capital charges and capital expenditure decisions in core government. *Journal of Public Budgeting, Accounting, and Financial Management*, 10(3), Fall: 354–374.

Ryan, T.P. (1989). *Statistical methods for quality improvement*. New York: John Wiley.

Sanches, L.C., Brown, S.A., and Izzo, J.A. (2020). A century of not-for-profit accounting: A historical perspective. *The CPA Journal*. www.cpajournal.com/2020/12/09/a-century-of-not-for-profit-accounting

Savage, L.I. (1951). The theory of statistical decisions. *Journal of American Statistical Association*, 46: 55–67.

Savas, E.S. (2000). Privatization and new public management. *Fordham Urban Law Journal*, 28(5): 1731–1737.
Schlaifer, R. (1959). *Probability and statistics for business decisions.* New York: McGraw-Hill.
Schwartz, E. (1987). Inventory and cash management, in J.R. Aronson and E. Schwortz (eds) *Management policies in local Government finance.* Washington, DC: ICMA, 342–363.
Shafritz, J.M., Russell, E.W., and Borick, C.P. (2013). *Introduction to public administration.* New York: Pearson.
Shank, J.K. and Govindarajan, V. (2008). *Strategic cost management: The new tool for competitive advantage.* New York: Free Press.
Shim, J.K. and Siegel, J.G. (1991). *Modern cost management and analysis.* Hauppaauge, NY: Barron's Foundation Series.
Simpoon, R. (1997). *Managing finance and information.* Washington, DC: Pitman.
Smith, L.R. (2014). *Financial accounting and reporting.* New York: Wolters Kluwer Tax & Accounting.
Solenberger, H.M. (1995). *Managerial accounting.* Cincinnati, OH: Southwestern (College) Publishing.
Sorensen, J.E. et al. (1996). Managerial accounting, in J. Rabin et al. (eds) *Budgeting: Formulation and execution.* Athens, GA: Carl Vinson Institute of Government, The University of Georgia, 452–461.
Staehr, K. (2006). *Risk and uncertainty in cost-benefit analysis.* Denmark, Copenhagen: Institute for Miljovurdering.
Starling, G, (1982). *Managing the public sector.* Homewood, IL: Dorsey Press.
Starling, G. (1979). *The politics and economics of public policy.* Homewood, IL: The Dorsey Press, 491–494.
Steiss, A.W. (1982). *Management control in government.* Lexington, MA: Lexington Books.
Stewert, J.D. (1984). The role of information in public accountability, in T. Hopwood and C.R Tomkins (eds) *Issues in public accounting.* Oxford, England: Phillip Allan, 14–25.
Stout, R. Jr. (1980). Management, control, and decision, in R. Stout, Jr. (ed.) *Management or control? The organizational challenge.* Bloomington: Indiana University Press, 98–124.
Stramatis, D.H. (1997). *TQM engineering handbook.* New York: Marcel Dekker.
Svara, J.H. (2013). *Public administrator's code of ethics.* Phoenix, AZ: Lincoln Center for Applied Ethics, Arizona State University.
Swift, J.A. (1998). *Principles of total quality.* Boca Raton, FL: St. Lucie Press.
Swiss, J.E. (1991). *Public integration systems.* Englewood Cliffs, NJ: Prentice-Hall.
Taguchi, G. (1992). *Studies on mathematical statistics for quality control.* Doctoral dissertation, Kushu University, Japan.
Tague, N.R. (2004). Seven basic quality tools, in *The quality toolbox.* Milwaukee, WI: American Society for Quality.
Taha, H.A. (2010). *Operations research: An introduction.* New York: Prentice Hall.

Tankersley, W.B. and Grizzle, G.E. (1994). Control options for public management: An analytical model for designing appropriate control strategies. *Public Productivity Review*, 8(I), Fall: 1–18.

Tenner, A.R. and Detoro, I.J. (1992). *Total quality management*. Reading, MA: AddisonWesley Publishing.

Thai, K.V. (1997). Govt'l auditing, in R.T. Golembiewski and J. Rabin (eds) *Public budgeting and finance*. New York: Macel-Dekker, 585–608.

Thiel, D.V. (2014). *Research methods for engineers*. Cambridge, England: Cambridge University Press.

Thompson, F. (1997). Matching responsibilities with tactics: Administrative controls and modem government, in R.T. Golembiewski and J. Rabin (eds) *Public budgeting and finance*. New York: Marcel-Dekker, 551–574.

Thompson, M.S. (1982). *Benefit-cost analysis for program evaluation*. Beverly Hills, CA: Sage.

Tolley, K. (1995). *Evaluating the cost-effectiveness of counseling in health care*. New York: Routledge.

Truett, L.J. (1995). *Managerial economic analysts: Problems, and cases*. Cincinnati, OH: Southwestern Publishing.

Tyndall, D.G. (1951). The relative merits of average cost pricing, marginal Cost Pricing, and price discrimination. *The Quarterly Journal of Economics*, 65(3): 342–372.

US Chief Information Officers Council. (1995). Chief Financial Officers Act, 1990. *Information Technology Laws*. Washington, DC: Chief Information Officers Council.

US General Services Administration. (2023). *Digital strategy*. Washington, DC: GSA. Public Law 115–336, "21st Century Integrated Digital Experience Act." 2023 Annual Report. www.gsa.gov/technology/government-it-initiatives/digital-strategy

US Department of Transportation. (2002). *Life cycle cost analysis primer*. Office of Asset Management. U.S. Department of Transportation.

US Logistics Management Institute (LMI). (1965). *Lifecycle costing in equipment procurement*. Washington, DC: US Logistics Management Institute.

Vatter, W.J. (1967). Operations research and management accounting. *Nebraska Journal of Economics and Business*, 6(2), Autumn: 65–79.

Vazakidis, A., Karagiannis, I., and Tsialta, A. (2010). Activity-based costing in public sector. *Journal of Social Sciences*, 6(3): 376–382.

Villanova University (2020). *Six sigma in government*. Villanova University, March 12, 2020. www.villanovau.com/resources/six-sigma/six-sigma-government/ [Retrieved July 31, 2020].

Von Neumann, J. and Morgenstem, O. (1969). *Analysis of decisions under uncertainty*. New York: McGraw-Hil.

Wade, J. and Herman, M. (2021). Accelerated depreciation. *Investing Answers*. https://investinganswers.com/dictionary/a/accelerated-depreciation

Wantuck, K.A. (1989). *Just-in-time for America*. Milwaukee, WI: Forum.

Weiss, B. (1997). *Activity-based costing and management: Issues and practices in local government*. Chicago, IL: Government Finance Officers Association.

Westinghouse, G.E. (1985). *Work measurement IIE micro software.* Atlanta, GA: Industrial Engineering and Management Press.
Weygandt, J.J., Kimmel, P.D., and Kieso, D.E. (2015). *Managerial accounting: Tools for business decision making.* Hoboken, NJ: Wiley Global Education.
Wheeler, K.M. (1994). *Effective communication: A local government guide.* Washington, DC: International City Management Association (ICMA), Local Government Management Series.
Woods, M.D. (1994). *Total quality accounting.* New York: John Wiley.
Ziebeli, M.T. (1991). *Management control systems in non-profit organizations.* San Diego, CA: Harcourt Brace Jovanovich.
Ziegenfuss, Jr., J.T. and Bentley, J.M. (2000). Implementing cost control in health care: Strategies driven by organizational systems approach. *Practice and Systems Research*, 13(4): 453–474.
Zimmerman, J.L. (1997). *Accounting for decision making and control.* Chicago, IL: Irwin.

Index

Made in the USA
Monee, IL
13 September 2026

62980175R10221